Sex Versus Survival

Sex Versus Survival

The Life and Ideas of Sabina Spielrein

John Launer

OVERLOOK DUCKWORTH

New York • London

First published in the United States and the United Kingdom in 2015 by
Overlook Duckworth, Peter Mayer Publishers, Inc.

NEW YORK
141 Wooster Street
New York, NY 10012
www.overlookpress.com
For bulk and special sales please contact sales@overlookny.com,
or to write us at the above address.

LONDON
30 Calvin Street, London E1 6NW
T: 020 7490 7300
E: info@duckworth-publishers.co.uk
www.ducknet.co.uk
For bulk and special sales please contact sales@duckworth-publishers.co.uk,
or write to us at the above address.

Cataloguing-in-Publication Data is available from the Library of Congress

A catalogue record for this book is available from the British Library

ISBN: 978-1-4683-1058-0 (US)
ISBN: 978-0-7156-4741-7 (UK)

Typeset by Ray Davies
Manufactured in the United States of America

2 4 6 8 10 9 7 5 3 1

Contents

Plates between pages 148 and 149

Preface and Acknowledgements

MY INTEREST in Sabina Spielrein began through pure serendipity. For many years I was on the staff at the Tavistock Clinic in London, a major centre for psychological treatment in the United Kingdom. One of my regular tasks there was to run a management training day for people who were about to become qualified psychiatrists and psychologists. We usually spent most of the day doing an exercise in which they had to act as the boards of two imaginary mental health institutions. Over the years I had fun inventing the names of these institutions. For some time I called one of them 'The Spielrein Institute'. I chose the name as a joke – at least, I thought it was a joke. I took it from a real historical figure called Sabina Spielrein. Like many people, all I knew about her was that she was a patient of Carl Jung and had become his mistress. I knew that Sigmund Freud was somehow connected with her, and thought maybe she had been his patient too. I also liked the sound of her name, which I assumed was probably Viennese.

One day, I decided I should pay Sabina Spielrein the respect of finding out more about her. I read about her affair with Jung, and how Freud helped in a cover-up to protect him. Much had been written by Freudians attacking Jung over the whole business, by Jungians defending him, and by feminists wishing a plague on both their houses. It certainly seemed that Spielrein conducted herself with greater dignity and restraint than either of the men. Apart from reading about this episode, I discovered that Spielrein was a psychiatrist and psychoanalyst in her own right. I felt contrite at having used her name in a flippant way and decided to make amends by reading some of her professional articles. She wrote them in the first thirty years of the last century in German, French and Russian, though they were translated into English only in the 1990s. Her most significant paper was entitled 'Destruction as the Cause of Coming into Being'. This was originally published in 1912 and was based on a lecture she had given the previous year in front of Freud and his circle in Vienna.

I can remember the moment I started to read the paper. I almost fell out of my chair with astonishment. I felt I was reading something written a century ahead of its time. It seemed that Sabina Spielrein had anticipated many of the biological and psychological ideas of our own age. These included the need for understanding the mind in terms of its evolution, and the role of the reproductive drive in human psychology. From a modern perspective, there were flaws in her argument. All the same, I was shocked to discover that her theory was completely rejected – indeed mocked – by those who heard it at the time. I found it incomprehensible that these ideas had disappeared into oblivion. I started to read her letters, diaries and other scholarly papers. These deepened my respect for her as an original thinker. In all the existing books and articles about her, I could find no account that did her full justice. A number of writers argued that she was underestimated as a thinker, but this was in the context of showing how Freud, Jung and others adapted some of her ideas. No one had ever re-examined her life and ideas as a whole, or properly challenged the way she was marginalised in the history of psychology. I closed down the imaginary Spielrein Institute and became interested in the real Sabina Spielrein. I started to collect materials about her, intending to write a book about her one day, perhaps in old age. The announcement of a Hollywood movie about her, *A Dangerous Method*, caught me by surprise. I pulled together a small self-published volume about her in time for the launch of the movie, hoping that it might gain some attention for her ideas rather than the imaginative scenes of her sex life that were the main attraction of the film. This led to a commission to write the present book.

I am pleased to have completed the book before reaching old age, but as a result I have had to do so while working full time. This would have been entirely impossible without the indulgence and love of my wife Rabbi Lee Wax and our children Ruth and David. I want to express my enormous gratitude to them. This acknowledgement must precede all those that follow.

Although I know some German and French and a minuscule amount of Russian, I have been dependent on prodigious amounts of translation into English carried out by dedicated friends who were able to do this better than I. These were Tom Carnwath, Jens Föll, Andrew Levy, Judith Prais, Annie Swanepoel and Neil Vickers. All of them offered helpful reflections on the material they translated and on earlier drafts of the book, especially Neil Vickers who was able to draw on his extensive knowledge of psychoanalytic history. I am immensely grateful for the many hours of work they put in simply through friendship.

At an early stage of my interest in Spielrein, two tolerant editors allowed me to summarise her story in print for a medical readership: Christopher Martyn at the *Quarterly Journal of Medicine* and Fiona Moss at the *Postgraduate Medical Journal*. Subsequently, Melvin Bornstein at *Psychoanalytic Inquiry* asked me to elaborate in print on Spielrein's ideas about sex and sexuality and what these might mean from a modern perspective. These were important steps towards developing my understanding of Spielrein and her relevance to contemporary thought. After I wrote my original short book about Spielrein's life and ideas, I was invited by Bernadette Wren and David Bell to give a presentation about her to a scientific meeting at the Tavistock Clinic. Subsequently Joan Raphael-Leff asked me to do the same to the academic faculty of the Anna Freud Clinic. The intelligent questions and challenges I faced at those events helped me to hone my ideas considerably. Arising out of the Tavistock meeting, I set up a small seminar group there, to explore the potential connections between evolutionary theory and psychotherapy of the kind that Spielrein pointed towards. The members of that seminar group are Jim Hopkins, Graham Music, Michael Reiss, Daniela Sieff, Annie Swanepoel and Bernadette Wren, with Sebastian Kraemer as a corresponding member. Our monthly meetings, email dialogues and exchanges of papers have played an important part in my attempt to evaluate Spielrein's theories. The use of the outstanding library at the Tavistock Clinic has been a great boon, and I greatly appreciate the help I have had from its staff.

While I was writing my original version of the book, I corresponded with a number of evolutionists and psychoanalysts to check out my ideas, and received useful comments from them. Apart from those already mentioned, they include Gillian Bentley, Linda Brakel, Jim Chisholm, Helena Cronin, Martin Miller, Aine Murphy and Randolph Nesse. When the movie about Spielrein was released, Sarah Ebner at the London *Times* asked me to write an article about Spielrein. On the day the article appeared, Peter Mayer from Duckworth and Overlook contacted me to ask if I would be willing to write a more extensive and scholarly biography. David Marshall and Andrew Lockett at Duckworth have been highly supportive during the project, especially in steering me through the murky forest of copyright law. Nicky Solomon and Kate Pool from the Society of Authors also provided helpful guidance.

Every biographer stands on the shoulders of previous researchers. I have been exceptionally fortunate in having the direct aid of many of them. Spielrein's German biographer Sabine Richebächer carried out many years of meticulous work trawling the archives in Zurich, Geneva, Moscow, Rostov-on-Don and elsewhere, culminating in her excellent German biography in 2008. She was generous with her advice and information, especially in the early stages of my work. Alexander Etkind has written a superb account of psychoanalysis in the Soviet Union, and I was fortunate to be able to meet him and learn some helpful background about Spielrein's years in Russia. Without the prior researches of these two outstanding historians, I could not have written this book. Magnus Ljunggren, the Swedish scholar who originally traced Spielrein's niece Menikha in the Soviet Union in the 1980s, has been kind enough to allow me to use copies of some of the photos that she gave him. Coline Covington, co-editor with Barbara Wharton of a seminal collection of essays about Spielrein, also helped me in relation to copyright issues. The polyglot New York psychoanalyst Henry (Zvi) Lothane has written many original articles challenging received myths about Spielrein, and I have benefited from his frank views, as well as encouragement to make contact with Professor Vladimir Shpilrain, representing the Spielrein literary estate. Professor Shpilrain's generosity in granting permission for extensive quotations from his great-aunt's letters, diaries and other documents has been a huge boon for which I am profoundly grateful. One of the coincidences that occurred while I was writing the book was the discovery that a Russian acquaintance of mine, Alexander Zhuravlyov, spent his childhood close to Spielrein's step-daughter Nina Snetkova.[1] He remained in frequent contact with Nina until her death in St Petersburg a few years ago, and interviewed her about her past. His recollections of her, and of her memories of her step-mother, established an unexpected closeness to the subject of my book.

Finally, I am very grateful to Katy Zaidman, the great-granddaughter of Sabina's brother Jan, who helped me to compile a family tree. As I approached the completion of this book, it was moving to discover that there are now more surviving descendants of Sabina's parents, Nikolai Arkadyevich and Eva Markovna, than there were before the family was devastated by the events of the Terror and the Holocaust. This book is dedicated to their living family and future generations, in memory of Dr Sabina Nikolayevna Spielrein-Sheftel, and her daughters Renata and Eva.

All quotations from the letters and diaries of Sabina Spielrein are reproduced by kind permission of Professor Vladimir Shpilrain on behalf of the Spielrein Literary Estate.

The records of Sabina Spielrein's hospital admission in 1904-5 are in the possession of the Psychiatric University Hospital Zürich, Burghölzli, and were originally edited by Dr Bernard Minder; extracts from them are used with permission of the Spielrein Literary Estate.

Photographs of Sabina Spielrein and members of her family appear by kind permission of Professor Magnus Ljunggren. The photograph of Nina and Olga Snetkova appears by courtesy of Alexander Zhuravlyov.

Original translations of Russian letters by Sabina Spielrein and Eva Spielrein appear by kind permission of Dr Henry Lothane.

The letters between Sigmund Freud and CG Jung were first published in 'The

Freud/Jung Letters: The Correspondence between Sigmund Freud and C.G. Jung Freud/Jung' edited by W.McGuire, translated by R. Manheim and R.F.C. Hull, Copyright © 1974 by Sigmund Freud Copyrights and Erbengemeinschaft Prof. CG Jung, and © 2007 Foundation of the Works of CG Jung, Zurich. Extracts are reproduced here with the permission of Princeton University Press, the Marsh Agency on behalf of Sigmund Freud Copyrights, and the Paul & Peter Fritz Agency on behalf of the Foundation of the Works of CG Jung.

The letters of Sigmund Freud to Sabina Spielrein were first published in '*Tagebuch einer heimlichen Symmetrie: Sabina Spielrein zwischen Jung und Freud*' edited by Aldo Carotenuto. Extracts are reproduced with permission of the Marsh Agency on behalf of Sigmund Freud Copyrights. The letters of CG Jung to Sabina Spielrein were first published in the same volume, Copyright © 1986 Erbengemeinschaft Prof. CG Jung, and © 2007 Foundation of the Works of CG Jung, Zurich. Extracts are reproduced with permission of the Paul & Peter Fritz Agency on behalf of the Foundation of the Works of CG Jung.

Extracts from the works of Sigmund Freud are from 'The Standard Edition of the Complete Psychological Works of Sigmund Freud', translated under the general editorship of James Strachey, and appear by permission of Random House, Basic Books (Perseus Books) and the Marsh Agency on behalf of Sigmund Freud Copyrights

Extracts from the works of CG Jung are from 'The Collected Works of C.G. Jung', edited by H. Read, M. Fordham, G. Adler and W. McGuire, and translated by RFC Hull, Copyright © 1979 by Princeton University Press and © 2007 Foundation of the Works of CG Jung, Zurich. They are reproduced here with the permission the Paul & Peter Fritz Agency on behalf of the Foundation of the Works of CG Jung.

Extracts from 'Memories, Dreams, Reflections' by CG Jung are published with the permission of Random House.

Introduction

SABINA SPIELREIN led one of the most remarkable lives of the twentieth century. Born in Tsarist Russia in 1885, she suffered abuse as a child and had a severe breakdown in her teens. She became a psychiatric patient, and then had an erotic relationship with her psychiatrist, Carl Jung. When he panicked and broke it off, she sought help from Jung's colleague Sigmund Freud, who instead conspired with Jung in a cover-up. She realised what the two men had done, but forgave them. Her restraint saved Jung's career, and possibly psychoanalysis as well. She qualified as a doctor, became a colleague of Freud, and tried for many years to bring about a reconciliation between him and Jung after their bitter rift. Later, she worked closely with some of the other great figures in psychology in her era, including Jean Piaget. After returning to Russia, she became caught up in a dispute between Stalin and Trotsky, before returning to her home town and pursuing a career there as a child specialist for the rest of her life. In 1942 she was murdered in the Holocaust, along with her two daughters.

By the time of her death, she had vanished from history. For most of the twentieth century, the main record of her existence consisted of a footnote in one of Freud's essays. When the correspondence between Jung and Freud was published in the 1970s, it hinted at the part she had played in bringing the two men together, and then as a cause of their bitter feud. Later, her own diaries and letters came to light in Geneva, revealing the nature of her relationship to them in her own words. It became clear that the two men had conspired to pacify her after she had been abandoned by Jung. Historians began to explore her life, more documents emerged, some of her own scholarly papers were republished, and her name became quite well known. People wrote articles about her, and produced movies and plays. With the release of the movie *A Dangerous Method*, directed by David Cronenberg and with Keira Knightley in the starring role, Sabina Spielrein became famous for the first time – albeit in a Hollywood version. The film included scenes of deflowering and spanking, mainly for entertainment.

However, there is a story about Sabina Spielrein that remains to be told. She was among the most original thinkers of the twentieth century. She was the first person to make the journey from being a psychiatric patient to becoming a psychoanalyst herself. Before almost anyone else, she took the thoughts and language of patients with schizophrenia seriously, and tried to make sense of what

1

they said. She made one of the first attempts to link human psychology with the biology of sexual reproduction, anticipating some key ideas from a century later. She took a woman's perspective on psychology long before it occurred to others that gender was important in studying the mind. She was one of the first people to use play as a form of therapy for children. She took a serious interest in child development and the language spoken by children before it was fashionable to do so. She was a bridge-builder and a peacemaker: between people, schools of thought, professional disciplines and ways of looking at the world.

Apart from studying with Jung in Zurich, Freud in Vienna, and Piaget in Geneva, she worked with some of the other greatest names in the history of psychology and neuroscience. After her collaboration with Jung and Freud, she moved to Berlin to work alongside Karl Abraham, who later founded the first psychoanalytic training institute. In Geneva, she joined the founders of child psychology as a discipline and took an active part in its development. As well as working closely with Piaget, she was his psychoanalyst. Melanie Klein and Anna Freud attended a presentation she gave in 1920 on infants and mothers. Afterwards, they began to write about ideas she had first proposed. When Spielrein returned to Russia in 1923, she was one of the pioneers of the new field of pedology, which brought together the medical, psychological and educational care of the child. While there, she worked with two of the other most eminent psychologists of the century, Alexander Luria and Lev Vygotsky, who both developed theories based on her ideas. She helped to run a residential children's home that was under the protection of Trotsky. One of her charges was Stalin's son, Vasily. After she returned to her home town of Rostov-on-Don, she continued to promote enlightened approaches to the care of children and the mentally ill, regardless of political pressure to toe the communist party line. Spielrein's entire career appears to have been one in which she had a profound effect on those around her, while remaining unacknowledged in her lifetime, and forgotten after her death.

This book is the first full-length biography of Spielrein in English. It covers her whole life from 1885 to 1942, not just the years when she was close to Jung and Freud, although I devote several chapters to that period because of its significance. I attempt to evaluate her life and ideas in the light of today's understanding, and to stake a claim for her stature as a thinker. I do this particularly in relation to her attempts to build bridges between psychology and evolution. A hundred years after Spielrein's encounter with Jung and Freud, we have a far better understanding of how the voices and ideas of women, victims of sexual abuse, and those with a psychiatric history have often been denigrated or ignored. We are in a better position to reassess her without the same prejudices, and we can redress some of the injustices done to her. My aim is to promote her recognition as one of the most original and underestimated thinkers of the last century.

I have written this book for the general reader with no specialised knowledge of psychology, and without assuming any views for or against psychoanalysis, or an allegiance to any particular school of thought. I have avoided a detailed technical discussion of how Spielrein's ideas contrasted with those of Freud, Jung and others, although, where necessary, I explain the innovative ideas and methods in psychological treatment that became important in Spielrein's time. I try to do so in as non-technical a style as possible, and generally without taking a position on which I consider more valid than others. I do, however, examine her views on sex and reproduction from an evolutionary perspective, as that was how she wished them to be judged.

Spielrein's story sheds light on Jung and Freud in a way that is not flattering. They were ambitious, conspiratorial and rivalrous – often to Spielrein's disadvantage. I do not intend the portrayal of their behaviour to be taken as an overall judgement on their achievements. Despite their failings and prejudices, they made towering contributions to psychiatry and psychology that Spielrein was the first to recognise. The idea that Freud and Jung promoted – healing through the telling and re-telling of personal stories – has become one of the dominant discourses of our time. It has been a source of liberation for millions of people. However, along with their pioneering zeal, both Freud and Jung introduced tendencies that have bedevilled the 'talking therapies' ever since (I use the term 'talking therapies' to cover not only psychoanalysis but all the forms of individual, group and family therapy and counselling that have been derived from it). These include dogmatism, the cult of the charismatic leader, schisms, resistance to a respectful exchange of ideas between different schools of thought, separation from the world of mainstream science and research, and hostility towards biology and evolutionary thought. This book shows how these tendencies developed, and what Sabina Spielrein did to fight against them. She was the first and possibly the most significant person ever to do so. Only now, a century later, are some of these tendencies being challenged to anything like the degree she would have wished.

The sources and what they reveal

The principal source of information about Spielrein lies in what she wrote in her letters, diaries and papers. She wrote perceptively, vividly, and with passion. She wrote about her family, relationships, dreams, fantasies and theories. In keeping with the habit of her time, she made copies of her letters, including those she sent to Jung and Freud. She kept drafts of letters she may never have sent: sometimes these are more revealing than the ones she did. She preserved many of the letters people wrote back to her, including those from Freud, as well as her extensive correspondence with her family. In accordance with the conventions of her era, she also had little hesitation in including personal disclosures in her professional writings.

All these documents are a precious gift to posterity. The approach I have taken in writing this book has been largely a documentary one. Selections from Spielrein's diaries and correspondence are scattered across many books. Most of these have been out of print for many years, or are not available in English translation. Until the arrival of internet archives, her professional papers were obtainable only from specialist libraries. Now many are available online, but most of these have never been translated. I am the first biographer to have obtained permission from the Spielrein literary estate for unrestricted quotations from her correspondence and diaries. This generous gift enabled me to do what I hoped: to build much of this biography around what she wrote. There are other sources of information about Spielrein too. Miraculously, the hospital notes from Spielrein's admission following her breakdown were preserved, and have been published in a number of books and journals. Jung and another colleague, Feiga Berg, described Spielrein's case history in various publications, although the accounts are inconsistent and need to be read with caution. All the letters between Freud and Jung, including around twenty-seven alluding to Spielrein, are available in their published correspondence, as are many of the letters that Jung and Freud sent to Spielrein. Taken together, the documentation provides a unique portrait of a single individual through diaries, case descriptions, professional papers and intimate correspondence with some of the greatest thinkers of the age. The granting of copyright permission from several sources has enabled me to interleave her own writing with quotations from her correspondents. This is the first time this has been possible in any language, and has allowed a coherent and consecutive narrative of her life to emerge.

I originally set out to write this book mainly in order to make Spielrein's ideas better known, intending simply to cover her personal story while doing so. I expected that recounting her life would be straightforward. It was not. In the course of my researches, I discovered that many of the facts that are generally assumed to be true about her life are unsubstantiated, or directly contradicted by the evidence. Most previous accounts of Spielrein's life have been derived from two books written a long time ago, each inaccurate in different ways. The first is *A Secret Symmetry: Sabina Spielrein between Jung and Freud*, edited by Aldo Carotenuto and published in 1980. This included some of Spielrein's diaries and correspondence, together with a commentary. The diary extracts were highly selective, with no explanation why this was the case. The editor was a Jungian analyst, and his commentary was slanted towards exculpating Jung. The other influential book about Spielrein is *A Most Dangerous Method* by John Kerr, published in 1993, which later became the principal source for Cronenberg's movie.[1] Kerr's interest was mainly in the early history of psychoanalysis, and Spielrein herself is absent from long stretches of his book. He wrote it before Spielrein's hospital records and other key documents were available and included a great deal of speculation, much of which has proved to be wrong. There are few references to his work in subsequent scholarship about Spielrein. The absence of any proper biography in English has meant that these two problematical accounts of Spielrein's life have created an image of her that is highly distorted. I hope that anyone coming to the story for the first time will find my account of her life and ideas convincing. Those who already know the received version will find that this book challenges their pre-conceptions. I hope they too will be persuaded by the evidence.

In order to write this book from a fresh perspective, I have read, re-read, and in many cases copied out large sections of what Spielrein and her contemporaries wrote, in order to get a sense of what really happened. As a result, I have formed a view of her life that is very different from the popular versions. Without ruining the suspense for readers, it may be helpful if I briefly summarise how my account diverges from these.

I do not believe that Jung undertook psychoanalysis of Spielrein during her hospital admission in 1904-5, or at any time thereafter. I concur with the Swiss historian Angela Graf-Nold that it was probably Jung's director, Eugen Bleuler, who was most instrumental in bringing about a swift improvement in her mental state during her hospital admission. I endorse the conclusions of the psychoanalyst Henry Lothane, who has established that Jung never provided therapy for Spielrein after she was discharged from hospital, nor did she or her family ever pay for sessions. When Jung's transgressions took place he was her former hospital psychiatrist and current university teacher and friend, not her therapist. John Kerr's imaginative reconstruction of her weekly sessions as an outpatient was based on a false assumption.

I consider as flimsy the claim that the maverick psychoanalyst Otto Gross persuaded Jung to have an erotic relationship with Spielrein: Jung had already

5

had affairs and needed little persuasion. His intense affair with Spielrein was not a long one, probably lasting just over five months in 1908. The belief that Freud's intervention helped Spielrein and Jung to end their relationship is also incorrect. After the initial crisis had resolved, they had intermittent erotic encounters for a further year or so. Spielrein then became tired of Jung's erratic moods and philandering. When she graduated from medical school, she left Jung and Zurich immediately on her own initiative. Spielrein's and Jung's feelings were unequal. He only ever wrote four letters to her in which he expressed anything like the degree of love she felt for him, and these were written within the space of a few months during their affair. At other times his letters to her were harsh, critical, anti-Semitic or anti-woman. The evidence that Jung based his conception of the 'anima' on her – the archetypal female image within each man – is circumstantial and tenuous. However, she may have given him the idea that lay at the core of his system of psychology and treatment – the importance of pursuing one's personal destiny or individuation. I explore all these issues by examining the documents themselves.

I do not think that Jung's relationship with Spielrein requires a psychoanalytic explanation. He was neither the first nor the last male doctor with a strong sex drive and a pregnant wife to become dangerously entangled with a young female admirer for a while, break it off when his wife discovered it, and then resume it once things had calmed down. A great deal of what he wrote to Freud explaining the relationship can be read as the kind of story that any young man caught in that situation would construct. Much of it was demonstrably untrue. I do not believe the general reader needs anything beyond intelligence and empathy to relate to what happened. Whether Jung and Spielrein had intercourse remains an unresolved question. The evidence is contradictory. The idea that Jung spanked her is a figment of one film director's over-heated imagination.

Another area where I diverge from some commentators concerns the lifelong effect on Spielrein of her relationship with Jung. After she left him of her own volition in 1911, she sought a meeting with him on only one further occasion. She felt longing for him for several more years, but had distanced herself from him both intellectually and psychologically by 1920. I do not share the assumption that Spielrein's life was forever tinged with the masochism that was recorded as a feature of her sexual fantasies when in hospital. I do not believe it is either appropriate or possible to base interpretations of what she did in later life – let alone how she dressed, or designed her apartment in Stalinist Russia – on her adolescent sexual fantasies. These kinds of interpretations belong in the consulting room with the living, not on the written page relating to the dead.

I do not see Spielrein's life back in Russia as a sad anti-climax to her career.[2] After two years under the Bolshevik spotlight in Moscow, she worked as a children's doctor back in her home town of Rostov-on-Don for at least fifteen years while she brought up two musically gifted daughters. She published original work in psychology for as long as it was safe in the Soviet Union, and possibly longer. She may have been the last person ever to mount a vigorous public defence of Freud and psychoanalysis in the Soviet Union, and probably went on seeing patients after this was banned. The image of Sabina Spielrein as an adult that I like to hold in my mind is the one portrayed by her niece Menikha, who knew her in the late 1930s: 'Sabina Nikolayevna was by her upbringing a very well mannered, friendly, and gentle person. At the same time she was tough as far as her convictions were concerned – she could not be convinced of the contrary.'[3] The other image is the one that shines out of her personal and professional writings: that of a gifted and immensely original scholar, thinker and doctor, who was determined to be her own woman.

The rediscovery of Sabina Spielrein

The story of Sabina Spielrein's rediscovery is almost as remarkable as that of her life. When Spielrein returned from Switzerland to Russia in 1923, she left nearly thirty years' worth of diaries and correspondence behind her. She gave every indication that she expected to return to Switzerland in a few months. Her journals and letters had always meant a great deal to her, and the restitution of memory was central to her professional work. Spielrein left her papers at the place where she worked, the Rousseau Institute. Its director was an eminent psychologist called Édouard Claparède. She expected to return to Geneva shortly. In the event, she never came back, and they remained there for fifty years.

When the correspondence between Freud and Jung was published in 1974, scholars began to scrutinise it. Inevitably, they looked at the more puzzling references, including those that might shed light on the two men's turbulent relationship. Aldo Carotenuto was among these scholars. Based on the references to Spielrein and a great deal of intelligent guesswork, he came to the conclusion that she must have been crucial in Jung's own psychological development. In 1977 he published a book about Jung where he put forward this idea. By good fortune, he had a friend who had carried out research on Édouard Claparède. This friend, Carlo Trombetta, spoke to Claparède's nephew and heir Georges de Morsier, and mentioned Spielrein. In October 1977, de Morsier phoned Trombetta to say that some documents had been found in the basement of the Palais Wilson, where the Rousseau Institute was sited. These appeared to relate to Spielrein, and were indeed the cache of papers she had left behind. Carotenuto examined them and realised their significance. He published around thirty extracts written between 1909 and 1912 in his book, *A Secret Symmetry*, which also included letters from Sabina Spielrein to Jung dated 1911 to 1918, and correspondence between Spielrein and Freud dated 1909 to 1923. His book, together with the Freud-Jung letters, finally showed Spielrein's importance in the lives of the two men and the fate of their relationship. For unknown reasons, Carotenuto did not state that the diary extracts were taken from only one of a number of diaries that Spielrein started to keep at the age of ten and continued to write, in exercise books and on loose sheets of paper, for at least seventeen years.[4]

Since Carotenuto's book was published, further documents have emerged from the archive. In 1983, extracts from a diary of around 1906-7 appeared in a French journal: they took the form of some extended letters that Spielrein had drafted to send to Jung. Jung's own letters to Spielrein were finally released by the C.G. Jung Estate in 1986, and included in the German edition of Carotenuto's book. Ten years later, the researchers Irene Wackenhut and Anke Willke presented a dissertation to the University of Hanover Medical School entitled 'Sabina Spielrein: Abuse Victim and Psychoanalyst'. This contained a large amount of further material, including selected extracts translated from Spielrein's childhood diaries in Russian and further student diaries in German, as well as family letters. Although the dissertation was never published, portions have been widely quoted in other books and articles. A significant selection was issued in Germany in 2006, in an edition by Traute Hensch. In her German biography of Spielrein, Sabine Richebächer also cited some further diary entries, as well as quoting from around a hundred letters and other documents that she was able to examine in Geneva. Other letters, or fragments of letters, have appeared in various journals over the years as different scholars have been granted access to the archive. Some important letters were seen in the Geneva archive and translated from the original German and Russian by Henry Lothane.

The rediscovery of Spielrein's papers remains frustratingly incomplete. Spielrein's literary estate reverted to her niece Menikha in Russia in 1999. Following her death the next year it passed down to her first cousin Evald Shpilrain. It now resides with his son, the mathematician Professor Vladimir Shpilrain in New York, who is Spielrein's great-nephew. However, her papers remain in a private home near Geneva, with the de Morsier family. Much of Spielrein's correspondence with her family and friends has never been examined, let alone catalogued, published or translated. The same may be true of her diaries as well. All the available editions simply indicate where sections are absent, without specifying their number or length. Attempts have been made to arrange for their transfer to a state archive so that scholars might have access to them. These efforts have been caught up in issues of ownership and copyright and have so far failed. For whatever reason, my own attempts to contact the custodians of the archive met with no response, although I had already decided that there was enough material in the public domain to justify a new biography. Having the support of members of the Spielrein family was a great bonus. It would be a wonderful achievement if the custodians of the archive and the inheritors of the literary estate could honour their forebears by agreeing to deposit the archive with a suitable institution. A long overdue assessment of all her private papers could then proceed.

Taken together, the available material seems like a collection of glittering fragments, each one immensely precious in its own right, and probably large enough to guess at the appearance of the whole mosaic. It is tantalising not to know what is missing. It is impossible to know how it would affect our understanding of Spielrein if we had a scholarly edition of all her diaries, her entire correspondence and her professional writings. She was a wonderful writer, and they would make far more compelling reading than anything a biographer could ever hope to offer.

Finally, I have chosen the title of this book, *Sex Versus Survival*, for two reasons, which will become clear in the course of the book. First, it is clear from her writings that Spielrein in her youth experienced sexuality as something demonic, imposed against her own wish to attain an independent identity. In addition, this gave her an intuitive understanding of one of the principles of modern evolutionary thinking: the central challenge of our lives is to balance the drive for reproduction with the need to survive.

Notes on the text

1. All translations of Spielrein's diaries and letters, and of correspondence to her, are original except where indicated. Other translations are from published collections listed in the bibliography, including the Freud/Jung letters.

2. I have recorded dates as they appear on the original documents. Russia used the Julian calendar until 1918, so dates there were twelve days behind Western Europe until 1900, and thirteen days behind between 1900 and 1918.

3. I have used Sabina Spielrein's first name until her adulthood, and then her

surname, except when writing about other family members in the same passage. Spielrein's first brother was called Yasha in childhood and Jan as an adult so I have used these names, not his formal name Yakob. Her second brother Isaac used the name Sanya in childhood, Oskar while living in Germany, and Itshe when publishing in Yiddish. To avoid confusion I have used the first two names only. I have transliterated all Russian, Yiddish and Hebrew names phonetically, using 'kh' to indicate the sound in 'loch', e.g. Khave Mordekhayevna Lublinskaya.

4. In quotations from diaries and letters, I have used italics to indicate words that were underlined. Three dots signify that I have omitted words from the text for brevity, unless there is a footnote stating the ellipsis was in the original. Three dots in square brackets […] indicate a gap in the source. Phrases within square brackets are glosses to explain a foreign phrase or technical term. I have sometimes altered punctuation, capitalised a quotation or inserted a full stop at the end, for ease of reading.

5. It is impossible to cover a vast amount of detail without making mistakes, for example through miscopying or using an inaccurate source. Please can readers let me know when they discover any of these so that I can correct them in any future editions.

1

Childhood 1885-1904

18 October, 1910. Instead of working – writing my diary!¹

I T IS a week before her twenty-fifth birthday. Sabina Spielrein has barely slept during the night. A comment from the previous day kept running around her head. It was made by her former psychiatrist, now teacher and lover, Carl Jung. His comment called into question her most cherished conviction: that she had a 'higher calling', of divine origin. Now, in the morning, she cannot manage to study, even though her final exams at medical school are due in only two months. Instead, she is writing in her diary, and trying to come to terms with Jung's remark:

> For that is what robbed me of my night's rest: the thought that I might be only one of the many, my achievements might not rise above the average, and my 'higher calling' might be a ridiculous dream that I now have to pay for. The question is: how did this need to believe in a higher calling ever become so strong within me?

From childhood, Sabina Spielrein felt called to an extraordinary destiny. Her belief drew her to some of the greatest men of her age. It governed her career. At the time she wrote those words, it was the main source of energy in her life. She once thought this destiny meant that she would have an enduring relationship with Jung, and that they would inspire each other to great achievements. At other times she realised such a relationship would never happen, but she might still bear his child: a son named Siegfried, who would himself have a heroic destiny. Now, she was beginning to accept this too would never happen. Jung was, after all, a married man with three children, a successful career and many other girlfriends. She had persuaded herself that her 'higher calling' would take the form of a new theory instead: a ground-breaking idea about sex and death that would transform people's understanding of the human mind. One way or another, only one thing really mattered to her. She must do something exceptional with her life. She could not be 'only one of the many' – whether that meant sharing Jung with his other mistresses, or turning out to have only a mediocre talent.

To strengthen her resolve, she decided to take a new approach in her diary. Instead of writing obsessively about her relationship, as she had often done, she started to set down the facts of her childhood and the history of her family. Much of what we know of Sabina Spielrein's origins comes from those pages of self-analysis, written after that turbulent night. Her family story anticipates, to an uncanny degree, many of the themes of Spielrein's own life: passion, prophetic abilities, forbidden liaisons, religious divisions, disappointment, transformation, and the risk of oblivion.

*

In the middle of the nineteenth century, Sabina Spielrein's family on both sides were traditional, orthodox Jews. They all lived within the Pale of Settlement – the area on the western edge of the vast Russian empire where Jews were legally permitted to live. Her father's family lived in Warsaw, formerly the capital of the Polish kingdom, but absorbed into Russia in 1815 after Napoleon's defeat. Her mother's family lived in the eastern part of the Pale, in the province of Yekaterinoslav in the Ukraine, near the Black Sea. Their family name – Lublinksy – suggests that they probably originated from Poland too, and the city of Lublin. In spite of the geographical distance between the Spielreins and the Lublinskys, the two families led similar lives. They observed traditional Jewish practices of living and worship. As Jews, they were restricted to a small number of occupations. They were excluded from universities and most social institutions. They were subject to periodic outbreaks of violence by local Poles or Ukrainians. However, they also saw what the historian Martin Gilbert has described as taking place during the middle and late nineteenth century: 'a great flourishing of Jewish literary, cultural, political, educational, journalistic, religious and spiritual activity'.[2]

The lives of the Spielrein family reflected this in every way. By the time Sabina was born, the family had experienced huge social advancement. They become highly educated. Her father went to university in Berlin. Her mother's family moved to the port of Rostov-on-Don, near the Black Sea. They joined the 'merchant guild' class. This entitled them to property, the right to trade abroad,[3] and exemption from conscription – a crucial privilege in a country where young Jewish men, unlike ethnic Russians, were subject to conscription for up to twenty-five years. They mixed freely among their Russian contemporaries and intellectual society. They travelled widely. As we shall see, their views about women, religion and sex were as liberal as those of anyone in Vienna or Paris.

Rostov-on-Don was a thriving industrial city, with a population of around 120,000 by the end of the nineteenth century. Look at it on a map and you will get a sense of its importance. It lies thirty kilometres upstream from the Sea of Azov, a huge sheltered bay at the north-east corner of the Black Sea, diagonally opposite Istanbul. Just as Istanbul was the gateway to the Mediterranean and the west, Rostov was the point of entry to the vast hinterland of Russia, stretching thousands of miles to the Pacific Ocean. Positioned south of Moscow, and just across the Caucasus from Georgia, Armenia and Iran, Rostov was a trading centre for fish, wheat, tobacco, wool and oil. It was a meeting place for dozens of cultures, and connected by a growing railway system with Western Europe. One Jew born in Rostov at the turn of the century wrote about his memories of the city as a child as follows:

I always pictured my city as a river city; I always surveyed her from the river shore ... In my time, if a traveller came to Rostov by steamer from the north or south, he could see the city at her decorative best. She made a pretty scene dominating the Don and the flat steppes beyond. The domes of the two cathedrals, the old one and the new one, led to the smaller churches and older buildings in what I liked to imagine as a dishevelled procession.[4]

He described the wide avenues ascending from the port, and the bazaars where Cossacks from the steppes and peasants from Armenia and the Ukraine sold their wares. He wrote of the fisherwomen and tricksters, the pedlars, palm-readers and somnambulists, and the parades, fires, demonstrations, sensational murders and cholera outbreaks that he remembered from his youth. In his memory, Rostov-on-Don was a 'young, naïve, enthusiastic, cruel city'.

Someone else who knew Rostov was Chaim Weizmann, later the first president of Israel, whose wife Vera Chatzmann originated from the city. He wrote:

Rostov-on-Don, in southern Russia, is the gateway to the Caucasus; the Jewish community there was small, and though subject to all the disabilities which crippled Jewish life in the Pale, its material condition was on the whole easier. The district was wealthier, competition was less keen, and if a family belonged – as my wife's did – to the class of so-called "guild merchants", they enjoyed special privileges – for Jews, that is – and consequently a more comfortable existence.[5]

Weizmann observed that Jews from Rostov had relatively little contact with the poorer Jewish masses in western Russia and Poland. He also noticed how levels of anti-semitism were lower in Rostov than elsewhere. Jewish and Russian doctors and lawyers mingled with little difficulty.[6] In spite of this, it is important not to romanticise the situation. There were periodic waves of pogroms in nearby Ukraine, including in Yekaterinoslav in 1883.[7] Massacres of Jews and lootings of Jewish property were to affect Rostov itself during the revolution of 1905, and again during the Bolshevik revolution and civil war. The fear of sudden eruptions of anti-Jewish violence was always present in times of political instability.

Between 1885 and 1915, the Jewish population of Rostov increased tenfold.[8] Although most Jews were traders and craft workers, the community included many doctors, lawyers, teachers, mining engineers and wealthy merchants like Sabina's father. The main Choral Synagogue included a house of prayer, a library and a school. There was a Soldier's Synagogue for retired soldiers from the Tsar's army, and later a Handcraftsmen's Synagogue as well. From 1881 there was a Jewish hospital.[9] Many of the Jewish children attended secular schools. At the time of Sabina's birth, around a third of the children in the girls 'gymnasium' or high school were Jewish. Moisei Aisenstadt, the main rabbi of the town from 1889 to 1910, was an advocate of Zionism, unusual for a religious figure of the time. An edict of 1888 placed Rostov outside the Pale of Settlement and closed it officially to further Jewish settlement. This does not seem to have prevented immigration into the town. In a census in 1897, there were around 12,000 members of the community.

Sabina's mother was the daughter and grand-daughter of rabbis. She was born in 1863, as Khave Mordekhayevna Lublinskaya. As the family rose socially, she Russianised her name to Eva Markovna. When Sabina set down her family history in her diary, she wrote first of all about Eva's grandfather, Rabbi Lublinsky the elder:

I knew my great-grandfather until I was 3 or 4 years old. In my memory he was a large friendly man dressed in black, nothing more. What was far more important was what I heard about him. He was a much loved rabbi in Yekaterinoslav. People would carry him around our town on their shoulders. There were stories about his prophetic abilities. I particularly remembered one that was told about his death: he quite calmly predicted the moment of his death, even the exact time. He did not really die, but rather made his farewell and went to God, who was calling him.[10]

His son, Rabbi Mordekhai Lublinsky, inherited his character (see plate section no. 1). He was still alive at the time Spielrein was writing her family history. By then he was senile, but still 'cheerful and loving':

> My grandfather loved people. His house was always open to all comers ... Numerous relatives lived there and were allowed to take as much money as they needed. There was none left for the dowry for his daughter, but that did not trouble him. He firmly believed that God would provide for his daughter and he was right.

There were many stories about him. He defended people in court. He overpowered two boys trying to beat up an old woman on the street. He gave his last three roubles to a poor woman. He was also allowed to deliver speeches in public places, in a way that was usually not tolerated in Russia.[11] Sabina described how her grandfather had suffered a big disappointment in his youth. Many women adored him because of his loving nature and his good looks, but he fell in love with the daughter of a Christian doctor. His father forbade the match. Instead, there was an arranged marriage to Sabina's grandmother. 'Nana' was evidently 'loving and long suffering but not very intelligent'. Rabbi Lublinsky moved with his family from the Ukraine to the community in Rostov – joining the more liberal Jews who now formed the backbone of the community. He was an advocate of secular learning and social assimilation. He sent his daughter Eva to the Russian high school. Sabina believed this had something to do with his thwarted love:

> Apparently the image of his first love lived on in his unconscious, because he regarded study of the Christian sciences higher than anything else. His daughter had to study, always just study; she was not allowed to help with the housework.[12]

Eva was one of the first Jewish women in Russia to go to university. She had been brought up with two brothers that Sabina described in her diary as 'stupid' and 'limited', but her third and youngest brother Moishe or Mosya was highly intelligent and also went to university, training to be a doctor. (Eva's mother evidently had many other children who died very young, but there is no further information about them.[13]) Eva herself trained as a dentist, although she did not practise for long. By adulthood, she had become an eligible match for any Jewish professional. She was first engaged to a physician, but the families were opposed. Her fiancé's parents spread rumours about her, and their son believed them. They separated. Eva felt her life was 'ruined' by the rumours.[14] She then turned down a Christian suitor, 'a respected figure in St Petersburg'. She told him it would destroy her parents if they married. The next day he shot himself.

In due course, her father introduced her to a more suitable match: Naftul Aaronovich Spielrein. He had been born in 1861 and was already a successful businessman, a dealer in fertiliser and animal feed. He was one of five children – three boys and two girls. Like Eva's family, his own family in Warsaw spoke Yiddish, the traditional language of eastern European Jews. The family name itself is Yiddish for 'fair play', or more strictly 'pure play'. Like many educated Polish Jews of his time, his affinity was for western European and particularly German culture. By the time he met Eva he had acquired many other languages, including not only Polish and Russian but also Hebrew, French, German, English, and the classics. He developed an interest in music, a passion his daughter was to inherit. One of his brothers, Adolf, qualified as a doctor just as Eva's brother Mosya had done. Naftul studied agricultural science in Berlin and appears to have been something of a polymath, with a lifelong interest in politics and philosophy. He was a vegetarian and refused to wear a hat or overcoat all year round, eccentricities that probably would have marked him out more then than nowadays.

After moving from Warsaw to Russia, Naftul changed his name to Nikolai Arkadyevich. This signified a shift of social class, and one of nationality as well. Eva's parents were impressed by Nikolai's intelligence and piety. However, Sabina described his piety as a double-edged sword: it took the form of 'a vague belief in a destiny-like force'. In the eyes of believers, he was 'a straightforward heretic'.[15] Eva turned down the marriage three times. In the end, impressed by his intelligence, 'his firm and noble character', and his concern for her, she assented. Sabina wrote: 'He knew how to win over Mother's parents ... They became a couple. One could scarcely think of two more different people.'[16]

On 25 October 1885, at the age of twenty-two, Eva gave birth to her first child: Sabina Nikolayevna. In the Jewish birth register, she was recorded with the Yiddish name Sheyve.[17] Later, Eva was to have four more children. The first son Yakob, or Yasha, was born in June 1887, only a year and a half after Sabina. The next son Isaac, or Sanya, arrived four years afterwards, in 1891. When Sabina was eight and a half, in 1894, there was a second girl, Emilia. Finally, the last son, Emil, was born in 1899. All three boys were to become nervous and troubled in childhood, like Sabina. All three also grew up to become notable scientists. By the time the family was complete, the Spielreins were extremely well off. They were one of the wealthiest families in the city, as well as among the best educated (see plate section no. 2). They moved from an apartment and built a lavish house, a 'sugar-cake' rococo palace on one of Rostov's principal avenues, named after the poet Pushkin, a couple of kilometres north of the river Don. As well as Nikolai's business office, Eva had a consulting room there, as did her medical brother Mosya. As the years passed, and the family's wealth increased further, they acquired other properties in the surrounding town.

We have an unusual amount of information about Sabina's childhood. This comes from several sources. When she was admitted to hospital in her teens, it was at the time psychiatrists first became interested in the events of childhood and recorded them. Sabina's own diaries date back to the age of ten. Later, she wrote about her memories in her adult diaries and professional writing too. The information from these sources helps to explain many aspects of her personality, including her emotional disturbance and also her resilience and creativity.

As a small child, Sabina was sickly. She suffered from recurrent sore throats, stomach pains and intractable constipation. She had two life-threatening infections, measles and diphtheria.[18] She was also a troubled child. She enjoyed being hurt or watching others being hurt, although it made her furious as well. She masturbated a lot, particularly after she had been excited by being beaten or witnessing a beating. Later, she developed an obsession with the sight of her father's hand, and also with images of him defecating. In time, these problems extended to her brothers and other men as well. They continued throughout her childhood and adolescence, and contributed to her breakdown in her late teens, as the following chapters will show. Punishment by beating was extremely common in families in Russia at the time.[19] Sabina's problems were probably not triggered by those alone. More likely, they were a consequence of far wider unhappiness within the family, of which the beatings were a part.

Sabina's father was prone to depression and suffered outbursts of rage. He took to his bed for days at a time, refusing to eat. Sometimes he threatened suicide.[20] His daughter's descriptions of him create the impression of someone with a dominating presence: ferociously intelligent, imaginative, critical, autocratic, moody, driven and at times cruel. He disliked physical contact with others.[21] Sigmund Freud, who was to meet him on one occasion, described him as 'a man I found so interesting, even if inflexible'.[22] According to her later hospital notes, Sabina loved him 'painfully', while at the same time feeling a 'curious abhorrence' towards him. He began punishing his children from when they were three or four. With Sabina, he would sometimes lift up her skirt and smack her on her buttocks, doing this in front of her siblings in order to humiliate her. Later, one of her medical school contemporaries was to describe how Sabina's

17

beatings 'built up inside her mind as enormous and overwhelming suffering'.[23] In spite of this degree of cruelty, Nikolai was a complex man, with a lifelong passion for literature, philosophy and psychology. Sabina's relationship with her father was complicated too, and in some ways contradictory. As an adult, she wrote admiringly of his qualities, and was close to him at the end of his life.

Eva Spielrein was always described as 'nervous'. Throughout her life, her letters to Sabina convey a high degree of anxiety, concern and protectiveness – although the circumstances often warranted this. When Sabina was admitted to hospital, the notes describe her mother as having 'hysterical absences of a childish kind'.[24] Sabina later described how Eva had the habit of buying everything she saw. She would borrow money from relatives in order to conceal this from Nikolai. When he found out, there would be a 'huge row'.[25] In her letters and diaries, Sabina rarely wrote warm comments about her mother. In her adult life, she stayed away from her for many years, waiting until her death before returning to Russia.

At a young age, Sabina developed tremendous powers of creative imagination. A paper she wrote when she was twenty-six shows how her sense of a 'higher calling' first started:

> My imagination was vast. I was a goddess, and ruled a mighty realm. I had a power that I called 'Partunskraft'[26] ... With this power I could know everything, and obtain everything, which I only had to desire ... I had so much power in me, unknown to anyone else, and I was certainly God's chosen. My parents knew nothing about this aspect of my emotional life ... I did not want to hear stories from other people at that time, I could produce as many of those as I wanted.[27]

According to the same paper, her mother kept the facts of sex from her. So did her school. She only learned about it properly from zoology lectures at university. Nevertheless, as a child she thought a great deal about how humans were created. On one occasion she 'tirelessly dug a hole in the ground' and asked her mother how long it would take until she could pull out an American by the legs. 'It then became my burning wish,' she explained, 'to create a living man, in the same way as our loving God.' She tried to do so from earth and clay, and from olives and soap. Inspired by an uncle who was a chemist, she spilt the remains of food and drink onto a table, and mixed them together making a big mess:

> It gave me great pleasure when one colour changed into another, or a new shape or consistency emerged. So I cannot forget the mixture of pleasure

and fear that I felt, when a piece of material through the mysterious power of a fluid turned into paper.

She kept fluid in flasks and 'wonder-stones' from which she expected creation to occur. She was also a bold child. On one occasion when she was three or four, a teenage uncle came to visit.[28] He took her and Yasha into a dark room, pretending to be God. He told them scary stories and played the violin. Two-year-old Yasha was frightened, but Sabina thought it was funny. According to her recollections, she continued to be fearless until she was around seven, but then she started to become preoccupied with illness and death:

It had not escaped my parents' notice that I was scaring my brother, and one day my father said to me: 'Just wait, fate will certainly punish you. One day you will suffer fear, and then you will know how your brother felt.' I don't think I took this threat seriously, but nonetheless it had definite consequences, for one day I became really frightened when I saw two black kittens sitting on the chest of drawers in the next room. It was certainly an illusion, but nonetheless so vivid, that I can still see the little creatures just as they were, sitting peacefully together. 'That means Death, or Plague,' I thought.[29]

After hallucinating the kittens, she remembered how she once asked a young mother if she could have a baby herself. The woman told her she might be able to give birth to a kitten instead. She became scared she would indeed bear a kitten. When she wrote these memories down in her paper, she commented how often women regard pregnancy and birth as a dangerous illness, fearing that new life will always come at the expense of the old one. It was an idea that would preoccupy her for many years. She also described how she used to imagine frightening creatures, and feared that an unknown force would pull her away from her parents. She was fascinated by hearing descriptions of different diseases, and worried at the same time. At night, she thought of these diseases as people who wanted to attack her or take her away.

Sabina was religious and prayed a lot. From the age of seven or eight, she had her own imaginary 'guardian spirit' and held conversations with her in German. Her mother used to tell the children traditional Hasidic stories — Jewish tales of angels and demons — acquired from her own heritage. Sabina loved these. Her mother explained that all their sins would be written in down in heaven, in red. On one occasion, Sabina and her two brothers alarmed their mother by kneeling on top of a cupboard, praying to God to go to heaven.[30]

19

Sabina and Yasha attended a small elementary school that was part of the Fröbel movement, renowned for its enlightened and liberal approach to education in the early years.[31] At home, she learned to speak French and English fluently, as well as German. 'Papa speaks French with me and Yasha and German with Sanya,' she wrote.[32] Sometimes they would speak different languages on different days. Later, Sabina chose to learn biblical Hebrew.[33] As well as servants, the family also employed a music teacher and a private tutor. They had a Polish nanny nicknamed 'the bomb', whom Sabina described as 'wicked, thin, tall, and very dirty. She hates us and always argues with us.'[34]

Throughout her childhood, punishments could be arbitrary and ruthless. Nikolai would confiscate his children's belongings and threaten to burn them.[35] An account from Sabina's diary, aged twelve, depicts one particularly unpleasant episode. At the time Yasha was eleven and Isaac (Sanya) seven:

> At tea-time Yasha found the picture of the orang-utan in Sanya's book. Sanya said Yasha had torn it out. Yasha kept saying 'No.' But finally he said: 'Yes, maybe I did.' Then Sanya began punching him with his fists, but Yasha held his hands back. Papa then ordered them to beat each other for a whole hour. Sanya howled twice. Papa gave Sanya a fork, so he could poke out Yasha's eyes, but Yasha would not let him do it. It became so noisy that Mama came in and took Sanya away. Papa said when two people argue like this, he will lock them in somewhere and make them fight for three whole hours.[36]

The brothers became moody and aggressive in their turn. As her hospital notes testify, Sabina was just as afraid of them as she was of her father.

At the age of eleven, Sabina gained admission to a competitive high school for girls, the Yekaterinskaya Gymnasium (named after Empress Catherine the Great). She concentrated on languages and classics, with relatively little time for sciences. Out of school, she studied singing, the violin and piano. Her father put her under tremendous pressure. While other girls felt proud of scoring three or four out of five in class assignments, her father teased her if she got less than top marks. She would tremble with fear that he would ask her.[37] She used a code to write things in her diary that she did not wish him to read,[38] but he would threaten to burn it if she spent too much time writing rather than practising the piano.[39] Sometimes she needed time off school for nervous symptoms. Her father told her to lie and say that she had been physically unwell. She objected to this, knowing why she felt unwell, and believing that it was better to be honest about it.[40] An ambiguous entry in her diary suggests she may have been scared of his physical advances: 'It is time to sleep, otherwise papa will come ... it always seems that papa comes and I freeze ... Goodbye day. And it is 5 past 9. And papa is coming ... it is time.'[41]

Following her twelfth birthday, Sabina had a party to celebrate becoming 'bat mitzvah', an adult woman according to religious law.[42] Shortly afterwards, all four children had a mock marriage ceremony in which she married Yasha, and Isaac married their little sister Emilia, accompanied by comical incantations and a feast. Even their mother joined them in the festivities.[43] On that occasion, Sabina decided she would have a baby girl, followed a year later by a baby boy – just like her mother. The account makes it sound as if the family could sometimes have fun. However, the beatings carried on. At thirteen, after being beaten by her mother, Sabina hid away in a cellar hoping to die from the cold. Her father threatened suicide, then tried to beat her too. He gave in to her pleas to stop, but forced her to kneel down and kiss a picture of her grandfather and to swear always to be a good child.[44]

Around this age, Sabina lost her belief in God. This 'left a void'. She kept her 'guardian spirit', and dreamed of having a girl friend, a Jewish girl who would be the best pupil in the class after herself. Such a girl appeared in reality and Sabina loved her 'with all the intensity of childish love'. The friendship lasted a year.[45] She then chose a Christian girl as her best friend. This girl pursued Sabina's brother Yasha for a while, and afterwards went out with his best friend.

Around the same age as Sabina lost her religious belief, she acquired an interest in science. She determined to become a doctor, following in the footsteps of two of her uncles. Her grandfather, Rabbi Lublinsky, gave his approval. 'I believe no-one could have been happier than my grandfather,' she wrote, 'when he learned that I had decided to study medicine.'[46] She wrote a school essay describing a man for whom science meant more than anything in the world and was ready to sacrifice his own life for it. She imagined how all his family had died of cholera, but his wife came back to him as a ghost and told him he should remain loyal to science and serve it unconditionally.[47] In some ways this defined her own future attitude to science.

In the vacations, there were walking trips in the Russian steppes, journeys on the steamer down the Don estuary, through the Sea of Azov and around the Black Sea, and visits to the extended family in Warsaw. When Sabina wrote about these trips, the writing was mature and beautiful:

I will never forget the impression that the sea made on me. It caused me no anxiety at all. I was charmed by the wonderful view, a splendid level surface like silver, it was as if little waves were catching and swallowing each other ... Light clouds moved gently across in turn, each enjoying its own dignity. A huge mother-cloud had linked arms with the little ones, for fear they might make some unseemly movement.[48]

Then, when Sabina was fourteen, her grandmother died. She wrote:

It is very difficult for me to live in this world without my grandmother. I often suffer from anxiety, and it seemed to me that only my Nana could protect me. I can't write anything more ... I remember how often she looked out for me, and persuaded Mama that there was no need for her to get cross with me. How she comforted me when I was upset. How she agreed with me that Sanya was naughty and not ill, and taught me how to deal with him. How I used one time to climb into Mama's and Nana's bed and dream about the future. With what great love Nana played with my hair, and how good I felt at those times. Now I am alone with my worries. I've got nobody with whom I can speak freely, nobody to talk to, about the things that interest me. All the worries that had piled up on me over a few days I used to spill out to Nana.[49]

This is a loving eulogy, but also a worrying one. Without the protective influence of her grandmother, she was exposed to all the turbulent cross-currents of her father's rage, her brothers' provocations, her mother's constant anxiety, and the academic pressure to excel.

In her teens she developed her first crush, on her Christian history teacher. Initially she felt revulsion for him, but over time she was captivated by his 'great intelligence and the serious, sad expression in his black eyes'.[50] At first, her infatuation led her to laugh a lot in his presence, but when she discovered the depth of his knowledge and her own eagerness for learning, her crush progressed by leaps and bounds: 'I wanted to make some sacrifice for him, I wanted to suffer for him.' Then the teacher began to show a distinct sexual interest in her and paid visits to her house. There was a rapid cooling off in her own feelings: 'In the end, he became simply a bore,' she wrote. Later, Jung recorded that the real reason she cooled off was because her love for him had brought on troubling fantasies about him, to do with beatings and excretion.[51] The contrast in these accounts alerts us to how much we need to read beneath the surface of the original documents. In the course of Spielrein's story, we will often come across different versions of events.

After Sabina rejected her teacher, he found a confidante in her mother and fell in love with her too. When Eva left for a vacation in Paris, he jumped out of a window, intending to take his own life. He was diagnosed as suffering from schizophrenia. Next, Sabina fell in love with her father's brother in Warsaw, Uncle Adolf. She felt he was not as intelligent as her teacher, but he had her father's 'noble character and a decidedly artistic bent'. To complicate matters Uncle Adolf fell in love with Eva, just as the teacher had done.[52] These were Sabina's first two experiences of infatuation and its unpredictable consequences.

The year after her grandmother's death, Sabina travelled with her mother and her youngest brother Emil to Berlin. She wrote vivid descriptions of everything, including the discomfort of the journey, and the independence of mind she found among people in Germany. She noted how women and men there were more equal. In anticipation of her later interests, she expressed curiosity about the way children acquire different languages in different ways.[53] Even at times like these, she was conscious of her mother's neediness: 'I am struggling with such an anxious mother,' she wrote, 'for whom I have to carry a serious responsibility.'[54] She described how Eva forgot she needed to show their passports at the border, and did not know she had to buy a ticket for Emil.[55]

Later that year, there was another death, far more tragic and unexpected than her grandmother's. Sabina's only sister Emilia died suddenly, at the age of six, from typhoid. This was devastating. 'I withdrew completely from other people,' she wrote later. 'After the death of my little sister, my illness began. I took refuge in isolation.'[56] Sabina had been ten when her sister was born, and was approaching her sixteenth birthday when Emilia died. A photo of the two daughters with their mother shows Emilia as a bonny, confident child, while Sabina looks at the photographer solemnly (see plate section no. 9). Sabina wrote little about Emilia, so we are left to imagine how much she had spent the six years of her sister's life playing with her, teaching her, and observing her with the attention that she was often to give children later. We know that Sabina's mental deterioration began from this time.[57] Her troubled family background and personal difficulties had made her vulnerable, but evidently this was the breaking point. The timing of Sabina's decline in relation to her sister's death seems clear from the records, but has rarely been the focus of any comment.[58] Today we might regard her breakdown as being triggered by a bereavement reaction.

Sabina continued to function well at school, and left with a gold medal. In every other respect, she fell apart. She stopped seeing her friends. The rows with her mother escalated. She developed tics and grimaces, and alternated between crying and laughter. Her psychosomatic problems worsened, including abdominal pains and headaches. She was now eighteen. It must have been clear to her parents that there would be no possibility of her securing a place at medical school, either in Russia or in the west. Nor would she be an eligible young bride. Her mother took her to stay with the family in Warsaw. Sabina's strong feelings for her Uncle Adolf, and Adolf's own feelings for her mother, cannot have not have made the stay an easy one. Her mental condition deteriorated further.

It would have been unthinkable for a wealthy and cosmopolitan family like the Spielreins to consider treatment for these kinds of problems in either Poland or Russia, where care for the mentally ill consisted of incarceration. Their choice could only be in a western country where psychiatry was most developed: France, Germany, Austria or Switzerland. Given Sabina's language skills, and her father's wealth and connections, they could have chosen any of these. Perhaps they considered Vienna, where Professor Sigmund Freud was experimenting with the radical and controversial new 'talking cure' known as psychoanalysis. Instead, they chose Switzerland.

2

Asylum 1904-1905

Anamnesis. Uncle Lublinsky is the informant. Patient was an intelligent pupil, received gold medal at Gymnasium. Always rather hysterical. Around 3 years ago, became more seriously ill. Has just been in Interlaken with Dr Heller for a month. Very dissatisfied there. No-one had done anything. She should have gone to Monakov. But M did not take her as she was too agitated. (As he is an old Russian Jew, he continually gives only meagre and evasive answers, and in addition he has not mastered German properly.) Today calmed down in the course of the day.[1]

THIS ENTRY in the hospital records, dated 18 August 1904, is by Dr Carl Gustav Jung. Sabina had been admitted to the Burghölzli Hospital, on the outskirts of Zurich, at ten o'clock the previous night. She had been given a diagnosis of hysteria. The entry starts with the word 'anamnesis' – literally, 'the uncovering of memory'. This was the standard term at the time for what doctors now call 'taking a history'. Later, in the world of psychoanalysis, it came to mean something different – the recollection of forgotten memories from the past. Here, Jung was simply taking down some standard information, including the fact that Sabina had already had an unsuccessful admission elsewhere. His informant was Eva Spielrein's youngest brother, medically qualified, described by his niece Sabina as 'very intelligent' and probably not much older than Jung.

How could Dr Jung have formed a view of him as an 'old Russian Jew'[2] whose answers were 'evasive'? This is a puzzle, but it alerts us immediately to the fact that medical notes are no more objective than diaries. They are complicated texts, displaying prejudices of the writer and the time, as well as being a medium for promoting their beliefs and theories.[3] We are incredibly fortunate that Sabina's hospital records have been preserved. At the same time, they need to be treated with caution, and sometimes read against the grain. Jung's perceptions of Jews were often negative, as later events will show. In addition, he may have been subject to common western stereotypes of Russians as temperamental and less civilised than westerners.[4] For his part, Dr Moishe Lublinsky might have been troubled by the fact that the Swiss psychiatrist never carried out a physical examination, something that would normally have happened both in western and eastern Europe.⁵

It is worth noting that Sabina calmed down in her first day in hospital. Even before treatment had begun, she was more settled. Is it possible that being in a place of safety, away from her family, was already having its effect? And had the handsome young physician already made an impact on her?

*

The Burghölzli was not the first place in Switzerland where Eva Spielrein and her brother had sought help. As the entry shows, she had already been to a sanatorium in Interlaken, run by a Dr Heller, and specialising in mental disorders. Her admission there was not a success. She developed a crush on the medical assistant, then felt let down by him. Dr Heller considered her level of disturbance unmanageable. Next, her family took her to the psychiatric clinic at the University of Zurich. It was run by an eminent Russian émigré, Professor Monakov, an expert in physical brain trauma. He felt she was too agitated for treatment there. It is not clear why he did not arrange her immediate admission to hospital instead.⁶

Finally, on the evening of 17 August, with Sabina in a state of extreme agitation, a Dr Bion was summoned to the hotel where they were staying. The doctor wrote a brief letter of referral to the Burghölzli, Zurich's local mental asylum, explaining that she was in a hysterical state, laughing and screaming. She could no longer stay at the hotel, and was a danger to herself.⁷ Bion believed that she was paranoid and psychotic – in other words unable to tell delusion from reality. Uncle Mosya and a medical police official took her to the hospital. Eva did not come, possibly because her presence might exacerbate her daughter's state. The short journey to the outskirts of Zurich would bring her into contact with some of the most radical doctors and thinkers of the age, changing her life – and theirs too.

The place where Sabina Spielrein arrived was one of the safest places in Europe for her to be. Attached to Zurich University, the Burghölzli was among the most advanced mental hospitals of its time. Its former director, Auguste Forel, was a pioneer of psychiatry who had turned it into a centre of international repute. He had abandoned the coercive methods of other mental hospitals at the time: the bed bath, the bed strap, and the straitjacket. He was an enthusiast for hypnosis, and one of the first doctors to carry out serious research into its use and efficacy. Sigmund Freud admired him, and had been a contributing editor of his *Journal of Hypnotism and Suggestion Therapy*. Forel took an interest both in the anatomy and physiology of the brain and in abnormal mental states. He was one of the first psychiatrists to promote a united view of the brain and mind. He regarded these as different perspectives on the same phenomenon, a view that has become common in our own age. He was also a passionate evolutionist. He spoke of how 'the longing of the human soul and the social experiences of the different human races and historical periods could be reconciled with the findings of natural science and with the laws of psychological and sexual evolution'.[8] He was one of the world's foremost researchers into the behaviour of ants as social creatures. He campaigned vigorously against alcohol consumption and promoted open discussion of sex and sexuality. As well as being a compassionate doctor, he was an outstanding manager and scientist.

Forel set exacting standards for his staff. The historian Angela Graf-Nold describes these as follows:

> He demanded of the doctors that they relinquish all private practice, and forbade them to accept gifts from relatives; he allowed only a joint kitty for tips for nurses and attendants. Under Forel ... there were 'residential duties' for medical and care personnel: apartments were available for the director and senior physician; assistants and trainee doctors had rooms; nurses did not have rooms of their own but slept on camp beds in the patients' rooms or in the corridors. Even married people had only one day a week off.[9]

By the time Sabina arrived, Forel had left the Burghölzli to pursue scientific studies in evolution. The director of the Burghölzli was now Forel's former assistant, a man named Eugen Bleuler. He too was one of the founding fathers of enlightened psychiatry. Brought up with a schizophrenic sister, he devoted himself passionately to the humanisation of psychiatric care. He anticipated much that we now regard as good care for the mentally ill. 'The most important tools for treating the psyche,' he argued, 'are patience, calm and inner goodwill towards the patients, three qualities that must be absolutely inexhaustible.'[10] Bleuler believed that a mental hospital should be a therapeutic community. Every patient contributed to this. So did all the staff members and their wives, who joined in everything from gardening to concerts, drama and scientific meetings. Bleuler's wife, Hedwig Waser, was a distinguished philologist but also joined in organising these events. Like Forel, Bleuler also made great high demands of his staff. They lived in the hospital, working from six in the morning till late in the evening. They ate alongside the patients. All the doctors were considered equally responsible for each patient, and had to report to him at regular morning and evening meetings.[11] One of Bleuler's disciples later described how 'the spirit of unconditional acceptance of the person, of the healthy as well as the sick, reigned in the hospital'.[12]

Bleuler took overall charge of Sabina's care, but most of her recorded contacts were with his acting deputy, Dr Carl Jung. At the age of twenty-nine, Jung was at the beginning of his career and only ten years older than Sabina. An imposing and passionate man, Jung was the son of a Protestant pastor and his troubled wife Emilie, herself often a psychiatric patient. While at medical school in Basel, Jung had acquired an interest in occult phenomena. Supervised by Bleuler, he wrote his doctoral dissertation based on his observations of séances carried out by his cousin, Helene Preiswerk. His work followed the ideas of Théodore Flournoy, a professor of experimental psychology in Geneva who had studied spiritualism and believed it was a psychological rather than a psychic phenomenon.[13] Jung traced elements of his cousin's séances to aspects of her own unconscious mind. This laid the foundations for his lifelong belief that our minds inherit shared cultural patterns which show themselves in myths, works of art, dreams and mental disturbance.

Jung had joined the Burghölzli in 1900 as second medical assistant. There were no other applicants and virtually no pay. Two years later, another doctor resigned because of overwork, and Jung was promoted to first assistant. By now, Bleuler had established an experimental psychology laboratory at the hospital. He hoped it would help to put psychological treatment on a sounder scientific footing. Bleuler invited Jung, together with his colleagues Franz Riklin and Ludwig Binswanger, to carry out research into Jung's current area of interest – word association tests. These tests explored connections that patients made between different ideas, as well as the time they took to respond to words, and any changes in the electrical resistance of their skin while they did so. This was believed to be a good way of diagnosing mental disorders. It also helped Jung to discover the notion of 'complexes': emotionally charged patterns of thoughts, feelings and images that he believed lay at the heart of mental disorders. Jung had no intention of staying at the Burghölzli. He had become engaged to Emma Rauschenbach, the daughter of a wealthy manufacturer. After two years, he resigned from the hospital and went to study in Paris. On his return, he and his new wife moved into an apartment in Zurich. In the normal course of events Jung would never have returned to the Burghölzli, but in the summer of 1903 he agreed to come back to cover two of the medical assistants who were on military service. While he was there, the senior physician Ludwig von Muralt fell ill with tuberculosis. Jung took over as his locum too.

At the time of Sabina Spielrein's admission, Jung was effectively covering the jobs of three doctors. He was not enjoying the work. His ambitions to move back to Basel had been thwarted by the appointment of someone else to the post of senior physician there. In the week following Sabina's admission, he wrote to a friend that he felt his academic career had been wrecked *'for ever'*.[14] He found himself writing letters, carrying out interviews, 'running all over the place and getting very annoyed'. He complained that he had lost six kilos in a year through overwork. However, the senior physician continued to take sick leave and Jung moved into his post in October 1904, two months into Sabina's admission. The following April, von Muralt resigned, and Jung was officially appointed as Bleuler's deputy. He was to remain at the Burghölzli until his resignation in 1909. Jung's tenure in the post continued exactly to the day he disclosed to Freud that his relationship with Sabina Spielrein had got out of hand.

Jung's new young Russian patient was suffering from hysteria – in the formal medical sense of suffering from uncontrolled emotions and gestures, with alterations in her physical sensation and function.[15] At that time, florid hysteria of the kind Sabina was displaying was quite common. It was one of the few ways that women from oppressive backgrounds could attract attention and help. There were various theories current at the time to account for the condition. The great French neurologist Jean-Martin Charcot believed it was an inherited neurological disorder. By now, a different kind of belief was emerging: that psychological trauma could cause the condition. Charcot's pupil Pierre Janet had proposed this idea. Both Bleuler and Freud had studied with him, and Jung had attended his lectures when he was in Paris. There was only one established treatment for hysteria: hypnosis. Although Sigmund Freud in Vienna had been developing his new method of psychoanalysis as an alternative, no one else was using it yet. As well as prescribing hypnosis, Bleuler also believed it was important 'to alter the conditions in which the syndromes grew' and 'to create a purpose in life for the patients by taking into account not only external relationships but also the internal ones which have caused the patients to reject their sense of purpose in life'.[16] As a rule, hysterical patients were not admitted to hospital but treated in the outpatient clinic. Out of the 332 patients admitted in 1904, only eleven suffered from hysteria.[17] The other residents of the hospital were mostly older than Sabina and suffered from more serious conditions such as schizophrenia. Jung himself had probably treated only eight such patients before.[18] However, he was now starting to experiment with word association as part of treatment as well as for diagnosis.

Sabina's hospital records cover the period from her arrival on 17 August

1904 to her discharge on 1 July the following year – around ten and a half months. By modern standards, the notes are sparse, consisting of only thirteen pages. There is a standard 'pro forma' cover sheet, and a second sheet with family details. There are six entries in the first week, covering her 'anamnesis'. The remaining pages include only fourteen written or typed entries, mostly by Jung. After the first week, these occur only weekly, then at much longer intervals, more or less stopping in January 1905. There are some additional documents about Sabina in Bleuler's file of correspondence as director. In a helpful comparison with other notes from the hospital, the Swiss psychiatrist Bernard Minder, who first published her records, pointed out that this reflects the fact that five doctors were looking after around 400 residential patients, as well as having to write reports, liaise with the authorities and engage with research and training, and spend some time with every single patient each day.[19] Much of the day-to-day care was carried out by the 97 nurses. In spite of the thinness of Sabina's notes, they make one thing clear. Her mental state improved rapidly, albeit with setbacks. By October, her progress was sufficient for Bleuler to support her wish to go to medical school in Zurich the following year. Later, her improvement became more rapid and sustained. From January 1905, she was effectively studying for medical school, and working alongside the doctors and medical students.

In almost every account of Sabina's story, there is a claim or an assumption that treatment by Jung brought about a rapid improvement. A careful reading of the hospital records does not support this. Her notes are in fact made up of several interwoven narratives. The central narrative concerns her disturbance at the time of her admission, and the pattern of her improvement. A parallel one relates to a small number of conversations Jung had with her about her childhood, her family and her sexual fantasies: what he was later to describe as her 'analysis'. Another important thread involves the interactions between Bleuler and the Spielrein family in the course of the year. Finally, there is a narrative that is only hinted at in the hospital records themselves, but was in time to become the dominant one: while she was Jung's patient, Sabina fell passionately in love with him. It is worth teasing these elements apart and examining them one at a time. The remainder of this chapter is devoted to the first of these narratives, summarising Sabina's overall progress during the course of the months she spent at the hospital. The next chapter is devoted to examining the exact details of what Jung and Bleuler did, and how each contributed to her improvement. The last and most important effect of Sabina's admission – her love for Jung – are the subject of the ensuing chapters. One of my purposes in separating these narratives is to challenge the pervading myth that has connected Sabina's improvement solely with Jung's treatment in spite of the documentary evidence.

After her arrival, Sabina was admitted to a private room in the women's wing, with a nurse assigned to her. Her parents agreed to pay the standard 1250 Swiss Francs per quarter, roughly the equivalent of what Jung would have earned once he became senior physician. A fortnight later, the fees were increased when it became apparent she would need intensive observation with a live-in nurse in her room.[20] Her identity as a wealthy and highly educated Russian Jew made her unusual in the hospital. In fact, she had far more in common with the medical students and assistant doctors there than with the vast majority of her fellow patients. Zurich University was already a magnet for Jewish students like herself who could not obtain placements back in Russia, while young Russian psychiatrists flocked to learn with Bleuler.[21] Sabina had in effect joined a small expatriate colony in the hospital, where Russian professionals almost certainly outnumbered Russian patients.[22]

The picture of Sabina at the time of her admission and on several occasions afterwards is of a deeply troubled, agitated and at times provocative adolescent. On the evening of her arrival, Jung wrote:

Patient laughs and cries in a strange combination with a compulsive manner. A mass of tics; she rotates her head jerkily, sticks out her tongue, twitches her legs. Complains of a terrible headache. She says she is not mad, she was only agitated at the hotel, she could not stand people or noise.[23]

The next morning, Jung completed the cover sheet of her file, with Uncle Mosya as his informant. Sabina's weight was recorded as 47.6 kilos, which was probably underweight for her.[24] In spite of Dr Lublinsky's reticence, Jung managed to elicit some more information – or perhaps added it later as more emerged from Sabina. He wrote that Sabina's father was 'Healthy, active, irritable, overwrought, neurasthenic, hot-tempered to an unreasonable degree.' After writing this, Jung deleted the word 'Healthy', suggesting that Dr Lublinsky gave one version of the story but he later found out a different one. Her mother was described as 'Nervous (like patient), *hysterical?*' We learn that 'one brother has hysterical weeping fits, another suffers from tics and is very hot-tempered, the third is melancholic and also does wrong in order to suffer'.[25]

In the days following her admission, Jung met Sabina regularly to take her history in more detail. Her mood fluctuated between calm and agitation. After a week, we learn of the kind of incident that was going to plague the staff for quite some time:

> On the evening of 22.8, 10pm, a tremendous noise. When the nurse (a replacement) was going to bed, the patient demanded she should leave the room for 5 minutes ... The nurse laughed and said 'no', whereupon the patient replied 'perhaps she thought she was going to kill herself.' Patient suddenly pulled off the curtain cord and while the nurse was trying to get it from her, she threw the nurse's watch on the floor, poured lemonade all over the room, pulled the bed apart, beat up the nurse, and then, wrapped in a blanket, sat in an armchair.[26]

And so it goes on. After an upsetting visit from her mother, she 'behaved badly'. The next day, after reading a letter from a friend, she 'tied a curtain cord round her neck (not in a very dangerous way)' and then tried to swallow a medallion on a gold chain. When Jung was absent for a week, she used his return as an opportunity to 'produce a few scenes'. First she climbed up a window grille in the corridor, them she sat for a long time in the doorway of her room, covered only in her nightdress and a blanket. When Jung did not come, she had a hysterical fit, became exhausted and let herself be put back to bed.[27]

However there were intervals of calm. These began in the first week, when she was put on strict bed rest with 'no books, no conversation, no visitors'. Gradually, as her stay continued, these intervals became more common. Barely a month after her admission, and before Jung had recorded any conversations other than his anamnesis, Bleuler wrote to her father to say there were now days which passed uneventfully.[28] At this point she was already participating in the examination of patients and going for walks in the hospital grounds with the nurses. Three days later, Jung was able to write that 'the states of agitation have become less frequent'.[29] However she still played 'childish pranks (suicidal gestures to drive the nurses crazy, running away, hiding, giving people scares, disregarding prohibitions.)' At times she was depressed, or developed physical symptoms. She also seemed to enjoy 'playing mad', although with an innocent and even humorous aspect:

> Patient entertains the other patients by telling them fantastic stories from Mars.[30] She claims that she travels to Mars every evening, and she projects all her counter-sexual fantasies onto this. People on Mars do not eat but are nourished by osmosis. They do not propagate, but instead children develop

quickly within the unconscious minds of different individuals and appear ready made and without further difficulty.[31]

At some point in her admission, Sabina wrote a 'Last Will'. It is her first recorded writing in German, so was presumably meant for her attendants to read:

When I die, I will only allow my head to be dissected, if it is not too horrible to look at. No young person must be present at the dissection. Only the keenest students may observe it. I bequeath my skull to our school. It should be placed in a glass and the following should be inscribed on the container (in Russian): 'And let young life play at the entrance to the tomb and let indifferent nature shine with eternal splendour'. I give my brain to you. Just place straight into a beautiful vessel decorated in the same way and write the same words on it. My body is to be cremated but no one must be present for this. Divide the ashes into three parts. Place one part in the urn and send it home, scatter another part on the earth in the middle of a big, big field (near us), plant an oak-tree there and write: 'I too was once a human being. My name was Sabina Spielrein'. My brother will tell you what is to be done with the third part.[32]

A poem written in October 1904, this time in Russian, testifies to how depressed she felt at times:

Empty, dark and cold,
Empty and dark around me,
I am alone in the world,
All alone.
No dear little father,
No dear little mother,
No roof for a home,
No one to tell my worries.
Oh my head,
My poor little head,
No way can I give you peace,
Nowhere give you rest …[33]

Despite such moods, there had been a sustained improvement in her mental state by now. Bleuler wrote to her parents that she was 'assisting one of our doctors with a scientific project'. The doctor in question was his deputy Jung. The project was a post-doctoral thesis he was writing on word association, in order to apply for a university lectureship later in the year. Bleuler also informed her parents she was now planning to go to medical school in Zurich the following Spring.[34] By now – late October – Sabina's status in the hospital was unprecedented: research assistant to the new senior physician, and medical student in waiting. At this point, Jung had recorded only one extended conversation since the week of her admission, and Bleuler did not mention that Jung's support went beyond letting her help with his research.

For several more weeks, there was an oscillation between calm and her 'pranks'. In early November, Bleuler recorded that she had absconded over the wall leaving a note that 'if I'm not back by tomorrow morning, it doesn't necessarily mean that I'm dead'. She then returned after five minutes. Bleuler's entry continues: 'Enjoys putting obstacles in the ward corridor (benches, etc.) for the writer to jump over, is pleased when he jumps ... Or she composes songs featuring the clinic doctors but she cannot recite them for laughing.'[35]

As Christmas approached, Sabina was taking walks to the local village of Seefeld. In January she was becoming 'slowly reacquainted with the city, walking with other people and dining with them', as well as reading psychological books that Bleuler lent her. She joined the assistant doctors for lunch and spent several hours a day in scientific studies. She spent more time assisting Jung in carrying out word association tests in the laboratory.[36] As the next chapter will show, it was during this period that Jung had a small number of extended conversations with her about her symptoms and their origins. In February Bleuler wrote to her mother: 'She is largely free of hysterical symptoms, and she can therefore be regarded as having recovered.'[37] By this point, all clinical entries in her hospital notes had come to an end, except for the following brief note in April, when she had already entered medical school:

In the last few weeks, definitely improved and increasingly calm. Now listens to lectures conscientiously and with interest (zoology, botany, chemistry). Fluctuations in mood still occur from time to time, particularly in connection with letters from home.[38]

The entire second half of her hospital stay consisted of pure asylum in the original sense of the word, namely being in a place of safety. Bleuler had already raised the possibility that she should move into town, but she preferred to stay in the protected environment of the hospital to study and work as an unpaid assistant.

During the last few months of her stay, Sabina may have had as many conversations with colleagues in Russian as she did in German. We know of at least five Russian medical students who were there around the same time. The list is impressive. Fanya Chalevsky was later to become the first woman ever to publish a psychoanalytic case report.[39] She also became engaged to one of Jung's closest colleagues, Alphonse Mäder. Feiga Berg was training to be a psychiatrist, and later published an account of Sabina's case history.[40] Esther Aptekmann came from Yekaterinoslav, the home town of Spielrein's mother. She later worked as a psychiatrist back in Russia. There was also a student named Tatiana Rosenthal, who went on to became the founder of psychoanalysis in St Petersburg.

The most significant Russian at the Burghölzli was Max Eitingon. Born into a wealthy Jewish family of fur merchants in Russia, Eitingon had been brought up in Germany and was now studying medicine in Zurich. Later on, he used his independent wealth to fund the development of the psychoanalytic movement, before emigrating and setting up the Israel Psychoanalytic Society. Alongside the students, there were also Russian psychiatrists who had come to work under Bleuler, and distinguished figures from elsewhere. These included the German psychiatrist Karl Abraham, who soon became one of Freud's closest confidantes and founded the first psychoanalytic institute in Berlin.

Before examining the contacts that Sabina had with Jung and Bleuler, it is worth asking how much of her improvement was due to her circumstances alone. These included the tolerance that Bleuler induced by his presence and principles, and the social activities like walks, dancing and drama. In addition, there was kind and attentive nursing although, both then and now, medical files remain silent on such matters. Jung later wrote that the nurses showed more psychological interest in the patients than the doctors, and were often better at diagnosing them.[41] In Sabina's case, there was also the scientific learning: the books that Bleuler and Jung lent her, attendance at lectures and case presentations, the engagement with her fellow Russians, and working with Jung in the laboratory. If we knew nothing else about her treatment or her love for her physician, the preceding account of her care would be enough to make her improvement credible. The question is: did talking therapy of any kind play a part, and if so, what was it?

3

Treatment 1904-1905

This morning, constant alternation of laughter and tears, jerking of the head, seductive glances ... Symptoms from earliest childhood. Could not observe someone being humiliated without falling into a pathological fury in which she finally had to masturbate ... Patient loves her father 'painfully'. She cannot turn to her father, he does not understand her properly, he uses insulting words towards her. She cannot give in to her father out of self-respect, and when her father is then sad she cannot talk to him and she is then even more pained. He has hit patient and she has had to kiss his hand for this. (At this point lots of tics, grimaces and gestures of revulsion) ... It finally emerges that the father has hit her a number of times on her bare bottom, most recently in her 11th year, now and again in front of her siblings. It needed a huge battle to elicit this confession from the patient. Here the tics matched the affect, as they showed horror and revulsion. Insisted several times she would and could never talk about it, and anyway did not want to be cured.[1]

THE WRITING is Jung's. He was recording his first direct conversation with Sabina, on the day after her admission, and just after he had spoken to her uncle. A year later, Jung was to write about Sabina to Freud and claim 'By using your method I have analysed the clinical condition fairly thoroughly and with considerable success from the outset.'[2] It is a bold claim. Along with similar statements, it has formed the basis of the canonical view of Sabina's treatment. This depicts it as a course of psychoanalysis through the length of her admission, a phenomenal success, and the experience that converted Jung to Freud's method. This view became established when Carotenuto published her letters and diaries, and when John Kerr wrote his book – although neither had seen the hospital notes. It has become fixed in the popular imagination. It has overshadowed subsequent scholarly critiques, which have called much of it into question.

The last chapter recounted the overall narrative of Sabina's admission. This chapter covers two of the other narrative threads from her records. First is an account of the conversations that took place between Sabina and Jung, with an assessment of what he meant by his 'analysis'. After that I examine Bleuler's interaction with her family, and the degree to which he apprehended the real danger that her father and brothers presented. I hope that a detailed consideration of these elements of her care will provide a clear view of what did and did not occur. First, we need to start with an account of psychoanalysis at that time.

*

In 1904 psychoanalysis was in its early days: Freud had founded his 'Psychological Wednesday Society' in Vienna only two years earlier, with four other members. He had first conceived of his 'talking cure' following a case described by his mentor Josef Breuer, who had spent long periods of time with a young hysterical patient he saw in the 1880s, described as 'Anna O'. Breuer allowed Anna to tell him 'fairy stories', letting her take as much time to do so as she wanted. Breuer also hypnotised her, encouraging her to make connections between her symptoms and past events.[3] Anna was the first person to dub this 'the talking cure'. Freud adapted Breuer's method. He abandoned hypnosis and in its place introduced two innovations. One was the analysis of dreams; the other was the use of 'free association' – asking patients to speak whatever came into their mind, however irrational this appeared. By doing so, he believed patients would discover links that would make sense of their neurotic symptoms and relieve them. He introduced the use of the couch, and of regular fifty-minute sessions, six days a week, to facilitate this process. Around 1904, he was seeing patients in this way for periods of up to several months. Later on in the century, it became commoner for a course of analysis to take some years.

As well as his method, Freud also developed a new theory to account for mental disturbance. He proposed that these had their origins in sexual conflicts in childhood. At first, he believed that they arose from actual trauma, in the form of sexual abuse. By this time, however, he had abandoned this 'seduction theory' in favour of the notion that children fantasised sexual relationships with their parents, most commonly the parent of the opposite sex, in the form of the Oedipus complex. According to this revised view, conditions like hysteria were due to an inability to come to terms with an incestuous desire that could never be fulfilled. He used his clinical method – dreams, free associations, the couch and regular daily sessions – aiming to help his patients understand and resolve such conflicts.

By the early years of the twentieth century, Freud had become clear that the success of therapy depended not just on the analysis of associations and dreams, but more on the strong emotional bond that patients formed with their analysts, including sometimes falling in love. He was starting to discover how to use these feelings to help patients discover the difference between dependence on a parental figure and self-reliance. Freud had written little about this aspect of therapy, and Jung knew nothing about it – although like most psychiatrists he had probably had the experience of patients falling in love with him. In the next year alone, at least three of them would do so, including Sabina.[4] Bleuler admired Freud and encouraged his juniors to become acquainted with his ideas. These were sometimes discussed at the regular fortnightly meetings to review interesting patients, held at the hospital or in Professor Monakov's laboratory. Under Bleuler's influence, Jung had read some of Freud's work. He was interested in his ideas about sexuality, although with reservations.[5] He had not yet met Freud, and had no direct practical knowledge of how he worked. When Sabina was admitted to the Burghölzli, Jung was certainly not a follower of Freud. He saw himself in the psychiatric tradition of Janet, Flournoy and Bleuler, all of whom were far better known.[6] In this context, we can now examine how Jung treated Sabina.

In the course of her admission, Jung made just twelve entries that recorded conversations with her. Five were made when he took her history in the first week. The remaining seven were spread over five months: one in September, two in October, one in December, and three in January. He made a few additional entries for different reasons, for example when he was called in at night to pacify her. Apart from one occasion, he did not record how long the conversations lasted. A small number of his notes seem to relate to a series of meetings over two or three days, but there is no indication this happened regularly. Given the prodigious scale of Jung's workload, the shared responsibility of four or five doctors for around 400 patients, and the fact that he was quite often absent on military conscription and for other reasons, it is hard to imagine he was able to have many conversations beyond those he recorded, although it is possible he saw her more briefly on most days as part of his daily hospital round visiting every patient. The few entries Jung did make are of compelling interest. They help us to understand Sabina, and they show how skilled Jung was as a psychiatrist.

On the second day of her admission, while Jung was still taking his history, Sabina described an incident that happened around the time of Emilia's death, although that detail is not recorded:

Three years ago the patient happened to say to her father that she could give up her parents in exchange for the company of others. There was a big scene, her father went wild and threatened suicide. Scenes like this happened very often, and they lasted for days. It also distresses the patient that her father insults and tyrannises everyone in the house. She is upset that he is so unhappy and always talks about dying etc. When he is nice towards her, she feels sorry that she has behaved badly towards him. She is always frightened that one day he will kill himself.[7]

Even though this was only her second day in hospital, she then made a remarkable confession:

She cannot say 'good morning' to her father, she cannot speak French with him. This sense of shame has been present since childhood: 'When I see his hand I cannot bear him.' She cannot kiss him. During punishment, the peak experience was that her father was a *man*.

Jung underlined the last word. There can be little doubt that Sabina had already told him, on day two of her admission, that she was sexually aroused when her father beat her. This made sense of her confession on the first day: 'Could not observe someone being humiliated without falling into a pathological fury in which she finally had to masturbate.' Jung continued his entry by recording that Sabina's father also occasionally made 'improper remarks'. Sabina's relationship with her mother was similar. Eva had even tried to beat her in front of her brothers the previous year, when she was nearly eighteen. Sabina then told Jung about the beating at the age of thirteen, when she doused herself in cold water and hid in the cellar in order to die. She also described how she had tried to starve herself to death on holiday in Karlsbad 'because she made her mother so angry'.

The day following these disclosures, Eva Spielrein came to the hospital. It was Jung's first meeting with her. Eva told him how Sabina had always been ill as a child. She had periods of apathy from the age of twelve, brooded on the purpose of living, and 'pitied all human beings'. Eva told Jung how Sabina had fallen in love with her Uncle Adolf and then had a similar reaction to Dr Heller's assistant. It is noticeable that she dated Sabina's problems from puberty rather than 'from earliest childhood', which was Sabina's recollection. Not surprisingly, Eva omitted to mention Adolf's own feelings for her. She did however confirm that 'Father used to be very strict'.[8] Jung's professionalism is evident here: he dispassionately recorded Eva's version without noting he already knew some of these details, or commenting on any discrepancies.

Two days later, Jung saw Sabina again. He made a short entry, noting that her tics appeared at points in the conversation 'that have a particular connection with her complexes'. He presumably meant they occurred when the conversation turned to the issues of masochistic pleasure and shame that she had already told him about. He also wrote that she was extremely sensitive, especially to stimulation, and ordered strict bed rest.[9] When he returned the next day, she told him she had just had a 'big fright':

> She felt as if someone was intruding on her, something[10] crawling in her bed, something human (what?). She felt as if someone was shouting in her ear – and that she herself was totally repulsive, like a dog or a devil. (Wrote on a piece of paper the Russian word for devil, 'chort'.)[11]

Jung noted this down without additional comment, and moved on to asking about her siblings. He recorded: 'Patient was sixteen years old when the sister died (of typhoid). She loved her sister "more than anything in the world." Her death left a terrible mark on her.' He then moved straight on to her religious beliefs, writing down that she received a very religious upbringing, and prayed a great deal as a child. God answered her in the form of an inner voice which spoke to her in German. 'Gradually she came to the realisation that the voice was not God but an angel sent to her by God because *she was an extraordinary person.*' His style of note-taking suggests he was using a conventional psychiatric approach, asking questions according to a list of subjects he wished to cover, rather than inviting Sabina to talk in more depth about any one of her experiences in the way that Freud might have done at the time. The session seems to have completed his initial history-taking, although the following day he saw her again to record the episode when she tore down the curtain cord because the nurse had upset her. He wrote:

> If one displays the least sign of any lack of respect or trust, she retaliates at once with negativistic behaviour and with a succession of bigger or smaller devilish behaviour. Every conversation to try and find anything out from her, is as difficult as walking on eggshells.[12]

These accounts give us a vivid picture of the external torments Sabina had suffered, and the internal ones that continued. They bear witness to her courage in sharing such shameful thoughts, and to Jung's empathy in eliciting them. Yet Jung does not state anywhere that he is using a Freudian approach. The following year, he did so explicitly in the notes of other patients.[13] There is also no indication that he employed Freud's method of analysing dreams or 'free association'. Again, Jung was to mention both these techniques with patients he saw in the next year. As Bernard Minder has remarked, the notes gave 'hardly any indication' of the method.[14] In one sense, there was no call for Jung to use Freud's method. The sexual causes of Sabina's distress poured out of her. The task that Freud described – bringing a patient to the realisation that a symptom arose from early sexual conflict – was unnecessary. As many commentators have pointed out, Jung also ignored some worrying clues regarding the nature of Sabina's abuse. I will examine this topic later in the chapter.

Following Jung's initial 'anamnesis', he went on leave. This upset Sabina. There was an entry by an unknown doctor recording that this had made her headaches so bad that he had to give her morphine.[15] There was then the episode when she tied the curtain cord around her neck again, and tried to swallow a medallion. When Jung returned in September, he did not resume any lengthy conversations – or at least none that he recorded. He made one brief descriptive entry to say she had made some scenes.[16] In another entry at the end of the month, he recorded her request that he should never display the slightest sense of being in doubt about her, but 'only the utmost strength and a firm belief in her recovery'. He added that she had no attention span when she was reading by herself, but 'only the personal presence of the physician can focus her, but if this is the case it can go on for hours'.[17] Some commentators have assumed this meant Jung abandoned all his other duties and sat silently in her presence for hours at a time, while she read. For an assistant doctor in a mental hospital with 400 patients, this seems inconceivable. It is equally inconceivable that he would do this without recording such encounters for two to four weeks at a time. His entry is far more likely to mean that his presence calmed her and its influence continued for hours.[18]

The next entry in early October is a short note describing a page with three drawings that Sabina made on a receipt from the sanatorium at Interlaken. The receipt is pasted above his note. One drawing shows a person under a shower, with the caption 'water treatment sanatorium'. Another shows Dr Heller giving a patient electrical treatment, although he appears to be sitting astride her. It is labelled 'electrocute'. As Jung comments: 'The position is a remarkably sexual one.' The third drawing shows two people in a circle labelled 'Dr Heller' and

'Dr Hesselbaum'. Underneath all these sketches Sabina again wrote the Russian word for devil or 'hell': 'chort'. Jung also wrote that she was now inviting him to hurt her:

> Patient reveals many other masochistic features for example, the relationship with her father, for whom she feels a remarkable revulsion. The chastisements form her central complex. She always asks the writer to do something painful to her, to treat her badly in some way; we should never ask her for something, only command it.[19]

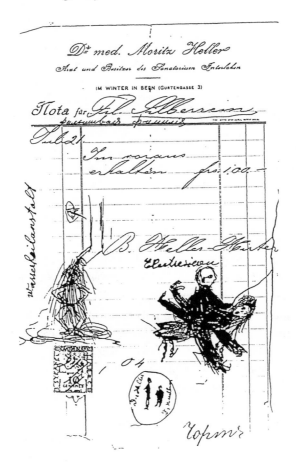

In the same entry, Jung noted that Sabina had 'great insight' into her condition, but 'not the slightest inclination to improve it'.

In mid-October, shortly after Bleuler had let her parents know she intended to go to medical school, Sabina's symptoms changed. Because she was so much better, Jung took her for a walk. She started to limp, and complained of unbearable pain in the ball of her foot. He examined her feet and found that there was nothing wrong. He then visited her over the next two days to assess her. He wrote: 'On the second day there was a deep abreaction [emotional catharsis], following which the pain had completely gone on the third day.' Jung then 'analysed' what had happened. It was his first use of the word, and the first conversation that he had recorded in any detail since his history-taking two months previously.

> Analysing it reveals that patient used a walk with the writer (their first) as an external cause for the pain in her feet. She developed unbearable pain in her feet for the first time after a particularly violent row between her parents. After that incident father stayed in bed for 2 days, sick with rage, neither speaking nor eating. On the second day, a relative visited who was not to know what had happened. Patient had to ask father to get up, which was very embarrassing for her. The same evening the whole family went for a walk with their guest, and everyone behaved as if nothing had happened ... On this walk her feet started to hurt so that for a long time afterwards she was unable to go out ... Patient now knows she must gradually get used to a freer life again.[20]

Unless Jung was leaving a lot out, Sabina's associations were not with her central problems of sexual arousal through humiliation. They were connected with a recent family event. Her wish to get used to a 'freer life' may be a reference to her recent resolution to stay on and study in Zurich. Some people have assumed that the walk must have been the famous one when Jung beat Sabina's cloak, provoking her into a furious reaction. This incident has played a prominent part in plays, movies and mythology. In fact, this incident is not in the records. Jung wrote the story later and for different purposes, as the next chapter describes.

After this 'analysis' Jung was absent for another day. On his next visit, Sabina demanded that he should squeeze her left hand tightly until it hurt. She explained to Jung calmly: 'I only want to feel pain. I want you to do something really bad to me, to force me to do something that I object to with all my might.' Jung was then absent again for two weeks. Once more, Bleuler recorded that Sabina developed a host of physical complaints including headaches, pains in her limbs and chest, and tiredness. She tormented the nurses and made scenes at night. The entry included his criticism of the head nurse who dealt with the situation 'stupidly' by forcing her back to bed. He gave Sabina some phenacetin as a sleeping draught, but she did not take it. He clearly recognised these episodes as minor setbacks. By now, in early November, Bleuler was treating her as a medical student: he recorded how she saw a letter from the clinic and 'made a correct diagnosis of epilepsy'.[21]

When Jung returned, the pains in Sabina's feet came back so badly that she was unable to walk. She was also refusing to eat, saying she wanted to starve herself to death. She also 'spontaneously admitted to masturbating, which greatly exhausts her'.[22] However there is no record of any further 'analysis' before Jung went away again for three weeks on military duties. When he returned, the same pattern repeated itself: she had intense pain in her feet. For only the second time, Jung used the word 'analysis' to describe his conversation. He found out that the pain had recurred on a walk to a nearby village, when she met a lady who spoke loudly. Sabina imitated her with expressions of disgust. This revealed that the lady reminded her of her mother's extravagance and the scenes that occurred whenever her father learned about it.[23] Jung had now asked on two occasions for Sabina's associations with her foot pains. Both times, she simply reported recent family incidents rather than talking about the beatings and sexual feelings she had spoken of in August. The long intervals between the conversations are striking. Jung did not comment on the fact that Sabina was asking him to do things she found sexually arousing. Nor did he apparently ask her to enlarge on this.

The most significant conversation Jung had with Sabina during her admission was in the New Year. His wife Emma had moved into the hospital at the end of November. She gave birth to their first daughter Agathe there on 26 December. Spielrein would no doubt have been aware of this. As her German biographer Richebächer suggests, the timing of some of her symptoms in hospital might have been triggered by real events such as these.[24] Two weeks later, Jung made his first entry of 1905 in the records. He reported that Sabina had another 'great fright' during the previous week. She felt there might be a cat or someone else in her room. Someone was also speaking in her ear. She felt 'something moving along her back like a snail and something grasping her side like a hand'. When he asked for her associations with this, she recalled that 'on New Year's Day exactly a year ago' there had been a big row at home. She then recalled 'with great effort' the scenes in which her father had beaten her. She told Jung about the occasion at the age of thirteen when Nikolai ordered her to lie down and tried to lift her skirt but relented, forcing her kiss the picture of her grandfather instead. Jung then wrote:

Finally, a three hour encounter showed that she has experienced sexual arousal in connection with the beatings since she was four years old, she cannot hold her water any more, has to press her legs together, later she also has to discharge this with an orgasm. In the end she only had to see or hear her brother being beaten to make her want to masturbate – or someone merely needed to threaten her and she had to lie on her bed and masturbate. In the last few years, it progressed to the point where that the slightest hint could trigger off this urge. She explained that someone only needs to laugh at her, which symbolically means humiliation for her, to cause her to have an orgasm ... Fundamentally all her expressions of disgust and her negative behaviour can be traced back to this complex. She sees herself as a totally bad and corrupt person, she therefore feels she should not be among other people ... During the act, the patient wishes all kinds of torments that she pictures as vividly as possible, she particularly imagines being beaten on the bare bottom and, to excite herself, that this is taking place in front of a large audience.[25]

The mention of 'three hours' is striking. Here too, some commentators have drawn the conclusion that this was typical of the time Jung spent with her. In fact, this is the only mention in the notes of how long a consultation lasted, suggesting Jung devoted an especially long period of time to it. It is one of the two longest entries in the notes since her original 'anamnesis'.[26] It is also likely that Jung started it with a session of word association in the laboratory. Although there is no record of any tests in the notes, there is apparently evidence of these in the Geneva archive.[27] In addition, Feiga Berg, one of the Russian medical students, later wrote an account of Jung's treatment that made no mention of psychoanalysis or Freud, but attributed Spielrein's improvement to the use of word association tests:[28]

> Jung treated the patient. When the treatment began, he asked her to pay attention, with associations in the association test. In this way he found out the patient's complexes and persuaded her to talk about them.[29]

Jung made two more entries during the rest of January, saying that Sabina had maintained her improvement. She admitted to him that until the New Year she 'could not resolve whether to abreact this central and most important part of her complex' but had resolved 'to make the first step into the world'.[30] Later that month she tried some word association tests in Jung's laboratory with acquaintances. These showed she could not say the word 'beat'. In his last entry in January, Jung also wrote: 'Yesterday during the evening visit, patient was reclining on the sofa again in her usual voluptuously oriental manner, with a sensual, dreamy expression.'[31] There were no more entries of any significance in the notes. The single extended confession recorded on 8 January was evidently the culmination of what he called her 'analysis'.

Is it possible that Jung regarded a single conversation, or even a few conversations scattered over several months, as psychoanalysis? Jung provided the answer to this question himself, with an account he published of another case the following year. In an essay entitled 'Psychoanalysis and Association Experiments', he wrote of how he used his word association tests to elucidate a patient's complexes, following this through with Freud's technique of free association – similar to what Feiga Berg described in Spielrein's case.[32] The patient in his essay was a governess with obsessional ideas, and he carried out analysis 'strictly on Freud's lines'. After three sessions over three weeks, the patient's obsessions 'disappeared'.[33] In that account, he stated that this was his 'first analysis'. What he did with Sabina the previous year may have been a rudimentary attempt to work in this way. He may have believed, in good faith, that he was trying out some elements of psychoanalysis. Yet apart from the amount of detail he elicited, there was nothing different from what he had learned from Sabina on her first day in hospital: 'Could not observe someone being humiliated without falling into a pathological fury in which she finally had to masturbate.' In the long January session, she offered him a moving and powerful confession. It was also evidently the first time she had been able to talk at length about being excited by punishment. It might have had a profoundly therapeutic effect. But it was not an 'analysis' by any standards, including those of the time.

Jung also ignored – or at least failed to record – any questions about the 'creature in her room' that spoke into her ear, crawled down her back like a snail, and then grasped her hand. In his commentary to the notes, Minder writes: 'It seems highly astonishing to me that incest was never brought into the discussion, either by Jung, or later by Freud.'[34] Similarly, Graf-Nold has pointed out how Jung's notes drew attention to Sabina's sexuality as if it originated from her, without at any point alluding to any likely cause, let alone the possibility of abuse.[35] Jung's inattention is especially puzzling as he was aware of the effects of sexual abuse and claimed to have been a victim himself.[36]

There is another intriguing aspect of these records. Jung's description of the final 'analysis' uncannily resembles Freud and Breuer's first case description: that of 'Anna O'. Like Sabina, Anna O was a highly intelligent and multi-lingual young woman who suffered from hysteria.[37] When Josef Breuer described his treatment, he wrote of spending several hours at a time with her. She would then recall disturbing scenes that had occurred in connection with her father exactly a year previously around Christmas and the New Year![38] Jung had certainly read *Studies in Hysteria*, where Breuer reported the case. Sabina had probably read it too.[39] Was this an extraordinary coincidence, or were Jung or Sabina in some way imitating – innocently or otherwise – what they had read, including even the time of year these recollections took place? One hypothesis is that Jung had just read, or re-read, *Studies in Hysteria*, and was looking for exact parallels in Sabina. She then obliged by behaving exactly like Anna O. Freud would not have approved. By now, he was using the case to illustrate what could go wrong in psychoanalysis. This included the way Breuer ignored the obvious sexual nature of their encounters, his abrupt termination of the treatment when he realised this, and Anna's subsequent collapse.[40]

To summarise Jung's involvement in Sabina's treatment: apart from taking her history, he recorded a few sporadic conversations with Sabina over the course of five months. These took place when she was already much improved and waiting to go to medical school. In only one of them did he record at any length the problems that tormented her. That single long consultation probably included word association tests. What Sabina told him came from a resolution to disclose more details of what troubled her, but Jung did not elicit anything of which she was previously unaware. Jung did not at any stage record that he had used Freudian techniques, as he did later, nor did he include her among the cases he described shortly afterwards as his first attempts to use such an approach.

Jung was not the only doctor looking after Sabina. Bleuler remained in overall charge of her care. He was in communication with her family throughout her admission. It is now worth examining his own involvement with her care. The first record of this took place in the week of Sabina's admission. It was a note requesting her mother to bring 'everything she has asked for in her letters to you'.[41] The tone is characteristic: a mixture of respect with a commanding manner that is not to be brooked. When Nikolai visited Zurich early the following month, it was also clear who was calling the shots. 'Dear Sir,' Bleuler wrote, 'You may visit your daughter tomorrow.'[42] Nikolai presumably did visit his daughter the following day, because later in the week Bleuler wrote to him again concerning – of all things – who should measure her for a new dress. He recommended that Nikolai should either arrange to send a seamstress or pay the one at the hospital to do so.[43] It is a mystifying message for the director of a large hospital to take the trouble to write. It suggests that Bleuler was making sure Sabina's father did not carry out the measurements in person.

The letters in the next few weeks are straightforward and business-like, keeping Nikolai informed of Sabina's progress and requesting advance payment of her fees. In October, the same note of peremptory politeness reappears. In the letter where Bleuler wrote of Sabina's decision to go to medical school, he also pointed out they had not replied to their daughter's last letter and 'she eagerly awaits news from home'.[44] Two weeks later, he wrote again. He had received no response either to his plea or, more surprisingly, to the news about Sabina's decision. He stated it once more. He then continued:

> We very much recommend that she should not return to Russia for quite a long time. In our opinion, even a reunion with her family would be highly inadvisable before she begins her studies ... Your daughter needs to become self-reliant and develop independently, and must therefore be freed from all emotional worries for her family and all the restrictive conditions that family life brings ... Your daughter also takes the view that these are the conditions needed for her recovery.[45]

There are two unusual aspects of this letter. One is the conviction with which Bleuler delivered the injunction. The other is that Spielrein family complied with it. Was their silence at this point an indication that Nikolai understood something Bleuler had now established? Was there an unspoken agreement that it would be best if everyone did as they were told? Later letters only deepen the mystery. In November, Jung wrote to Nikolai about some recent letters that his daughter had sent home. He explained that she had written these in a childish mood and 'sincerely regrets this unconsidered course of action'.[46] He appeared to be mollifying Sabina's father. Yet early in the New Year, Bleuler did exactly the opposite. He delivered the 'coup de grâce'. Nikolai was to be entirely cut off. Bleuler explained that the New Year 'with its reminders of home' had brought Sabina to a 'serious state of agitation'. She felt exhausted and had asked her doctor to write on her behalf:

> As her memories of you greatly agitate her, we are of the opinion that it would be better for Miss Spielrein not to write to you directly over the next few months. In order to relieve her responsibility for this, we have therefore forbidden her to write to her father.[47]

The date of this ban is exactly two days before Jung's entry on 8 January describing Sabina's three-hour analysis a few days earlier. Is this another extraordinary coincidence, or could Sabina's final, detailed confession be related to Bleuler's letter? Since these events are among the most striking in the entire notes, and occurred within days of each other, it seems very likely they were connected. There are two possible explanations. One is that Sabina's 'abreaction' involved disclosure of her abuse, which Jung relayed to his director, leading him to take action. The other possibility is that Sabina was emboldened to 'take her first step into the world' because she knew Bleuler had authorised her to stop all contact with her family. This might fit with the element of theatre that may have been present in the conversation, with her taking on the role of 'Anna O'. Jung's note of 8 January does not make it clear if the 'abreaction' happened before or after Bleuler's letter on the 6th, so either explanation is possible.[48]

There was little further correspondence until May, when Sabina was due for discharge. Jung then wrote to point out that she did not want her father to regard her silence as 'a lack of affection' but 'it is characteristic of your daughter's nervous disposition that she connects all kinds of pathological obsessions with your person, and these worry and trouble her'.[49] To reassure Nikolai, Jung added that 'she retains only feelings of love for you'. Exactly a week later, Bleuler again wrote to Nikolai, once again in an entirely different tone. He expressed alarm at the plan for one of Sabina's brothers, presumably eighteen-year-old Jan, to move to Zurich to study:

> *Miss Spielrein* has become extremely agitated that she is being expected to look after her brother. In order for her to remain in her improved condition she must be *absolutely free* from any obligations towards her family for a long time. Miss Spielrein has today found herself an apartment which she is expected to rent today, so that a move can be carried out the next few days.[50]

Jung then wrote to Nikolai to ask him if he could arrange for Jan to attend a university elsewhere.[51] He apologised that they had originally recommended Zurich for Jan because they were 'as yet unaware of the obsessional fantasies which are attached by our patient to her brother'. Isaac had now apparently now joined Jan in Switzerland, and Jung suggested that both brothers could share an apartment in whichever other city they went to.

Once again, Nikolai and Eva did exactly as they were told. They moved both their sons away from Zurich. In one way or another, they understood what the letters were saying, even if we do not. It must remain uncertain whether Sabina's fantasies about her father and brothers were connected to her sexual feelings towards them on her own part, or to her experience of physical assaults, or to any form of sexual abuse. What is clear is that Bleuler was convinced Sabina's admission would only remain a success if the men in her family stayed away. He would probably have seen the record of Jung's conversations in the notes, but did not refer to them in his own entries or letters as playing any part in her treatment.

There is a striking contrast between Jung's conciliatory tone and Bleuler's commanding one. This may simply have been due to seniority, but there were other differences in their approach too. In April, Sabina needed a certificate to enter university. Jung had penned a couple of lines mentioning that she had been institutionalised. He stated, inaccurately, that she was 'likely to spend some considerable period of time with us'.[52] It was evidently not the message the university wanted to hear. A week later, Professor Bleuler corrected the matter by sending his own meticulously worded and typed substitute certificate: 'Miss Sabina Spielrein from Rostov/Don, who has been living at this local institution and planning to matriculate at the medical faculty in the summer term, is not mentally ill. She was here for treatment for a nervous condition with hysterical symptoms. We therefore recommend her for matriculation. The Director, Bleuler.'[53]

Looking closely at Bleuler's interventions and comparing them with Jung's, it is easy to understand the view of Graf-Nold, who argues that Bleuler played the greater part in her recovery: 'What was unusual in Sabina Spielrein's case,' Graf-Nold writes, 'was how unreservedly Bleuler stood up for her: she could rely on his unwavering backing for her apparently almost hopeless struggle for independence from her father and from her whole family by whom she felt literally "possessed" ... Although Spielrein made it clear to him that she had been traumatised since her early childhood, it remains unclear whether and how Jung comprehended her traumatisation.' She concludes: 'The result of his ambitious scrutiny of Spielrein's complexes was that the trauma and the perpetrator faded into the background.'[54]

It has to be said that Sabina did not see things in this way. For beneath the text of the hospital notes, there is a quite different subtext. As she would reveal before long, she had fallen in love with Jung.

4

Medical Student 1905

Hell! I've been at the university. I've had so many impressions that I can hardly begin to describe them. The Professor of Zoology, Lange, really struck me as wonderful. I was on fire with interest, but now a reaction has set in and everything feels so difficult again. I don't feel as if I'm the same as the other students. I feel cut off from them ... I feel as if I'm far more thorough, serious, critically developed and self-sufficient but unfortunately I don't yet know if I'll be scientific enough for the work, whether my health will allow it. And the most important question is: am I capable enough? In the meantime, life without science is unimaginable. What else would there be for me to do apart from science? Get married? That's awful even to think about: sometimes my heart aches for tenderness, love; but it's only a deceptive, fleeing, superficial moment hiding the poorest prose ... No! I don't want that kind of love: I want a good friend to whom I can explain every train of thought: I want the love of an older man who will love and understand me (spiritual affinity) the way parents love and understand a child. My own parents – they weren't like that at all. I still want to know if I will turn out to be anything. If only I was as wise as my Junga![1] ... And how stupid that I'm not a man; they have it so much easier. It's outrageous that the whole of life is organised just for them. I won't be a slave![2]

THE DAY before she started her lectures at medical school, Sabina Spielrein began to write in her diary again, still in Russian. She continued as a resident in the Burghölzli. She would be commuting from there to university for the next few weeks until moving into an apartment. The diary extract includes virtually all the moods that were to characterise her life during the coming years at medical school: volatile moods, a commitment to scientific study, a longing for love, a fear of marriage with its disappointment – and her feelings for Carl Jung. Two things are particularly noticeable at this point. One is her passion for science. The other is that her love for Jung does not seem to be predominantly erotic. It is more like hero-worship.

53

*

When Sabina Spielrein started at Zurich University, she was carrying on where she left off two years earlier at the time she finished school. She was at a disadvantage through having lost some time. In other ways, she had benefited. She was further into adulthood, and had already had a year of independence from her family. She had friends among the students at the university mental hospital, and had come to know some of its most distinguished staff. She had had time to study. She also presumably spoke even better German than she previously, and must have understood the local dialect. From her regular walks, she was already accustomed the city, its lake and the surrounding mountains. Rather than being thrust almost overnight into an unfamiliar city, she had time to look for a suitable apartment.

Zurich was around the same size as Rostov, and a main European railway hub. It was only two days' journey by train to Rostov. Zurich was also one of the most sedate and liberal cities in Europe. Although women were excluded from suffrage, Zurich University was the first in Europe to admit female students. Scientifically, it was also among the most advanced universities in Europe. Among its Nobel laureates was Wilhelm Röntgen, who first detected X-rays. The city also had a large population of immigrants and refugees. It was becoming a haven especially for Russian political émigrés. Georgi Plekhanov, the founder of Russian Marxism and leader of the Socialist Revolutionary Party, lived there. Trotsky was soon to arrive after the abortive revolution in Russia in 1905. During the First World War, Lenin stayed there.

Spielrein, as we have seen, was far from being the only Russian woman at Zurich University. They generally went there because it was almost impossible for them to gain places at a medical school in Russia. In 1865 Nadezhda Suslova, the daughter of a serf from near Nizhny-Novgorod, had applied to Zurich University to test its claims to being liberal. They agreed to admit her as their first woman student. She studied alongside August Forel, and qualified as a doctor very quickly. She returned to Saint Petersburg to become a gynaecologist.[3] Large numbers of Russian women followed her example and flocked to Switzerland, as did Russian Jews of both sexes. Many identified with the rising radical movements in Russia. By 1910, there were 362 Russian students at Zurich University. The majority were women, and more than half were studying medicine. Out of eighty-four students who qualified in medicine there at the same time as Spielrein, no fewer than fifty-two were Russian women.[4]

Spielrein's contemporary from Rostov-on-Don, Vera Chatzmann, was a medical student in Geneva at almost the same time. In his memoirs, her husband Chaim Weizmann described his wife's student group in Switzerland in a manner that could have applied to Spielrein and her circle. The group 'differed in a marked way from the general run of Jewish girl-students in the Swiss universities of that time. Their looks, deportment and outlook on life set them apart.'[5] They were less absorbed in Russian revolutionary politics, paid more attention to their studies, and avoided the public meetings and 'endless discussions' which seemed to take up so much of the time for the average Russian student abroad. While the majority of the émigré Jewish students seemed 'underfed, stunted, nervous and sometimes bitter', the women medical students were entirely different. Some were involved in the Zionist movement. The first Zionist publishing house was founded in Geneva, and plans for a Hebrew University in Jerusalem were first discussed there.[6]

Socially, the Russian students lived more or less in isolation from the local Swiss. Sabina lived in the Russian 'colony', and the friends she described in her diary, together with their boyfriends and girlfriends, were nearly all from Russia as well, although they included other foreign residents. Russians were not universally popular. Swiss newspapers purveyed all the usual xenophobic stereotypes, from terrorism to the risk of innocent Swiss men being helplessly seduced by 'these fearful sirens'.[7] Spielrein could not have been further from the stereotype. She steered clear of radical groups. She was also one of the wealthiest students. She received a stipend from her father of 300 Swiss Francs every month.[8] She took holidays in and around Switzerland. Although she moved accommodation about a dozen times during her medical school years,[9] this was not for financial reasons. She sometimes made a point of wearing shabby clothes, but that too was out of choice and to indicate where her priorities lay.

Spielrein's early weeks at medical school were not easy. We learn from her diary that she still suffered from headaches, and felt sick and weak. In June, a week after moving into an apartment in town, she wrote in her diary about how she was keeping herself isolated:

Somehow I'm afraid to get close to people. I fear for my freedom. The only thing I have now is my freedom, and I'm protecting this last treasure with all my strength. I cannot bear the tiniest criticism of my personality, not even in the form of a simple instruction: it feels like a punishing sermon ... Only from Junga can I tolerate everything. It is unbelievably painful to me when he reprimands me. I want to weep, to beg him to stop, because I feel my personality being suppressed, but on the other hand, I can't resist him at all.[10]

The 'reprimands' presumably came when she visited Jung at the hospital and perhaps in the laboratory. There is no record of social engagements at this point. Her feelings come over as adoration rather than desire, and her sense of rejection seems more on account of criticism from her hero rather than the rebuff of someone she saw as a potential lover. In spite of her low moods, she applied herself diligently to her studies. She attended lectures in botany, anatomy, physical anthropology, human measurement, group behaviour, and genetics. The breadth of studies is impressive, and a reminder that Zurich University was at the cutting edge of intellectual endeavour. Spielrein also enrolled to study psychiatry under Professor Bleuler. In contrast with his enlightened attitude to psychiatry and his humanity towards individual patients, he shared with many of his medical and psychiatric peers a belief in racial doctrine, the superiority of some races over others, and in eugenics. It would be interesting to know how Spielrein and the other Jewish medical students dealt with this. Their teachers may have reassured them that they were 'untypical' of their degenerate race as a whole.

She continued to play pranks. She wrote a letter to Bleuler on scraps of paper, explaining she had no energy to buy proper paper – but then wrote again to say she had made this up.[11] She played tricks on her classmates – on one occasion, she feigned spraying them with potassium cyanide.[12] She also fooled her mother by forwarding an awkwardly effusive letter from her friend Louise Rähmi, pretending it was from Jung.[13] Louise Rähmi was one of her closest friends, a Swiss working-class woman who had been admitted to the Burghölzli with persisting physical symptoms following an accident when she was knocked down by a horse.[14] Louise remained in the hospital after Spielrein's discharge to train as a typist, but Sabina continued to visit her, and took her on a three-week hiking trip in the mountains. She lent Louise money for the trip, but on Jung's advice applied to Bleuler for reimbursement from charitable funds.[15]

In August she wrote to her mother somewhat breathlessly about the loan to Louise, being short of money, and much else. She made no attempt to disguise her delight at developments in her friendship with Jung:

I am insanely happy in a way I've never been in my life before. At the same time it's painful and I want to cry with happiness. You've obviously guessed the cause of all this is Junga. I visited him today. He calmed me down about Rähmi, he said that in his opinion her condition has improved a great deal and he advised me not to ask for the money back that I'd spent on her. I should therefore request it from the charitable society ... We touched on this subject after Junga declared that I shouldn't be wearing a hat with holes in it and that I must have my shoes repaired. I told him that I didn't have any more money, but that it wasn't possible to ask my parents for any more ... So he made a proposal to lend me 100 francs and write to you about it, but because I totally protested, he made me take 10 francs from him for the hat and repair of the shoes ... Now, can you see what he's really like, my Junga? When I left the Professor [Bleuler] today I felt as if I'd been sentenced to death, but he restored my faith in my own powers, and made me so happy! He is going to visit me on Friday (1 September) at 3 o'clock. If only I could learn how to cook borsht before then! Today Jung and I went on rounds in our hospital. There are so many women there who admire me! Now sleep is overcoming me. I'm going to bed.[16]

Sabina was clearly besotted with Jung. She also gives the impression that he had taken on a protective role towards her, possibly in order to help her adjust to her independent life. However, the strength of her daughter's feelings and Jung's response to the invitation must have alarmed Eva Spielrein. She came from Rostov to see him and demand a referral to another physician, in order to help her daughter overcome what seemed like an inappropriate passion for him. We do not know whether she asked him explicitly to write to Sigmund Freud but it is possible. Freud's reputation for the treatment of hysteria was growing. Eva may also have wanted an opportunity to take her daughter away from Zurich, to remove her from her physician.

Jung complied by writing his first ever letter to Freud. The procedure would normally be to send a confidential report direct, perhaps with a brief letter of introduction to give to the patient. Jung did something quite different. At the time, he was occupying Professor Bleuler's office and deputising for him.[17] He reached for a sheet of Bleuler's own notepaper and typed a referral letter to Freud, for Eva to use 'if the occasion arises'.[18] Effectively, it disclosed every last detail of Sabina's private fantasies. In the words of Bernard Minder: 'It is unusual to say the least to produce a report for use if the occasion arises, which contains detailed information on the patient's pathology.'[19] Jung had now crossed two professional boundaries: accepting a social invitation to meet a recent patient with a crush on him, and disclosing her intimate sexual fantasies to her mother.

Jung began the report by describing how Spielrein suffered from hysteria. He explained this was due to an inherited weakness, with both father and mother suffering from hysteria, 'especially the mother'. He noted that one of Sabina's brothers also suffered from this severely. He explained that Sabina's problems started about three years before, although their roots went back to her early life. He then added his retrospective claim: 'By using your method I have analysed the clinical condition fairly thoroughly and with considerable success from the outset.' Jung laid out explicitly that her father had administered physical punishments that became connected with her 'premature and now highly developed sexual awareness'. He continued by giving the details of her technique of masturbation by rubbing her thighs together, how she was aroused by threats and humiliation, became sexually aroused at the sight of her father's hands, and imagined her father to be defecating and then thrashing her on the buttocks. Jung added further detail about how she was obsessed by fantasies including eating food and defecating it at the same time, and being whipped in front of a large crowd.

He went on to explain that Sabina's condition noticeably improved and she emerged as a highly intelligent, gifted and sensitive person. He added: 'There is a certain callousness and unreasonableness in her character and she lacks any feeling for situation and for external propriety, but much of this must be put down to Russian peculiarities.' He ended the letter by writing that Sabina had started at medical school, but she still suffered a great deal when meeting with members of her family. He mentioned that this was something Eva 'was unable to understand', adding the hint that Freud should nevertheless be able to make sense of it. Nevertheless, he explained that Sabina's mother knew about the most important aspect of her daughter's 'complex'. He ended the letter with this statement:

During treatment the patient had the misfortune to fall in love with me. She raves on to her mother about her love in an ostentatious manner, and a secret perverse enjoyment of her mother's dismay seems to play a not inconsiderable part.

His method of referral is unaccountable. Why would any doctor write in this manner and give it to the patient's mother? There are several possibilities. He may have wanted to let Eva know quite how much the family's behaviour had damaged Sabina. Perhaps he wanted to alert Eva to the possibility of sexual abuse. He may have composed the letter to make it impossible for her to forward it, so that the side effects of his treatment would not be exposed.[20] Or it may have been a completely unreflective act. Whatever the case, Eva did not send the letter to Freud. Instead, she shared it with her daughter, who quoted from it later.[21] Sabina herself never seemed to mind that her mother had seen the letter. This is also puzzling, unless we assume she wanted Eva to know how miserable a child she had been.

The letter does not make it clear when Jung realised Spielrein was in love with him. The warning signs had certainly been there. There had been previous crushes, her 'seductive glances' from day one, her agitation when he was absent, her requests for him to hurt or command her, and finally her 'voluptuously oriental' manner towards him. Setting all of this aside, vulnerable young women who spend time with handsome and attentive men are prone to fall in love. The kinds of intimate interviews Jung had conducted with Spielrein were also likely to amplify such a reaction. Freud had observed this phenomenon with his patients and gave it the description of 'transference': in other words, transferring onto the person of the analyst erotic feelings that he believed had once been directed at their parents. But Spielrein's feelings for Jung did not develop solely because of these. They were part of a pattern of infatuations with men. They latched onto Jung almost as soon as she arrived in the hospital. They became 'raving' – to use Jung's word – when she worked in close proximity to him in the laboratory, received friendly advice from him, and when he accepted her invitation to come to her apartment for a meal. The irony is that her love had probably been one of the most important factors bringing about her recovery. To a significant degree, it seems to have replaced her yearning for punishment and the obsessive images that had tormented her. In spite of the other elements that contributed to her improvement, she emerged from the Burghölzli with the conviction that it was Jung himself who had made the difference. Her love for him energised her. If Freud had ever seen the letter, he might have questioned Jung's use of the word 'misfortune'. He might have suggested that her love represented a provisional success, and could be turned into a more substantial one by a more careful kind of therapy. For Jung, this was unknown territory.

If Jung believed that Spielrein needed help from Freud, he evidently took no further steps to encourage it. Nor did he offer her treatment himself. There has been a tenacious myth that Jung gave Spielrein therapy as a private patient following her discharge from the Burghölzi. The myth arose because Jung gave several different accounts of her 'case' and these are contradictory. In the referral letter he gave to Eva, he made it sound as if Sabina's treatment was over. In the same year, he published his story about beating her cloak, and also implied it was over.[22] Similarly, when he presented her case at a conference a couple of years later, this too sounded historical.[23] However, he also mentioned her two or three times in letters to Freud in the same period, as the next chapter relates. On those occasions he wrote as if she was a current patient, rather than someone he was looking after protectively. Once their relationship had got into trouble, he then retracted this claim. Indeed, he took pains to emphasise to Freud that he had pulled Spielrein out of her illness 'years ago' and she had subsequently abused his 'friendship'.[24] Spielrein herself was clear that she had been his friend and not his patient. In June 1909 she wrote to Freud: 'Four and a half years ago, Dr Jung was my doctor, then he became my friend.'[25] Her dating is precise: she ceased being a patient in January 1905. This is exactly when Jung regarded her 'analysis' as complete, and when the entries in her hospital notes virtually stopped. In other words, she was only ever a hospital patient of his, not an outpatient.

There is a parallel myth that her family paid fees to Jung for therapy. They did not, although Spielrein later explained to Freud that her mother sometimes sent Jung food and other gifts.[26] There were receipts in the Burghölzli records which researchers originally misconstrued as being for therapy, but these related to other items.[27] The varying claims by Jung's biographer Deirdre Bair that Jung offered 'confidential talks several times a week',[28] or that her father paid for 'regular Friday afternoon sessions'[29] are groundless. So is John Kerr's elaborate reconstruction of Spielrein's 'weekly sessions' as an 'outpatient'.[30] It is a shame this account has become one of the best known 'facts' about Spielrein.

Before returning to the main story, it is worth pointing out that Jung's various descriptions of Spielrein's 'case' contained other discrepancies too. One of the best examples is the famous story of Jung beating Spielrein's cloak. This appeared in Jung's first published account of her, not long after her discharge. He included it in an essay on 'hidden memory', to illustrate how people could forget traumatic events but still be influenced by them. He described how he had to treat 'a hysterical young lady' who had been 'brutally beaten' by her father. He gave an account of how he went out for a walk with her and she dropped her cloak. When he picked it up and tried to beat off the dust with a stick, she threw herself at him 'with violent defensive gestures', and tore the cloak away from him. Jung claimed he immediately guessed the reason, while the woman was 'nonplussed'. She could only say it was very unpleasant for her to watch. Jung explained that an unconscious memory had acted on his patient exactly as if it had been a conscious one.[31] The story is puzzling. Spielrein never had any difficulty connecting her feelings of fury, sexual arousal and shame with the idea of being beaten. Indeed, this was her main symptom. Jung's story cannot be true. We are left guessing which parts were closer to the truth than others. It seems as if Jung's relationship with Spielrein was now serving different purposes – not just a protective friendship, but a source for material he could adapt as necessary for his academic career.

Jung's career was certainly going from strength to strength. He had become an acknowledged expert in giving legal evidence, based on word association tests.[32]

Zurich University had accepted his research treatise and appointed him as a lecturer. His lectures were becoming so popular that they had to be moved to the largest room in the building and were frequented by large numbers of women from the town. The fact is, he had many things on his mind apart from one of his ex-patients who had a crush on him. After he wrote the letter to Freud, he may even have distanced himself from her for a while. There is a gap of several months in her diaries for the rest of 1905 and the first half of 1906, so this is unclear.

However great her own concerns were, Eva Spielrein took no further action either. She too had other things on her mind, of a far more serious nature. Her middle son Isaac was in trouble, and her daughter's crush would have seemed trivial by comparison. Isaac had been caught up in the '1905 Revolution' in Russia. Earlier in the year, a peaceful demonstration in St Petersburg had ended in the shootings of hundreds of unarmed civilians, on the so-called 'Bloody Sunday'. Civil unrest had now spread across Russia, with further demonstrations, strikes, mutinies and uprisings against landlords. In St Petersburg, the Social Democrats organised the first 'soviet', or worker's council. Although the Tsar made a conciliatory response to these protests at first, by the end of the year the members of the St Petersburg soviet were arrested, and troops put down a workers' rising in Moscow. By the Spring, there had been an estimated 14,000 executions and 75,000 arrests. Like most episodes of civil unrest in Russia, the uprising led to pogroms against Jews. Nationalist groups attacked Jews in Odessa and Kiev.

On 18-20 October 1905, just a few weeks after Jung had given his letter to Eva, a pogrom took place in Rostov for the first time ever. With the aid of Cossack units, rioters massacred 150 Jews and wounded another 500. They also ransacked Jewish stores, warehouses and mills.[33] There is no record of whether any relations or friends of the Spielreins were harmed, or if their property was damaged. The scale of the violence was terrifying for the community, not least because of the city's reputation as being safe for Jews. Isaac Spielrein was by now a feisty fourteen-year-old. He had already hit back at his father, bringing his assaults to an end.[34] He now joined a Jewish self-defence patrol, and shortly afterwards became a member of the Socialist Revolutionary Party.[35] While Isaac does not seem to have been involved in violent political activities himself, he became involved in a conspiracy. When police searched the Spielrein home they found leaflets and revolutionary appeals. Isaac evidently responded by shooting himself in the mouth. His father Nikolai managed to bribe the police and take Isaac to Paris for treatment.[36] A doctor there asked him if he had shot himself for love and he replied that it was 'for the revolution'.[37]

Nikolai must have been more convinced than ever that he had done the right thing to bring his children up speaking several languages and with the expectation that they could make seek a career anywhere in Europe. Jan was already at university in Berlin, where he was studying engineering. Isaac was back in Russia for a while, but later went to Germany as well, to study in Heidelberg and Leipzig. Whatever her other troubles, Sabina may have counted her blessings that she too had settled in a city where riots, pogroms and revolutions were entirely unknown, and where she could get on with her medical studies and the pursuit of her 'higher calling'.

5

Man's Talk 1906-1907

But your lecture was so wonderful (not just in the scientific but the ethical sense as well.) How can you create such enthusiasm and emotion? You have fantastic potential energy and could achieve hugely more than you have. If only you had any idea how morally beautiful you were (when you treat patients so carefully and lovingly.) ... Although I went home in complete misery, I was calm and strong in my decision. I don't need anything else, everything just comes from 'poetry' ... I love you so much, that possibly I imagine something that isn't really true (or perhaps it is?) For example, that you despise me, and that you don't want me to keep crawling around after you etc. ... For that reason, I've wanted to leave Zurich for the past three years, but I haven't found a suitable university ... Well, what do you think about it? Should I leave you in peace for 3 years?[1]

ALMOST A YEAR had passed since Spielrein's mother had asked for referral to another physician. Spielrein had entered her second year at medical school. She was now writing gushing letters to Jung, and copying them into her diary. We do not know how many of them she sent. Sometimes they read more like private ruminations. There may also have been an element of fantasy in what she wrote. She had been in Zurich for only two years, not three as she states here. It is also difficult to know if her question about moving away was serious. There were many 'suitable universities' across Europe. These included Heidelberg, which she considered later, and the Sorbonne, where one of her future sisters-in-law was training as a doctor.

Spielrein must have posted at least some of the letters, because she mentions a few of Jung's replies, although we do not have them. She confessed to him they brought her joy. She implored him to keep writing even if she did not always answer.[2] She begged him not to let anyone know how much she adored him, and asked his praise for not mentioning this to her own friends, including Feiga Berg.[3] In the passage above, she talked of 'poetry'. Later on, she was to use the word to mean erotic contact, but it does not seem to convey that meaning here. It probably describes the intense excitement she felt in his presence, only to be followed by 'complete misery' on separation. With what may be realism, she also admitted the possibility that he sometimes regarded her as a stalker. Without any documentation from his side, it is impossible to guess at his feelings or reactions at this point. Possibly he regarded her effusions as a form of self-therapy, expecting she would get everything out of her system. He may simply have enjoyed the adulation. The communications we have later on from his side nearly always show a discrepancy between his view of her and the feelings she expressed.

Her diaries and letters also never make it clear how often their encounters happened, nor where. Presumably they met at university lectures, and in the wards and clinics at the Burghölzli. Spielrein may still sometimes have helped him in the hospital laboratory or visited him in his office for friendly chats. In later accounts, she was to give the impression that their friendship was more or less continuous after she left hospital. However, this letter draft does not make it sound as if they were seeing each other a great deal at this point. There must also have been periods when Spielrein had to concentrate on other subjects like surgery and could not spend much time at the Burghölzli. As later events were to show, Jung may not have been seeing her as often as he was seeing several other female students, and was less intimate with her at this point than with some others.

*

As well as gushing tributes, Spielrein was sending Jung more mature thoughts. She recorded her first psychological theory. It concerned one of Jung's own central interests: emotional complexes. She argued that these served the function of holding the personality together. She suggested that hysteria only took over an individual when healthy complexes could no longer work. From her own experience, she believed it was an attempt to build an alternative personality that was an artificial performance.[4] She also proposed a new theory of dreams. She regarded them as a form of auto-suggestion, a way of hypnotising oneself into certain kinds of actions.[5] She put forward the notion that human beings possessed a drive towards personal transformation, which was in continual conflict with forces of repression that held it back.[6] Each of these theories only took up a page or two, but they indicate the originality of her thinking and her early intellectual confidence. They also contain the seeds of her later ideas.

In one of her letter drafts, she tackled Jung on his views on concerning socialism.[7] She reminded him that he had once remarked to Feiga Berg that 'all socialists were thieves'. He had quipped: 'One takes your chain, the other your watch.' Spielrein wrote that she could not really believe he was serious: he was, as usual, just going 'over the top'. She argued that his familiarity with comfort had made him associate everything with people's complexes. In a discourse several pages long on socialism and the theory of labour, she challenged his belief that the richest were also the ablest in society. She pointed out that they could also leave their inheritance to less able descendants. She cited her friend Louise Rähmi as the most intelligent of all her fellow students, in spite of having come from a poor background. Even adoration had not dulled her sense of social justice nor – in some respects – her critical appraisal of Jung. Much of Spielrein's time was spent studying and reading. In her diary she referred, among other writers, to the philosopher Ernst Mach and the biologist August Weismann. Mach believed that the personality was something continually changing rather than fixed. Weismann was the greatest of Darwin's followers. He established the crucial difference between the sex cells (eggs and sperm) and the other cells of the body. Later, in her most important theory, Spielrein was to invoke both of these writers in different ways. It is clear that she was developing the passion for science that was to be with her for the rest of her life. It is also clear that she was able to keep her obsession with her friend within sufficient bounds a great deal of the time.

It was during 1906 that Jung did finally made contact with Sigmund Freud. The story of their profound friendship and its catastrophic breakdown is one of the great sagas of twentieth-century intellectual history. In the course of it, they exchanged over 700 letters.[8] These letters hold a fascination of their own. The rest of this chapter is devoted to the developing relationship between the two men, and the thoughts they occasionally exchanged about the Spielrein 'case'. Jung's first successful attempt to contact Freud was in early 1906 when he sent him a copy of his *Diagnostic Association Studies*. In it, he described the technique he had first pioneered for psychiatric diagnosis and then for treatment. He included the essay containing his account of the three-session 'analysis' of a woman with an obsessional disorder, described in Chapter 3. He also described other patients with whom he had used psychoanalytic technique for the first time. These did not include Spielrein. The book made it clear he saw himself as a proponent of his own method of word association and regarded Freud's approach as an adjunct to this.

Soon after Freud had received the book, he responded by sending Jung his own *Collected Short Papers on the Theory of the Neuroses*. A great deal hinged on this exchange for both men. Jung was making contact with a senior colleague with a reputation for being innovative. Freud, for his part, was concerned that psychoanalysis would not thrive if it was restricted to a small circle of Viennese Jews including a fair number of cranks and oddballs – as he was the first to concede.[9] Jung was now in the academic mainstream. His first paper, with Riklin, on word association, was described by the psychiatrist Adolf Meyer as 'a remarkable piece of work' and 'the best single contribution to psychopathology during the past year'.[10] From Freud's perspective, a connection with Jung, his director Bleuler, Zurich University and the wider gentile world, was just about the best possible one he could make.

Once he had read Freud's papers, Jung wrote back approvingly – to an extent.[11] While he appreciated his colleague's views, he said, he was still a long way from understanding the therapy or Freud's theory concerning the origins of hysteria. He also noted that Freud's therapy seemed to depend on 'certain personal rapports'. He conceded that hysteria might well be a predominantly sexual problem, but he could not agree this was always the case. What Jung wrote was a frank account both of his knowledge of psychoanalysis and his reservations. It also foreshadowed the main theoretical disagreement that would arise between him and Freud: whether mental disorders arose exclusively from sexual conflicts. However, these reservations were set aside in Jung's next letter to Freud three weeks later, when he presented Freud with the first of many case histories he was to share with him:

At the risk of boring you, I must abreact my most recent experience. I am currently treating a hysteric with your method. Difficult case, a 20-year old Russian student, ill for six years.[12]

Although he did not name her, the 'difficult case' was clearly Spielrein. After Jung's introduction, he went on to describe her first trauma taking place at the age of two or three, when she saw her father spanking one of her brothers on the bare bottom. According to Jung, this had a very strong effect on her. Afterwards, she could not prevent herself from thinking that she had defecated on her father's hand. Jung then described how, up to the age of eight, she liked to sit on the floor with one heel pressed up against her anus, trying to defecate and prevent it. She could end up being constipated for two weeks as a result, but the action brought her 'blissfully shuddersome feelings'. In time, Jung explained, this was superseded by vigorous masturbation. He wanted to know Freud's view of all of this.

Quite apart from the phrase 'currently treating', there are many odd aspects of this letter. Why did he fear 'boring' Freud with such an interesting case? What emotions were there for him to abreact – in other words, to discharge – through narrating them? Why did Jung fail to mention that he had referred the patient the previous year? He wrote of a specific 'trauma' of witnessing Yasha's spanking on one specific occasion, but did not mention that Sabina received frequent beatings herself. He described an anal obsession he had never previously recorded. As other commentators have noted, the oddest aspect of the letter is that Jung does not state that the patient was functioning well at university, and seeing him as a friend rather than a patient – a point that he was to make emphatically later on. For a moment, we might wonder whether this is indeed Spielrein, except that later on he described the same symptoms in a context that made this clear. As the scholar James Rice has commented, there is a strong suspicion that Jung was slanting the narrative towards Freud's own interests, including trauma at a specific age, anal eroticism, and extended analytic treatment.[13] It is also noticeable that Jung did not make any claim that she was a 'test case' or that he had tried to psychoanalyse her two years previously.

Freud responded by offering his view of the case. He said he was pleased that the patient was a student, because uneducated people could not be reached by the method. He thought the defecation story 'nice'. He explained how the sight of a brother being spanked could reawaken a forgotten memory trace from infancy, when she no doubt had the experience of soiling her father's hand, and therefore the pleasure of anal excitation. He added that such people were often neat, stingy and obstinate. He reassured Jung that cases of 'repressed perversion' like this could be analysed successfully.[14] If Jung noticed that none of Freud's epithets except 'obstinate' fitted Spielrein, or that her 'perversion' was hardly 'repressed', he did not point this out.

Between October 1906 and the following summer, Jung and Freud exchanged around sixty further letters. There is no mention at all of Spielrein, but one can trace the men's growing mutual affection. On Freud's side, the project was partly educational. He wrote about the importance of the transference of strong feelings towards the analyst. He explained that it was not the quality of interpretations that made a difference, but the quality of the relationship: 'Essentially, one might say, the cure is effected by love.'[15] The two men exchanged more papers and ideas. They planned congresses and journals. They plotted a future for psychoanalysis that combined Freud's radical ideas with Jung's respectable, Christian, university milieu and his commitment to experimental research. In March 1907, Jung and Emma travelled to Vienna to meet Freud. The two men had a thirteen-hour conversation that has attained a mythical status.

The next time Jung referred to Spielrein in his letters was in July 1907, eight months after his first mention of her. On intimate terms with Freud by now, he began with another apology for boring him with some recent experiences.[16] He then launched into some humorous anecdotes about two women he had met at a party. He had apparently flirted with one of them, and the other then flirted with him. He told Freud that his wife Emma had taken this in good spirit and had joked about it. He then moved on to an account of a 'patient' who was also vying for his erotic affections. From the description, there is no doubt that this again was Spielrein. Jung described her as a 'hysterical young Russian woman'. He explained how she had told him how a verse from the poet Lermontov was continually running around her head. The poem was about a prisoner whose only companion was a bird in a cage. The prisoner had opened the cage and let the bird fly out. Jung described how her wish was 'to help someone to perfect freedom through psychoanalytical treatment'. She had also admitted she wanted to have a child by him. In the letter, Jung quipped that he would have to 'let the bird out'. In case his Viennese friend did not understand the crude Swiss slang, Jung referred Freud to a well-known pornographic picture by the artist Kaulbach, showing winged penises looking like cockerels.

There are several striking features of the letter. First, Jung's account of the poem is full of errors.[17] It is by Pushkin, not Lermontov. The poem is about a religious ritual. The man in it is not a prisoner, and there is no cage. Spielrein was highly literate and would not have given a garbled version. Either Jung had been inattentive when she was describing the poem, or his memory was at fault. Another notable point is that Jung wanted to create the impression that he was treating her as a patient, even though he was not. We discover for the first time that Spielrein had aspirations to become a psychoanalyst, and had confessed she wanted Jung's child. The way in which Jung pokes fun of her does not make this narrative any less disturbing. Freud replied simply by noting the 'many charming "trifles"' in the letter.[18] He failed to connect this story with Jung's last 'boring' one about the student with anal eroticism. There was no reason for him to do so. Jung had not included any detail that was the same as his previous account.

As well as case histories and professional plans, the men's letters were full of tittle-tattle and humorous character assassinations. Two of the people who figured in their correspondence were the most colourful in psychoanalytic history. They were also to play a part in Spielrein's story: Otto Gross and Max Eitingon. Gross was an Austrian doctor, psychoanalyst, drug addict and sexual libertine who had been previously been admitted to the Burghölzli under Bleuler's care. A man of charm and imagination, he was the first psychoanalyst to preach promiscuity as a cure for neurosis. The other man, Max Eitingon, had been one of the students present at the Burghölzli, but had recently gone on to study with Freud. Eitingon also had a well-deserved reputation for promiscuity. This may explain Jung's outburst in a letter to Freud later in 1907 where he expressed his feelings about the two men. He started by describing Eitingon as 'a totally impotent gasbag', but then conceded that he envied 'his uninhibited abreaction of the polygamous instinct'.[19] He predicted that Eitingon would never amount to anything from a psychoanalytic point of view but might one day become a member of the Duma – the (famously impotent) Russian parliament set up by the Tsar in response to the 1905 revolution. He then moved on to a critique of Gross, who had told him that he put a quick stop to the transference by 'turning people into sexual immoralists'. Gross had argued that transference to the analyst was itself a 'symbol of monogamy' and hence evidence of repression. Jung expressed his own view that sexual repression was absolutely vital to keep civilisation going, even if it caused psychological problems for 'inferior people'. He concluded by criticising Gross for his preference for the 'sexual short-circuit'. Jung regarded this as stupid, in bad taste 'and therefore anything but a civilising factor'. It is not difficult to guess that Jung was either trying to talk himself out of the 'sexual short-circuit', or putting up a smokescreen because he was already trying it out.

The following month, Jung wrote a letter to Freud that also probably related to Spielrein. He described a lady who had been cured of an obsessional neurosis but made him the object of her sexual fantasies, which were torturing her.[20] She wanted to separate from him and deal with them on her own. He was unsure whether to continue her treatment or discharge her. If this was a disguised narrative about Spielrein, he once again omitted any details to connect the story with previous ones. Freud's response is not recorded, but Jung thanked him for his advice and said he had put it into practice.[21]

In September 1906, Jung attended a conference for neurologists in Amsterdam. Freud did not attend, but Jung used the occasion to present a robust defence of Freud's view of hysteria. The centrepiece of his presentation was another version of the Spielrein case. He began by pointing out there was an increasing consensus that hysteria had a psychological origin, and praised Freud for trying to establish the exact causes. He cited 'Anna O' as an example of how memories could be forgotten and converted into physical symptoms. He recommended Freud's method of free association as a way of penetrating this more deeply than hypnosis, so that the patient 'gradually gains complete insight into the illness'. His claimed to have proved these findings with association tests. He also commented that, once the chain of associations was clear through these tests, it was no longer necessary to do any special work of interpretation. In other words, association tests could act as a form of psychoanalysis in their own right.[22]

Jung proceeded to describe a case of 'psychotic hysteria in an intelligent young woman of twenty'.[23] Spielrein was never psychotic, but Jung probably exaggerated the diagnosis for effect. He began by describing her method of anal stimulation, as he had described it to Freud, and how this progressed to masturbation. This time he did not talk about her witnessing Yasha being spanked. Instead, he mentioned how there was 'once' an occasion around the age of seven when her father spanked her and she became sexually excited. He explained how her perverse and obsessive fantasies then began at puberty, and she started to imagine people defecating as they ate. He added more details than previously, for example saying she had the same fantasy about her teacher, and in the end she could never eat with other people around her. He described how any reproach would lead her to imagine being punished. She would then become sexually excited, and cover this up with laughing, cries of disgust, and gestures of horror. Much of this account is recognisable. It sheds new light on Spielrein's behaviour when she arrived at the Burghölzli. However, the story has an even more Freudian twist than before, especially with the single beating trauma, and the onset of her obsessions at puberty. Jung made a point of emphasising that Spielrein's complexes did not involve her mother. He did not refer to relentless family conflict, or the possibility of actual sexual abuse. He concluded by pointing out how effectively the history demonstrated the key principles of Freud's view. As he presented it, it was indeed a textbook illustration of the Oedipus complex.

His presentation was a disaster. This was not because he had slanted the history. The audience simply regarded Freud's sexual theory as unacceptable. The great Parisian psychiatrist Pierre Janet was present, and declared the theory 'a bad joke'. Jung went over his time limit and refused to respond to the chairman's request to stop after his allotted half hour. When he was forced to do so, he stormed out of the hall.[24] He wrote to Freud complaining that they were 'a ghastly crowd, reeking of vanity, Janet the worst of the lot'.[25] Freud reassured him that the doctors were really not yet capable of understanding even the simple things. They should just go on working and not get into any arguments.[26] It was no doubt sound advice, although ironic in the light of the arguments they were soon to have with one another. Before that happened, however, Jung was to get into serious arguments with someone else: Sabina Spielrein.

70

6

Woman's Talk 1907-1908

I cannot bear it when you speak to me like this. Either we should decide not to mention these subjects or, if we do discuss them, I must be able to react to your remarks accordingly. Naturally my wishes cannot change after only one conversation, because I need a long period of reflection for it to work. But my wish never took the form: 'I want to have a child by you.' Because that would first mean: 'I undertake to give you up for ever.' And that only seems possible for me in specific moments when I feel badly offended by you; then the wish to have your child takes over from everything.[1]

THIS PASSAGE comes from the draft of a letter that Spielrein wrote to Jung probably in late 1907 or early 1908. It is evident here that their friendship has got into difficulties. She still adored him, but they were having arguments. Spielrein does not spell out exactly what Jung said that upset her, but everything else is fairly clear. They had just had an argument about her wish for his child – the subject of the 'bird' joke in his letter to Freud. Jung had told her she should give up this wish. Whatever response she gave, he then told her off for that too. His reprimand had upset her terribly. She was now telling him she needed time to let go of the wish. As she explained, he had totally misunderstood her wish. It was not erotic desire. Quite the contrary: she only felt an intense wish for his child when she feared he would not return her love, and there was no other way of keeping hold of him. Jung's ban on speaking about her fantasy, and his reprimand, might have had something to do with the missing advice he had requested from Freud about a female patient. Perhaps Freud had advised Jung to tell his 'patient' she should stop dwelling on her 'sexual fantasies' and try and get to the root of them instead. If so, Jung was applying the wrong solution to the wrong problem: Spielrein was not his patient, and her fantasies were not primarily sexual.

Spielrein's letter drafts and a later diary make it clear that Jung had now decided to try and sort out her fantasies by analysing them during their social or educational encounters. She felt he was acting without her consent, and dangerously. As far as she was concerned, her treatment had ended three years ago. She did not want to go back to being his patient. She was also worried such conversations would expose his own feelings towards her in an unmanageable way. Later, one of her Russian medical school peers would describe what Jung was doing as an 'experiment'.[2] This was a perceptive comment. It suggests the possibility that Jung was testing out more of Freud's ideas on his friend, just as he did when she was his patient in hospital. In the words of psychoanalyst Henry Lothane, Jung was 'mixing friendship with an ambiguous therapy without a fee. It is an ethical dilemma just as weighty as mixing ongoing therapy with a sexual relationship.'[3]

The letter drafts appear in a notebook that has come to be known as the 'Transformation Diary'. It is named after a section near the beginning that Spielrein headed: 'The theory of transformation and related matters.' The name is misleading, since the notebook is not really a diary. It contains three long letter drafts intended for Jung. They were probably written over a period of several months. The style of the first one is similar to the drafts she wrote in 1906, covered in the previous chapter, and may have been written not long afterwards. By the time she wrote the last one a year or eighteen months later, including the passage above, she had become seriously disturbed by their friendship. Reading the drafts therefore enables us to trace their friendship over that period, from a manageable crush to a serious crisis.

*

The 'Transformation' letters end with an outpouring of emotion, but they do not begin that way (I use the term 'Transformation' letters for these drafts from now on, rather than the less accurate 'Transformation Diary'). The first reads like an academic essay, with complex arguments and intricate examples. It was here that Spielrein first tried to formulate a theory of sex and death, drawing on a wide range of sources from literature, philosophy, psychology and biology. To understand what she was writing about, and why, we need to step back and consider some of the different contexts in which she was living and working. Spielrein was a formidable young intellectual. She had left school three years previously as a gold medallist, able to speak and read fluently in at least three major European languages, and with wide-ranging interests including music, art and literature. It is no surprise that we find references in her diary to Goethe, Ibsen, Galileo, Marx, Wagner and Leonardo da Vinci, as well as her compatriots Gorky, Gogol, Dostoyevsky and Pushkin. These were set down in the manner of one highly literate and cultured adult writing to another.

Just as cultural literacy was evident in what she wrote, so was scientific literacy, and particularly knowledge of biology. She was attending a leading medical school. It was part of the German-speaking scientific world, which had taken the leading role in biological discoveries in the generation following Darwin. Spielrein wrote of Darwin's key principle of evolution, using his phrase 'the preservation of the species'. We know she had read August Weismann early on in medical school.[4] Among his other discoveries, Weismann had realised that primitive organisms only die because of changes in the environment, so that sexual reproduction might be connected with the fixed life cycles of higher organisms like humans. This connection between sex and death informed Spielrein's own thoughts. In her drafts, she described how organisms surrender their identity in order to create the next generation, and how even humans must give up their individuality, and eventually their existence, in the interests of reproduction. From her later writing, it is clear that she learned about Oskar Hertwig, who first showed images of how a sperm penetrated an egg.[5] She also no doubt knew of the eminent Swiss scientist Friedrich Miescher, who isolated the genetic material DNA and called it 'nuclein'. Just before she started at university, a number of biologists rediscovered Gregor Mendel's work on the laws of inheritance. She later referred to these too.[6]

Beyond culture and science, there was a third strand of Spielrein's thinking that was even more important. This was her wish to become a psychiatrist and psychoanalyst. According to Spielrein, Jung had urged her to take up psychiatry even while she was still at the Burghölzli. 'A mind like yours will advance science', he had said: 'You must become a psychiatrist.'[7] From Jung's letter to Freud, we already know that she had conceived an ambition to become a psychoanalyst. Although there were no women who were recognised as psychoanalysts,[8] there were several she had met in hospital or at the university who had ambitions to achieve this, including Esther Aptekmann and Tatiana Rosenthal. A close involvement with psychoanalysis must have offered many attractions for Spielrein. It provided a reason to stay close to the man she adored. It offered an opportunity to carry on resolving her turbulent emotions. By serendipity, she had found herself cast as a player in a radical movement that all Europe was beginning to talk about. The man who had been her psychiatrist was on his way to being anointed as the 'crown prince' to its founder. She must have been aware that the narrative of her treatment had become an important currency in her doctor's own advancement. She had seen Jung's description of her case history for Freud in the letter her mother possessed.[9] She followed Jung's publications and would have read the account he gave of her at the Amsterdam Congress.

Whatever she made of these, there could be no stronger indication that her place at the heart of this movement was fated. With this background in mind, we can now return to the 'Transformation' letters themselves.

The first draft begins with a short story, or drama. It is headed 'Two speakers'. One speaker is clearly meant to be herself. The other is a portrait of Jung. It is a frank one. She describes how he would try to present his case passionately, 'even violently and thunderously', but this was generally unsuccessful. His exaggerations and omissions 'make one doubt the sincerity of his cause'. He would suddenly change his manner into a cold and rejecting one. He was only at the height of his power when he was able to hold back his emotions and tease himself, so that his spirit could 'come out of its hiding place'.[10] After this prologue, Spielrein proceeded with a case example: a married woman with schizophrenia, probably drawn from a patient. Over the ensuing paragraphs, she then posed a number of questions: 'What really is this abominable thing called love? What do we love in the other? How is the love of a woman different from that of a man? How can this essentially human feeling be distinguished from sexual attraction? And what enables us to renounce it? How do we move from erotic attraction to affection, or create something out of unbearable separation?'[11] For Spielrein, these were not simply theoretical questions. They were urgent personal ones as well.

In this draft, she began by pursuing answers through literature, philosophy and psychology. Then she turned to biology for an answer:

Every individual as such must disappear. In an amoeba the entire 'personality' disappears, with people or other animals only a tiny part does ... but the instinct is always towards death, the destruction of the personality, in which two individuals are merged into one. This is how you can explain the numerous depictions of the [sexual] instinct as destructive, demonic etc.[12]

Using her own feelings as examples, Spielrein developed the argument that human beings are torn between self-preservation and the instinct for transformation. In her view, the instinct for transformation is driven by the need for the 'preservation of the species' – in other words, for reproduction. She believed that this instinct draws us powerfully to people whose 'complexes' are similar to our own. It provides the motivation for great discoveries. It also stands in opposition to our own interests as individuals, which is why we experience it as 'demonic'. Her argument shows how she was exploring a singular notion: the reproductive drive is overriding, but it involves destruction before transformation is possible. For her, the ideal outcome of this mixed creative-destructive urge – such as love between her and Jung – would lead to a transformational act of artistic or scientific creation. Her argument is often convoluted and hard to follow. These are the jottings of evolving thought, not a fully formed theorem. However, they contained ideas that she would continue to develop over the next ten years.

As the drafts proceed, there is a gradual diminution of the theoretical side of Spielrein's meditations. Strong emotion comes to the fore. The logic seems to unravel in places, with the associations between one thought and the next becoming looser. One has the sense that Spielrein is losing her grip on both the argument and her feelings. She wrote the second letter draft while on vacation at home, in Rostov-on-Don, in what seems to be a disturbed state of mind.[13] She veers between theory and feelings in a way that makes it hard to follow either very clearly:

> You see, I do not love you now, I mean, not in the ideal sense, and this state is much more horrible than death. Nothing matters to me ... The preservation of the species is obviously more important than the preservation of an individual. Why don't you want to kill me, if you love me although you know I am a degenerate? ... I implore you, do not be impatient right away. I don't want you to misunderstand this totally. There is a fundamental difference between your view and mine, and if we cannot agree, I won't be able to prove to you why anything appears to have a different cause, and this torments me.[14]

Near the end of the second draft, she wrote about the treatment of hysteria, and what should and should not happen during it. She explained that sexual desires could be over-analysed to the point of humiliation. She was evidently referring to herself, and to the unwanted therapy Jung was trying out on her. She also described how she was affected by being back at home: 'Here, my family has now made sure that, taken away from my studies, I've been pulled back into my complex again. My misery is limitless again. Will I be able to emerge from it unscathed?'[15] She was presumably indicating that some of her old masochistic symptoms had returned.

It is unclear where she wrote the third letter draft, but she was probably back in Zurich. All intellectualisation has now disappeared. There is pure emotional pain. The psychoanalyst Jeanne Moll has remarked that 'in the last pages her passion overcomes her, revealing the prolonged, loving lamentation of a lonely woman'.[16] This is where she protested that her wish to have Jung's pure love was far stronger than her wish for a child, who could only ever be a proxy for Jung:

Oh you! If you knew how dear you are to me, without the least thought of the child. Isn't the wish to have a child above all the wish to have at least a small version of you? ... You try to suppress every strong feeling you have for me. The result is that you are made of diplomacy and lies.[17]

She made it apparent that Jung himself had now proposed they should terminate any attempt at using the friendship for interpretations. She completely agreed:

I don't feel comfortable speaking to you like this. But what should I do? I cannot let you retaliate by humiliating me. It is infinitely more awful for me than if I died just so you could be at peace. What should I do? I completely agree with you that we should never speak to each other again about the unconscious. I am now going to Locarno and hope that new impressions and a longer time without seeing you will make things clearer.[18]

Following the distraught passage that appears at the head of this chapter, she concluded: 'When the time comes when I have to leave you for good ... then I really don't know ... no-one knows what fate will bring, and I don't think it's impossible that I may fall in love with someone else, and that will have another destiny in that respect.[19]

Comparing the Freud-Jung correspondence during this period with Spielrein's letter drafts, she and Jung appear to have inhabited different universes. Jung and Freud were caught up in a world of mutual admiration, ambition and political strategy. She was immersed in soul-searching in relation to her own destiny and also to find theoretical meaning in what she was going through. She was also utterly confused by what was happening in her friendship with her former psychiatrist. There is still no evidence at this point that she meant anything like as much to Jung as she believed. There is far more to imply that it was a one-sided love that he was now trying to analyse away. If he had shown her any sign of love, she would surely have mentioned it, as she was to do later. In the two years leading up to the summer of 1908, he had only mentioned her two or three times in his letters to Freud. It is striking that all his accounts during this time were emotionally distant and inaccurate, and one was jokey and dismissive. However much Jung was dissembling, there is no evidence for asserting, as John Kerr does, that she meant 'a great deal to him personally' during this time.[20]

Jung had many things to distract him. At the beginning of 1908, his wife

Emma became pregnant for the third time.[21] Together, they decided to build a new home on the shore of Lake Zurich, in the village of Küsnacht. It was to remain their home for the rest of their lives. In April they received a three-day visit from Freud himself, in reciprocation for the visit they had paid to Vienna. Later the same month, Jung organised the First International Congress for Psychoanalysis in Salzburg: forty-two people attended, including Freud, Bleuler, Gross, Eitingon and the leading neurologist and psychologist from Geneva, Édouard Claparède. In his letters, Freud's salutation changed from 'Dear colleague' to 'Dear friend and colleague' and then 'Dear friend', although Jung remained careful to address the older man as 'Dear Professor Freud'.

On the clinical front, matters were not so rosy. In May 1908, Otto Gross was admitted to the Burghölzli again, this time under Jung's care. Bleuler had insisted that that Freud should formally request an admission. Freud obliged, promising to take over his care once he had withdrawn from opium and cocaine under medical supervision.[22] Gross's behaviour in the Burghölzli was not encouraging. He refused to eat anything except specially prepared vegetables. He wore several shirts one on top of another, and kept taking off his underpants 'to warm them'. He made odd scribblings of people on the walls and floors of the hospital, which Jung examined to try and understand his unconscious mind. Somehow he managed to obtain drugs, presumably from hospital staff, to mix with Jung's prescription drugs. He became violent and broke furniture if Jung did not come immediately on request. When Jung refused to admit Gross's wife so that Gross himself could psychoanalyse her, he determined to analyse Jung instead. Jung appears to have consented, and informed Freud of this. When he got stuck, they changed roles. As a result, Jung felt his own psychological health had definitely benefited. Gross was now voluntarily going through opium withdrawal, and was really 'an extraordinarily decent fellow with whom you can hit it off at once provided you get your own complexes out of the way'. Jung confidently announced that he had finished the analysis after a few weeks, leaving only 'minor obsessions of secondary importance'.[23]

Freud raised an eyebrow slightly at this report. He expressed amazement at how young people were able to work, confessing that he would have taken longer.[24] If he had stronger reservations about the speed and nature of Jung's analysis, he held them in suspense. His suspense did not last long. Three weeks later, Gross jumped over the wall of the hospital garden and vanished. Jung let Freud know, predicting he would come to a sad end before long.[25] Jung's prediction was accurate, although it took longer than he expected. Gross continued on his erratic journey for several more years, preaching and practising his manifesto for free love. He followed a diverse career as a writer, anarchist agitator, cultural critic, psychoanalyst and psychiatric patient until 1920, when he was found freezing and half-starved on a street in Berlin, and died of pneumonia soon afterwards.

Gross almost certainly used some of his conversations with Jung to advocate sex with patients. If so, he was preaching what many analysts apart from himself were already practising. Many, like Jung, had come from sexually conservative backgrounds. Freud's ideas had given them permission to explore their own and each other's sexual histories and fantasies freely. Apart from conveying his view that a great deal of moralising about sex was due to denial and hypocrisy, Freud had so far given no guidance about the limits of relationships with patients or ex-patients. He had also been tolerant of analysts' sexual adventures.[26] Jung was not the only analyst who was simultaneously exploring the practice of psychoanalysis and on a voyage of discovery to find the right way to conduct his personal life – or the wrong one.

Poetry 1908

My dear friend, I have to let you know what a lovely impression you made on me today. Your image has completely changed, and I would like to tell you how very, very happy it has made me to be able to hope that there are people similar to me, for whom living and thinking are one; people who do not abuse the power of their mind to make fetters, but much more in order to create freedoms. Because of this, a feeling of beauty and freedom has awakened within me ... You cannot believe how much it means to me to hope that I can love a person that I don't have to condemn, and who does not to condemn herself, to suffocate in the banality of habit.[1]

IT WAS the summer of 1908. Four years since he first took her medical history Carl Jung was writing to Spielrein to confess he had fallen in love with her. How could this have occurred? The first and most obvious answer is: such things happen. When a young, intense and adoring young woman persists in trying to attract her older male teacher, it is not entirely unknown for this to affect how he sees her. This is especially the case if the man is susceptible to affairs and his wife is starting to show the signs of pregnancy. In addition, Jung's failed attempts to 'analyse away' his friend's love may have had exactly the effect she feared: created greater intimacy, exposed Jung's own vulnerability, and led him to mirror her idealisation of him. Jung's 'feeling of beauty and freedom' seems to have developed in a short space of time. Only ten days earlier, he had written a quite different kind of letter to Spielrein. It is the first of his surviving letters to her, and has a harsh, even persecuted tone. He was writing in response to something she had just written to him. She may have been expressing the troubled feelings that appeared in her third 'Transformation' letter. Alternatively, she had perhaps commented on the disappearance of Otto Gross from the Burghölzli, which happened a few days earlier:[2]

My dear Miss Spielrein, You were really skilful at getting under the skin of my unconscious with your biting letter. That kind of thing could only happen to me.[3]

He explained he was engaged the following Monday as he was meeting Freud's colleague, the Welsh psychoanalyst, Ernest Jones. However, he was coming into town on Tuesday morning, 25 June, and wanted to meet her at the landing stage. He proposed they should take the boat onto Lake Zurich, so they could be alone and undisturbed. He hoped that in the sunshine and open water it would be easier to find a clear direction in this 'turmoil of feelings'. Something must have happened on the boat trip or shortly afterwards to convert bitter mutual recriminations into the most passionate reconciliation. From feeling fond and protective of her, but determined to analyse away her crush on him, he suddenly saw her as sexually attractive and a source of personal liberation. Later, Jung was compelled to inform her that this was not first time he had experienced this with a young woman.

*

As the opening passage to this chapter shows, Jung made it clear from the outset that this new relationship would not replace his marriage. It would be one where neither would demand, nor offer, the 'banality of habit'. A few days later, he reiterated this in another, similar letter. He disclosed what a releasing effect it had had on him that there were people like her who would behave just as freely as they thought. This would compensate him for 'many disappointments'. He felt calm and free.[4] There are several short letters following this, mostly to set up assignations. His salutation had already changed from 'My dear Miss Spielrein' to 'My dear friend'. He now progressed to 'My Dear'.

At the end of July, Spielrein returned to her family in Russia again for her summer vacation. She did not write to him for a couple of weeks. When she did so, she revealed that she had taken a momentous step. She had told her parents about the latest developments in their relationship. Jung's reply showed he had no objection to this disclosure: quite the contrary. He was more concerned that her silence signified that 'the devil had a hand in it'. He now expressed his admiration for her parents' 'truly great broadmindedness'. While Nikolai as a man of ideas would have find this easier, he observed, it would be a great and unexpected achievement for any woman, since they were naturally conservative. He confessed he felt very much more attached to Spielrein than he had ever realised. There are the faintest of hints in the letter that Jung had reassured Spielrein earlier that his wife might take a 'broadminded' view of polygamy, as she would later claim. He continued:

I happen to be terribly suspicious, and always think other people are trying to exploit and tyrannise me. It is only with great difficulty that I can muster a belief in man's natural goodness. That certainly does not apply to you however![5]

After these reflections, Jung continued his long letter with his concerns that cholera had broken out Rostov, and advised Spielrein about her diet. He let her know about two American professors who were visiting, and a German one who was coming to study with him. Tellingly, he asked her to continue to send her letters to the Burghölzli for forwarding, rather than writing direct to the family home in Küsnacht, which suggests that Emma might not have been so broadminded about polygamy after all. He ended with the news that Freud would be coming to visit him in September, and thanked her for the money she had sent him – possibly to return a loan. The letter ended 'With an affectionate kiss from your friend ...'. The tone and material of the letter leave little room for doubt: Jung and Spielrein had become lovers. Eva Spielrein – for whatever reason – had come to tolerate the relationship. Nikolai thought it was entirely acceptable and in keeping with his modern beliefs.

Spielrein must have responded to his letter straight away, because only a week later, in the middle of August, Jung wrote back. This time, his letter is brief. His tone is noticeably more measured. He wrote of how she had received a large 'bonus' of friendship. He offered her a heartfelt wish for a successful life and the fulfilment of all her goals. He reassured her that if she performed all her work with love, it would always go well. He ended with a reminder to keep addressing letters to the Burghölzli.[6] There is a slightly valedictory feel to the letter, as if he was already preparing to distance himself. At the beginning of September, Jung was able to thank her for sending him some photographs of herself, as well as detailed descriptions of life in Russia.[7] Once she set off back to Zurich to complete her studies, however, another letter arrived belatedly from Jung, and her mother could not resist opening and reading it. The turbulence of the letter she then wrote to Sabina speaks volumes not only about Eva, but about the fluctuating passions of all three parties to this drama:

Dear Sabinochka, I cannot find peace after your departure and I do not know where to write ... At night I thought of you and him, and after having lost all hope of receiving any news, and when my suffering for you reached a climax, I suddenly received a letter addressed to you. I was so upset I could not read a word. I ask you a thousand times to forgive me for opening the letter, but I opened it because you would have let me read it anyway and I had to know what it held for you, because my entire mood depended on it. His letter calmed me down. It expresses deep friendship, lightly coloured by something else, which is quite natural. He often thought of you, of the cholera, of your soul. He is probably in the throes of a conflict and his counsel to you and to himself is not to let the feeling of love grow but to suppress it, though not to kill it completely ... He writes that this is necessary for the sake of the loved ones, that is, his wife and children. And what about you? Perhaps I got it wrong? Anyway, I like the tone of his letter very much, especially the limits within which he places you and himself. It seems to me that it could not be any better. You have in him a person devoted to you, with a touch of love (more than that is not permitted and you have to remain content with that).[8]

Eva advised her daughter it would be different if she wanted him to divorce his wife, but as things stood 'you must not go any further'. Sabina could no doubt succeed in taking him away from Emma, but it would not be worth it. She advised her daughter to continue meeting him as a friend. 'He also needs you,' she wrote, 'but he is not suffering, on the contrary, he is getting better.' Eva begged Sabina not to disclose to Jung that she had opened his letter.

Eva's letter testifies to her genuinely loving feelings for Sabina. It also ends on an almost perfect note for a Jewish mother: 'As far as the jam is concerned, tell him that you brought along food for him but were unable to bring more.' She then advised Sabina to rent a lavish apartment, invite Jung, and to keep her informed of all the details. 'You can talk to him about love but remain unyielding, you only stand to gain from it. For the time being, do not hide your feelings.'

One of the things Eva Spielrein implies in this letter is that, separated from Sabina, Jung was finding little difficulty in calming his feelings towards her. Her supposition is confirmed by Jung's next letter to Spielrein at the end of the month, written from one of his spells of military service. He apologised for not having written for a few weeks, explaining that Freud had been staying with him for quite a long time. The rest of the letter is taken up entirely with Jung's admiration for Freud. There is no mention of his own feelings for her. If the correspondence stopped at this point, one might assume that both he and Spielrein had followed Eva's advice by reining in their passion and continuing as good friends.[9]

There is a gap in any correspondence for a couple of months. However there are a couple of undated letters by Spielrein in the Geneva archive that clearly come from the latter part of 1908. The first depicts a scene that has become material for the movies:

Dear Mamochka,

Truly miracles happen in this world. No more, no less, without intending to, I managed to hypnotise Junga. How did it happen? He came to me 5 minutes earlier than agreed upon. Knocks and I answer 'Ja!' He enters and I am greatly embarrassed because I did not expect it was him and I stand there with my hair half-loose, comb in hand [...] He sat down on the couch and promised he would not look, even though I had known in advance that 'not looking' to him means he covers his face with his hands and peers through the spaces between the fingers ... Then, as always, he launched into long speeches about him not having slept all night thinking about me, him wanting me to be happy forever etc. ... I tell him that such speeches are a disturbance to me, that I love him anyway, that if one day we have to part then that will be that, but now I am not thinking of anything and I am fine. Then he kisses me and bawls. '*Was ist?*' [What is it?] and he immediately glows with happiness. I am a mother for him, he a father for me, the best of all possible worlds! But the best of all, he had the idea to make me a new hairdo: he pulled the comb out of my hairdo and loosened my hair, whereupon he became jubilant that I looked like an Egyptian woman (!)[10]

The second letter says everything we need to know about the wild, oscillating emotions of their 'poetry' together:

That I love him is as firmly determined as that he loves me. He is for me a father and I am a mother for him, or, more precisely, the woman who has acted as the first substitute for the mother (his mother came down with hysteria when he was two years old): and he became so attached to the substitute woman that when she was absent he saw her in hallucinations etc. Why he fell in love with his wife I do not know ...[11] Let us say, his wife is 'not completely' satisfactory and now he is in love with me, a hysteric; and I fell in love with a psychopath, and is it necessary to explain why? I have never seen my father as normal. His insane striving to 'know himself' is best expressed in Jung for whom his scientific activity is more important than anything in this world [...] An uneven dynamic character coupled with a highly developed sensitivity, a need to suffer and be compassionate *ad magnum*. You can do to him and get from him anything you want with love and tenderness. Twice in a row he became so emotional in my presence that tears just rolled down his face! If you could only hide in the next room and hear how concerned he is for me and my fate, you would be moved to tears yourself. Then he starts reproaching himself endlessly for his feelings, for example, that I am something sacred for him, that he is ready to beg for forgiveness etc.[12]

She reminded her mother how Nikolai always used to apologise in exactly the same manner after marital arguments. She did not want to quote Jung's self-reproaches as she knew she was just as guilty as he was. She knew how many female patients went to see him and fell in love with him, but he had explained that as he was their doctor he could not do so in return. They had both considered the possibility of separating from each other. He felt responsible for her fate, 'and howled as he pronounced these words'. When that particular conversation came to an end, they stood still, 'in the most tender poetry'. A week after this encounter, he visited her apartment again:

Poetry again, and as usual, will I ever in my life forgive him what he had concocted with me; he did not sleep that night, became exhausted, cannot fight it any longer ... The question for me is whether to surrender with all my being to this violent vortex of life and to be happy while the sun is shining, or, when the gloom descends, to let the feeling become transferred to a child and science? ... *So far we have remained at the level of poetry that is not dangerous, and we shall remain at that level, perhaps until the time I will become a doctor, unless circumstances will change ...*[13]

It is clear from this context that Spielrein was by now using the word 'poetry' for explicitly erotic contact, drawing on the word for sex used by a patient she was writing her dissertation about. There is of course no precise physical description here of what 'poetry' actually constituted, and it would be absurd to expect this. For better or worse (probably the former), few lovers oblige historians with anatomical descriptions of who did what to whom. Readers will no doubt be able to draw on their own experience and imagination rather than depending on biographers or movie directors to do it on their behalf. Whether the couple ever went beyond the 'dangerous' level is discussed in Chapter 9, in the context of a narrative that Spielrein wrote the following year, intended for Freud. What is apparent is that their erotic contact was tender and loving, not sado-masochistic. In the remaining part of her letter to Eva, she described how one of Jung's patients tried to get over him by taking to the mountains, where she became infatuated with a young man. This patient was now pregnant and the man 'turned out to be the most small-minded person and abandoned her forthwith'. Spielrein continued: 'Now she cannot stand him and in desperation wanted to end her life, and would have done it, had Junga not saved her once again.'

On 1 December 1908, Emma Jung gave birth to her first son, Franz. Three days afterwards, Jung wrote again to Spielrein. It is the confession of a distressed and confused man, and the most poignant he was ever to write to her:

My dear, I regret so much, I regret my weakness and curse the fate that is threatening me. I am fearful for my work, for my life's mission, for all the tremendous perspectives that this new philosophy is revealing to me … My mind is torn to its depths. I, who had to be strong person for so many weak people, am now the weakest. Will you forgive me for being what I am, and how I am? For offending you in this way, and forgetting my duties as a doctor towards you? Will you understand and grasp that I am the weakest and most unstable of people? And will you never take revenge on me for that, either with words, or with thoughts and feelings? I am looking for that future person who will make it a reality to love independently of social advantages or disadvantages, so that love can be an end in itself and not always just a means to an end. My misfortune is that I cannot do without the joy of love – tempestuous, ever-changing love in my life … When love for a lady awakens in me, my first feeling is a feeling of regret, of pity for the poor woman who dreams of eternal faithfulness and other impossibilities, and is destined for a painful awakening from all these dreams.[14]

He continued by making it clear that he had no intention of making the same mistake over and over again by further marriages, since it was far better to stay engaged in a dishonest marriage rather than repeatedly disappointing each wife. 'What on earth is to be done for the best?' he asked Sabina. He proposed a meeting the following Tuesday morning in her apartment. Since the last 'upset', he had been completely unsure where he stood with her. Now he wanted assurances about what she intended to do. Most of all, he was concerned his work would suffer, and he knew that was far more important than any passing difficulties like his current ones. He begged her to return some of the love, patience and generosity he had given to her when she was ill. He concluded: 'Now I am ill [...]'[15]

There is an honesty here that will never reappear again in his correspondence with her. As he admitted, this was already an established pattern for him: sudden infatuation with a woman, passionate erotic contact, followed after a short time by guilt and regret. We do not know who his previous loves might have been, but we do not need to. Spielrein was definitely not the first. From the sound of it, she may not have been the second or third either. He knew he wanted everything: his marriage and family with Emma, an endless succession of 'ever-changing' loves, and above all his work. Reading between the lines, Spielrein by now had understood that he meant exactly what he said about wanting free love. Jung, for his part, was seriously worried what might happen if she would not settle for a love that was 'an end in itself'. If she refused, what might she do in consequence? His mind was now in as much turmoil as hers. The most striking part of his confession is that he openly recognised that he had failed in his professional duty towards her as her former doctor. He was asking her not to take the revenge at her disposal. He wanted to place her in the role of his physician instead.

So far, their love affair had lasted only five months, from around the time of the boat trip on 25 June to the birth of Franz on 1 December. Her love continued as it had done for the past four years. For him, this affair was ending as others had before: in remorse, confusion, and a confession that what he wanted was a succession of ever-changing mistresses. It is tempting to share Spielrein's belief that she had been exceptional in his eyes. How much would our judgement alter if diaries and letters came to light from some of Jung's other female assistants, students, patients, and ex-patients from that time? This was the last of Jung's letters to Spielrein for nearly a year. By that time, there had been another dramatic alteration in his feelings, and three more individuals had been drawn into the drama. They were Emma Jung, Eva Spielrein and Sigmund Freud.

8

Crisis 1909

A woman patient whom years ago I pulled out of a very sticky neurosis with the greatest devotion, has violated my confidence in the most mortifying way imaginable. She has kicked up a vile scandal solely because I denied myself the pleasure of giving her a child. I have always acted the gentleman towards her, but before the bar of my rather too sensitive conscience I nevertheless don't feel clean.[1]

IT WAS three months since Jung had written his letter of profound remorse to Spielrein. Now, he was writing to Sigmund Freud about a 'vile scandal' he claimed Sabina Spielrein had kicked up about him. The person whom he portrayed to Freud less than two years previously as a current patient had once more become a patient he had treated 'years ago'. Writing man to man, he used a strikingly precise phrase – 'I denied myself the pleasure of giving her a child' – without saying what other sexual pleasures he failed to deny her, or himself. He went on to claim that her shocking response only happened because he had been so honourable, and his conscience so sensitive. He admitted to Freud that he had made her into a friend up to a point – perhaps even an inappropriate one – but the reason she was now taking revenge was simply because he stopped short of conception.

Jung confessed that his sense of his polygamous inclinations had been 'totally inadequate', in spite of all the self-analysis he had done. Now, he was aware that the devil could use even his best motives for 'the fabrication of filth'. He felt churned up 'hellishly', although certain the experience would build up his moral strengths. His relationship with Emma had 'gained enormously as a result'. It is striking how completely the feelings of love and remorse he expressed to Spielrein only three months earlier had now vanished. Instead, he was mixing half-truths together with downright lies – carefully packaged among a great deal of innocent news relating to house-building, invitations, concerts, lectures and other trivia.

This letter is the first in an astonishing exchange that took place over the ensuing four months between Jung and Freud, and between Spielrein and Freud. Taken by themselves, the letters between Jung and Freud present a shifting, inconsistent and puzzling account of events. Interpolated with Spielrein's side of the story, they make more sense and are far more gripping. As we will see, Spielrein was telling the truth, while the men were doing something entirely different. In the words of Sabine Richebächer, 'a shabby game unfolds in which, out of calculating power politics, and in an endeavour to avoid any public scandal around psychoanalysis, Freud and Jung together draw up a design to checkmate the queen ... She is led up the garden path, pathologised, appeased.'[2]

From all the different accounts, including Spielrein's later letters to Freud, it is possible to piece together the events of early 1909 that led to this second dramatic turnaround in Jung's feelings. An initial summary will be helpful, although the finer details will emerge in the course of this chapter and the next. In brief: someone wrote to Spielrein's mother anonymously in the early part of the year. In Spielrein's own account, it 'minced no words, saying she should rescue her daughter, since otherwise she would be ruined by Dr. Jung'[3] – in other words, become pregnant. Spielrein believed the anonymous letter came from Emma Jung. She must have had grounds for this: her mother may have forwarded it and perhaps she recognised Emma's handwriting. The letter also persuaded Eva Spielrein that there was an imminent danger of her daughter's 'poetry' with her lover now becoming 'dangerous'. Eva wrote to Jung, asking him to desist. Jung's response was to break off the friendship altogether. He insisted on seeing Spielrein only once a week, in formal medical consultations in his office at the Burghölzli. At one of these, she physically attacked him. He then refused to see her at all. He sent Eva Spielrein a series of highly compromising letters. In one of them, he invited her to Zurich to hear his side of the story. She came, but in the end they never met.

*

At the time he wrote his letter to Freud, Jung may really have believed that Spielrein was kicking up a 'vile scandal'. He may also have been making the story up, before Freud heard about the affair from someone else. As he knew, it was his own wife who had kicked up a 'vile scandal' by telling Eva Spielrein what was going on. Emma had a warm friendship with Freud in her own right, and might well confide in him. Eva Spielrein herself had arrived in Zurich by this point and could easily spread the word. If one of Sabina's friends and fellow students, or Sabina herself, was going to expose him, he needed to get his retaliation in first. He had to convince Freud as quickly as possible that any rumours were due to the malicious lies of a disappointed ex-patient. Meanwhile, the atmosphere in the house at Küsnacht with a new baby, a wronged wife, and a husband who had to terminate an affair abruptly, cannot have been easy.

In fact, Freud had already heard a rumour that Jung was sleeping with one of his patients. A mutual colleague named Muthmann told him that a patient was boasting about being his mistress. Freud wrote to let him know. He reassured him that he and Muthmann had drawn the only possible conclusion: the woman's claim was a neurotic fantasy. 'To be slandered and scorched by the love with which we operate,' Freud wrote, 'such are the perils of our trade.' He then flattered Jung with a quotation from Goethe, whom Jung sometimes claimed as his own great-grandfather: 'In league with the Devil, and yet you fear fire?'[4] Jung was relieved that it never crossed Freud's mind that he would take a patient as his mistress. In his reply, he protested his enduring loyalty to psychoanalysis in spite of his patient's ingratitude. At the same time, he was genuinely puzzled by Freud's report. He must have realised that the rumour that reached Freud could not have come from Spielrein. If she was going to kick up a 'vile scandal', she would not boast about being a current mistress. She would complain about being an abandoned one. 'The story hawked around by Muthmann is Chinese to me,' he wrote. 'I've never really had a mistress and am the most innocent of spouses ... I simply cannot imagine who it might have been. I don't think it is the same lady.'[5] His claim to marital fidelity may have been false, but his perplexity sounds real.

On the day that he wrote his letter about the 'vile scandal', Jung resigned from his post as Bleuler's deputy at the Burghölzli. He explained that he wanted to devote himself to the pursuit of science.[6] He asked if he could keep his voluntary status in order to run the research laboratory. He planned to continue as a university lecturer. His departure from the job was probably inevitable anyway. Bleuler had passed him over for a teaching post, giving it to Jung's laboratory colleague Riklin instead.[7] Jung's relationship with Bleuler had deteriorated badly, and he had already complained to Freud about Bleuler's 'intolerable infantilisms'.[8] All the same it is amazing that he failed to tell Freud that he had just taken the most significant career move of his life: leaving hospital practice to become a private psychoanalyst. As later revelations would show, his resignation may have occurred at exactly the moment when he feared exposure was inevitable.[9] In other words, he had panicked.

Over the next two months, everything calmed down. The hospital accepted Jung's resignation. The Jung family moved out of Zurich to the village of Küsnacht. No one had exposed his affair with Spielrein. No one seemed to believe the other rumour, or mind about it. His complaint to Freud had, if anything, impressed his mentor. Jung was presumably trying hard to build bridges with Emma. It was now Spielrein herself who threw the spanner in the works. She was finding the manner of the break with Jung intolerable. She had no wish to revive the affair, but wanted to separate without rancour. She decided the best person to help her so was Sigmund Freud. She was aware she had once been referred to him anyway, and knew that he was now close to her friend. She hoped he would see her as a patient to help her deal with her feelings. She also wanted him to explain to Jung that she was not pursuing him, either with marital hopes or for revenge. At the end of May, she wrote to Freud, in somewhat cryptic terms:

> Dear Professor Freud, I would be most grateful if you would grant me a brief audience. It concerns a matter of the highest importance, that would probably interest you to hear about. If it is possible I would like you to let me know of a suitable time a little in advance, since I am a trainee here at the hospital and therefore will need to arrange for someone to cover my absence. Maybe you will imagine that I am an audacious seeker after fame, planning to bring you some twisted, 'earth-shattering' piece of work, or something of that kind. No, that is not what leads me to you. You, too, have made me feel embarrassed. With expressions of esteem. I am looking forward to your reply.[10]

Spielrein did not mention Jung in the letter. Nor did she explain that the 'matter of greatest importance' concerned him. She did not need to. Freud presumably saw the Zurich postmark, remembered Jung's complaint, and put two and two together. Quite clearly, this letter was from one of the neurotic female fantasists circling around his Swiss colleague. He forwarded the letter to Jung with the comment: 'Weird! What is she, a busybody, a chatterbox or a paranoiac?'[11] He asked for a brief reply by telegram. Jung evidently obliged.[12] His reply put Freud in a position to give Spielrein a disingenuous brush-off. Freud wrote to explain he could not ask her to travel to Vienna simply on a matter concerning himself, without knowing why she might want to make such a 'sacrifice'. Please could she let him know more in writing what it was all about, so he could form his own opinion.[13]

Jung needed to do a careful calculation at this point. He had no idea that Spielrein wanted to separate amicably. He feared she would either demand a renewal of their affair or kick up a stink. Either way, she would tell Freud what had happened. His previous narrative would no longer serve the purpose. He needed a new and more detailed story: one that would endear him to Freud, while continuing to cast Spielrein as a mischief-maker. This was precisely what he constructed. In his next letter to Freud, he named Spielrein for the first time, confirming she was the person he had written about in March. He explained she was the case he had presented at the conference in Amsterdam. She was also, 'so to speak, my test case, for which reason I remembered her with special affection and gratitude'.[14] He did not explain that she had been under his care in hospital, or point out that she had already appeared two or three times in previous letters as a patient and not a friend.

He now elaborated on how he had managed her treatment. From experience, he explained, he was worried she would relapse after discharge from hospital. That was why he felt obliged to become her friend. It took him quite a while to realise that she was ruthlessly planning to seduce him. As soon as he realised this, he broke off with her at once. He believed she was now getting her revenge by telling everyone he was going to divorce Emma and marry her instead. Jung warned Freud that she would ask him to be a match-maker between them. He likened her to Otto Gross in the scale of her 'father complex'. He had tried to cure both of these difficult individuals *'gratissime'* [completely free][15] and with 'untold tons of patience'. Each of them had then abused his friendship. He admitted that certain other factors had had led him astray. One was a tendency to serial infatuations with Jewesses. He explained this by saying how charmed he had been by one of Freud's daughters (presumably the eldest, Mathilde, who was twenty-two). This was the first time he had alluded to Spielrein being Jewish, or connected her with his other sexually delinquent Jewish patient. He also admitted that 'Gross's notions flitted about a bit too much in my head'. Dealing with these two impossible patients were 'bitter experiences', he wrote. 'To none of my patients have I extended so much friendship,' he lamented, 'and from none have I reaped so much sorrow.'

The letter is, in many ways, a masterpiece. Jung managed to emphasise his 'special affection and gratitude', in contrast to the 'seduction' and 'revenge' that motivated Spielrein. His warning that she wanted Freud to be a matchmaker would be guaranteed to keep him off the field. Jung could be fairly certain of winning favour with Freud by offering some tokens of self-awareness, such as the effect exerted on him by Mathilde Freud and Otto Gross. In passing, he staked a claim for the first time that Spielrein was 'so to speak, my test case'. This slightly guarded claim may reflect his recollection that his conversations with her were his first tentative attempts to try out Freudian ideas. It is also understandable in the context of trying to flatter Freud. Taken together, the whole confection almost makes one forget the truth of the matter: his wife had found out he was having an affair, and told the young woman's mother, who then blew the whistle on it.

Jung's stratagem worked. Freud replied to say he had already written a letter to Spielrein in which he affected ignorance, pretending to think she was exactly what she explained she was not: 'an over-zealous enthusiast'.[16] He consoled Jung that these kinds of romantic pitfalls were painful, but hard to avoid, indeed necessary. Freud added that he had never been fooled so badly himself, but he had certainly come close to it a few times and once had 'a *narrow escape*'. Really, he confessed, the only reason he had never got into this kind of situation was simply because his work kept him so busy and he was ten years older than Jung when he started practising psychoanalysis. Such experiences, he reassured Jung, would help him to develop the thick skin needed to overcome 'counter-transference'. They were in fact a '*blessing in disguise*'. He concluded:

The way these women manage to charm us with every conceivable psychic perfection until they have attained their purpose is one of nature's greatest spectacles. Once that has been done or the contrary has become a certainty, the constellation changes amazingly.

As Freud was teaching the younger doctor, psychoanalysis presented a risk of the patient falling in love, particularly if the patient was a young woman and the analyst a man. In many ways, this letter was a crux in the history of psychoanalysis, as well as in the way Jung's relationship with Spielrein came to be seen. For the first time, Freud introduced the notion of 'counter-transference' as the mirror image of the transference that he had realised lay at the heart of the therapeutic relationship. The term defined the *special* risk of psychoanalysts becoming attracted to their patients, just as their patients could to them. There is a consensus that these events led to Freud's insistence the following year that all intending psychoanalysts must undergo analysis, in order to become more aware of how patients could form strong erotic feelings for those treating them, and vice versa.[17] For the moment, at least, it appeared that Freud was willing to ignore every other aspect of the circumstances. These included Spielrein's varying status as friend and patient, and the tendency of other male doctors to misbehave with their female patients with a fair degree of frequency. Freud decided not to publish anything about counter-transference because of the furore it might cause to admit that psychoanalysts had sexual feelings for their patients, but he suggested that analysts should circulate the information privately.[18]

Although her next letter has not survived, Spielrein must have responded to Freud's request by explaining some more details of their relationship. She enclosed one of Jung's love letters, possibly his first one from the previous summer. Freud could no longer pretend that he considered her merely a 'zealous enthusiast'. He wrote back at once, admitting he had 'completely misunderstood' her previous letter.[19] However, he still made no offer to see her. Instead, he launched a vigorous defence of Jung. As his friend and colleague, Freud said, he believed Jung could not possibly indulge in any 'frivolous or ignoble behaviour'. He certainly did not think he should act as a judge. Even if he had to, he would need to observe the legal maxim '*auditur et altera pars*' [hear the other side]. He told her that Jung's love letter had helped him realise that the two of them must indeed have been close friends, and possibly this arose from a medical consultation. He advised Spielrein that the best way to deal with it in the circumstances would be to suppress her feelings herself, without involving anyone else in the matter. He sent her back Jung's letter, remarking that he did not hold the 'somewhat gushing effusion' against the young man. As an older man, he said, it had made him smile. He then wrote to Jung, explaining how he had cast himself as 'Sherlock Holmes', pretending to guess everything from tiny hints. He told Jung how he had advised Spielrein to deal with her problems 'endopsychically'– in other words, as the productions of her own mind.[20] He cautioned Jung against contrition and reaction, and reminded him of a saying by the philosopher Lassalle about a chemist whose test tube cracked, who just got on with his work:

In view of the kind of matter we work with, it will never be possible to avoid little laboratory explosions. Maybe we didn't slant the test tube enough, or we heated it too quickly, In this way we learn what part of the danger lies in the matter and what part our way of handling it.[21]

One of the temptations in reading this correspondence is minutely to analyse every inconsistency and – it has to be said – every example of evasion, deceit and hypocrisy in them. To state only the most obvious points: Freud was pulling the wool over Spielrein's eyes by pretending to deduce a great deal he already knew. While protesting he would need to hear 'the other side' in order to form a judgement, he had in fact already heard it in considerable detail. He was also pulling the wool over Jung's eyes by not disclosing that he had seen one of his love letters. He feigned thinking that Spielrein wanted him to be a matchmaker, knowing she had never asked for this. Freud also knew perfectly well that her feelings were not due to a single 'medical consultation' but a long and troubled relationship. His advice to manage her own unresolved feelings was entirely out of character. That was her previous doctor's responsibility and, if that failed, for a colleague. His response placed his Swiss colleague's reputation above any interest in helping a distressed patient. As for the metaphor of the slanted and over-heated test tube, one can only speculate what image was in Freud's conscious mind when he wrote it.

Jung wrote briefly to thank Freud for his fatherly tolerance: 'It is too stupid that I of all people, your "son and heir" should squander your heritage so heedlessly, as though I had known nothing of these things.'[22] And that, it seemed, was the end of the matter – except that Sabina Spielrein knew she had been tricked and fobbed off. She had more to say. One way or another, she was going to say it.

9

Free Associations 1909

I begged him many times not to provoke my 'ambitia' [proud hopes] with various probings, because otherwise I would be compelled to uncover similar complexes in him. In the end the unavoidable happened ... it reached the point where he could no longer stand it and wanted 'poetry'. I could not and did not want to resist, for many reasons. But when he asked me what was going to happen next, (because of the 'consequences' of this) I said that first love does not want anything, that I wasn't thinking of anything and did not think to go beyond a kiss, which I could even forego if necessary. And now he is saying that he was too kind to me, that I wanted something sexual with him because of this, and of course he never wanted it etc.[1]

SPIELREIN HAD RECEIVED Freud's 'Sherlock Holmes' letter, making it clear he had no intention of seeing her. In response, she drafted a number of letters to Freud over the next three weeks. The printed versions cover over twenty pages. In them, she described her relationship with Jung from the day she entered the Burghölzli. As the passage above shows, they describe how Spielrein tried repeatedly to deter him from analysing her in the context of their friendship, and how he persisted in doing so. According to her account, it was then Jung who first wanted 'poetry' – her term for physical and erotic contact. The letter drafts take us through the vicissitudes of their involvement with each other, from the time she entered the Burghölzli to the moment when he abruptly ended their friendship. Interwoven with this, there is an account of the bewildering events of the past few weeks, when Jung behaved in a way that was erratic and at times seemed deranged. Although she may have sent Freud some sections of these drafts, she probably decided to use her writing more for self-reflection. It therefore makes sense to read them as a diary, where she tried to review the history of the relationship, and come to terms with its inevitable end. It may also help to see them as an imaginary analysis with Freud. She perhaps visualised herself lying on his couch in Vienna, with Freud sitting behind her, which is what she had hoped for when she first wrote to him.

Unlike the 'Transformation' letters, these ones are not hard to follow from an intellectual point of view. Spielrein was not trying to explain her theoretical ideas. Apart from a sentence or two, she did not even refer to them. The difficulty for the reader is that she poured out what was essentially a stream of consciousness. The sections that she did send to Freud, he found well-nigh impenetrable. Subsequent readers have had the same reaction. Spielrein referred to different events, conversations and feelings in her relationship with Jung, but often connected by their emotional links, and not necessarily in the order in which they happened. She repeated herself or returned to complete her earlier descriptions. In places, important information is missing so we are left to guess at the context, or the dates when something happened. Thus, rather than presenting extracts in the order she wrote them, I have re-organised them in this chapter into a more or less continuous narrative. Because of its power as a work of self-analysis as well as a history, I have also chosen to present it here in this one chapter, rather than distributing the information through earlier chapters as 'factual' detail alone.

*

Before beginning her story, Spielrein wanted to disabuse Freud of two ideas. The first was that she was Jung's enemy. She absolutely denied this: 'I am in no way his enemy. I see him as my oldest little baby upon whom I have bestowed so much effort that he can now live independently.'[2] The second error she wanted to correct was that she wanted Freud to mediate between her and Jung as lovers. Quite the contrary, she protested: *'My dearest wish is to part from him in love.'* This would enable her to move on in her life. She rejected Freud's suggestion that she should suppress her feelings. She explained that it would not work for her. If she did this for Jung, she said, she would never be able to love anyone else again. If she held on to her capacity to love, someone might turn up who would be similar enough for her to love him.[3] She also wanted to state that she had refrained from ever boasting about her friendship with Jung. This suggests she may have heard the other rumour. She wanted Freud to know she had kept everything confidential, even though she had proof of Jung's high regard for her: the abortive referral to Freud where he described her as a 'highly intelligent and gifted person of the utmost sensitivity'.[4] She wrote how relieved she was by Freud's last letter to her so far, because it showed his trust in Jung, even after he had seen the love letter.[5]

Spielrein now laid out her history of their affair. It explains many aspects of their relationship that would otherwise seem obscure. She confessed she had loved Jung 'more than anything in the world' for the entire time since they first met.[6] From the beginning of their relationship, she believed he had regarded her as a colleague, friend and confidante. While she was still in hospital, he gave her some work to do on his first paper on word associations. From early on, he also gave her indications he was dissatisfied with marriage. For example, she had once dreamed about his wife complaining how dictatorial he was. When she told Jung, he sighed and said he had realised early on that living together was difficult. Jung told her she was an exceptional woman, while his wife was an ordinary woman and accordingly 'only interested in whatever interested her husband'.[7]

Spielrein made no claim that he returned her love during the first four years after she had met him. Instead, she described how they were 'very good at reading each other's minds'.[8] They began to share their intellectual and artistic passions, especially concerning Wagner and his music. When she said she loved *Das Rheingold* best, his eyes filled with tears. He told her he was just writing exactly the same thing. She spelled out that such moments of telepathy had happened long before there was any question of sexual relations. It was Wagner who 'planted the demon' in her.[9] She described how this turned the whole world into a melody for her. 'The earth sang, the lake sang, the trees sang, and every twig on every tree.'[10] From that moment in the friendship, she said, that conceived her image of Siegfried, an ambiguous symbol that sometimes signified a creative work, and sometimes a child:

> Then Siegfried came into being, he was meant to be the greatest genius, because Dr Jung floated in front of me like a descendant of the gods and from childhood on I had the notion that I was not destined for an ordinary life, I felt flooded with energy, all nature spoke directly to me, one song after another came to me ...[11]

It is worth stopping to consider what Wagner and Siegfried meant in Spielrein's imagination. The figure of Wagner – German nationalist and anti-Semite – would hardly have been a neutral one. She made the choice that many cultured Jews of her generation (and subsequent ones) have done. This was to turn a blind eye to the composer's politics, because of his musical and literary genius.[12] All the same, a relationship between a Jewess and a Gentile that centred on Wagner signified a step beyond this: a wish to merge her ethnic origins and traditions with Teutonic ones. There are resonances here from her mother's family, where such liaisons were repeatedly attempted. There are also resonances with Freud's wish to 'lose' the Jewish identity of psychoanalysis by fusing it with the Christian world of Swiss psychiatry.

Her preoccupation with Siegfried had other implications. In Wagner's *Ring*, Siegfried is the son of an incestuous coupling. His parents are twins. His mother Sieglinde dies while giving birth to him. He is a hero who 'does not know fear'. He wins the love of Brünnhilde, daughter of Wotan ruler of the gods, after awakening her with a kiss. When Siegfried is murdered by a rival, Brünnhilde lights a funeral pyre for him and commits suicide by riding into it. At the same time, Valhalla the home of the gods catches fire, consuming Wotan and all the gods. These rich associations of Siegfried's story would not have been lost on Spielrein. The relationship between her and her former psychiatrist would be, in metaphorical terms, an incestuous one. Spielrein's consciousness of death as an aspect of conception and childbirth was ever-present. So too was her sense of a heroic destiny. Finally, the mythic notion that such events contained within them an apocalyptic climax, both destructive and transformational, remained a central one for her.

When Spielrein confessed her 'Siegfried complex' to Jung, he treated her 'with the most tender friendship, like a father'.[13] He evidently admitted he had to consider such matters in connection with her, but the real world 'was arranged in a certain way ...'. She felt entirely calmed by this confession: the thought of his love for her, she wrote, made her want to keep him perfectly 'pure'. What is striking about the account is that nothing suggests these conversations were either therapy or a love affair. They read as what they almost certainly were: the conversations of a passionate young woman in love with her ex-psychiatrist and teacher, with him leading her on in a somewhat naïve and flirtatious way, but without any serious intention of going anywhere.

At a certain stage, she explained, their relationship then got into trouble: not sex, but difficult conversations. Evidently she was describing the difficulties that arose when they had been friends for around two years and he tried to cure her of her obsession with him. She explained the problems she had set out in her 'Transformation' letters. She had warned Jung of the risks he was taking by analysing her. It was not something she had asked for, she insisted. It would expose her to an even more profound love, and might lead him to fall in love with her too. She described how she had 'defended herself in letters against every attack' but had been 'forced as a patient to confess my love for him'.[14] Her use of the word 'patient' is interesting in the light of her insistence elsewhere – and Jung's – that she was never in that position. She presumably meant she felt forced into the role during this period.

According to her account, what happened next was the opposite of what Jung described to Freud. Far from Spielrein being the seductress, it was his own advances that prevailed over her resistance. Her words at the beginning of this chapter describe how he initiated a discussion about how far they should go physically. She had said she could cope with just a kiss, or even less, if necessary. This may not be totally honest: no doubt her physical desire fluctuated from moment to moment, especially after the first kiss had actually taken place. At the same time, it is consistent with her claim that she hoped for mutual adoration, not sex. Jung's advances the previous summer were connected from the first with his desire for polygamy. Two passages, drawn from different points in the drafts, spell this out:

> 4½ years ago Dr Jung was my doctor, then he became my friend, and in the end my 'poet' i.e. my beloved. Finally he came to me and everything went as it usually does with 'poetry'. He preached polygamy, he wife was supposed to be in agreement etc. etc.[15]

> Now he turned up, radiating pleasure. He explained to me with strong emotion about Gross, about the great insight he had just acquired (i.e. about polygamy), he did not want to suppress his feelings for me any more, he confessed that I was his first, deepest woman friend (his wife excepted, of course) etc. etc. and he wanted to tell me everything about himself.[16]

Jung's claim that Gross's ideas 'flitted around his head' suddenly falls into place, although not quite in the way he told Freud. The conversations with Gross about polygamy must have taken place during the two men's crazy mutual analysis early the previous summer, before Gross absconded on 17 June.[17] This means that Jung must have told Spielrein about his conversion to polygamy *before* they went on their fateful boat trip on Lake Zurich on 25 June. The 'coup de foudre' at that time may have felt genuine on Jung's part. However, as Spielrein's account shows, Jung had set the terms for their erotic relationship in advance. He had warned her it was not going to be exclusive. In any case, as he confessed only a few months afterwards, he had already been indulging in 'tempestuous, ever-changing love' for some time. Gross had been preaching to the converted.

From that time onwards, according to Spielrein, she and Jung did more than talk about Wagner. They sat in 'speechless ecstasy' for hours, with him sometimes weeping.[18] He gave Spielrein his diary to read, saying that no one other than his wife had ever seen it, and asserting that no one could understand him as she could.[19] They kissed, they cuddled, and probably more. In this respect, there is one passage in the drafts that must give us pause. Spielrein wrote about how she had suffered disdain at the hands of the person 'to whom I sacrificed my maidenly pride, allowing myself to be kissed etc., for the first and perhaps the last time in my life'.[20] This is an intriguing claim. The phrase 'maidenly pride' in the German text is 'Mädchenstolz'. It was used at the time as a euphemism for virginity. Was Spielrein claiming here that she and Jung did in fact have full sex, or did she mean it literally in terms of her pride? Some writers, including Richebächer, believe penetration did take place.[21] Others, like Lothane, believe it did not.[22] A paragraph in a paper Spielrein published in 1912 seems to imply she had personal experience of intercourse.[23] On the other hand, it would be odd to write about 'losing my virginity' and then continue the same sentence with 'allowing myself to be kissed etc.'.[24] On the whole, it depends on which phrases you pick and what you make of them. The German psychiatrist Johannes Cremerius dismisses the whole virginity debate with this question: 'Are not disappointment, betrayal, humiliation and the abuse of trust, and the destruction of dignity and self-worth, of more consequence for a young girl to whom all this has happened?'[25]

In her letter drafts, Spielrein explained to Freud that she was fully aware that Jung was 'no hermit', and saw many other women than herself. She mentioned an association experiment carried out on Jung and reported by his colleague Ludwig Binswanger. Jung associated the word 'faithfulness' with 'ruefulness'.[26] Nevertheless, she was insistent that she had never wanted just 'a little affair' like his other women.[27] Nor could she believe, even now, that this was all it had been: 'He cannot deny that he viewed me and his love for me as something sacred,' she wrote. 'He cannot deny that he assured me many times over that no one could understand him the way I could.'[28] She quoted from Jung's letter of remorse, sent after his son's birth in December.[29] Reading this, one cannot help feeling she was trying to convince herself the relationship was exceptional for him, when it probably was not. At some level, she knew all along that Jung was a womaniser. Like so many other women in that situation, she may have believed she could cure him. One commentator, Henry Lothane, has been highly critical of Jung's unwanted attempts to analyse Spielrein, but regards it as hypocritical to condemn his erotic involvement with her. After all, they were both adults, Jung had not been her doctor for a long time, and she knew what kind of man he was. 'Whether they had sex,' he writes, 'is nobody's business.'[30]

In the course of writing the drafts, Spielrein also included an account of the crisis that ended the relationship. The details now allow us to understand what motivated Jung's panic, and hence his letters to Freud. Following the 'anonymous' letter, Eva Spielrein wrote to Jung saying he had saved her daughter in the past and should not now undo her.[31] She begged him not to exceed the bounds of friendship. Spielrein did not learn until some time later that there had been some further compromising correspondence between Jung and Eva. Meanwhile, she found Jung's attitude to her had changed beyond recognition. Clearly in a state of desperation, he told her he would have to run away to America, or even Africa. He then insisted she should become a patient formally, allotting her an hour a week 'like all of his female patients'. Unless Spielrein was making it up, this means that Jung was fully aware his medical registration was in jeopardy and he might have to flee in disgrace. His insistence on making Spielrein an official private patient, when he might simply have refused to see her, may have been a tactic to emphasise that he had now formally taken Spielrein on as his patient, and hence she had never been one previously.

Spielrein described in her letter drafts how she attended three of these consultations, but then heard from friends about several more of Jung's conquests, including 'a tragedy that occurred with a woman patient whom he first led on, then rejected'.[32] None of her friends would say anything good about him. When she confronted Jung with this at her fourth session, he gave her a long sermon about everything he had done for her and was continuing to do. He informed her she 'wanted too much because he had been too good to her'.[33] She described how at this point she 'took leave of her senses'. Her realisation that she was really just one in a long line of women completely overwhelmed her. She boxed his ears. Then she grabbed a knife from his desk and assaulted him with it. She saw that Jung had gone very pale and clapped his left hand against his left temple, saying: 'You hit me!' She had no idea what had happened. The next thing, she found herself sitting on the trolley bus on the way home with her hands over her face, in floods of tears, and people asked her if she had injured herself. When she reached her destination she rushed to see some women friends and they told her she was bleeding. At that point she noticed that her hand and forearm were covered in blood. 'That's not my blood, that's his,' she babbled. 'I murdered him!'[34]

According to her account of events, she raged and wept for quite some time. Then she wrote a letter to Jung, describing her state. Immediately afterwards, she left for Lake Maggiore on the Italian border, intending never to see him again. She drafted an anonymous letter to Freud, which she never sent. To her surprise, she received two 'brief, dry' letters from Jung telling her they should stop meeting even as doctor and patient. He informed her that on the coming Friday, the day for their next appointment under the new arrangements, he would be leaving town. 'In this way, the entire painful matter will be laid to rest more easily.'[35] Spielrein next explained in her letter drafts how her mother had arrived in Switzerland to discuss her daughter's situation, as Jung had requested. Before any appointment, Eva exchanged some more letters with him. Whatever he wrote had outraged her. She told him she was now going to visit Professor Bleuler, presumably to expose the entire business. She also asked if she could meet Jung at her hotel, as she was not willing to compromise herself by being alone in his office.[36] He sent no reply. She never met Jung. She never went to see Bleuler either. Although Spielrein does not spell this out, by far the likeliest reason is that she talked her mother out of it as soon as she got back from Lake Maggiore. From her point of view, exposing Jung would have ruined her hopes of an amicable parting. It would also probably have meant she had to leave the university. The timing of Eva's visit to Zurich is uncertain, but it would fit with the period just before Jung's resignation on 7 March, and his letter to Freud about the 'vile scandal'. If so, Eva's threat of visiting Bleuler almost certainly triggered both.

Spielrein described how her mother initially tried to conceal Jung's letters from her. When Eva handed them over, she saw how appalling they were. In the first, he had written that he stopped being her doctor the moment he 'ceased to suppress his feelings for her'. He claimed it was easy for him to change his role because he had never charged her a fee, and therefore felt his professional obligation was at an end. In a defiant gesture, he suggested that if Eva Spielrein wanted him to stick to his role as a doctor, she should compensate him for his trouble: 'My fee is 10 francs per consultation.' He then advised her to accept matters as they stood, since this 'would not set up any obligations on either side for the future'.[37] Understandably, Spielrein regarded all of this as 'insulting'. She added that her mother thought Jung could not see private patients anyway. It seems from her account that Eva appreciated his protectiveness towards her daughter, but never imagined she was in any kind of treatment with him. Eva had, however, given him gifts instead of money over the past few years. These were 'also meant to show her friendly attitude towards him'.[38]

Spielrein then wrote of how Jung's letters got even worse. In a second letter, he appeared to be backtracking about the affair. He protested he had always told Sabina 'a sexual relationship was out of the question'. Instead, 'being in a very gentle and compassionate mood', he wanted to give her proof of his trust and friendship, in order 'to liberate her inwardly'. This turned out to be a serious error, he wrote to Eva, and he much regretted it. He summarily informed Eva Spielrein that her daughter's headaches were the consequence of not fulfilling her desires, which regrettably he was unable to do himself.³⁹ Jung apparently followed this with a third letter that was even more insulting. Spielrein could not bring herself to paraphrase it. Regarding the fourth letter, Spielrein was only able to say she had underlined a 'classic' passage with blue pencil. Finally there was a fifth letter. Without giving any details of its contents, Spielrein explained to Freud that 'one scarcely needs to be a psychiatrist' to understand why her mother felt deeply offended by it. It was this letter that led her mother to refuse to see Jung alone at the Burghölzli.⁴⁰

Spielrein explained how she had told her mother of her assault on Jung. Eva had evidently relayed the story to Nikolai, who said: 'People have turned him into a god, and he is nothing other than an ordinary human being. I am so happy that she boxed his ears! I would have done it myself. She should do whatever she believes she must: she can look after herself very well.'⁴¹ Sabina confessed that at this point she had thought of all kinds of further revenge, but realised that a scandal would do nothing to improve his behaviour: he 'could not be saved by public disgrace'. Indeed, he would then be completely incapable of realising what he had done. Having behaved so disgustingly out of cowardice, she wrote, he would then 'turn into a scoundrel from conviction'.⁴² The news that Spielrein was now hearing from her friends can scarcely have lessened her thoughts of revenge. Her letter drafts tell of how she discovered Jung was telling people he had treated someone for free, but had been forced to write to the patient's mother to say that she should pay him for his services. Somebody challenged him with the story that a student from the Russian colony was having an affair with him. He replied that that it was nonsense, but confessed he ought to be more careful 'about treating patients for nothing'. Another acquaintance told her that Jung simply wanted 'to paint himself lily-white for his wife's benefit'.⁴³ Hoping to hear a different view, Spielrein showed Jung's love letters to a medical student friend called Rebecca Babitskaya, whom we will encounter in more detail in the next chapter. Rebecca had no doubt about Jung's true colours. He was a 'good for nothing' and 'beyond saving'. It was Rebecca who expressed her view that he had used Spielrein as 'his first experiment'. By this point, all her friends were trying to convince her of what had really happened: he was a philanderer who had led her on and then abandoned her. The suspicion that this was the case began to weigh on her thoughts continually.⁴⁴

She was now cut off from Jung even as his patient. The only way she could see him at all was in his university lectures. Rebecca was present at one of these, and noticed Jung go pale. She turned around to see Spielrein, who had also gone white in the face. Spielrein walked out of the room, fearing she might commit a folly.[45] How could this end? If she was to avoid 'folly' and 'revenge', what else was there left for her to do? If Freud would not see her, where could she turn? Spielrein had now been writing her letter drafts on and off for three weeks. It had helped her to reach a bold decision. She went to see Jung in person.

10

Reconciliation 1909-1910

Yesterday afternoon ... I spoke to the 'culprit' himself between 4.30 and 6.00 ... He promised me he will write to you honestly about everything. If only he was really able to be honest with himself, if he was really able to be honest with you, I would then be so happy! You are cunning too, Professor: '*auditur et altera pars*.' The first outcome of this is that you should have agreed to give me an audience, without showing the slightest resistance. But you would rather spare yourself an unpleasant moment. Isn't that correct? Even the great 'Freud' cannot always ignore his own weaknesses[1]

I T WAS three weeks since Spielrein had written her first letter draft to Freud. This passage is one of the last drafts, reporting on her decision to confront Jung. It demonstrates how completely she had seen through the 'shabby game' that the two men had played on her, and how astute a judgement she had formed of their weaknesses. It also demonstrates her determination – one might almost say her compulsion – to forgive him. Once again, we do not know if she ever sent a version of it to Freud. It would be nice to think that she did, and that it laid the foundations of Freud's future respect for her. She gives no reason here for her decision to tackle Jung. The most likely one is that it came from her own self-analysis, in which her letter drafts had played an important part. In one respect she had done exactly what Freud had advised: to sort matters out on her own, and through reflection. What she had not accepted was Freud's view that the problem was mainly inside her own mind.

*

Spielrein wrote accounts of the meeting both in her letter drafts and subsequently in her diary. She described how Jung wanted to hurry away at first because he still thought she was 'his bitter enemy'.[2] Evidently she reassured him that she did not want to start anything up again, but wanted to discuss his horrible behaviour towards her mother and herself, so she could see him as a 'fine, noble person' again. His manner changed 'at once'. He showed 'deep repentance', and talked about a malicious person who had been telling tales maligning him. This sounds like an elaborate bluff: if he ever believed in the 'malicious person', he thought it was Spielrein herself. However, by now it was clear nothing disastrous was going to happen, and he must have realised that Spielrein had almost certainly played a part in making sure of this. Since she was taking the initiative to resume the friendship, it would have been imprudent to provoke her again. The wound Sabina had inflicted on his face had also probably healed. In her account of this moment to Freud, Spielrein described how Jung offered some excuses for his behaviour. He told her about his tendency to become infatuated with Jewesses, starting with Mathilde Freud. He explained he had already confessed this to Mathilde's father. Spielrein did not believe this rationalisation for a moment, but was touched that he had tried to endear himself to Freud by making it up.[3] Jung does not appear to have added the motif of Otto Gross's influence on him. Spielrein knew in any case that the story of Gross converting him to polygamy for the first time was bogus. She now wrote of how they parted 'the best of friends', just as she had hoped.

Following this resolution of the crisis, Jung wrote to Freud to express relief, so we have his account too.[4] He reported a '*very decent*' talk with Spielrein. It convinced him that the 'rumours' did not come from her. He told Freud he now wanted to withdraw his accusation. He wrote of how Spielrein had 'freed herself from the transference' and had suffered no relapse 'apart from a paroxysm of weeping'. He confessed he was 'largely to blame for the high-flying hopes of my former patient'. He then launched into another explanation of what happened, different from his previous versions. He told Freud that it all started because of his principle of taking everyone seriously, which meant that he was obliged to analyse her wish to have his child. He had been blind to the fact that 'Eros was lurking in the background' all the time. He now had insight into the fact that he had attributed such wishes only to her, when in fact they were also true about himself. Things had only come to a crisis, he wrote, when they came close to having 'sexual acts'. At that point he defended himself in a way that was clearly unacceptable. He described how he had written to her mother saying he could not comply with her daughter's sexual desires because he was her doctor. He reluctantly confessed this to Freud 'as a father'. He asked if Freud could let Spielrein know he had owned up to everything, including the letter to her parents. He particularly wanted her to know he had been 'perfectly honest' with Freud. He concluded by saying how glad he was that he was not mistaken about his patient after all, confirming the soundness of his own judgement.

Jung's honesty was far from 'perfect'. To spell out just a few of the imperfections, he was under no 'obligation' to analyse Spielrein's wish for a child, because she was not his patient and had expressly asked him not to do so. The crisis did not happen because they came close to 'sexual acts'. It happened because he had taken the initiative sexually, then felt remorse, and was then discovered. His account of the letter to Eva is the exact opposite of what he had actually written to her: namely, that he *was* entitled to gratify Sabina's sexual desires, precisely because he was *not* her doctor. In this context, the final note of self-congratulation for his 'soundness of judgement' is rather jarring. Freud, to his credit, immediately wrote to Spielrein, saying that Dr Jung had now sent him some information that helped him to understand why she had wanted to come to Vienna. He now realised he had 'divined some matters correctly' but 'construed others wrongly and to your disadvantage'. He asked her to forgive him, conceding that it was the fault of 'his young friend', and not her. He expressed satisfaction that this would allow him to hold women in high esteem. He concluded: 'Please accept this expression of my entire sympathy for the dignified way in which you have resolved the conflict.'[5] The last sentence describing Spielrein's dignity is faultless. Yet a certain amount here is disingenuous too. Freud once more feigned at guessing things he already knew. He was careful not to spell out exactly what Jung told him. Intriguingly, he ignored Jung's request to mention that he had owned up to his letter to Eva. Perhaps Spielrein sent him the actual letter, so that he knew how big a lie Jung had told him. At any rate, he had seen at least one love letter that Jung had written, and knew some of his claims to be falsehoods. Freud was holding his cards close to his chest, and would only reveal to her many years later what he had really thought.

Freud then wrote to Jung again.[6] He reported having sent Spielrein 'a few amiable lines' and had already received an answer from her. Her letter was 'amazingly awkward'. He asked: 'Is she a foreigner by any chance?' He advised Jung not to find fault with himself, saying 'it was not your doing but hers'. He declared that he felt no anger about anything, but was marvelling instead at 'at the profound coherence of all things in this world'. The overall tone of the letter is one of indulgence. Freud seems to be indicating that he cares little about what did or did not happen between Jung and his patient by way of physical contact. Presumably this was what happened when you slanted a test tube the wrong way and overheated it. His question as to whether Spielrein was a foreigner must have reassured Jung. Freud had clearly not joined up his 'test case' from the Amsterdam congress with the 'anal erotic' student, the 'Russian hysteric' or the sexual fantasist of his letters, all of whom he had presented as different patients in continuing analysis. Freud's only real concern had been to pacify the young woman, get his young colleague off the hook, and make sure psychoanalysis was not torn apart by the sexual scandal that its opponents were now waiting for eagerly. Even if other analysts were sleeping with their patients, such a misdemeanour by a married 'crown prince' with someone who had been under his hospital care and was now his university student could still have been catastrophic. Jung acknowledged Freud's help in closing the matter, and did so briefly. He had nothing to gain by supplying the missing links in Freud's recollection. 'First of all I want to thank you very much for your kind help in the Spielrein matter, which has now settled itself so satisfactorily. Once again I took too black a view. Frl S is a Russian, hence her awkwardness.'[7]

Summarising the conspiracy that Freud and Jung undertook to deceive Spielrein, the psychiatrist Johannes Cremerius wrote as follows:

> When Jung wants to extricate himself from the relationship because a public scandal threatens (Sabina's mother, alerted anonymously to the 'affair' by Frau Jung, plans to call on Professor Eugen Bleuler, Jung's boss), she must stand aside to save his career and marriage ... The cynicism of this complicity from the point of view of the patient, who is sacrificed in a manner which severely disturbs and damages her, is shocking.[8]

The two conspirators may have felt the matter had been laid to rest. This was not the case for the woman. 'My project is coming to an end,' she wrote on the day after the meeting with Jung, 'and deep depression is possessing me.'[9] Even though she had brought about a resolution in her estrangement from Jung, her emotions were far from resolved. Her outpourings in her letter drafts continued for many more pages. She anatomised his 'Jewess' excuse further, looking at it from different angles. She revisited the stark contrast between his passion for her in earlier times and the aloofness she had seen from him more recently. In the light of what she seemed, briefly, to have achieved for herself, it makes painful reading. If Jung thought she had 'freed herself from the transference', he was badly mistaken.

Spielrein spent the rest of the summer travelling.[10] She joined up with her Polish Uncle Adolf in Berlin, and then with the rest of her family at the resort of Kolberg on the Baltic. Once there, she was able to talk to her mother face-to-face about what had happened with Jung. Eva's view of the matter at first disappointed her, but she soon managed to talk the relationship up again:

> Mother says it is impossible for me and my friend to stay friends once we

have already given each other our love. A man cannot keep up a pure friendship for long. If I am nice to him – then he will want to have love, if I am always cold – then it will spoil everything for him. That made me so low, so low! O dear, what should I wish for? If I could implore Fate, I would pray: Fate, let my friend and me be exceptions, let us always meet each other glowing with pleasure, supporting each other in joy and sorrow so that even when we are 'à distance', we form one soul, that we aspire to go 'higher, farther, wider'.[11]

Because of the turbulence of Spielrein's relationship with Jung, and its fascination, it is easy to lose sight of the other dimensions of her life. Fortunately, during her summer holiday of 1909, she began once more to write about other things in her diary apart from her feelings about Jung (see plate section no. 5). It includes the wishes, fantasies and observations that any twenty-three-year-old female diarist of the time might have recorded. Here is an entry written in a hotel in Berlin, en route to meeting her family at Kolberg:

My room is certainly extremely clean, but not homely: small, basic furniture, tasteless yellow wallpaper ... But I did allow myself a little entertainment this morning. If I want to be totally honest – I must also be able to record things that give a little insight into the psychology of so-called modest girls, which I also count as. It only lasted only a short time, now it is over, and ... well, it is a little uncomfortable to write about. Let's get over this: when I went to wash this morning, I closed the curtain, but in a way that left a gap for someone to look into the room. I did not do this on purpose; but when I spotted the mistake while I was at the sink, I did not want to change it. As I remember this, I can feel myself blushing; I believe – I would never be able to think something like this, but only half an hour ago I was standing by the sink and thinking: it's so nice when someone admires me; down to the waist I am not embarrassed; I take pleasure that I have the shape of a grown women, that my skin is soft, curves that are nice and well-developed. Even if I have a very ordinary face, I can still be attractive. What can be more beautiful than a healthy young girl, if she is 'maidenly'.[12]

Her pleasure in her own body seems remarkably normal, as does her fantasy that a man might glimpse her breasts. From her diary the following day, we learn that her wish was fulfilled.[13] After dressing, she noticed 'a nice young gentleman' in the building opposite, gazing into her room. Once again, she found herself blushing deeply 'and this mild manifestation of the unconscious, which I noted quite objectively, pleased me very much'. A little later, 'an older gentleman' looked out of a higher window, and Spielrein noted how 'a wave of deep disgust' washed over her. As she makes clear, she was finding as much pleasure in noting the reflex responses of her own physiology as she was in the sensations themselves.

Although Spielrein now spent her university vacations with her family, the records she made of these were sparse. Here too, what is striking about her reflections is that any passionate young woman might have written them. She even allowed herself the luxury of some purple prose. Following a break on the Rhine, she wrote:

> I am calling to mind the rolling, lush, leafy area north of Lake Constance with its picturesquely scattered stretches of conifer forest. And also the wonderful illumination, when the sky is a little cloudy. And yet it always made me feel so low when I sank down into the atmosphere of the lonely cottage in the midst of that green carpet. I could not give myself up to a peaceful life within the circle of my family. I become anxious with perfect quiet. I must have people with passionate strivings around me ...[14]

With her family in Kolberg, she wrote:

> Perhaps it would be much, much better if I did not have so much worldly wisdom, and if I could therefore just 'fall into' a situation. ... My mind is still youthfully fresh, my intellect already very old, and this constant examining, weighing, caution, mistrust ...[15]

Following her return from summer holiday, Spielrein tried to work on her medical school dissertation – a study of a schizophrenic woman. Writing such a dissertation was a compulsory element in medical training at the time. While some of her contemporaries had done this in other specialties, including gynaecology, ophthalmology and paediatrics,[16] Spielrein chose to do hers in psychiatry. However, she was now in despair over it. Bleuler was her supervisor, but their meetings were not going well and had reduced her to tears. She was drawing on Jungian ideas about the mythic underpinnings of the unconscious mind, while Bleuler no longer felt sympathetic either to the man or his theories. Guided by a dream, she ran to Jung, whom she had not seen for a long time – possibly since they had made up three months earlier in June.

At first she was tongue-tied, but she was eventually able to confess that she wanted him to look at her dissertation. Jung's response was to laugh at his former boss, whom he now held in contempt. Although this 'perfidy' tormented Spielrein, she knew that Jung could offer her better supervision, and agreed to retrieve the work from Bleuler. According to Spielrein's record, the encounter took them back to where they had been the previous year:

> The most important outcome of our conversation was that both of us loved each other deeply again. My friend said we will always have to be on guard, so that we do not fall in love again; we would always be dangerous to each other. He admitted to me that until so far he had not met any female who could take my place. It was as if he had a necklace in which all his other admirers were – pearls, and I – the medallion.[17]

At the end of their meeting, he pressed her hands several times and said this should mark the beginning of a new era in their relationship. She asked herself: 'What could he mean by this? Will we see each other or not? ... How will things develop?' To use a modern term, one has the impression that she is going round the loop with him once more. The only difference is that Jung's expressions do not sound convincing. In spite of Spielrein's hopes, they seem like the well-rehearsed flatteries of a Don Juan – a judgement she was to make herself before long. At this point her diary breaks off for a year.

Just before this, Spielrein had begun to write about her medical student friends for the first time. Generally she referred to them by an initial ('Frl. B') or an epithet ('the Christian'; 'my colleague'). Sabine Richebächer, her German biographer, has been able to identify some of them from cantonal and university records, as well as other sources. Several of Spielrein's medical student friends appear to have had parallel biographies to her own, including (in various combinations) Russian Jewish origins, hysterical or depressive symptoms that led to them spend time in the Burghölzli, student placements there, treatment with Jung, and becoming emotionally or sexually involved with him. A number of her friends have already appeared in earlier chapters. One was Feiga Berg, the intern who wrote the only account of her case history apart from Jung's. Another friend, Esther Aptekmann, had been in and out of the Burghölzli as a patient, and was now one of Jung's 'pearls'. Fanny Chalevsky came from Rostov like Spielrein: she was the student who had been engaged to Jung's colleague Alphonse Mäder. They had now split up. Jung wrote to Freud about this, saying Mäder was to be congratulated: 'Such marriages, as we know, never work out.'[18] If he was referring to marriages between young Russian Jewish medical students and older Swiss doctors, he may have been congratulating himself on avoiding such a fate.

111

Spielrein had made other friends as well while at medical school. There was a Christian girl called Alexandra Florov from Rostov, whom Spielrein may well have known from high school years. Spielrein possibly confided in her about her entanglement with Jung – or at least Alexandra guessed something was going on. When things were at their lowest ebb during Jung's attempts to analyse her, Alexandra said she looked as if she 'had blood-spattered boys in front of her eyes'. The phrase was a Russian idiom for 'blind with rage', from Pushkin's drama about Boris Godunov, describing him after he had ordered the murder of Ivan the Terrible's son.[19] Another Russian friend, Shaina Grebelskaya, was scholastically brilliant but suffered intermittently from depression, and was sometimes psychologically dependent on Spielrein.[20] She also became interested in psychoanalysis and published her dissertation on a case of a paranoid patient alongside Spielrein's most significant paper.[21] Spielrein was later to seek her advice too, concerning what to do about her relationship with Jung. Spielrein remained friendly with Louise Rähmi, her fellow patient from the Burghölzli. Louise left Zurich for a while and had an affair with an Austrian that ended in pregnancy in 1907. After her daughter Alice was born, she returned to complete her medical studies in Zurich.[22] Her example of doing this despite the prejudice that surrounded single mothers must have given Spielrein pause for thought.

One particular friend from medical school, Rachel Leibovich, stayed in touch with Spielrein for many years. Unlike many of her Jewish peers, Rachel remained religious. She visited Spielrein in Berlin and Lausanne, and wrote letters to her until at least the 1920s. After the First World War she married a Swiss Jew named Meer Simon Nachmansohn, who originated from Jaffa. He had studied philosophy and law, and had acquired an interest in psychoanalysis. The couple had a son and planned to return to Jaffa or emigrate to the United States. Their marriage was short lived, however, and they divorced after barely two years.[23] Given the general conservatism of both Switzerland and the Russian Jewish community, it is noticeable how many of Spielrein's circle ended up living as single mothers or divorcees. The various ingredients of displacement, mental disturbance, radical ideas on psychology, intellectual advancement, and sometimes loss of traditional faith, cannot have made it easy to sustain relationships. Spielrein's experience of turbulent relationships followed by frustration in marriage was, for her circle, reasonably typical.

In her diary, Spielrein gives the general impression that while she was at university she found her contemporaries silly and unworthy of much interest. Here is a typical entry:

I went to see a woman colleague to recover and help her overcome her weariness with life. Another colleague called by, a woman I dislike, then a Russian doctor from the surgical clinic, a little redheaded, totally insignificant individual. We started up the usual silly discussion about men and women: pointless, knowing remarks, just to have something to say, and the world struck me as so dull. Is this the youth, the strength and blossom of humankind? Is it also possible I will never find a different milieu, among people who love life as much I do, who know how to find beauty in everything and do not always just sneer at everything?[24]

There is one passage in her diary where she describes a pair of friends at some length. She does so in the context of comparing four similar 'pairs' of Christian and Jewish friends, beginning with the two girls she knew at high school, and then her history teacher and her Uncle Adolf. In this instance, the Christian is unidentified but may be Alexandra Florov. Her Jewish counterpart was Rebecca Babitskaya, the most vividly portrayed person among Spielrein's circle, and the one who had shared her frank opinion of Jung. Spielrein describes how the Christian woman's relationship with Rebecca was imbued with sexuality:

The Christian girl was and still is up to her ears in love with her mistress. Even if they never had a sexual relationship with each other, the stronger woman abused her charms as a woman on the stupid girl. Thus I once heard her say 'V, don't you want to admire my body any more?' At the same time she was also trying to make her colleague more of a young lady, even to find a fiancé for her ...[25]

Rebecca was already married, to an Armenian Christian called Mirkirtish Ter-Oganessian.[26] Spielrein recorded the parallelism with her two childhood girlfriends, where the Jewish woman got married but the Christian became dependent and did not.[27] According to Spielrein, Rebecca was not only dominating, but also selfish. Spielrein contrasted Rebecca with herself. While her friend was gregarious and a pragmatist, Spielrein was a 'hermit' and an idealist. Rebecca would tell her off for not haggling in shops. Rebecca also regarded her and her father as 'psychopaths' for paying the fees for her surgery course rather than just turning up at the lectures like everyone else. During the time of her break with Jung, she and Rebecca had a bust-up. Spielrein had been weeping day and night and trying to distract herself with mechanical work at the hospital. Rebecca was doing a placement at the Burghölzli and showing off as the 'most impressive female' there.[28] She was also writing her dissertation, and including an 'analysis' of a patient. Spielrein helped her with this, but then agonised over whether Bleuler and Jung would prefer her friend's work. She imagined Jung reading the dissertation and deciding that Spielrein's dissertation was not so special after all. He would then fall in love with Rebecca. An image of Rebecca sitting next to Jung at a psychiatric congress came into her mind: 'She – proud and contented as a wife and mother, myself a poor psychopath with mass of desires and unable to fulfil any of them.'[29] Spielrein's critical view of Rebecca may have been influenced by the fact that she was the friend who described Jung as 'good for nothing', and as using Spielrein for 'his first experiment'.

In her diary, Spielrein recounted how her friends were all embroiled in love lives of considerable complexity, while she herself desperately tried to hold on to her idealistic view of life, men and her mission in life:

In the morning the Jewish girl from the third pair [Rebecca] came to me ... Her first romance was with a Jewish doctor; now she is with someone else and is already in her sixth month of pregnancy. This and the conversations about our work made me very agitated. I became very worried that I might be useless all my life or stay sterile. That afternoon I went to see my new acquaintance. Instead of a peaceful experience I only found woes here as well ... So I went home. Here a colleague was waiting for me, a woman who has been recently been seriously depressed. She has given her heart to a doctor from the eye clinic. For her it was her first love. For him? ...[30] They just went on together since he did not consider her suitable for marriage ... Now I was alone and thought how beautiful love is when you can give yourself up completely to your emotions, when even for a short while you can have someone entirely for yourself and only for yourself; when you are certain that your happiness does not bring pain to anyone, which was always the case for me.[31]

It is notable that, looking back on her relationship on Jung from this point, what she valued was not the eroticism of the previous year, but the times they had earlier, when she experienced a sense of immersion in each other's souls. There is also every indication in Spielrein's diaries that she sailed through medical school, as did her close friends. There is no mention of any struggles to complete assignments or obtain good grades. There is, however, one document that indicates she considered leaving Zurich and completing her medical training in Heidelberg instead. It is in the form of a note from Bleuler, dated October

1909.[32] One can only assume that this represented an attempt to distance herself from Jung, rather than testifying to any difficulty with her studies in Switzerland. Bleuler may well have been aware of her reasons for wishing to make such a move. In the event, she remained in Zurich to complete her studies there – and to bring her relationship with Carl Jung to an end.

11

Separation 1910-1911

I often feel the force of my passion and of our emotional affinity so powerfully that I ask myself whether I should try to wrest him away from his wife, especially since my Guardian Spirit tells me I can do anything I want to ... But should I really want this? Could we even then be happy? I think — neither of us would be, because the thought of his wife and children would give neither of us any peace. I am far from being his wife's enemy; I can understand her position in relation to me only too well, and even though I scarcely know her, I believe she must be a good person, if my friend chose her ... How often have I asked her forgiveness for the pain I brought into her quiet home. Overall, my love has brought me almost nothing except pain.[1]

IN SEPTEMBER 1910, three months before she was due to take her final medical exams. Spielrein took up her diary again. There may have been another cooling-off period after her reconciliation with Jung the previous summer. Now, they were clearly meeting again. She could not let go of her fantasy of a Wagnerian unification of their souls. However, with the passage of time, and with graduation close, there was a change of tone. While she used the present tense for some of the time, she was also starting to use the past tense as well. Some of her thoughts about Jung were the typical musings of 'the other woman', but there was some detachment as well. She seems to have accepted there would now be a loss. She also realised that the 'status quo' was not tenable. While Jung could appear anywhere with his wife, she wrote, she herself had to skulk in dark corners, and to accept being called immoral, his lover, 'maybe *maitresse!*'[2] She dreaded the pain of parting, and the loneliness that might follow. She recognised that having a child with Jung would mean — or would have meant — never finding a new love. She ruminated on a suggestion Jung had made that he should 'introduce her in his house, make me his wife's friend'. It held no attractions for her. It was to be a further three years before Emma acceded to such an arrangement with Toni Wolff, another patient and pupil of Jung's. In her diary, Spielrein urged herself to be firm and not to give way to 'idiotic emotionalism'. She ended this same diary entry:

117

And now – may he be happy! If only I could get a quicker response to the paper I sent him. The suspense doesn't allow me any peace, especially as I expect I shall surely go through another great tempest over it.[3]

It is no coincidence that her desire for her friend to be happy is now counterpoised with her wish to get on with her own professional career. This was the year that Spielrein emerged for the first time as a writer of serious, original academic works.

*

While Spielrein was preparing to distance herself from Jung, his own progress as the 'crown prince' of psychoanalysis had been relentless. He was already editor of the movement's flagship journal, the *Jahrbuch* (*Yearbook*), of which Freud and Bleuler were joint directors. In September 1909, he and Freud travelled together to the United States where they both lectured at Clark University in Worcester, Massachusetts, and received honorary doctorates. During the course of his lectures, Jung paid great respect to Freud, but also laid out significant areas of difference between his colleague and himself. In March 1910, Jung was elected president of the International Psychoanalytical Association at its congress in Nuremberg. Through all of this time, he was working on the book that was to define Jungian psychology and, in effect, its irreconcilable differences from Freudian psychoanalysis. This was his *Psychology of the Unconscious*, which was eventually published in 1912, and renamed *Symbols of Transformation* in later editions.[4] It was an encyclopaedic work of psychology, anthropology and mythology in which Jung laid out his belief that certain universal myths could be used as the basis for explaining the workings of the human mind. He argued that the roots of both creativity and mental disorder lay not in the sexual drive but in collective cultural patterns, passed down from one generation to the next. Starting the book with the fantasies of one particular spiritual medium,[5] as he had done in his doctoral dissertation, Jung widened his scope to take in a vast range of references from Egyptian, biblical, classical, oriental, Renaissance and modern texts in order to support his case. It is possible that Spielrein was one of the students who assisted him with research for this.[6] During 1910 Jung prepared the first part of this 'magnum opus' for publication in the *Yearbook* the following year.

Meanwhile, Spielrein had completed her own dissertation – the 'paper' she mentioned she was anxiously waiting for Jung to look at, in the passage quoted above. Before she could publish the dissertation it also had to be assessed for her doctorate. Although he was no longer her supervisor, this was Bleuler's task as professor. His response was a curious one. He was friendly towards her, but said he had only had time to look over a tenth of it. He thought that part was fine, and was entirely happy to trust her concerning the rest of it. He inquired whether she wanted to publish it in a Freudian journal, and if she wanted to ask Jung directly about this, or let him write a proposal. She asked if he would do this.[7] It is hard to know what to make of Bleuler's reaction. It would be an unusual practice, then as now, to sign off a dissertation without reading it. He may have tired of Spielrein's Jungian approach after a few pages, but wanted to encourage her on the career she was determined to follow. His respect for Spielrein's current supervisor was now close to rock bottom, and his sympathy for Freud was soon to go in the same direction. The acceptance of her dissertation was an important moment for Spielrein personally, but it also marked a significant moment in the history of psychoanalysis. She had in fact become the first person ever to succeed in a doctoral dissertation using a psychoanalytic approach. Freud was certainly aware of this, because it was the first ever to appear in a psychoanalytic journal. It also led to her formal acceptance the following year as a member of the Vienna Psychoanalytic Society. This historical 'first' was to be one of many that would characterise Spielrein's career for many years into the future. The contents of the paper itself – and its originality – are covered in the next chapter.

The day after he had seen her, Bleuler followed up his comments with a letter confirming that she should submit her dissertation to Jung's *Yearbook*. She was delighted: 'The dear, good little Father! So he did not forget!'[8] A few days later, Jung gave his own response. It was highly positive – until the inevitable sequel:

I received a nice note from him at once addressing me as his dear friend and concluding 'your friend'. Many passages in my work had moved him to ecstasy. Yesterday another letter arrived, and the tone was entirely different: he was vexed that I left out his name everywhere, as if on purpose, that I do not cite his writing, and in the end even make fun of him a little. Good God, if only he had the slightest notion how much I have suffered on his account and still suffer! Is it a surprise if I was worried about reading his works, because I was afraid to become a slave to emotion again? Is it so amazing that I also fell unconsciously into a negative view because of this? In his latest letter he called me 'Dear Fräulein' and closed with 'Sincerely, Dr Jung'. At first I almost collapsed with misery when I read it.

Then I calmed down, and was even pleased that he reacted so strongly to my behaviour that he wanted to hurt me with that cold tone.[9]

Quite apart from what this passage shows in terms of Jung's over-sensitivity, it contradicts the myth that he and Spielrein constantly exchanged ideas during the development of their thinking. Although he had been her dissertation supervisor for a year, he had never read it, even before she submitted it for her degree. For her part, she had actively avoided reading his works. In spite of her frustration with his moods, she paid what was probably her first visit to the house in Küsnacht. She complimented him on it, but he seemed not to hear it and immediately took up her case study, which pained her. In spite of this, everything went off peacefully:

I can scarcely believe I could love anyone in the way I love my friend. I fear that my life is ruined. The only salvation would be for him to be mine, but because of his wife that would be impossible, and I could not wish her the pain of being abandoned, so there is one only one outcome worth hoping for, that is for both spouses to grow tired of each other and for his wife to run off with some 'Frenchman'. Yes, of course that is a childish fantasy in relation to a Swiss woman, an almost impossible wish, but during that crazy night I could not console myself any other way apart from imagining this little drama. What would I give to make that possible![10]

What is apparent is the magnetism of Jung's personality, and the immediate effect it has each time Spielrein meets him. Whatever understanding she gained in the intervals between seeing him, his personal presence had the same effect on her every time. But she is clearly also preparing herself for separation. Later the same month there was more torment, as she met all his children – also probably for the first time. They came running to meet her in the waiting room, 'two sweet little girls and a little boy'.[11] She felt as if she had been 'plunged into cold water'. In front of the children she felt small and powerless. She wrote that 'any "desires" seemed revolting'. She managed to speak rationally but 'swallowed one tear after another'. On the way there, she had an accident on the trolley bus, hurting her knee. Jung laughed and told her she should not go about 'fulfilling anxiety desires'. In her diary, she lamented her fate at being 'one among the many who languish for him, and in return receive his kind gaze, a few friendly words'. She acknowledged that one needed to 'fulfil his every wish, so as not to bring down his wrath upon oneself':

If you don't take his vanity into account, you have to atone for it horribly: he takes on a very cold, official tone, and who then suffers badly as a result of that? Not him, obviously. He can get rid of any slight vexation by working, love for one woman can be replaced by another; you can also be sure that this next one will finally be humiliated, and she will be the one to have agonising days and sleepless nights, the silly little girl.[12]

As if things could get no worse, she had to see another woman supplant her. When out walking, she met Esther Aptekmann, her fellow ex-patient and student. Spielrein knew that Esther was now 'one of the many'. She was 'not particularly intelligent' but 'a beautiful and decent girl'. She loved Jung and, like Spielrein, believed he loved her:

And now I must come early in the morning, am drained, weary, because I must renounce love. She, on the other hand, hopes and glows with passion. Who knows; me he considers 'dangerous'; he is on his guard with me, and the love for me which he suppresses may find a new object in her ... I simply cannot be one of the many. It is absolutely necessary to me to see his love for me aglow from time to time, and under the right conditions I can channel it into a calmer form. It is a necessity to me to know that he did not exchange me so soon for another girl, and such an unprepossessing one ...[13]

September 1910 seems to have been an exceptionally volatile time. On the 27th Spielrein turned up for an appointment with Jung that he had already cancelled. His telegram informing her had arrived too late. That evening she learned the reason for the cancellation: Emma had given birth to another girl that day, her third daughter, Marianne. Back at home, Spielrein looked into the mirror and saw a 'stony grey face' with grim, black, burning eyes, 'a powerful, baleful wolf'. However, by the next morning 'she felt transformed', breathing in the cool air ecstatically. She again felt 'destined for something great'. She visited Jung to work on her paper. As well as her current paper, she told him about her next project: a theory that would describe the reproductive instinct as having two components: a creative one and a destructive one.

This was the idea she had first explored in her 'Transformation' letters, two or three years previously. She had evidently been thinking about it ever since. It seems to have been the first time she told Jung she was proposing to develop this further. He said he thought that the idea of a combined 'sexual instinct-death

121

instinct' was 'well worth working out'. He encouraged her to write it, with a view to publishing it alongside one of his own papers. They talked 'on and on'. He showed her a paper he had written and some correspondence with Freud. He explained how he had been deeply affected by parallels in the way they thought and felt, and was now worried that this would make him fall in love with her again. Once more she was able to convince herself that she was not 'one of the many' and that he was battling to suppress his strong feelings for her. She told herself that it was easy to suppress erotic desire in exchange for such a 'beautiful, noble friendship'.[14] For a short while, it appears she was able to put out of her mind the image of Esther Aptekmann and the rest of the 'many', but the cycles of ecstasy and dejection were becoming shorter. A week or two later, in early October, she considered suicide:

> The night is so wonderfully dark and treacherously warm ... Siegfried, my little son! One day you must relate everything that your mother is now feeling. You must be able to find a worthy father for yourself! If this does not happen, if all my intelligence and great sensitivity has been given to me only to help me understand more easily that I am useless for life and to see the dream of my youth melt away, then ...[15] I cannot go on living. I will be very cautious in what I claim, but I think I am capable of destroying myself with cyanide in the presence of the idol of my youth. In my feelings I have no fear of death![16]

Spielrein now embarked on writing the family history recorded at the beginning of this book. As we have seen, she was impelled to do so by a remark from Jung that undermined her sense of having a 'higher calling'. We can now understand that exercise in its full context. It was a continuation of her self-analysis and also part of her attempt to put Jung behind her. It was also a crucial part of the transition from seeing her higher calling as one that must be solely connected with Jung, to one that she might fulfil by intellectual achievements in her own right. One of the tasks she set herself was to try to understand the influences that her own family history exerted on her. She was particularly interested in the way that relationships between Jewish family members and Christian partners had recurred down the generations, and how they ended. She set down a description of the four comparable 'pairs' of individuals who came to play prominent roles at various points in her life, each consisting of a Christian and a Jew. Three have already appeared in this book: the Christian and Jewish girl friends she had at school; her history teacher and Uncle Adolf;[17] and her Christian friend from medical school and Rebecca Babitskaya.[18] She now described the fourth pair: Carl Jung and Sigmund Freud, in that order:

> At the time when our poetry began, he had two girls, and held the potential for a little boy, which my unconscious extracted from him at the suitable time by 'prophetic dreams'. He told me he loved Jewish women, and he wanted to love a dark Jewish girl. So in him too, there is an attempt to hold to his religion and culture, but also the drive to revitalise it through a new race, the drive to be liberated from paternal obligation though an unbelieving Jewess. His friend is Prof Freud – a Jew, an old patriarch. ... I do not love Freud because he robbed me of the most beautiful thing in my life: that is my friend.[19] Now my friend will possibly fall in love with Freud's daughter. Why should I go on tormenting myself? ... But I will hold fast to my belief that a great destiny awaits me. And now, what shape will matters take? I just played the piano. There is so much fire and so much love in me. *I feel it as something firm and unshakeable: Siegfried lives, lives, lives!* No one can rob me of that faith except my own death.[20]

She spent two days writing out her family history and the account of the four Jewish-Christian 'pairs'. It may have been this self-analysis that enabled her to make a firm resolution a few days later: 'Siegfried' was to not to be a joint production by Jung and herself, either scientific, or a real child. He was to be an intellectual achievement of her own:

> Almost 5 in the morning. Since 3, I have been unable to sleep. Both of us love each other as much as it is possible to love. If only he was free! But he is not, and in those circumstances, let me record my fixed decision: I want to be free of him! I still want to live and be happy ... Oh God, I would like at least to have some peace at night, so that I may gather my strength to begin my new work, 'On the Death Instinct'. ... Oh, Guardian Spirit, may I not be harmed in these emotional storms. I am totally determined now to be free.[21]

It would be a neat conclusion if this marked the end of the affair, but it had a while longer to run. A couple of weeks later, Jung was back in the picture again. There was the first mention of 'poetry' since before the crisis: 'The stronger poetry probably occurred the Tuesday before last.' Jung told her that he loved her for her magnificent, proud character, but he could never marry her because there was a great philistine inside him, who longed for narrow limits and a typically Swiss life style. Spielrein recorded his protestations word by word in her diary. From time to time, he said, he thought of changing the course of fate. The idea of possessing such a splendid woman was 'almost too tempting', but the philistine within him would resist it. Yet again, Spielrein convinced herself he would certainly marry her if he was free 'for he is capable of enthusiasm for greatness'. Nevertheless, something about his oration this time led her to conclude her diary entry: 'Adieu my little son, farewell!'[22]

Following her diary from day to day, it is hard not to share Spielrein's feelings each time Jung moves from passionate exuberance to coldness and rejection, and each time she mirrors this with messianic fervour alternating with suicidal despair. At moments, it is possible to convince oneself he may sometimes have shared her fantasy of a conjunction between the male Swiss protestant soul and the female Russian Jewish one: a Nietzschean heroic dream that might be fulfilled through a second marriage, by giving her a child, or even by acceding to the arrangement he was soon to establish with his wife and Toni Wolff – in defiance of the 'typically Swiss life style'. Yet it is still unclear what he felt for her when she was absent, or whether he made similar protestations to other young women friends that they too were unique soul-mates. Spielrein also had to face the fact that Jung had been married to Emma for nearly eight years, had four children by her, owned a magnificent house and a successful private practice on the strength of her wealth, and now had an international career that would scarcely benefit from a scandal. Emma was a thoroughly capable individual who was accustomed in Jung's absence to dealing with distressed patients, answering his professional correspondence, managing and liaising with Bleuler over the *Yearbook*, as well as managing the household and writing to her husband in detail almost every day.[23] As Kerr writes: 'If she was not the brilliant, mysterious consort her husband might have preferred to accompany him on his excursions into psychoanalytic netherworlds, all available evidence suggests she was likeable, down-to-earth, earnest, devoted.'[24] Another aspect of reality was that the short period when Spielrein had his undivided love was now two years in the past. She had four letters that expressed the passion she had always felt for him, and they were all written during those few months.[25] For much of the time, her passion was one-sided. She was increasingly able to see this.

Now aged twenty-five and on the verge of a medical career, Spielrein was eminently marriageable. This exercised her parents. In the summer of 1910, they had made their wishes for her clear. Nikolai wrote to let her know that traditional Jewish marriage brokers in Rostov had already approached them with suggested matches. Her parents had set aside a substantial amount of thirty thousand roubles for her dowry, equivalent at the time to eight thousand Swiss francs.[26] At this stage, she gave no sign of yielding to these proposals. Yet at times she could now imagine the possibility of marrying someone else, and how she would adjust her feelings for him to accommodate the changed circumstances:

> We would go hiking in the open air and spend the long winter evenings in our warm, finely furnished lounge. In the evening I would enjoy sitting on the sofa and knitting, and he would read to me from his work ... And how about my friend? He will stay dear to me, very dear, like a father. I will introduce him to my husband as my old friend, and give him a kiss in my husband's presence. If he is so proud, and sure of his power over me, that he can do the same thing to my friend, then I will know how to reward him![27]

In November 1910, while Spielrein was preparing for her medical finals, her father Nikolai came to stay. So far as we know, this was his first visit to her in Zurich since Bleuler's ban, although she had seen him during her vacations in Rostov and elsewhere. There are hints that he used the opportunity to put pressure on her to accept a husband from among those who had been proposed in Rostov. He came without Eva. Given his tumultuous and abusive relationship with her in the past, it is surprising to read her perspective from her mid-twenties:

> What still torments me is that I cannot give my father the love he properly deserves, so I am partly passive toward him, and partly show my feelings in a negative way, but fundamentally I feel that I have an unusually good, very unselfish father, and I owe him a lot of gratitude.[28]

Her description of Nikolai as 'unselfish' is surprising. On the face of it, the description seems to rule out the possibility that she ever regarded him as her abuser. It is also possible to interpret it in other ways: for example as a demonstration of the way victims try to suppress the past, or make excuses for their abusers. Either way, there is no hint that she now feared any violence or sexual advances from him. They had been corresponding for some time about matters of philosophy and psychology, in which he had always taken an interest. In one of them, he apologised for the academic pressure he had put her under at a child.[29] If anything now troubled her about his presence, it was that he seemed positively enthusiastic about her being her friend's mistress, while she was increasingly aware of the indignity of her situation. She had almost certainly made a decision by this point to leave Zurich as soon as she could.

After Nikolai left, Spielrein was able to concentrate on preparing for her final exams in December. She was also able to turn towards writing her next paper, on the connection between sex and death. It built on ideas she had tried to put together in her 'Transformation' letters. Although Jung had encouraged her to take this forward, she was concerned he might have another, less altruistic motive:

> I must confess that I am very worried that my friend, who wanted to mention my ideas in his paper in July and said I should first have the priority, may borrow the whole development of the idea, because he now wants to mention it in January ... How could I adore someone who lied, who stole my ideas, who was not my friend but a petty, cunning rival![30]

In December 1910, Spielrein took her final exams. In her diary, she described them as a 'swindle', noting that many students cheated by various means, including taking books into the exam room and copying from them.[31] She intended to do this herself, but recorded Jung's claim that he had got through his finals without any dishonesty. Later, he confessed this was untrue.[32] She sat her first paper on 9 December with an essay on regeneration, and her second the following week with a short paper on severe fever in childbirth.[33] The subjects are so central to Spielrein's preoccupations that this seems a strange coincidence. Perhaps she was able to choose them. One of her examiners made a note that he suspected her of plagiarism but could not prove this.[34] Whether by fair means or foul, Spielrein completed her finals successfully. She achieved top marks in psychiatry, high grades in surgery, internal medicine and hygiene, and did well in all her other subjects.[35] Her family duly showered her with letters and telegrams, with Eva assuring her she would achieve at least as much as Madame Curie, while taking another opportunity to suggest she should no longer meet with Jung.[36]

Her daughter finally took her advice. The last mention of 'poetry' with Jung took place in early December, just before the exams started:

> My friend and I had the tenderest 'poetry' ...[37] last Wednesday. What will happen to this? Fate, may something good come out if this, and let me love him nobly. A long, ecstatic kiss in farewell, my beloved little son![38]

Two weeks afterwards, she recorded what was to be almost their last meeting:

> He also said that in matters of love I would be honest, in contrast to him, who is dishonest in this respect. Instead of showing me calm love ... he fell back into the 'Don Juan' role that is so repulsive to me. Although he considers me honest in love, he believes I should belong to the category of women created not for motherhood but for free love. What should I say? I have to blush deeply for myself when I remember it. I was deeply depressed, I said a lot of stupid things ... I want to be a wife and mother, not a kind of pastime. I want him to see what I can do, what I am worth. I want him to love me madly and want to be able to defy him ... But I do still want to love someone! Where is the person I could love?[39]

Having finished her written exams in December, Spielrein faced her medical school 'vivas' from 16 to 19 January 1911. On the final date, she entered the following note in her diary, possibly the briefest she had ever made. It seems to reflect an acceptance of the inevitable:

> 'He is gone, and it is good thus.' At least my parents are now happy. Ah yes, what will happen now?[40]

She left Zurich almost immediately. She had lived there for seven years. She had had a relationship with Jung of some kind – patient, research assistant, student, friend and lover – throughout that time. Although she kept up an intermittent correspondence with him for some time, she only ever saw him once more in person. She carried on yearning for him for many more years.

However we may judge Jung, it is important to understand Spielrein's own appraisal of her experiences with him, and why she continued to love him. His devotion as a psychiatrist had helped her to recover from a terrible breakdown.[41] Her love for him replaced her far more troubling obsessions. She formed a friendship with him. In her eyes at least, it was always a close one. She set out on a single-minded mission to prove she was worthy of his love. In the end, she achieved this, even if for only a short time. Her erotic experiences with him may have been her first experience of tender physical contact. When their affair was exposed and he terminated the friendship, she still wanted to part as friends. She succeeded in this too. Meanwhile, she discovered what many young women do. Married men are susceptible to determined pursuit, especially if they have succumbed before. They will then have an erotic relationship on their own terms, lie their way out of it, denigrate their mistresses and go on to have other affairs. In time, Spielrein recognised all of this, and realised it would not stop. She remained grateful to him for what had happened. She also decided to leave him, of her own accord.

12

Munich 1911

My new acquaintance is the son of a tailor; using only his own resources, he has turned himself into an artist, and so far as circumstances permit, he now he wants to dedicate himself only to composing music. I have told him nothing about myself; but he feels I have such a good understanding of art that he cannot grasp why I am staying on in medicine. The other candidate for the art exam, who is an anthropologist, also felt my chosen field should be art history, not medicine. I talked about the Swiss a little with the musician (he is from Bohemia), then he spoke about Goethe and said: Goethe was enchanted by Switzerland, but not by its inhabitants, who seemed much too prim for him. The same person also thinks the stiffness of the Swiss will loosen up in a few generations. Blessed are the believers![1]

AFTER LEAVING Zurich, Spielrein took a break in Montreux,[2] and then moved to Munich to take a course in the history of art. She continued to write to Jung from Munich, although we do not have his replies. Some of her letters were in much the same style as before, and yet again it is hard to judge how one-sided her sentiments really are. But some of what she wrote to him, like the passage above, suggests a normalisation of their friendship. Not only was she able to report everyday conversations, as any friend might do, she was even able to tease him about the prospect of the Swiss 'loosening up'. Her decision to study art history for a few months reflects the breadth of her interests, but it may also signify that she just wanted a break to recover from her separation. She wanted to write her paper on sex and death while she was in Germany, and then go on to Vienna to meet Freud finally, and to explore the world of psychoanalysis there. Although she would meet people in Munich who would try to persuade her she had the makings of a great art historian, there is no indication that she ever seriously considered doing anything other than become a psychiatrist and psychoanalyst. However, there was no hurry about starting her career, as she remained financially independent. She certainly does not seem to have entertained the possibility of returning to Russia at this stage.

One of her first diary entries in Munich suggests that the move had done her good. Within a month of arrival, she was able to write:

Calm superiority rules in me, free from 'high tension' in the depths of my soul, which is a sign of the capacity for powerful achievements ... As I am the descendant of several generations of religious men I believe in the prophetic force of my unconscious. You can actually come so close to this 'God' so that you can speak with him and learn what he wants.[3]

*

Back in Rostov, the Spielrein family were celebrating the arrival of their first grandchild. Having completed studies in Paris and Leipzig, Jan had gone home for what he described as a 'petit-bourgeois' Jewish wedding ceremony. His new wife, Sylvia Ryss, was the sister-in-law of the revolutionary, Karl Liebknecht. After the wedding, Jan and Sylvia went back to Berlin. In 1911, they had their first daughter, Irina.[4] The younger brother Isaac was also now in Germany. After spending a term in Heidelberg, he moved to Leipzig and began to study psychology with Wilhelm Wundt, the original founder of the discipline of experimental psychology[5] (see plate section no. 4, with father Nikolai). Isaac and Jan almost never appear in Sabina's diary, although shortly after her final exams she recorded a dream in which her family all turned up at the Burghölzli. It seems to be based on her sister's death scene. She prefaced it by calling it 'old, shop-worn stuff'. She complained that it 'lacked any prophetic power'. She may have meant that she had relived this scene many times over the years.

The dream involved her father, mother, and the oldest and youngest of her brothers: Jan and Emil.[6] She explained that Jan always represented Jung in her dreams, and Emil clearly stood for Emilia. Sabina herself was there too. In the dream, Emil had contracted typhus. Her parents sent her and Jan into the next room to look after him. She became terrified of contagion and death, and could not understand why such kind parents could not sacrifice themselves, rather than exposing their children to danger. Once she and her brother were in the room with Emil, Sabina reproached Jan with being too superficial in his diagnosis. The little boy did not have either a temperature or a rash, so could not have typhus. Jan then examined Emil and showed her that he had a swollen abdomen and blue spots on his back – in other words the signs of *Typhus abdominalis*, or typhoid, another lethal disease with a similar name. The most striking feature of the dream is that the parents had abandoned both children to catch a fatal disease. This report of her dream is the only indication we have that Spielrein was still possessed by her little sister's death ten years previously.

Spielrein was a busy correspondent at the time, not only with Jung. In the Geneva archive there are letters to Munich from a wide range of her contacts.[7] A Dr Schlesinger and a Dr Lenz both approached her expressing interest in matrimony. Her mother wrote to her to request more information about this, and expressed frustration at not hearing more. Her father thanked her for a song she had written and said this moved him greatly. He exchanged thoughts with her about life and death, and gave an account of his meeting with the great Polish paediatrician and educator, Janusz Korczak. He also told her he had consulted Freud in Vienna while on a visit to a spa for his own nervous disorders. We know nothing about their encounter other than Freud's comment many years later that he was interesting but inflexible.[8] However, the range of his preoccupations and contacts demonstrates how far he shared his daughter's interests. Sabina's friend Rebecca Babitskaya wrote, counselling her not to keep away from people and not to be mistrustful. Shaina Grebelskaya wrote about missing her, complained about her own depression and poverty, and thanked her for a gift of money.

Jung was never far from her mind. She still cherished hopes of converting him from a 'repulsive Don Juan' into a great platonic lover. In the letter where she told him about her art school friends, she wrote:

My main purpose is always to cultivate everything glorious in you, and for it is of course essential for that purpose that you love me. Your idealistic moods coincide with your love for me. I am your 'first success'; your doubts about your different strengths etc., are manifested as resistance towards me ... I want you to be great![9]

This is the only time she described herself as his 'first success'. It is noticeable that she did in quotation marks. She was presumably quoting the claim he had made in his original referral letter to Freud, which her mother had shown to her.

While she was in Munich, her first paper was finally published. It was the revision of her dissertation that Jung had helped her to revise. It appeared in Jung's *Yearbook* alongside the first part of his *Psychology of the Unconscious*. The same volume also included Freud's famous paper on the paranoid judge Daniel Schreber,[10] and papers by a panoply of other key figures from the formative years of psychoanalysis. These included not only Bleuler, Binswanger and Mäder, but also Ferenczi, Pfister and Rank – names that will all reappear later on. This was a huge achievement for a newly qualified doctor, let alone one who had been a psychiatric patient herself. It was the first of what were eventually be around thirty-six published works over the course of the following twenty years. It broke new ground both intellectually and clinically, in a way she was to repeat many times.

In her paper, Spielrein presented the first ever detailed description of schizophrenia from a psychoanalytic point of view.[11] It consisted of an intensive case study of a patient she had been seeing at the Burghölzli: an intelligent well-read woman, married with two children, with paranoid schizophrenia. Spielrein discussed the material that arose in her conversations with the woman, including the patient's accounts of her experiences with Jung and the association tests he applied. Although the woman appeared to talk nonsense, Spielrein concentrated on the underlying meaning, pointing out the definite if troubled logic behind her language. She also followed a scrupulous research method by not checking facts in the hospital notes until she had reached her own conclusions, based on the woman's utterances. Spielrein incorporated Jungian thinking into her work, pointing out how the woman's ideas had similarities to mythology, seeming to confirm Jung's ideas about the existence of a collective unconscious. The psychoanalyst and historian Adeline van Waning has commented on the paper as follows:

> Spielrein did something very unusual for the time: she showed an interest in the utterances of a disturbed person, rather than merely categorising her and locking her away. She managed to decode meanings and demonstrated the parallel between the woman's thought mechanisms and the pattern of ideas on which mythologies are founded – the latter strongly inspired by Jung. It is significant that the patient's dreams and delusions not infrequently involved 'Dr J', who was studying sexuality and bringing it into practice on her at the time [*sic*] ...[12]

Whether or not Jung had brought sexuality 'into practice' with her, the patient certainly made many sexual allusions to 'Dr J'. She remarked that everyone fell in love with him, and that he wanted to get divorced each year. She reported that she had been 'flogged through Basel', Jung's home town, and that he had 'prostituted her'. Spielrein may have strongly identified with her schizophrenic subject as someone who had fallen for his sexual charm like so many others. Spielrein was no doubt drawn to the woman because of other similarities to her own situation too. The patient was a highly intelligent protestant woman married to a Catholic, and struggling with their religious differences, as well as with her husband's serial infidelities. She was preoccupied with images of sex, punishment and death. Spielrein saw this as confirmation of her own intuitions concerning the close relationship between the creative and destructive aspects of sexuality, as well as an indication of how schizophrenic thinking came close to the symbolism of myths. Jung referred to Spielrein's paper around a dozen times in his *Psychology of the Unconscious*.[13] Freud also made a reference to it in his paper on Judge Schreber.[14]

Jung had already written about Spielrein's paper in a letter to Freud. He spoke about it positively, pointing out how it supported his own theory of schizophrenia.[15] In the same letter, he mentioned that his evenings were taken up largely with astrology 'in order to find a clue to the core of psychological truth'. He also mentioned that Bleuler had declined the presidency of the Zurich psychoanalytic group. These were both ominous signs for the future relationships between the three men. In time, they would have grave consequences. If Freud disliked anything more than Bleuler's caution about psychoanalysis, it was Jung's passion for astrology and the occult. Soon he would not be able to tolerate either view, or either man.

While in Munich, Spielrein was able to focus on her next paper: her theory concerning the connection between sex and death. It had a dual purpose: to act as a replacement for the relationship with Jung, but also to draw on her experiences to formulate a ground-breaking theory. She sent Jung a draft of her paper. She also explained that she planned to go to Vienna in the Autumn. She asked him if he could supply a recommendation to Freud, or whether she should just go anyway. After an interval, Jung wrote back to say he had been unable to find the time to finish the paper, but he felt he had read enough to offer a provisional judgement.[16] He felt there were some excellent thoughts in it, anticipating various ideas he had already had himself. Rather than offering to publish them in the *Yearbook*, like her first paper, he suggested she should turn it into a small independent book, or try to include in Freud's series of *Papers on Applied Psychology*. He wrote of his hope that 'grandfather Freud' would have the same joy as himself over her work. He advised her that she did not need a recommendation to visit Freud. She could just go.

The highlight of the year was to be a psychoanalytic congress in Weimar in September, where Freud would be present. Jung organised an invitation for her.[17] He also included her on a list of participants that he sent to Freud: 'This time the feminine element will have conspicuous representatives from Zurich: Sister Moltzer, Dr Hinkle-Eastwick (an American charmer), Frl Dr Spielrein (!), then a new discovery of mine, Frl Antonia Wolff, a remarkable intellect with an excellent feeling for religion and philosophy.'[18] Jung's 'new discovery' was the one destined to be his long-term mistress. Their affair probably did not start in Weimar but during Emma's fifth and last pregnancy in 1913. Two weeks after the baby was born, he took Antonia on holiday to Italy. His triangular relationship with her and Emma was to last for forty years.[19]

Spielrein never made it to the Weimar congress. As the date approached, she had a relapse of one of her old symptoms – pains in her feet and difficulty in walking. Jung's response was reproachful. He saw it as a moral failure.[20] He told her there was nothing wrong with her foot and she was searching for a reason not to go.[21] He offered her the interpretation that the symptom represented a repressed wish about what the outcome would be if she came. Life required sacrifices and self-denials, he declared, 'the subordination of stubbornness and pride to the rules of devoted love'. He explained that she would only be granted happiness when she sought 'the happiness of others'. His 'frank admonition' was only possible because 'after long reflection by myself, I have removed from my heart all the bitterness which it still held against you'. It was not her work that had brought about this bitterness, he reassured her, but 'all the inner anguish' he had suffered because of her – and she because of him. The admonition continued for another paragraph before becoming dissipated in some good wishes: 'Get well again now! Freud will certainly accept you ... Approach him like a great master and rabbi, then everything will go well.' By the following month, she was well enough to move to Vienna. She was finally on her way to Freud, not just literally, but professionally as well.

13

Sex Versus Survival 1911

You feel the enemy inside yourself, in your own passion, which forces
you with an iron necessity to do something you do not want to; you feel
the end, and its transience, and you want to take flight. 'Is that all?' you
want to ask. 'Is this the climax and nothing more beyond?' What happens
to the individual in the sexual act that might justify such a feeling?[1]

THIS DESCRIPTION of sexual intercourse, and of the disappointment
that can follow it, is from the opening part of Spielrein's paper on
the connection between sex and death: 'Destruction as the Cause of
Coming into Being'. It was the paper she had been writing as her 'Siegfried',
to stand in for the son she never had with Jung. She used it to put the affair
behind her, and to transform what she learned from it into theory. It developed
from ideas she had first recorded in her 'Transformation' letters, and was also
to be her most important paper. She first delivered it in front of Sigmund
Freud and the Vienna Psychoanalytic Society in November 1911. The passage
above comes from the version she published the following year, adapted
from her presentation. Spielrein was describing sexual intercourse, as if from
experience. Did this actually take place with Jung after all, or did she wish
people to think it had? Almost certainly, she would have regarded the question
as irrelevant. From her point of view, all that mattered was that she wanted to
use all her experiences – whether real or imagined – to propose a theory of sex
and death that would subsume the theories of Jung, Freud and Bleuler, and
take everything back to Darwin's first principle: the preservation of the species.
In her mind, it was intended to bring together psychology with mythology,
philosophy, and above all biology. The theory, she was certain, would now
represent her 'higher calling'.

Her presentation followed the custom, in psychoanalytic circles at the time,
of mixing theoretical speculation with personal disclosure. While it might
nowadays seem embarrassing to do this, the study of psychology could never have
advanced without the courage of pioneers who did so. All the same, Spielrein's
topic, her theory, and her way of addressing it raised an important question:

did her sexuality lead her to see matters in a distorted or even pathological way, or did it give her the authority to speak about them with special insight? This was a question that certainly exercised Freud at the time. It remains a point of contention a century later.

*

Spielrein first turned up at the Vienna Psychoanalytic Society on 8 October 1911, unexpectedly. Their meetings were held every Wednesday evening, usually in a hired hall but on this occasion in a café. It was there she met Freud for the first time. 'She said I didn't look malicious, as she imagined I would,' he wrote to Jung.[2] It was not an auspicious evening. Some of the members present were followers of Alfred Adler, who had recently left the society over theoretical differences with Freud and set up his own group. Freud now told all Adler's followers that they would need to choose between his society or the rival one. Six members immediately resigned. By an ironic coincidence, one member who left was the only woman so far admitted to the Society, Margarethe Hilferding. Spielrein was then elected as one of three new members, immediately becoming the sole female: her admission was confirmed early the following year. In his report of the event to Jung, Freud was blunt: 'Rather tired after battle and victory, I hereby inform you that yesterday I forced the whole Adler gang (six of them) to resign from the Society. I was harsh but I don't think unfair.'[3] Such a baptism of fire might have put Spielrein off the movement, but in fact seems to have had the opposite effect: to encourage her to become a peacemaker.

Following the meeting, Freud took the opportunity to write to Spielrein about these events, evidently in response to some diplomatic reflections she had sent him about the evening. He remarked that she had probably been more emotionally attuned as a woman to what was going on. He admired the way she had wanted 'to remove our frowns and wrinkles with a soft hand'.[4] Describing the evening as 'not exactly a laudable one', he reassured her he had more of a sense of humour that must have been apparent. He expressed his gratitude for what she had written, and hoped she would feel at home in the Society. On the same day, he wrote to Jung to say that she was 'very intelligent and methodical'.[5]

The rumpus Spielrein witnessed was not unique in Freud's circle. By the time Spielrein arrived on the scene, Freud was already no longer on speaking terms with two of his other earlier associates – Josef Breuer, who had collaborated with him on *Studies in Hysteria*, and Wilhelm Fliess, who had helped in the creation of psychoanalysis. As well the Adler 'gang', more of his colleagues would face expulsion, or jump before they were pushed. Members present that evening who would depart in due course included Wilhelm Stekel, who had been Freud's most distinguished pupil, and Viktor Tausk, who was to fall foul of him in tragic circumstances.[6] Otto Rank, who was currently the secretary of the Society and later a member of Freud's 'inner circle', would resign in a few years, in protest at Freud's appraisal of him as a heretic. Ideological splits were to bedevil the movement for decades to come. Spielrein cannot have been deterred by the fractious atmosphere, because she not only turned up at the next meeting but spoke for the first time. She made a brief contribution on the question of time in the unconscious mind, an issue in which she would have a longstanding interest.[7] She also made a specifically Jungian point, namely that infant wishes represented 'phylogenetic' or ancestral ones. She spoke again the following week during a discussion on death and sexuality.[8] She explained that she had dealt with many of the issues that had been raised in the paper she had just completed. She offered to present it at a forthcoming meeting. This was exceptionally bold. It meant that her creative substitute for 'Siegfried' would now come under the direct scrutiny of Freud and his closest colleagues. Of more immediate concern, she did not have a copy. The only one was with Jung, who had held on to it for three or four months, but neither read nor returned it.

Spielrein now wrote urgently asking for it back. Jung wrote a long explanation of why he had been unable to read it properly, followed by an exhortation to represent his interests in Vienna.[9] He reassured her that his failure to return her paper did not represent any hard feelings towards her, but he wanted to keep the paper in order to be able to read it at a single session. He promised to send it immediately by registered post. He took note of her report of her first visit to the Society, informing her that there was no one really serious in Vienna apart from Freud, Rank and Hans Sachs. (Sachs was a lawyer and one of the few people present at Spielrein's début who remained close to Freud all his life.) Jung ended his letter by asking her not to betray him. His anxiety was understandable. Jung knew that he had many areas of disagreement with Freud. Most of all, there was the central place that Freud assigned to sexuality in mental functions and difficulties, in contrast to his own increasing interest in underlying mythical patterns.

Jung was not alone in fearing he would be the focus for the next schism. His wife Emma was also concerned. She and Freud had got to know each other well on their mutual visits in Vienna and Zurich, and had struck up an independent correspondence. Although Emma often seems a shadowy presence in comparison with her larger-than-life husband, the moving letters she wrote to Freud create an impression of someone more direct and self-aware, and certainly humbler than the man she married. In a letter that testifies to their degree of intimacy, she now reminded Freud of how he had once told her his marriage was 'amortised' – like a mortgage that had been paid off. He had clearly let her know that sexual relations with his wife Martha had ceased. He had also said at the time: 'Now there was nothing more to do – except die.' She knew these were signs that Freud hoped to abdicate in favour of her husband. She was concerned not so much for her husband, as for Freud himself. She wrote: 'Doesn't one often give much because one wants to keep much?' She cautioned Freud against handing over too much of a leadership role to Carl.[10] In another letter shortly afterwards, she wrote about the tendency of women to fall in love with her husband. She lamented how she was marginalised.[11] She did not mention any of his affairs, let alone the one she knew he had with Spielrein, but she complained about the role she had to play as wife: 'I can never compete with Carl. In order to emphasise this I usually have to talk extra stupidly when in company.' She may have foreseen the storm to come.

As the date of her lecture came closer, Spielrein kept Jung informed about developments in Vienna. He expressed his own anxieties about this. Having asked her earlier in the month not to betray him, he now warned her against excessive loyalty. He was worried how Freud would take the 'corrections' he was introducing into the theory of sexuality. He confessed that inwardly he was 'quite alien' to the spirit of the Viennese school. He advised her she was still too closely bound up with him and unable to judge his value accurately. '*You do not yet see who I am*,' he wrote. 'You will be set free only when you have completely purified your judgement.'[12]

Spielrein delivered her paper to the Vienna Psychoanalytic Society on the evening of 29 November. As usual, Freud chaired the meeting. Others present included Sachs, Tausk, and the physician Paul Federn who later wrote a mainly sympathetic review of Spielrein's ideas.[13] A summary of the paper appeared shortly afterwards in the minutes, taken by Otto Rank.[14]

The paper in many ways represents Spielrein's greatest achievement. Although it was a flawed work, both in its content and in its manner of presentation, she was attempting to do something immensely ambitious and unprecedented: namely, to anchor the 'talking cure' in Darwin's notion of the 'preservation of the species'. The rest of this chapter gives an account of what she said, and her central theme of 'sex versus survival'.

Spielrein's argument is complicated, and obscure in places, but its key ideas can be stated simply. She proposed that every human being is caught in a tension between two separate instincts: the instinct to survive as an individual, and the instinct to reproduce. The instinct to survive is a static one – a conscious desire to stay the same. The reproductive instinct is a dynamic one – an unconscious drive towards transformation. She also argued that the reproductive instinct has both a creative and a destructive aspect. The creative aspect is the desire to bring about a new conception, either in the form of a child or in a symbolic act of creation. However, this always requires destruction of what has gone before. She proposed to demonstrate this principle with a range of observations from biology, psychology, literature and mythology. In John Kerr's words, her argument 'had all the elegance of a new theorem in mathematics and physics'.[15] Rank's written notes from the live presentation are brief, so my account here is based on the published version from the following year.

Spielrein began her paper on a highly personal note: 'Throughout my involvement with sexual problems, one question in particular has always interested me: why does this powerful drive, the reproductive instinct, include negative feelings in addition to the expected positive ones?'[16] This opening statement is fascinating. Was she talking about her own sexual problems, her limited clinical experience, or both? Either way, she was pointing towards something she believed to be at the heart of human experience: the importance of the reproductive drive, and all the factors that lead us to resist it. Spielrein next described some of the existing theories that sought to explain the anxiety that surrounds sex. These had been proposed by Freud, Jung and others including Bleuler, who had coined the word 'ambivalence' to describe how each feeling is balanced by its opposite. Spielrein argued these explanations were all fine to an extent, but incomplete. In her view, a feeling of anxiety was an entirely normal aspect of sex and moved to the forefront of feelings as soon as 'the possibility of fulfilment of the wish first appears'. She then posed her opening question for a second time, with even more urgency, in the words that head this chapter.

The key part of her presentation now followed. In the published version, the section is entitled 'Biological Facts'. Spielrein described how a man penetrates a woman and discharges sperm into her vagina. Fertilisation takes place, and the egg undergoes internal destruction and reconstitution in order to form an embryo. She drew attention to the way this involves a number of parallel processes. For example, just as the man physically invades the woman, so one of his sperm invades her egg. In the same way, the genetic material of egg and sperm combines rapidly, with destruction and reconstruction of the original material. She drew a parallel between these physical events of sex, the feelings that surround it, and the conflicts to which it gives rise. She suggested that, through the different feelings that accompany sex, people surmise the internal events of creation and destruction that accompany this. 'Just as there is a joyful feeling of coming into being within the reproductive drive, so these are accompanied by defensive feelings like anxiety and disgust ... It is this feeling that corresponds with the destructive component of the sexual instinct.'[17] This was the core of her theory: at some level we know (or *feel* as if we know) that the act of procreation involves self-destruction.

After the 'biological facts', Spielrein addressed 'Individual Psychological Observations'. She examined how the basic conflict between the creative and destructive aspects of sex might be played out in different psychiatric conditions such as hysteria and schizophrenia. She took Nietzsche as a case example, examining how his mystical vision of 'eternal resurrection' represented the convergence of creation with destruction. She challenged Freud for suggesting that humans are governed by the pursuit of pleasure for its own sake. Spielrein disagreed, arguing that the pursuit of reproduction lay behind this and was even more important. Collective desires within us, she argued, do not correspond to personal desires. She backed up her argument by looking at masochism, the sexual desire for pain, which she herself had experienced. She suggested that a joy in pain would be incomprehensible if we believed we were governed by the pursuit of pleasure. She argued that pleasure might be the immediate cause of sexual desire, but desire itself only made sense in terms of the drive to reproduce, which was as much destructive as creative.

Following the psychological section, there was a section on 'Life and Death in Mythology'. Here, she tried to demonstrate how religious texts, great writers and cultural practices represented the unification of destruction and creation in human desire. Her examples included Adam and Eve, Christ, Romeo and Juliet, the Flying Dutchman, Siegfried in Wagner's *Ring*, and a great deal more Nietzsche. Her range of religious, philosophical and literary references was vast: Anaxagoras, Pliny, the Bible, the Talmud, Maimonides and Gogol as well as Wagner. Her scope of cultural reference covered the Arabs of Aqaba and Australian aboriginals. She examined sacrificial rituals, showing how they were aimed to placate a God who was destructive as well as being the Creator. Altogether, in the paper she quoted Freud twenty-five times, Jung eleven times, and other significant psychoanalysts at least twenty-five times. As well as the many writers she cited, she also drew on others she must have been familiar with but did not name. Her paper echoes the philosopher Schopenhauer, who emphasised how the sexual drive took precedence over the conscious wishes of the individual. According to the minutes of her live presentation, she also mentioned the Russian biologist Ilya Mechnikov, who suggested that human beings had a natural wish to die, and would appreciate this more if they led healthier lives.[18] As historian Alexander Etkind has shown, her argument drew on the culture of 'fin de siècle' Russia, where 'Love and death became basic, almost exclusive concepts of human existence ... and melded into a kind of supernatural oneness.'[19] There are particular echoes in her paper of two Russian symbolist writers. One was Vladimir Solovyov, a Christian mystic who saw sex as a means of achieving joyous victory over death. Spielrein's paper followed the same structure as his essay 'The Meaning of Love', which starts by describing procreation among insects and moves on to equating 'the god of life and the god of death'.[20] The other writer was Vyacheslav Ivanov, who wrote that 'the highest truth is reflected in the biological fact that the male of the species dies after copulation'.[21]

Spielrein's 'magnum opus' was without doubt a 'tour de force', but it was also confusing. Spielrein had fallen prey to some of the typical failings of an academic novice. She tried to cover too much ground. She showed off her erudition rather than staying close to her central argument. Having started from a Darwinian perspective, she seems to have moved over to a philosophical, Nietzschean one. She tried to demonstrate how her ideas were based on those of Freud and Jung, and how these could help to unite their two different approaches – something that neither man was going to appreciate. Perhaps unsurprisingly, her lecture did not have the effect that Spielrein hoped. Otto Rank's minutes of the discussion afterwards suggest that many of the audience grabbed hold of the wrong end of the stick. Spielrein was no doubt nervous, and her delivery may have been tremulous or over-enthusiastic. In the discussion, many of those present used her talk as a pretext for promoting their own ideas or pursuing quarrels, sometimes on unrelated topics. Tausk criticised her for using a deductive method, namely an approach from theoretical principles, rather than the inductive method held dear by psychoanalysts, proceeding from observation alone. Some attacked Spielrein's emphasis on philosophy, while others defended it. One person – Dr Stegmann, a guest and the only other woman present – almost understood Spielrein: 'The fear of love is the fear of the death of one's own personality,' she said, before lurching off into mysticism by adding: 'Love is indeed to be regarded as the transition from the small individual to the great cosmic life.' Some people thought that Spielrein was merely presenting Jung's ideas on his behalf, and they took the opportunity to have a go at him.

This was the line that Freud himself took at first. He used the occasion for his most explicit attack on Jung to date. In what may have been a prepared speech, he offered a critique of Jung's recent mythological studies. The material of myths, he said 'has been transmitted to us in a state that does not permit us to make use of it for the solution of our problems'. Having laid down the law in relation to myth, Freud then turned to biology, and directly to the heart of Spielrein's own argument. A psychological hypothesis, he asserted 'must be decided by way of individual psychological investigations. In contradistinction to our psychological point of view, however, the speaker attempted to base the theory of instincts on biological pre-suppositions.' Freud could not have been clearer: psychoanalysis must be completely separate from biology. It must not rest on biological principles. However, his remarks did at least pay her an indirect compliment: he fully recognised what she was trying to do – to square the circle between psychoanalysis and biology. There had clearly been many reasons why the lecture went down so badly: incomprehension, in-fighting, and no doubt sexism and concern about Spielrein's sexuality. But Freud made no attempt to conceal the main reason: hostility to biological thinking. At the end of the evening, Spielrein apologised for not having made the biological fundamentals of her theory clearer. However, she affirmed that 'the desire for extinction is a normal tendency and often expresses itself in women in the form of destructive ideas'.

In order to understand what Spielrein was trying to do, and why Freud opposed this so strongly, we need to go back to Darwin and the key pillars of his theory of evolution. We also need to consider how the relationship between evolutionary thought and psychology developed between Darwin and Freud. Spielrein's central argument was explicitly based on Darwin's idea of the 'preservation of the species'. Behind this main principle, Darwin had also proposed two others, and these are implicit in her paper. One was the variation of individuals from generation to generation. The other was 'natural selection' – the survival of the variations that turned out to fit the environment most effectively.[22] Later, Darwin added a further principle: 'sexual selection'.[23] This meant that individuals who selected the most resilient mates would end up with the most descendants. As discussed in Chapter 6 in the context of Spielrein's 'Transformation' letters, the biologists of the German-speaking world, including August Weismann, then discovered the processes that created variations in the first place, so that natural and sexual selection could occur. Just as Spielrein described, these were processes of destruction and reconstruction: between egg and sperm, and between the chromosomes within them.

Darwin was not only a biologist. He was also a pioneer in psychology. He believed that our mental capacities had evolved through selection in the same way as our anatomy, posture, or speech. He published an entire book on *The Expression of the Emotions in Man and Animals*.[24] There he speculated on how far our unconscious reasons for certain emotions, such as childhood fears, were evolutionary in origin: they were the result of selection, and hence were the ones that had proved most successful in the struggle for survival. He anticipated the day when 'psychology will be based on a new foundation, that of the necessary acquirement of each mental power and capacity by gradation'.[25] He may have expected this development to happen relatively soon, but sadly it did not. At his death, Darwin bequeathed his papers on psychology to his friend George Romanes, who tried to develop his ideas further.[26] Unfortunately, Romanes followed the fashionable 'biogenetic theory'.[27] This suggested that each organism 'recapitulated' its evolutionary history during its own lifetime. Romanes applied it to psychology, with questionable results. For example, he proposed that certain types of infant behaviour recapitulated that of reptiles. This style of thinking set the scene for a rash of similar speculation in psychology, particularly in the psychology of sex. Krafft-Ebing based his encyclopaedia of sexual problems, *Psychopathia Sexualis*, on the idea that such problems arose from degenerate evolutionary tendencies: for example that female masochism was an inheritance of the bondage of feminine ancestry. These kinds of ideas held considerable sway in the early twentieth century and influenced Freud, among others.[28]

Freud himself had started out his own career with a fascination for the science of biology and with evolution.[29] He carried out studies in the microscopic anatomy of the brain.[30] Like many psychiatrists of his generation, including Forel, he hoped that brain anatomy might reveal the causes of mental disturbance. Subsequently, along with others including Pierre Janet in Paris and Bleuler in Zurich, he became more interested in the psychological origins of such disturbance. Following the discovery of his new clinical method, he devoted himself to developing a theory based on the observation of patients and distanced himself altogether from biological theory. 'I try in general,' he wrote, 'to keep psychology clear from everything that is different in nature from it, even biological lines of thought.'[31] Some people regard it as Freud's genius to have developed a psychology based on clinical observation. Others see it as its central weakness. It meant that psychoanalytic theory was subjective. It made it dependent on the authority of one man, and vulnerable to disputes from rivals who drew different conclusions from what they observed.

There was another factor in Freud's rejection of biology too. He may have once been a skilled biologist in the technical sense, but he was never a great evolutionary theorist. To quote two modern psychoanalysts, his understanding of evolution was 'in some ways quite crude and quaint'.[32] He believed in the biogenetic theory. He also followed the beliefs of Darwin's predecessor Jean-Baptiste Lamarck, who had argued that environmental pressures could bring about variations that could be passed on to the next generation. This was entirely at odds with Darwinian thinking about natural and sexual selection, and it was wrong.[33] While Freud continued to refer in rather vague terms to the evolutionary origin of the human mind, he gave up any serious attempt to follow through this idea in a way that would have convinced any biologist of his time or since. As a result, he effectively ensured that virtually all the different forms of the talking cure that emerged during the rest of the century remained disconnected from their biological roots.

Some Jungians have argued that Jung was more in tune with evolutionary thinking than Freud.[34] This is because Jung later traced the workings of the human mind to enduring patterns of ideas, images and expectations – so-called 'archetypes' – that had been laid down in ancient collective experience. In fact, Jung's references to what we inherit as a species make it clear that he also took a Lamarckian view of the matter. He mistakenly imagined that cultures, races and social groups could acquire archetypal tendencies that would then be passed on through inheritance. There is no suggestion that he tried to understand the collective unconscious in terms of variation, or natural and sexual selection.

If we return to Spielrein's theory, it should now be clear why it was an explicit challenge to both Freud and Jung. It went beyond Freud's concern about what happens in childhood, or what adults describe as happening to them in the past. It went beyond Jung's concern with how human beings collectively fashion the images and myths that then govern their behaviour. Instead, Spielrein posed the question: what underlies both of these? Her answer was clear: we must look to biology to make sense of them. Although she paid tribute to both Freud and Jung, her project was more of an attempt to fulfil Darwin's hopes: a psychology based on evolution. Taking her own feelings as a starting point, she tried to trace these back directly to the biological processes she believed them to resemble. She also connected both the biological and psychological processes with their evolutionary purpose: reproduction.

From a Freudian point of view, Spielrein's argument was wrong because it started off from unacceptable premises. From a biological point of view, it looks rather different. She focussed on several aspects of biology that are emphasised by evolutionists today. One is the complementary relationship between sex and death. Weismann had pointed out that if death did not exist, sex would be unnecessary, but modern studies have gone further: sexual reproduction and life cycles of a fixed term may have arrived together and have a complementary relationship with one another. Sex is irresistible only because death is inevitable.[35] Another of Spielrein's topics that has moved to the fore in modern thinking is the intense battle that happens between male and female interests. This takes place not only between eggs and sperm, or between pairs of chromosomes. It starts with courtship and conquest, and continues within the womb and placenta.[36] It is also played out in the fights that take place between parents over the hearts, minds, and education of their children.[37] It is a battle where collaboration is delicately poised with rivalry, and the urge to create with the impulse to overcome or destroy.

In addition, Spielrein realised that human beings have to make fundamental choices in the course of their lives between the demands of procreation, and conserving their energy for themselves: we do indeed have to choose between sex and survival.[38] Spielrein also realised what might now seem obvious: the conscious reason we desire sex is out of pleasure, but the unconscious one is the need to have descendants. The desire for sex is also accompanied by an apprehension of its many risks, particularly for women. This includes a loss of physical identity through pregnancy – where the foetus literally becomes a biological parasite on the mother – and of psychological identity through marriage and motherhood. It includes the risks of violence, sexual abuse and rejection, all of which Spielrein had experienced. Spielrein also made an explicit claim, probably the first ever, that variations in sexual desire such as her own masochism could be seen as understandable strategies for achieving reproductive ends by different means, a remarkable insight for her time.[39]

Judged by the same standards of modern evolutionary theory, there were some serious flaws in Spielrein's argument. The instincts for survival and reproduction are not fundamentally in opposition to each other. Human beings need to pay more attention to one or the other objective at different times, and in different circumstances, but the two go hand in hand when raising progeny. If human parents did not survive after reproducing, their offspring would not stand much chance of survival. Spielrein was also wrong to say that the reproductive *drive* contains a wish to destroy oneself. We need to reproduce in order to ensure continuation in the face of death, but it makes no sense to describe death as a wish, an instinct or a psychological drive. The mystical self-immolation of a man and a woman in each other's identities, in the manner of Brünnhilde riding into Siegfried's funeral pyre, may be a compelling expression of idealised love, but it cannot be understood in terms of any psychological drive. Similarly, Spielrein's notion that a drive towards destruction is the cause of ambivalence before sex or disappointment afterwards is unconvincing. A sense of psychological merger during sex is common, and so is post-coital sadness, but there is no reason to imagine that this relates to what happens when a sperm merges with an egg – which in any case happens some hours afterwards.

It is not difficult to see how the insights and the flaws in Spielrein's argument both came from the same source. Her infancy and childhood, and perhaps her constitution, had endowed her with a desire for pain and abasement, together with a furious resistance to it. Later on, these developed into a passionate wish to subsume herself in a man's will, an overwhelming yearning to bear his child, and an intense apprehension of the consequences of doing either. This gave her some unique insights into the power of the reproductive instinct and the destructive aspects of sex. It also helped her to understand the crucial choices that need to be made between sex and survival. However, it led her to identify with notions of romantic self-sacrifice. In addition, she was constrained by the conceptual limitations of her time, and the fact that no one else around her had any interest in a project to anchor an understanding of psychology in the key principle of evolution.

Six years after her presentation, Spielrein managed to refashion her ideas about the reproductive drive without the distracting mystical elements that dominated here. She outlined these in one of her final letters to Jung, to be examined later in this book. Sadly, she would never publish a purely evolutionary account of the mind.[40] It was to be nearly a century before people would properly take up these themes again. Yet there seems no doubt that what she did in front of the Vienna Psychoanalytic Society in November 1911 was an attempt to sketch out some of the pre-requisites for a cogent Darwinian theory of psychology.

14

Aftermath 1912

My dear, Receive now the produce of our love, the work that is your little son Siegfried. It was hugely difficult, but for Siegfried's sake nothing was too difficult. If you do decide to print the article, I will feel I have fulfilled my duty towards you and your little son. Only then will I be free. This work is worth far more to me than my life, and that is why I am so fearful. You promised me that you will publish it in July, if it is of any value, naturally. It must surely be of some value, because so much love and persistence was devoted to it.[1]

SPIELREIN SENT this letter to Jung with the 'Destruction' paper, revised for publication. In spite of his original advice that it should be turned into a small book, it was going to go in his *Yearbook* after all. Although the presentation in Vienna had been a damp squib, she hoped that the additions and corrections she had included in the version for publication would make it more acceptable. It remained her 'Siegfried', the creation of the energy she felt between herself and Jung. The letter made it clear how much value she placed on the work. It was also her acknowledgement that their relationship was over, and that her theoretical work had replaced the desire for a real child by him.

Unknown to her, the ideas in the paper had already become ammunition in the battleground between Freud and Jung. As their mutual antagonism increased, one of the few things they could agree upon was their distaste for what she had presented in Vienna. Inevitably, their objections were not identical. Freud found the ideas too Jungian, and Jung found them too Freudian. Yet there were two issues on which they were in entire agreement. First, it was wrong to try and anchor psychoanalysis in biology. Secondly, the theory was too imbued with her own personal perspective, which – among other things – was a female one. The men's dismissal of Spielrein's embodied experience and insight as an abused woman, who yearned for a child and was scared of it at the same time, may say more about the failure of their imagination than it does about her theory.

Interwoven with the themes of biology and gender was another one. It was the question of science. Whether or not Spielrein was aware of this, Bleuler had resigned from the Vienna Psychoanalytic Society on the day before she gave her lecture. He had been in correspondence with Freud for some time on the 'closed door' policy of psychoanalysis, its intolerance of dissent, and the harm this had done to his relationship with Jung. Earlier he had written to Freud: '"Who is not with us is against us," the principle of "all or nothing" is necessary for religious sects and for political parties ... but for science I consider it harmful.'[2] In some ways the exchanges of the months that followed Spielrein's lecture in Vienna can be seen as a four-way struggle with Bleuler as a protagonist too.[3] At stake in the battle were Freud's view of sexuality, Jung's allegiance to mythology, Spielrein's allegiance to evolution, and Bleuler's trust in scientific dialogue. In the months that followed, each one of these threads for understanding human psychology was weakened by being pulled apart from the others.

*

The day after Spielrein gave her lecture, Freud let Jung know that Bleuler's letter of resignation had arrived. He had already sent him 'a critical answer'. He told Jung that 'the last trouser-button of my impatience has snapped'.[4] In what was possibly a comparison with Spielrein, he wrote that Bleuler's masochism was 'waiting for a good whipping'. He then turned to Spielrein's lecture, admitting cheerfully that he regarded her as a spokeswoman for Jung himself. Joking with Jung that he had almost written about 'your' ideas rather than 'hers',[5] he said he had some objections to her approach to mythology. He had discussed them with the 'little Spielrein girl'. Although she had a good head, he agreed with Jung that she was 'very demanding'. He then backed away from confrontation, with a laddish wink: 'I must say she is rather nice and I am beginning to understand.' He rounded off his comments with an attack on her biological approach, making it clear that this was no better than a mythological one: 'What troubles me most is that Fraulein Spielrein wants to subordinate the psychological material to *bio*logical considerations; this dependency is no more acceptable than a dependence on philosophy, physiology, or brain anatomy. PsA *fara da se* [Psychoanalysis will get along by itself].'[6]

Jung no doubt disagreed on the topic of mythology, but was happy to endorse Freud's other point. In his reply, he wrote that would take Spielrein's new paper for the *Yearbook* although it would need a great deal of revision.[7] He said the little girl had always been very demanding with him as well – although she was 'worth it'. He promised Freud that he would take account of his views concerning mythology, and asked for some more detailed feedback. 'I know of

1. Rabbi Mordekhai Lublinsky

2. Spielrein family 1896: Sabina, Emilia and Jan in front, Eva with Isaac middle row left, Nikolai and probably Dr Moishe Lublinsky at back, others unknown

3. Isaac Spielrein in Berlin

4. Nikolai with Jüdischer Wanderverein (Jewish youth organisation),
Leipzig, May 1914. Isaac behind his father

5. Wedding anniversary 1909: Eva, Sabina, Nikolai, Emil, Isaac, Jan

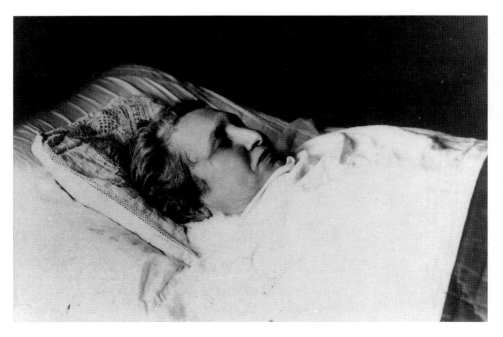

6. Eva on her death bed 1922

7. Jan, Emil and Isaac around 1930

8. Nikolai and Evald 1928

9. Eva, Sabina and Emilia around 1898

10. Sabina, identity document 1930s

11. Eva Junior, late 1930s

12. Nina Snetkova with her mother Olga

course that Spielrein operates too much with biology,' he wrote. 'But she didn't learn that from me, it is home-grown.' He was absolutely supportive of keeping psychoanalysis within its boundaries, although he wanted to point out it was worthwhile making occasional forays into other areas. Without spelling it out, he was content to dismiss biology so long as Freud did not dismiss mythology.

On the same day, he wrote to Spielrein in a different vein. He told her not to be too dejected about the way it had been received in Vienna, and he reassured her that the paper would definitely appear into the *Yearbook* if Freud was happy with it.[8] Later the same month, he reinforced this by saying that Freud had spoken 'very flatteringly' of her in his letters.[9] He congratulated her on this too, adding that there were 'other successes' he would wish for her 'even more'.

As requested, Freud wrote to Jung with some his objections to using mythology. He referred to a part of Spielrein's talk where she had spoken about the biblical story of creation. As Freud pointed out, this story appears in the Book of Genesis in two quite contradictory versions. Describing Genesis as 'a wretched, tendentious distortion devised by an apprentice priest', he argued that one could not take such muddled myths for comparison with psychoanalytic findings. Instead, it was necessary to look for their 'latent, original forms'.[10] Freud's contempt for the complexity of biblical texts is striking, especially for someone who was accomplished at teasing apart the contradictory themes of dream material. He was in effect promoting his own preferred approach to myths. This was to seek real historical events underlying them, as opposed to Jung's passion for collecting contrasting versions of common myths. For example, in *Totem and Taboo*, which he was writing at the time, Freud argued that the Oedipus complex arose from a primeval crime in which sons turned murderously against their father.[11] Later, in *Moses and Monotheism*, he put forward the theory that the story of Moses had its origins in the historical figure of Akhenaten, the Egyptian pharaoh who promoted a form of monotheism.[12]

Encouraged by the congratulations, 'the little Spielrein girl' returned to Rostov for the Christmas break in good spirits. When back at home in Rostov, she was 'practically buried under an avalanche of affection' from her family and friends. She had given a lecture on psychoanalysis at a local institute. The president thanked her for her 'excellent lecture' and asked her to give a few more. On her return, she recorded in her diary that she had now officially become a member of the Vienna Psychoanalytic Society, on the strength of her doctoral dissertation. She had become very fond of Professor Freud, who thought highly of her and praised her 'magnificent article'. He was also being very sweet to her personally. She now wrote that she had everything she had wanted with one exception:

'Where is the man I could love, whom I could make happy as a wife, and as mother of our children?'[13] She wrote that she had two women patients in Vienna whom she was treating free of charge. Both were doing well, particularly one, a singer, who improved very quickly. She was the illegitimate daughter of a count, and Spielrein felt deeply touched by her fate. The patient was now writing long letters and poems full of her praises.

Having completed her 'Destruction' paper and sent it to Jung, she waited eagerly for his response. Despite her passionate covering note, Jung sent only a standard editor's acknowledgement slip. As we can see from her next diary entry, it brought on suicidal thoughts again, followed almost immediately by something quite different: a prophetic dream.

How did it go? Exactly the same as with my first paper, in fact even worse: 'Dear Colleague, I confirm the receipt of both your manuscripts. With best wishes. Yours sincerely, Dr Jung.' This is how my friend wrote to me. I thought and felt a great many things. I do not have the strength to relate how I answered him. Today, yet more trouble followed. I had had more than I could take. I wrapped my collar protector around my neck and imagined myself blissfully released from this wretched existence ... A deep compassion for my parents then seized me. I hesitated, looked into the mirror, and found how well the blue-grey woollen scarf suited me. Then I thought of how lovingly my mother used to wrap a scarf around my neck to prevent me from getting cold, how she raised me until now, and then ... her only daughter ... because of a ...[14] Oh, because of a man who has crushed my entire life ... At this moment, I have not one iota of fear of committing suicide. Last night I dreamed that a young girl (obviously my fate) looked at my hand and told me I would marry an older man when I was 27.[15]

In addition, one of the members of the Vienna Psychoanalytic Society, Viktor Tausk, had read her palm. He predicted that she would experience something important when she was twenty-six or twenty-seven, and that her fate would take a new turn.

Jung had spent much of the winter defending psychoanalysis against its critics in Zurich. They were launching a fierce onslaught against it in the newspapers as an erotic pseudo-science.[16] Eventually, he found time to have a look at Spielrein's paper. Even though it was now almost a year since she had sent him the original draft of her lecture, and many weeks since he had received her final offering of their 'little son', this was the first time he had read her theory. In March, he wrote to say he found 'uncanny parallels' in this paper with his own *Psychology of the Unconscious*, which he was now preparing for publication.[17] He had never suspected this similarity before because until now he had always read her title incorrectly, thinking the first word was 'Distinction' instead of 'Destruction', and was puzzled by this. Now that he had realised his mistake, he found considerable parallels which showed the results people would get if they went about thinking 'logically and independently'. He told her that her destruction instinct was definitely correct: 'We desire not only the ascent but the descent and the end.' He added: 'This wish is commoner than we think.'

'*Distinction*' instead of 'Destruction?' How was it possible for anyone, let alone Jung, to read even the first page of her paper and fail to see it was about destruction and creation? Besides, according to her diaries she had been trying to explain her evolving theory to him for at least four years. How would Spielrein have reacted to his mis-reading, and the casual way he mentioned it? If his excuse was true it was utterly insulting. If he made it up because he had never looked at the paper, it was even more so. It cannot have helped that his paraphrase of her ideas was a caricature. Her reply to this letter no longer exists, but John Kerr speculates that she 'exploded'.[18] Jung's reply seems to confirm this. Again he appeased her, while planting the blame for any misunderstanding squarely on her.[19] He wrote that she was upsetting herself unnecessarily again. She had taken his phrase 'uncanny similarities' literally. He intended it much more as a compliment to her. He protested that her study was extraordinarily intelligent, containing wonderful ideas he was happy to acknowledge had first been hers. She had understood the 'death tendency or death wish' before it was ever clear to him. It would be quite impossible for anyone to imagine she had borrowed in any way from him. 'Perhaps I borrowed from you too,' he conceded. Certainly he had 'unwittingly absorbed' a part of her soul, as she doubtless had of his. He concluded by expressing pleasure that she was representing him in Vienna as his new work would certainly be misrepresented and she could defend his new ideas. Reading these letters, it is hard to avoid the impression that Jung had never really listened to Spielrein when she talked to him about her theory or ever read the paper closely. Historians Forrester and Appignanesi describe these letters as 'condescending and arrogant'.[20]

After offering praise to Spielrein about her 'Siegfried', he wrote about it disparagingly to Freud. He used a Latin quotation from Horace: 'What at the top is a lovely woman ends below in a fish.'[21] The comment could be understood as a reference to Spielrein simply as a strange creature like a mermaid, but it has obscene misogynist undertones. In the rest of the letter, he complained how much work he would need to do in order to make the paper publishable. He let Freud know he would not share his criticisms with 'the little authoress' herself. Jung and Freud voiced another concern to each other: her ideas could not be trusted, because she herself was so troubled sexually. Freud wrote that she was very bright and there was meaning in everything she said, but he did not like her version of the destructive drive because it was 'personally conditioned'. 'She seems abnormally ambivalent,' he wrote.[22] Jung replied: 'Her paper is heavily weighted with her own complexes.'[23]

Much of Freud and Jung's criticism of Spielrein's theory was based on their reservations about her as a person. In effect, she was claiming the right to use her untypical repertoire of sexual experiences and fantasies as a source of new psychological theory. This raises a fundamental question about personal conflict as a source of insight. Freud's own theory had arisen in the first place from an analysis of his own inner conflicts. All his immediate followers, including Jung, had analysed themselves in order to construct their own theories. They openly acknowledged that conflicts could be a source of discovery as well as discomfort. At times, members of the society offered theories that were valued precisely because everyone knew that these had arisen from their own psychological problems. At other times, their ideas were rejected for exactly the same reason. As a result, Freud and his followers were inclined to use one kind of argument when it suited them, and the other kind when it did not. Instead of evaluating a new idea from a colleague on its own merits, they tended to accept it when it fitted their own existing theories, reject it when it did not, and then praise or impugn the personality of the colleague accordingly. In the case of Spielrein, it is clear that she had drawn on her own troubled imagination to work out her theory of sex and destruction. In doing so, she put herself in double jeopardy. If people did not like her ideas, they could undermine them by blaming them on her mental state. Ultimately, this is the position that both Jung and Freud took. When they finally fell out, they used exactly the same tactic to criticise each other. This tradition has continued, with several modern writers examining Spielrein's theory mainly in terms of her own sexual conflicts.[24]

Freud maintained a dignified silence concerning Jung's quotation about a woman 'ending below in a fish'. But later on, he let Jung know that Spielrein had visited him to say she was leaving Vienna: 'Spielrein, to whom I was glad not to mention your criticism, came to say good-bye a few days ago and discussed certain intimate matters with me.'[25] This was the last time Spielrein's name appeared in their correspondence. We will never know what these 'intimate matters' were. Almost certainly they related to Jung. We know from her later letters that Spielrein talked with Freud about her feelings for Jung and her desire to have his child. She also took some dreams to him.[26] He may have learned that Jung had never given her any proper analysis, something that Jung had not made clear in their correspondence. It is likely that Freud's conversations with Spielrein helped to convince him of the need for an absolute ban on analysts having any kind of erotic relationship with patients. In 1915 he finally went public on this issue, declaring: 'The treatment must be carried out in abstinence.'[27] By that time, the two men were no longer on speaking terms. We can only speculate about the part played by 'intimate matters' in leading Freud to make his final decision about Jung, and to dissociate himself from the man he had once appointed as his 'son and heir'.

Spielrein remained in Vienna until March 1912. She attended meetings of the Psychoanalytic Society regularly, making points in the discussions from time to time. Several concerned the psychology of children. She submitted the manuscript of another paper to the society's *Zentralblatt*. It was the one on children's fantasies about pregnancy and childbirth in which she included so many details of her own childhood, and is covered more fully in the next chapter.[28] At the end of March, she attended the society for the last time, having resolved to return to Russia for the summer. Shortly afterwards, she paid a farewell visit to Freud in the apartment in Berggasse where he lived and practised. By June, he was writing to her to acknowledge a visit from one of her patients. This might be someone Freud had previously referred to her personally.[29] There are no extant letters to or from Spielrein for the next two months, and no entries in her diary between February and July. There is nothing to indicate what the next entry in her diary will reveal. For anyone reading it without prior knowledge, it comes as a bombshell:

On the 14th of June I married Dr Paul Sheftel. To be continued.[30]

15

Berlin 1912-1914

Our dreams after a tempestuous night. My dream: I have to pour tea for father and mother. At first I pour it into a bottle, then into glasses, but I cannot find a glass because the glasses are dirty and most are cracked. I believe I found only one glass but not 2, and then somehow I was prevented from doing so. Frau Ter-Oganessian (formerly Frl Babitskaya) with an ugly girl, then the child became as pretty as picture. Material for the dream: Yesterday afternoon my husband asked me to pour him a glass of tea quickly before he went to the synagogue in memory of his father. I wanted to do it soon, joked with him a little, but I didn't know he was in such a hurry, and he went off without drinking his tea. In the evening I imitated a little baby. Frl T-O as I mentioned, with whom we continually experience analogies in our erotic fate. With my marriage it also went just like hers. With her – an argument with her husband's mother. With me – ditto, because his mother felt hurt by him and left without seeing him. Now she has a one year old girl, Asia. At night – 'Freud'.[1]

PIELREIN WAS writing in her diary once more, a few weeks after her wedding to Pavel[2] Sheftel. In this description of her dream, she called the previous night 'tempestuous', presumably referring to their sex as newly-weds. Something else we learn from this account is that her husband was an observant Jew. On the day of this entry, he wanted to fulfil his obligation of going to his synagogue in Rostov to say the memorial prayer for his late father. Spielrein had responded teasingly, but afterwards regretted this. Play-acting a baby in the evening may have been her way of trying to entertain him, in order to make amends. We also learn that her relationship with her new mother-in-law may already have been in trouble.

There are other, darker suggestions in this entry. The tea glasses in the dream recall the glass that is ritually crushed underfoot by the groom at a Jewish wedding. Richebächer believes their appearance in the dream as cracked and dirty may indicate Spielrein's concern that she was not virginal.[3] The abrupt break in the document after the word 'Freud' suggests that Spielrein herself – or a subsequent censor – did not want us to know what followed.[4] We never learn of Pavel's own dream either, although the opening of the entry suggests that Spielrein originally placed this on record too. This is the last extant entry in any of Spielrein's available diaries. Although there are many more letters and scholarly articles, her own voice as a diarist will now be absent. The entry marks another kind of turning point as well. Until the year of her marriage, there was a strong sense of a forward trajectory in Spielrein's life. In spite of all her inner turmoil, certain things seem assured: her wealth, her academic success, her prospects of a fulfilling career. From 1912 onwards, this journey begins to falter. There are relocations, false starts, frustrations.

*

Spielrein married Pavel Nahumovich Sheftel on 1 June 1912.[5] Although she recorded the previous year that she had 'no religion',[6] her wedding to Pavel took place in a synagogue. A Rabbi Brailovsky officiated, and Pavel offered a traditional pre-nuptial 'guarantee' of thirty roubles as part of the Hebrew marriage contract. Pavel was tall, pale, bearded and handsome. Like his wife, he was qualified as a doctor, although he trained in Russia through a system of apprenticeship rather than attending university. His father died when he was young, leaving his mother to bring up her four children.[7] He remained with his mother and sisters until he married. The marriage of an assimilated, western-educated member of a Jewish community to a more traditional, observant one was not unusual. In spite of their advanced, liberal views, both Nikolai and Eva came from traditional backgrounds, and had been keen for their daughter to have a Jewish marriage. Pavel Sheftel may have attended the presentation that Spielrein gave on psychoanalysis in Rostov during her Christmas vacation. If so, this may have prompted her parents to organise a formal match.

The wedding in Rostov seemingly came out of the blue, but the influences leading to it are clear. Spielrein's parents had held discussions with professional Jewish matchmakers in Rostov while Spielrein was still at medical school. She turned down at least two suitors during her time in Munich. Spielrein was repeating the pattern of at least two previous generations, who had dalliances with gentiles before turning back towards the Jewish community for matrimony. She may have decided that liaisons with gentiles were more dangerous than going back to one's roots. There were also some other portents: Tausk reading her hand and predicting something major was about to happen, and the 'prophetic' dream of marrying an older man when she was twenty-seven.[8] Spielrein was still only twenty-six, but Pavel was indeed five years older. Most of all, the marriage may have been her conscious attempt to put her feelings for Jung behind her. The early weeks of the marriage in Rostov were certainly romantic. Pavel was to look back on these with nostalgia, recalling a time 'when silence meant more than words'.⁹ There is a poignant echo here of Spielrein sitting in silence for hours with Jung, four years earlier. But the differences between husband and wife were more than religious ones. Pavel was not as intelligent as Spielrein. Later, people were to describe him as moody. It is impossible to know if he was like this when he married, or became so as a result of the difficulties that soon arose. The fact is, we know vastly less about Pavel than we do about his wife. They were to spend many years apart. Even when they were together, the marriage never seemed to be one of Spielrein's principal concerns. In her later writings, she often used material from herself and her first daughter, but rarely anything that appears to be based on him, or on their relationship. This creates an inequality in the impression they make as individuals. In real life, he may not have been a shadowy figure, but there is not enough information to paint a more vivid portrait of him.

In the months between her visit to Rostov at Christmas 1911 and her return for the wedding, Spielrein discussed with Freud whether she should go into analysis with him. Spielrein now wrote informing him of her marriage. He offered his congratulations and observed this news must mean she was 'half cured' of her neurotic dependence on Jung. 'In retrospect,' he wrote, 'I have to confess that your fantasy of the birth of a Saviour to a mixed union did not appeal to me at all. In those anti-Semitic times, the Lord God arranged for him to be born from the best Jewish race. But I know that these are my prejudices.'¹⁰ He advised Spielrein firmly against pursuing analysis at this stage, saying this could badly prejudice the rights of her new husband, about whom she had written so warmly. If Pavel was given a chance to attach himself to her and make her forget her old dreams, he advised, a new person might appear in the shape of an infant who would 'have more rights than the old and new man put together'. Pavel almost certainly wanted to stay in Rostov, close to his own family, as well as to the Jewish community. Unlike Spielrein and her brothers, he had never mastered German properly, nor studied in the west. He was never to feel comfortable there. By contrast, Spielrein must have found Rostov provincial after her years of independence in Zurich, Munich and Vienna. She persuaded Pavel to move with her to Berlin.

Berlin was one of the most vibrant cities in Europe. There were many family connections there too. Nikolai had studied in Berlin in his youth. Her middle brother Isaac was currently there with his new wife Rakhil Potsharyova, who had qualified as a doctor at the Sorbonne (see plate section no. 3). Still only twenty-one, Isaac already had a formidable German education in philosophy and psychology. He had developed an interest in Jewish history and culture as well as the Yiddish language. Currently he was spending time at both the Institute for Experimental Psychology and the Institute for Jewish Studies. At the former, he had established a connection with William Stern, the pioneer of intelligence testing. During a visit back to Rostov, he had carried out a major study of high school graduates, using psychological tests, and sent a signed copy to Jung.[11] At the Jewish Institute he also worked with the philosopher Hermann Cohen, and later published a paper on Yiddish in Martin Buber's magazine *Der Jude*.[12] He was embarking on a brilliant career in his own right. The older brother Jan was also in Germany, with his wife Sylvia and their daughter Irina, born the previous year. They were in Stuttgart, where Jan was now completing a doctorate in physics.[13]

Spielrein's main reason for wanting to go to Berlin was because it was an emerging centre for psychoanalysis. Karl Abraham, the leader of the movement there, had known Spielrein from the time when he worked as an assistant at the Burghölzli. He then stayed in Vienna where he formed a warm and enduring friendship with Freud. He founded the Psychoanalytic Society in Berlin in 1910. Freud always regarded him as solid and imperturbable, and highly approved of Spielrein's plans to move to Berlin. He wrote to her that she could learn much from Abraham, adding: 'his sober manner is a good counterbalance to the many temptations you are exposed to in your work'.[14] Spielrein no doubt realised he was referring to both sexual and doctrinal infidelity. Once in Berlin, Spielrein enrolled on a short course for physicians and attended a clinic in psychoneurology. She began to write prolifically. Pavel, however, could not find work. They lived off Spielrein's dowry, together with hand-outs of money, food and clothes from her parents. He no doubt found this demoralising, if not humiliating. Eva wrote often, anxiously expressing concern about Sabina's weight and Pavel's health, asking for more information than her daughter was sending her.[15] The combination of distress signals together with gaps in information became a source of worry even for Freud. Spielrein had evidently mentioned that she needed to stay in a sanatorium and had an operation there. He wanted to know why: 'You don't write anything about it, and I must be satisfied with the fact that everything is all right with you.'[16]

Not long after Spielrein moved to Berlin, the relationship between Freud and Jung reached its bitter conclusion. In early 1913, Freud wrote to Jung: 'It is understood among us analysts that no-one need feel ashamed of his bit of neurosis. But one who while behaving abnormally unceasingly shouts from the rooftops that he is normal arouses suspicion that he lacks insight into his illness. I therefore propose to you that we give up our private relations altogether.'[17] Jung replied: 'I shall comply with your wish that we give up our personal relationship, since I never impose my friendship on anyone.' He ended with the Shakespearean flourish: '"The rest is silence."'[18] Both men kept Spielrein in the picture and tried to enlist her on their side. Freud indicated how important a part her affair with Jung had played in his disillusionment with his colleague. In early 1913, he wrote to her: 'My personal relationship with your Germanic hero is definitely broken in pieces. His behaviour was too bad. My opinion changed a great deal from the time I received that first letter from you.'[19] His reiteration of the racial theme was not new, but it was the first time he had connected Jung's treatment of Spielrein with the change in his opinion. For his part, Jung was unaware that his character and behaviour contributed to Freud's distaste just as much as his theories. He put the schism in a different light when he gave his own account of it to Spielrein. He explained that he had always been convinced Freud would never understand him. In his view, Freud always wanted to offer him love but he had just wanted Freud to understand him.[20] There has been endless debate about the split between Freud and Jung, and whether the underlying causes were theoretical, personal or a mixture of both. Freud himself linked Jung's personality and ideas together. In a letter to Karl Abraham, he commented: 'his bad theories do not compensate me for his disagreeable character'.[21] He also described Jung as 'brutal' and 'sanctimonious'. In the light of Freud's correspondence with Spielrein, and the meetings she had with him in Vienna, it is hard not to believe that Jung's behaviour towards her played a central part in their split.

Spielrein found it no easier to attract psychoanalytic patients in Berlin than she had in Vienna. Nor did she manage to establish any kind of presence among the psychoanalytic establishment there. By the time of Spielrein's appearance on the Berlin scene, Karl Abraham was caught up in the in-fighting that had engulfed the movement. He was one of the members of the inner circle or 'secret committee' that Freud had appointed to protect the theoretical purity of psychoanalysis.[22] The committee had been proposed by Ernest Jones, Freud's Welsh disciple, in response to Jung's heresies. Its purpose was to define what was doctrinally acceptable. In a quasi-religious ceremony that would have confirmed Bleuler's worst fears about the cultic nature of psychoanalysis, Freud bestowed antique Roman seal rings on the committee members. As well as Freud, the members included Jones and Abraham, Sándor Ferenczi from Budapest, and two of Freud's colleagues from Vienna: Hans Sachs and Otto Rank. Later, Max

Eitingon and Anna Freud were invited to join. At least two committee members, Sándor Ferenczi and Otto Rank, were later to fall out with Freud.

Abraham and his German colleagues may have regarded Spielrein as too closely connected with Jung, as Richebächer suggests.[23] Abraham certainly had a strong personal antipathy to Jung even before Freud did. Another possibility is that the Berliners regarded Spielrein as a victim of Jung – something that might have elicited their sympathy, but would not have enhanced her professional status. Abraham's recollections of Spielrein from when she was a patient at the Burghölzli may have coloured his view.[24] For whatever reason, she and Abraham did not get on personally, nor did she forge any other professional friendships there. Spielrein gave one presentation to the Berlin Society on psychoanalysis and ethics but had little further involvement.[25] A pattern was now beginning to emerge in her attempts to form any enduring alliance with other practitioners. Her independence of mind may have been one of her strongest qualities, along with her refusal to take sides in male squabbles. These qualities also ruled out the political moves that would have helped her career.

If Spielrein was isolated professionally, this was not the case socially. Pavel's mother and sister came for long stays. Eva came to visit. She took them to the theatre and tried to boost Pavel's confidence. She told him he could become a professor.[26] Just as she had in Zurich, Spielrein had a circle of Russian Jewish friends who were studying or working in Berlin. When her mother visited, she met Rachel Leibovich, whom she had known at medical school. Eva liked her because of her traditional manner. Spielrein kept up a lively correspondence with other friends from her Zurich circle, including Esther Aptekmann and Rebecca Ter-Oganessian, formerly Babitskaya. Esther was now a psychiatrist back in southern Russia, in an asylum with 1300 patients.[27] She told Spielrein how lucky she was to be in the west. However, married life was not easy. As the religious and intellectual divide between them widened, she wrote to her friend Rebecca, complaining about Pavel's limitations. Rebecca, whose marriage had turned out well, told Sabina that she could interest Pavel in psychoanalysis if she tried.[28] Nikolai also wrote urging her not to grieve at her fate:

Do not reproach your husband: he is a decent chap for you. Sadly, you don't have the ideal of a husband that you wished for, created on the model of your father. That is a shame: you will not find such undemanding and selfless men as me so easily, my dear, either as husbands or fathers. You have chosen very well. And anyway, where is the guarantee that you would be happier with another 'stronger' man? Be assured, the years will pass, you will come closer to each other, everything will sort itself out. You will achieve your aim in life and be happy.[29]

He also begged her to return to Russia – if not to Rostov, then to Odessa, Moscow or Petersburg: 'Bring light to the Russian darkness,' he wrote. For the time being, she ignored his pleas.

Although Berlin was disappointing in terms of establishing a private practice, it was productive for her writing. During her first few months in Berlin, her 'Destruction' paper was finally published, alongside papers by Freud, Jung, Rank, Bleuler, Ernest Jones and her friend Shaina Grebelskaya. In two years in Berlin, she published a total of ten more papers in psychoanalytic journals. This was almost the largest number she was to produce at any period of her life. The papers reflect many of the central preoccupations of psychoanalysis, including the interpretation of dreams and of literature. She wrote a paper on 'Mother Love' showing how subconscious images of one's mother could affect later relationships.[30] She also described two dreams that occurred during a menstrual period, both including fantasies of giving birth.[31] There were also two more substantial works. The first was the paper she had submitted the previous year, containing her memories of childhood. The other was about mothers-in-law, looking at them from a female perspective, and is discussed further below.

'Contributions to an Understanding the Child's Mind'[32] included her early experiences and fantasies, quoted in Chapter 1. It was the first psychoanalytic paper ever written about childhood fantasies. Thus all three of Spielrein's early papers had broken new ground. This one focussed on the beliefs of emotionally troubled children about pregnancy and birth. As well as her own memories, she described the creation fantasies of a thirteen-year-old called Otto and a four-and-a-half-year-old boy named Valli. Spielrein wrote about her attempts to pull an American out of the earth by the legs or create life from food and drink. She described how Valli thought he came out of his mother's blood. He believed his mother had given birth to his father, although his father had made his mother in the first place. Afterwards, he decided that that mothers made daughters and fathers made sons. Otto, by contrast, talked of dreams in which he was afraid of being overcome by an all-powerful mother, and seemed afraid of his growing sexual feelings. Spielrein pointed out the similarity of these themes to mythical ideas – a comparison that would have appealed to Jung. In her mind, they also seemed to confirm her core idea in her 'Destruction' paper, that sexual feelings and fantasies are strongly connected with destructive ones. Apart from the originality of Spielrein's subject she was also unique in the method she used. She insisted that the interviewer needed to be extremely careful not to pose questions, in order to elicit what children genuinely thought. Many of the children's expressions in the paper are reproduced verbatim. Her meticulous approach anticipates that of Jean Piaget, with whom she was to work a decade later. Her exploration of children's fantasies resembles those of Melanie Klein and Anna Freud, who carried out such work in the 1930s. The analyst Adeline van Waning describes the work as showing 'moving candour and not devoid of humour'.[33]

The following year, Spielrein published her paper on 'The Mother-in-law'.[34] She addressed the question of why it was so common for people to feel aversion to mothers-in-law, and why it seemed to make a difference whether this was the husband's mother or the wife's. She probably wrote the paper as a piece of self-analysis, while she struggled with the difficulties with Pavel's mother that she mentioned in her dream. The paper is sympathetic towards mothers-in-law, trying to see families from their own perspective. Spielrein began by pointing out how women have far less opportunity to fulfil their own desires in life than men, and often have to do so by experiencing life through others. She suggested that women create fewer works of art since this depends on an ability to 'objectivise' your own experience to some extent, which women find harder. She argued that this did not mean that men were superior, but reflected the woman's biological role as 'mother and governess of the human race'. These roles require so much use of 'the gift of sympathetic feeling' that women can usually only objectivise a part of what they experience. She then went on to describe the dilemmas that mothers-in-law face when they have known their children since infancy, and now see them trying to find their own way as adults: 'A mother lives her life first of all through her own children and wants to direct them the way that she would like to lead her own life, based on her own experience.'

Spielrein talked of how a mother-in-law wants to appear attractive to her son-in-law, but is easily hurt as she tries to get her new 'child' to love and appreciate her. This emotional situation would turn the most amiable women and gentlest of mothers into the most dangerous of mothers-in-law.[35] In what must be a reference to Pavel's situation, she then wrote: 'Particularly in families without a father, a mother will see her son as the man of the house ... Her daughter-in-law will continue to be a rival, until her love as a mother enables her to accept her son's good fortune in love.' She concluded the paper by discussing how children first idealise their parents, then break free, and finally find a balance. When prejudice against one's in-laws becomes a problem, she counselled, 'it is better to let the opposite feelings take over, in other words to treat others more kindly than your own relations'.[36] She may have been writing a prescription for herself, or describing how she had found a way of achieving a harmonious relationship with the older Mrs Sheftel. The paper was far more explicit than the 'Destruction' paper in claiming that psychoanalytic thinking needs to take account of how women experience the world, and how this differs from the man's view. There was also an endearing tentativeness in what Spielrein writes: 'When discussing such important questions, you always need to be careful and prepared to make mistakes.'[37] This contrasts strikingly with the dogmatic certainties that so many of her male colleagues were proclaiming. It is also consistent with an overall stance in the paper that we would recognise these days as explicitly feminist. The revolutionary nature of her approach is summed up by van Waning with the comment: '*Women's studies – in the year 1913!*'[38]

Spielrein's other papers from these years are mostly short, sometimes no more than a couple of paragraphs long. Some are theoretical discussions of how the mind creates unconscious associations. For example, she examined a passage from a Russian novel where the protagonist tries to work out what has made him suddenly anxious. He recalls being startled by a loud train whistle earlier in the day, and feels better on making that association.[39] In another paper, she used such associations to help a child overcome a phobia of monkeys. She traced this to a time when his mother had got angry with him and he had called her 'a bad marmoset'.[40] Spielrein said she was rarely able to see the boy, and admitted that the paper does not present a complete analysis. The account is indeed sketchy, but it provides evidence that she was one of the first people to try to treat children psychoanalytically.

By the middle of 1913 Spielrein was pregnant. Jung sent his heartfelt good wishes, saying that if Spielrein could really love her child, everything would turn out well: 'And why should you not love your child?'[41] Apart from this opening, Jung's letter is business-like, with a proposal that she should carry out a review of articles concerning schizophrenic writers and philosophers as her next academic task. Spielrein's own feelings for him were still far from business-like. Earlier in the year, she confessed this in a letter to Freud.[42] He replied to say how sorry he was to hear this, especially as the two men were on such bad terms.[43] He recognised it was pointless to complain to her about Jung. At the same time, he told her she still loved Jung because she had not managed to uncover her real hatred for him instead. He admitted that he had taken Jung's side at the beginning of their correspondence, when it looked as if his own relationship with Jung might work out. Now, he confessed, 'I am at least pleased that I am as little responsible for his personal accomplishments as I am for his scientific ones.' Freud's interpretation seems to have had little effect. Later in the summer, he wrote to say he could barely stand to hear her enthuse about her old love. He hoped the new baby would be an ally against Jung. 'As you know, I have been cured of any remaining fondness for the Aryan cause,' he wrote. He expressed a wish that if the child was a boy, he would turn into a convinced Zionist. 'We are and remain Jews,' he wrote. 'The others will always exploit us and will never understand or appreciate us.'[44]

Spielrein's pregnancy was difficult. She was concerned about her small physique and the problems this might cause.[45] There had always been a strong theme in her professional writings concerning the dangers posed to women by conception and childbirth. At some point in her pregnancy she did almost miscarry. In a letter to Jung several years later, she described how she regarded the near miscarriage as part of her inner battle between a real and an ideal child: 'The struggle was very hard for me, and the guilt from missing my life's goal was so great that Siegfried almost took my little daughter's life away.'[46] She wrote that the near miscarriage happened 'simultaneously with, or as a result of' a powerful dream about Siegfried himself. Spielrein no doubt recalled that, in Wagner's *Ring*, Siegfried's mother Sieglinde had died while giving birth to him. On 17 December 1913, her daughter was born safely after all, in their apartment in Thomasiusstrasse. Pavel wanted to call her Irma, while Spielrein wanted to choose Renata ('reborn'), referring to her birth after the inner struggle with 'Siegfried'.[47] They compromised on 'Irma-Renata'. Spielrein always referred to her as Renata, later also using the French version Renate, the German diminutive Renatschen, and the nickname 'Molli'. Jung sent a telegram of congratulation.[48] Freud wrote a letter to say it was far better that the child was a 'She'.[49] Spielrein, he remarked, could now think again about the blond Siegfried and destroy that idol, in case she really did have a boy in the future.[50] Spielrein described her little girl to Freud as energetic and sweet, a big strong little animal, 'totally auto-erotic and completely asocial'.[51] But having a child did not help the marriage. In summer, Spielrein was corresponding with her parents about two possible options: separation or divorce.[52] Eva came to stay for a short while, followed by Pavel's mother and sister.[53] This did not help her resolve her dilemma.

Spielrein was trying to find patients, as she had in Vienna. Once again, she was not succeeding. Just before the war, she wrote to Freud asking if he could send her some, and evidently complained when he did not. He fired off the fiercest letter he had ever sent her. He told her she was going crazy, with the same symptoms that Jung had started off with.[54] He explained how Emma Jung once passed on a reproach from her husband that Freud was withholding patients.

Adler had made the same accusation too. Freud explained that he had not seen a patient from Berlin himself for at least six months. He told her she was seeing him as more powerful than he actually was, in order to hold him responsible for her own failings. He linked this with her guilty conscience for not being able to liberate herself from her idol.

In spite of this, their friendship endured. Freud wrote offering her to put her name on the masthead of the new international *Zeitschrift*, or journal, for psychoanalysis.[55] Freud had founded it with Otto Rank to supplant Jung's *Yearbook*. He wanted her to show her partisanship, and to recognise who 'the enemy' was. He challenged her once again about still being in love with Jung, and for seeing him as a hero pursued by a mob. He reproached her for still writing in terms of Jung's theories, and for blaming Abraham for telling Jung the truth about himself. He said how much he wanted her to throw away her 'infantile ideal of the Germanic champion and hero' and stop resisting her Jewish background. At this moment, Freud's exhortations read more like those of a traditional rabbi. The hectoring tone also resembles some of Jung's letters to her. When Freud returned to analytic mode in the letter, he did so with more strength than ever before. He advised her not to expect that Jung would ever give her the child she must once have 'longed for' from her father. 'Warm up your life's intentions with your own inner fire, instead of burning yourself up with it. Nothing is stronger than controlled and sublimated passion.' If Freud had never fully accepted her as a patient, he was certainly addressing her as one now. Her love for Jung, he was arguing, arose from unresolved Oedipal love for her abusive father. She was, by implication, continuing to invest the same masochistic energy in Jung that her father had habituated her to invest in him. For whatever reason, Spielrein did not in the end give consent for her name to go on the *Zeitschrift*.[56]

At some point, Spielrein resumed her correspondence with Jung as well. She was one of the few people who still exchanged letters with both him and Freud. In time, she may have been the only one. We have none of her letters during this period, but the ones Jung sent to her do not suggest any strong passion on his side, apart from that attached to his detestation of Freud. In April 1914, he wrote to her about the 'painful experiences' he had been through before finally resigning as editor of the psychoanalytic *Yearbook*. He concluded: '*The tone of your letter affected me painfully, for I can see that you too despise me.* Respect for the human personality and its motives should not become undermined by psychoanalysis. Because I fight for this, I have suffered a great deal.'[57] He was not directing such sentiments at Spielrein alone. Battered emotionally by all the conflicts of recent years, of which his affair with Spielrein was a relatively small part, Jung had resigned from his university post, turned his psychological gaze inward, and embarked on his 'Nekiya' or night journey. The man who had tended to Spielrein during her own breakdown had now descended into a breakdown of his own. Following the break-up with Freud, Jung began to hear inner voices and experience troubling visions. Later he was to characterise this as a creative experience, but the Jungian analyst Anthony Storr has described it as a truly psychotic episode.[58] Although he did not go into hospital, this was more severe in psychiatric terms than anything Spielrein had ever experienced. If she had any hope of renewing a relationship with him, he was not in a state where this was remotely likely. The person who helped him through it was in fact Toni Wolff, who now changed from being his patient and mistress into becoming his analyst. There is no mention of her in correspondence between Spielrein and Jung, so we have no way of knowing whether Spielrein was ever aware of the part she played in his life.

16

Switzerland Again 1914-1919

I do not despise him at all, but I deplored his behaviour towards you, Professor Freud, and his attitude toward the Society – yes, if you will, I resented them. I could forgive J's attitude toward the Society even less than that business with me. I saw him only once after my marriage ... In spite of all his wavering, I like J and would like to lead him back into our fold. You, Professor Freud, and he have not the faintest idea that you belong together far more than anyone might suspect. This pious hope is certainly no treachery to our Society! Everyone knows that I declare myself an adherent to the Freudian Society, and J cannot forgive me for this.[1]

SPIELREIN WAS writing to Freud in 1914. It is clear she still felt a mission to reunite the two men, and to help them understand how their ideas complemented each other. Although this may have been fruitless, the mission preoccupied her for the rest of the decade. She gave no hint that her marriage was in trouble, although Freud had noticed that she now made no mention of her husband and had remarked on this.[2] Her comment about resenting Jung's attitude more than 'that business with me' is revealing. However strongly Freud believed that Jung had abused her, she never disclosed a significant alteration in her liking for him. Whether it was the magnetism of his personality, her gratitude for what he had offered her all those years ago, judgement that he had done her more good than harm, or just an enduring illusion, she never described her experiences in harsher terms. If her feelings for him did diminish, they did so by slow attenuation, not through the cathartic release of hate that Freud hoped to provoke.

It was spring 1914, but she made no mention of any fear of war. Few people expected war. When the First World War started, it did so with great speed. Freud himself had been unconcerned about the possibility. He sent his youngest daughter Anna on a trip to England during the summer, just before war broke out. Spielrein had visited Switzerland earlier in the year. It may have been the occasion of her final meeting with Jung, but there is no indication she planned to return there.[3] However, with the outbreak of war, there was little choice but to go back.

*

The Great War between Germany and the western allies broke out in July. Russia declared war on Germany the following month. Over the next four years around two million German soldiers died, and a further one million from the Austro-Hungarian Empire. Two of Freud's sons fought in the Austrian army. Both survived, although one, Martin, was wounded and became a prisoner-of-war in Italy. Most of Freud's younger colleagues were mobilised, including Karl Abraham, although Hans Sachs was exempted because of poor sight. The turmoil in Europe threatened to destroy psychoanalysis because of the conscription of both analysts and patients, and the difficulties of communication. Freud focussed his efforts on writing and helping to maintain the movement's journals. The effect of the war in Russia was even more catastrophic. Over two million Russian soldiers died, and there were almost as many civilian deaths through military action, famine and disease. Rostov-on-Don was far from the battlefront, but its population was swelled by refugees. The war was then succeeded by the revolution and the civil war. The city was not fully to experience peace again until the 1920s. Nikolai and Eva suffered less than millions of other Russians, but life was never as secure or comfortable for them again.

Spielrein was visiting a spa around the time the war broke out. She decided not to return to Berlin. She moved straight on to Zurich, getting Pavel to send on all the necessary documents.[4] For her, Zurich was the obvious choice. Switzerland was unlikely to be touched by war. She had spent most of her adulthood in the city and it no doubt felt like home. She had friends and colleagues there. She could try to find work in Zurich where she had professional connections and former teachers. For other Russians, the choice of whether go home was a hard one. Jan Spielrein stayed in Berlin, while his wife Sylvia returned to Russia with their daughter Irina. It appears that their own relationship had deteriorated in a similar way to Sabina's marriage. Isaac and his wife Rakhil stayed in Sabina's old apartment in Berlin, where their daughter Menikha was born in 1916. They were confined to Berlin, along with other Russian residents in the city. At the time, the choice to stay in the west, thus avoiding conscription into the Tsar's army, also meant choosing permanent exile. As events turned out, both brothers were able to return to Russia after the revolution.

In spite of wanting to go home,[5] Pavel joined Spielrein in Zurich. He presumably knew of his wife's former affair with Jung. Eva wrote to her daughter to say how unpleasant it was that she was back in the same city as Jung. She advised her to avoid him, while also telling her this was basically up to her and her husband. She should do whatever she wanted.[6] Spielrein sent her former correspondence with Jung to her friend from student days, Shaina Grebelskaya, who had completed medical school with distinction and was now a doctor in Odessa. Shaina also counselled her to stay away from Jung.[7] Pavel was in Zurich when Renata had her first worrying bout of respiratory illness. It was the first of many, thus repeating the recurrent sicknesses of Spielrein's own childhood. On at least one occasion, Pavel stayed up overnight, giving her regular doses of medicine.[8] Before he had been in Switzerland for long, however, he received his call-up papers for the Russian army. For him too, a decision to stay in Switzerland would have signified desertion. Pavel was not a strong individual, and already suffered from rheumatism and heart problems. In spite of this, he could not countenance spending all his life away from Russia. In early 1915 he departed,[9] to the disapproval of others including Jan Spielrein.[10] He ended up serving as a military doctor on the western front, until the problems with his heart and joints led to a safer posting.[11]

Spielrein hoped she might find a source of patients at the Burghölzli. She wrote to Bleuler asking if he could put her in contact with any morphine addicts. He could not help, but his reply was friendly. He suggested she should phone him.[12] Meanwhile, she kept up her membership of the Vienna Psychoanalytic Society. Freud wrote acknowledging receipt of her membership fee.[13] He offered his approval of the way she had described treating a patient, but suggested they should not talk too much about Jung since she would always find ways of excusing his behaviour. Freud took note of her comment that she might not seem productive on the surface but was working on herself psychologically, to adjust to her altered situation. In the same letter, Freud inquired after Nikolai Spielrein, 'a man I found so interesting, even if inflexible'. Freud speculated that the war might have affected him very badly. He also brought Spielrein up to date with news of colleagues she had met in Vienna. Otto Rank, who had taken the notes when she gave her presentation in Vienna, was keeping the movement's journals going. Victor Tausk, who had read her palm and predicted a change in her circumstances, was attached to the local hospital. Wilhelm Stekel was not doing so well. He had edited the Vienna *Zentralblatt* where she published her recollections of her childhood fantasies, but it had closed down. 'After the flood has receded,' Freud wrote, 'we hope to float our little ship again.' Although the boat was indeed to float again, two of these three men would not be crew members. Stekel had by now already spilt from Freud, Tausk was not to live for much longer.

By early 1915, Spielrein had moved from Zurich to Lausanne, where she and Renata lived in an apartment for the remainder of the war. It was not easy to find medical work, especially without a Swiss state qualification on top of her medical degree. She took up work as an ophthalmologist in a residential hospital for blind people.[14] Then she found some routine work as a junior surgeon.[15] Her mother wrote disapprovingly, saying she should stay at home to look after her daughter.[16] Her parents managed to send her money from Rostov so she could make ends meet and employ a nanny.[17] Renata continued to be ill, with frequent coughs that her mother thought were psychological.[18] Spielrein tried unsuccessfully to take up a post in a sanatorium in the Alps. Throughout the war, Eva wrote constantly to her daughter, sometimes daily. She expressed worries about her grand-daughter, and beseeched Sabina to respond. Replies were infrequent.[19] At one point she wrote to her daughter: 'For heaven's sake write to us more often and in more detail. We have not heard from you for ages, apart from a small postcard ... Write, write, write.'[20] She reported that Pavel was talking of divorce, but at other times that he missed his wife. When Sabina sent her a photo of Renata, Eva commented how sad she looked.[21] Pavel wrote, but also had to wait a long time for any answer.[22] Eventually, his wife sent him a photo of Renata too. He admired how beautiful she was and asked his wife whether she was coming back to Russia.[23] After witnessing a mass demonstration for the first time, Eva described how much there was to do to create a new order in Russia.[24] Nikolai was convinced his daughter would find work in Russia, although he was cautious about the best timing for a return.[25]

Spielrein found inspiration in playing the piano, musical composition, and singing together with Renata.[26] She made notes on her daughter's development, including her ideas and use of language, which she later used in some of her publications. She tried her hand at writing a novel in French: *The Winds*. It is inexpressibly desolate:

O south wind! You are the image of my heart's passion. I was sad that I had to do so much thinking. I became aware of the vanity of all effort, and was weary. All action seemed stupid, and all dreams pointless. I was sad and discouraged. The treacherous wind strangely desiccated my mind. The sky of my imagination was gloomy and grey. My despair was without any beauty, because beauty is made from mystery. *Mystery has died.*[27]

Spielrein was a woman with many gifts. However, it does not appear from this paragraph that writing novels was one of them.

Even in Switzerland, conditions were hard during the war years. At times, Spielrein barely had enough money for food or heating.[28] As her finances dwindled, Eva advised her to pawn her jewellery if necessary, and then suggested she should borrow money from Jung.[29] A Russian military censor examined one of the letters and appended his unsolicited view that she should go out and find some work.[30] In 1918, Spielrein took Renata, suffering once more from bronchitis, to stay in a clinic in nearby Ouchy. Her friend Rachel Leibovich had also moved from Germany to Lausanne, and came to look after them.[31] Renata continued to be unwell even after her discharge. By the end of the war Spielrein was unable to afford the rent, so she and six-year-old Renata gave up the apartment where they had spent the war and moved into a pension,[32] then to a small village in the Rhône valley, and then to a private children's clinic in Château d'Oex, where she may also have found work.[33] Spielrein fell ill herself, with toothache and ear pains, and needed an operation.

There is only sparse documentation concerning Spielrein's life in the war years, reflecting the circumstances of the time, so any account is necessarily short.[34] She published only two papers while in Lausanne: 'The Unconscious Judgement'[35] – concerning slips of the tongue – and 'The Utterances of the Oedipus Complex in Childhood'.[36] Although she did not see Jung, she resumed correspondence with him in a long series of letters including some of her most original ideas, as the next chapter relates. Near the end of the war, she wrote to him: 'I am ready to become active as a psychotherapist, but where will I find patients?'[37] After the war Spielrein considered returning to Zurich. She contacted Bleuler again, asking if he could lend her a book, and mentioning that she wished to cite some of her work at the Burghölzli in a forthcoming publication. His reply was as courteous as always, but signalled how far psychoanalysis had diverged from mainstream psychiatry. He offered to look for the book and send it to her, but requested her not to use the institution's address: 'You know that there is a great deal of hostility towards psychoanalysis, and I must add that even the public prosecutor has looked into it on one occasion.'[38] He advised her not to draw public attention to the hospital in such a sensitive matter, although she could use a pseudonym for the institution.

In her correspondence with Jung, Spielrein discussed taking on the project of translating his works into Russian. Her motive may have been mainly financial. She wrote to Freud letting him know of this offer, and tactfully said she could also do translations for him in due course if he wanted.[39] She also informed Freud she was no longer able to pay her fees to the Vienna Psychoanalytic Society. He responded by saying she could defer her payments for as long as she wished.[40] He also mentioned a meeting with her brother Isaac – by now the third member of the family to have consulted him. The war over, Isaac was free to travel, and one of his first ports of call was Vienna. In his late twenties, Isaac was establishing his own career in psychology, and would have had a professional interest in meeting Freud. All the same, it is impossible to resist speculating whether he too raised personal difficulties with Freud: his parents' personalities, the tempers that made Sabina so fearful of him, or maybe even sexual concerns. One wonders what Freud made of the family constellation, and how much his understanding of Sabina increased, as well as his respect for her.

In response to Spielrein's proposal to translate Jung, Freud said he had no right to dissuade her, since she would enjoy it and it would help her make a living. At the same time, he could not resist the barbed comment that people usually only made these kinds of offers if it fitted with their principles. But there was other news to tell her as well: Dr Tausk had taken his own life. Freud did not spell out the details. In fact, Freud had turned him down as a patient just as he had once declined to treat Spielrein. Freud instructed his pupil Helene Deutsch to analyse him but then advised her to terminate this since he was using it only to talk about his own relationship to Freud.[41] Tausk's bizarre suicide – he shot himself having already tied a noose around his neck – followed the cessation of this analysis. Like Spielrein, Tausk had been one of the first psychoanalysts to take a serious interest in the treatment of schizophrenia.

Spielrein's father now wrote to reproach her with complaining endlessly about her illnesses. He urged her to move back to Zurich, take the state medical examination and get some proper work.[42] Russia had been in continual turmoil since the October Revolution of 1917. It was now torn apart by civil war. As the former Russian empire descended into chaos, pogroms against Jews became common again. At least 50,000 Jews were murdered.[43] Rostov was the scene of fierce fighting between the Bolshevik army and their opponents in the civil war following the revolution. The city changed hands six times between the Red Army and the anti-communist White Army, until the Bolsheviks prevailed in 1920. In spite of this, Nikolai managed to keep his holdings of property intact. Jan began to plan his return to Rostov from Berlin and wrote to say that his sister would be welcome to join him.[44] Eventually he went on his own via the Ukraine, where he had to spend nine days hiding from bandits.[45] Isaac went to Georgia, where he worked for a while as a translator for the Russian Soviet legation.[46] He then moved to Moscow, where he used his language skills – he now spoke eleven languages – to scrutinise newspapers for the commissar for foreigners' affairs.

Spielrein had certainly thought at one point about joining in this homecoming.

In her letters to Jung, she reported having a dream in which Madame Bekhterev, the wife of the leading Russian neurologist, was returning to Russia with a little daughter. In the dream, Spielrein asked her to write a postcard to Eva and Nikolai once she arrived in Russia, because she thought this would provide more personal contact than sending one from Switzerland. Although Madame Bekhterev was not pleasant in the dream, Spielrein felt she would possibly accede to the request. Analysing the dream, she was in no doubt that Madame Bekhterev represented herself. She confessed that she had been thinking intensively about whether to return home. The dream signified a debate about where she would be more useful, and whether she could establish contact again with her fellow countrymen. She suspected that Madame Bekhterev had not been so pleasant to her because she had neglected her duty. She realised she always vacillated over the question of whether to go back, and was worried whether Renata could withstand the rigours of such an uncomfortable journey.[47] Spielrein made no mention of Renata's father in these deliberations. One has the impression that she did not really feel married any longer, or even connected with her family. At one point, Eva wrote to say she had heard nothing from her daughter for a whole year.[48] By now, Eva was seriously ill with severe arthritis and attacks of angina.[49] The prolonged silence indicates how little Spielrein contemplated returning to Russia at this stage. Now that war was over, there were new opportunities for her in the west. She wanted to seize them. Before that, however, there was some emotional work to complete.

17

Your Best Pupil 1917-1919

I am only answering now as I have been in England for quite a while. The love of S. for J. made the latter aware of something he only vaguely suspected before, namely a force in the unconscious that determines our destiny, which led him later to matters of the greatest importance. The relationship had to be 'sublimated' as otherwise it would have led to delusion and madness ...At times one needs to be unworthy in order just to live.[1]

FOLLOWING JUNG'S emergence from his 'night journey', or breakdown, he and Spielrein corresponded once again between September 1917 and October 1919. Their final letters constitute a dramatic dialogue. As she did in the 'Transformation' letters, Spielrein tried to engage Jung at a theoretical level, but also at an emotional and moral one. She asked him to clarify his ideas. She pointed out how much these had in common with those of his former colleagues Freud and Adler. She also put forward original ideas of her own. The letters are especially valuable to us because she never published these ideas elsewhere. She also wrote of her own feelings, memories and experiences. Increasingly, she attempted to evoke some kind of disclosure about Jung's feelings for her. As well as being a self-analysis, the letters are an implicit attempt to offer him some analysis as well. The passage above comes from near the end of their correspondence. Jung appeared to be offering her some kind of confession.

There are twelve complete drafts and fragments by Spielrein, all of which seem to have been sent. There are eleven responses from Jung. Parts of the correspondence are missing, but it is easy to fill in the gaps by examining the replies. Some of Spielrein's drafts are as long as scholarly papers, covering up to ten printed pages. Jung's are far shorter, but he did give substantial replies to most of her points and queries. One of the main themes of the letters was Spielrein's wish to tackle Jung on differences between his approach to the mind, and those of Freud and Adler. Her approach was bold and may have been unique. She wrote from the premise that each might be correct in his own way. She tried to explore whether the three different views might be different perspectives on the same realities. She raised the possibility that the fundamental principle that Darwin proposed – the preservation of the species – might underlie the different drives that each of them described. She was, in effect, proposing an overarching biological theory that would make sense at a scientific level, higher than any of the three men's personal and intuitive systems. The letters are rich in ideas and feelings. This chapter offers a summary of what they contain. It would take a book on its own to do proper justice to them.

*

The correspondence opened with Spielrein sending Jung some of her dreams. She wanted him to interpret them. In doing so, she also wanted him to show how he distinguished between the 'personal' parts of the unconscious mind and the 'collective' ones that he believed were expressed in art and mythology, and helped to guide one's destiny. Jung complied with her request. He explained that his own presence as a figure in her dreams could put her in touch with 'hieroglyphs'.[2] In other words, whenever he appeared in her dreams it was an indication they were directing her to deeper cultural symbols rather than her own personal unconscious. He advised her to observe this 'language of signs': it would provide her with special insight if she deciphered it correctly. The following month, Jung interpreted another of her dreams. This time, his counsel was blunt. He told her that she was falling fall victim to 'German technical intellectualism and its brutal power'.[3] As a result she would cry in vain for 'the sun's golden magic, the greenness of noon, and the scent of the earth'. He described how contemptuous people had been about this work. They slandered him, and mocked him and tore them to shreds. In spite of this, he insisted, he would persist with them until everyone else realised they were sitting in 'a dark, airless prison'. Jung passionately defended his view that there was more to the unconscious mind than a sexual drive. He bitterly reproached Spielrein for failing to acknowledge that he had the answer to what lay beneath this drive: a collective urge that united us with nature. For him, the exchange was not just about explaining his ideas but a way of revisiting his dispute with Freud. The tone of his writing is menacing. His metaphors carry hints of the anti-Semitic stereotypes that were to emerge explicitly in the correspondence later on.

Undaunted by this, Spielrein replied by arguing for an evolutionary view that could unite the approaches of all three great psychoanalysts: Freud, Jung and Adler. To make sense of her argument, it helps to distinguish the drives that these three different psychoanalysts identified. For Freud, it was the sexual drive.

For Adler, it was the 'will to power'. For Jung, it was a drive to individuation – in other words, to fulfil one's personal destiny. Each of the men believed that neurosis, or inner conflict, occurred when the principal drive failed to develop in the right direction. Thus, Freud saw neurosis as the result of misdirected sexual development in childhood. Adler believed it was the result of the infant's will to power being inappropriately thwarted. Jung saw it as a failure to discover and pursue one's destiny. A dispassionate person nowadays might see no contradiction between these three ideas. At the time, their proponents saw them as totally incompatible. They felt this justified not only rivalry, but enmity.

Putting forward her own view of the matter, Spielrein wrote: 'Natural history recognises only two drives, the drive for self-preservation and the drive for preservation of the species.'[4] She suggested that Adler's 'will to power' could in fact be equated with sexual wishes. To illustrate her thinking, she used a case example. As she often did, she drew on observations of her daughter. She described first of all how Renata had learned as an infant to bring her father into the room by fits of coughing. Later on, when Renata was a toddler and her father was no longer around, she used the same symptom to get their male doctor to attend, because she enjoyed his physical touch on her stomach. Spielrein then described how Renata had been ill with vomiting, but was willing to lie in bed absolutely still and quiet, without eating, if her mother sat by her and called the doctor in each day. In each case, Spielrein argued, Renata was doing whatever would ensure the presence of a parental figure and physical contact. What sort of power did it imply, Spielrein asked, if a child would sacrifice 'tranquillity, freedom of movement, play with other children and favourite foods', in order to receive more attention from those whose love she wanted? She then explained the purpose of these stories:

To express my personal view, I would regard the instinct for self-preservation as contained within the instinct for the preservation of the species. The need to survive is thus inseparable from the need to die and be reborn again. At first, the instinct for self-preservation goes alongside the instinct for preservation of the species. With tiny creatures you cannot yet say whether, for example, they love the mother's breast because it satisfies the need for nourishment, or whether this love is already so emancipated that the baby loves the breast 'physically' for its own sake, or – what I think likeliest – because it satisfies hunger while providing warmth and calm. Thus physical contact becomes pleasurable, and this is already the beginning of sexual feeling. And the feeling of power? What is it except the need to draw more love and attention to oneself? And the feeling of insufficiency? You suffer from a sense of inferiority if as a result you feel you have less right to recognition and love. Then you cannot survive and you also cannot procreate.[5]

This was her most complete and confident statement of the biological underpinnings of the unconscious mind. She was arguing that all drives, whether for power, for love, for nourishment, for warmth and peace, serve one single purpose: what she refers to as 'the preservation of the species'. Some of what she said here about the infant's desire for the breast, and for maternal attachment, anticipated thinking from later psychoanalysts such as Anna Freud, Melanie Klein and John Bowlby. In fact, Spielrein went further than any of them. She was arguing that all behaviour is driven by the reproductive instinct.

What Spielrein was doing was far more than trying to bring about a reconciliation between Freud and Adler. She was proposing that these ideas could be combined to form a unified theory at an evolutionary level. From the perspective of modern biology, what she wrote was also absolutely correct. As she had realised by this stage, the instincts for survival and reproduction are not opposed in the way she had claimed previously. In evolutionary terms, survival is necessary for reproduction, and serves its purposes. We are all the descendants of an unbroken line of ancestors who managed to survive in order to be able reproduce. According to all biological thinking since Darwin, human endeavour therefore has to be organised around reproduction, otherwise we would not be here. In that sense, sex drives everything, just as Freud realised – although as Spielrein argued in her 'Destruction' paper, quite correctly, it is reproduction that is in the driving seat and not pleasure, as Freud claimed. Biologically speaking, pleasure is only the means, not the end. Similarly, as Adler proposed, it makes sense to recognise that individuals have to exert power in the struggle for survival and reproduction – although they have to collaborate as well. Hence the behaviour of infants and children might be understood within either of these two schemes: preparing to succeed as sexual beings, and learning how to exert power in order to do so.

Judged by twenty-first-century standards, there were still some flaws in Spielrein's attempt to draw these ideas together. She used Darwin's term, 'the preservation of the species', just as she had done in her 'Destruction' paper. The notion of the 'species' has now fallen out of fashion, since species cannot promote their interests collectively. These days, it would be more appropriate to place an emphasis on the continuation of genes, or of co-operative groups such as families, clans or cultures. However, it is perfectly possible to translate Spielrein's thinking into such a framework. This substitution of concepts is regularly used to translate Darwin's ideas into current terms and affirm their validity. The same applies here.[6] A more obvious flaw in Spielrein's case is her idea that the need to survive goes along with a need to die and be reborn. This is a hangover from the mystical way she framed matters in her 'Destruction' paper. It is understandable in terms of her own adolescent fantasies of abasing herself before others, and her desire to merge her own fate with that of Jung. It echoes the romantic idea of transformation through love and self-sacrifice. It also recalls the experience of losing a sense of self during intercourse. However, from a biological point of view, reproduction requires not death but survival.

Jung's reply was once again dismissive, but not because of any detail in it. Describing her views as fitting with her personality type, and containing an 'average empirical truth', he launched an offensive against her entire theory that was reminiscent of Freud's attack on it after her lecture to the Vienna Psychoanalytic Society six years earlier: 'It is inadmissible for biological psychology simply to cut the throat of a psychology of the ego.'[7] In other words, it was a mistake to look at psychology in terms of biology – murderously so. There is a letter missing in the series here, but its contents are clear from Spielrein's response. Jung must have questioned her motives for giving case examples based on Renata. Her reply was assertive. She pointed out: 'For a number of years I was one of your best, if not your best pupil.'[8] She argued that it was perfectly self-evident that, following a period of personal development, she should take an interest again in Jung's scientific progress. She then proceeded to explain that she had chosen a concrete case to find out if he considered a Freudian or Adlerian one correct, and how he would personally interpret it. She commented: 'It is really instructive for me that you and Freud accuse each other of the same thing, namely applying biological assumptions to psychology. Yet neither of you considers instinct to be biological.'

Following this unequivocal claim that the instincts must be biological – indeed, what else could they be? – she then proposed a view that brought Jung's approach more fully into the picture as well. She wrote how much she admired the way he had built on Freud's theories to show how libido, or sexual energy in its broadest sense, could be 'sublimated' or 'domesticated' into cultural projects. She wanted to know if he believed that suppression of a 'life task' could also lead to inner conflict, which would then be expressed with infantile symptoms in the same way as a sexual problem. 'Have I understood you correctly?' she asked, regarding her summary of Jung's approach. 'If so – I believe this presents a very interesting and fruitful insight.'[9] It was indeed. She had brought all the three main psychoanalytical approaches within a single framework. In terms of modern evolutionary theory, she had understood that one can make indirect as well as direct contributions to continuation, through participation in acts with collective cultural value.[10] The only problem was that none of the three men, including the man she was writing to, was interested in such a framework. They were interested in being told they were right, and in proving the other two wrong. Inevitably, there were parts of Spielrein's argument that were flawed here too. She tried to fit in parts of Jung's thinking in a way that would neither have satisfied him, nor have made sense in terms of the 'preservation of the species'. Yet what she was doing was still enormously impressive: looking for commonalities rather than difference, and unity rather than exclusion. She realised that psychoanalysis would only gain a scientific status if it was properly anchored in a system of thought that the wider scientific community subscribed to: Darwin's theory of evolution.

Spielrein used her next letters to explore Jung's theory concerning different psychological types of people, and his view of the structure of the unconscious. She argued that it would be sensible to divide the notion of the 'non-conscious' mind into two separate components. The first was a 'subconscious' one, consisting of all the ideas, images and symbols we are not necessarily aware of at any particular moment but can summon into awareness when needed. The other was a truly 'unconscious' one, consisting of the impulses that lead us to do things for reasons of which we are genuinely unaware. This distinction too is consistent with a modern understanding of how some things are out of consciousness simply because they would be too distracting, while others are more deeply hidden because they could give signals to others that would put us at risk.[11]

Up to a point, Spielrein's claim to be using dreams, personal disclosures and observations of her daughter for theoretical discussion alone was credible. From December 1917 some more private material started to creep in. She disclosed to Jung that she had tried to work as a surgeon in order to 'renounce any aspiration to personal creativity', but found that her 'desire for self-surrender' blossomed in the form of a passion for musical composition.[12] Further on in the draft, she became even more personal. She told him about an occasion when she saw Freud in Vienna with a dream about giving a lecture that was as interesting as either he or Jung could deliver. Her own analysis of the dream revealed her wish to create 'a great Aryan-Semitic hero'. Freud apparently agreed with this interpretation and found the analysis 'most interesting and profound'.[13] It is surprising that Spielrein had ever needed a dream to make sense of her Siegfried fantasy in this way. It is even more surprising that she was letting Jung know she had discussed it with Freud. She also described a recurrent waking dream where she constantly tried to climb up a polygon or mesh, only for the image to change into a beetle falling down into a spider's web.[14] Although she does not offer this interpretation, it is tempting to wonder if she was the beetle and Jung the spider.

Jung replied patiently to each of her points, but the more intellectual their debate became, the more obvious it was that there were personal feelings behind it, at least on her side. Her first letter of the New Year began exactly as she might have written to him in the old days: 'Since the holidays, the "Monday morning blues" have set in.'[15] She told Jung that his last letter made her happy, because their thoughts were moving towards each other and they might reach an understanding. She then began a discussion of the best attitude for a psychoanalyst to take with a patient. She expressed the view that Freud's recommendation of a neutral attitude was best for the average patient, since disapproval would increase the patient's resistance, while displaying pleasure would 'drench his desire with blood'.[16] She remarked that these two extremes were especially risky 'in an analysis involving a doctor and patient of a different sex'. She described how Freud had breached his own rule when analysing one of her 'Siegfried' dreams. Freud had said: 'You could have the child, you know, if you wanted it, but it would be a great pity.' After that, she said, she stopped dreaming of Siegfried. Spielrein was entering dangerous territory here. She was letting Jung know how much she had told Freud about their relationship. She was cautioning Jung against mistreating anyone else as he had done with her. Quite possibly, she was 'fishing' to find out if he wanted to resume their affair. This seems to be confirmed by what she wrote next:

> There are some people who for example fall in love, and then love and are loved by free, youthful individuals; others fall in love with older, married individuals and love only when they are not loved ... *What in the end, prevents a normally developed person from fulfilling their life goal? Fear of* life?[17]

Her thoughts were starting to resemble the loose associations of her 'Transformation' letters. She reproached Jung about some advice he had given her in the past, when he counselled her against devoting her time to musical composition. Spielrein then approached the key question she wanted to ask: how can one ever distinguish between one's true destiny, and a mere fantasy? Suddenly, it seems as if a decade has rolled back. Spielrein is once again like a fourth-year medical student, living through the agony of finding out that her lover's wife has borne him a son:

> Another woman had the boy, and I had a girl ... You, as a grown, experienced person, knew what at all the implications were. I was still much too young, and my first love and 'vocation' were too sacred to me to follow what you were saying and recognise the symbols that the subconscious probably produced to warn me ...[18]

In a postscript, she finally stopped trying to create the impression that this was a purely theoretical discussion. Admitting she felt some resistance to telling him personal things, she felt that 'you learn the most from self-analysis, and anyway, I have no other analysis available following your method'.[19] She was, in effect, asking Jung to offer her an analysis through their correspondence. Her next letter posed the question even more urgently.[20] '*The solution of this problem would have extraordinary importance for me,*' she wrote. She was still fascinated by Jung's belief that each individual might discover, through self-examination and dreams, the fate for which they were destined. Not only that, she still believed Jung could answer the question for her. Seeking an answer from Jung was fraught with problems. She was trying to mix theory with therapy. She was doing so through correspondence alone. She had the frustration of being only 170 kilometres away from him, yet could not see him in person. Most of all, she was seeking answers from a man she had once thought to be part of her destiny, yet who was certain this was not the case. Crucially, neither she nor Jung felt able to tackle what had happened between them, how this might have affected her, and how this might disqualify him from offering her any impartial guidance. As Kerr points out, Spielrein was really seeking only one thing from him: a confession that their love for each other had once been as important for him as for her. It was a confession he was unwilling to offer.[21]

Jung seems by now to have become annoyed by how personal and direct her questions were becoming. He sent her letter back, underlining all the passages where he believed her thinking was too concrete. He pointed out that in relation to the real world she had to be a musician, doctor, or wife and mother. But the task did not end there.[22] These were only functions, but if she did nothing more than perform such functions, he said: '*You have not therefore become yourself.*' He complained that she was always trying to drag the Siegfried symbol back into the real world, when it was actually a bridge to her psychological development instead. In his next letter, however, he returned to the racial theme. He pointed out that she could become prophetic if she wished: 'the Jew also had prophets'.[23] He advised her that there was a part of the Jewish soul that she was not yet living, because she still had her eye too much on externals: 'That is – "unfortunately" – the curse of the Jews ... he is the murderer of his own prophets, even his Messiah.' Jung seemed unaware of what such comments might mean to someone whose family lived in a country where murderous pogroms against 'Christ-killers' had taken place repeatedly for generations, and were happening there on an unprecedented scale as he wrote.

Spielrein, the daughter and grand-daughter of rabbis, responded with dignity:

> It is not only the Jewish people who murdered their prophet, but simply the fate of prophets never to be recognised in their own fatherland during their lifetime ... I must counter that there is scarcely any other people so inclined to see mystical and prophetic significance everywhere as the Jewish people.[24]

Having taken up the cudgels on behalf of her people, she then launched a passionate defence of Freud. She argued that it was unfair to reproach Freud with one-sidedness, since anyone who first launched a major theory first appeared like a king, and was then denounced as one-sided:

> Do you have the courage to recognise Freud in all his greatness, even if you do not agree with him on every point, even if in doing so you might have to credit Freud with a large part of your own achievements? Only then will you be completely free, and only then will you be the greater one. You will be astonished to see how powerfully your entire personality and your new theory will broaden and become more objective by doing so.[25]

She returned again to Siegfried. It was here that she explained how her inner conflict over having a child had almost played itself out in a miscarriage. She described the dream about Siegfried that coincided with it. After recounting this, she wrote: 'What happened was too profound and shattering; so that I cannot talk about it yet.'[26] She inquired of Jung once again whether any indication could be found that Siegfried was meant to be a spiritual child or whether it really was her destiny to create 'a great Aryan-Semitic hero'? But she also wondered if this was just 'a pathological attempt at self-aggrandisement', a form of 'megalomania' that permeated all her dreams and fantasies. Spielrein ended the letter: 'Many other questions are pressing for answers, but enough for now. *Please be kind*

183

enough to send the letter back to me, as it is one of the building blocks for my further development and I shall need it again. With best wishes.'[27]

Jung wrote several further letters to her, in response to her questions and dreams. Spielrein's letters to Jung beyond this date are not extant, but one can infer the contents from his replies. It seems she repeated the same questions in different forms. Jung's tone is increasingly irritable. In March 1919, he told her that her dreams 'have a threatening character and show a murderous tendency'.[28] In his opinion, this was because she had a materialistic attitude and should recognise the divine spirit instead. 'You are cursed if you speak against your own conscience,' he warned her. 'I hope it is not too late.' Apart from being both Freudian and Jewish, Spielrein had two others failings in his eyes: she was a woman, and she had betrayed him. In his next letter, he addressed both these faults. 'My mistrust is aroused by the flightiness of the female spirit,' he wrote, 'and its vain and tyrannical presumption ... How you must accept Siegfried, I cannot tell you.'[29] After repeating the warning that she would be 'cursed' if she followed Freud's 'sinful violation of the sacred' rather than the spark that Siegfried represented, he concluded by spelling out the consequences of not following his way: 'I kindled a new light in you which you must guard for the time of darkness ... Whoever betrays this light for power or cleverness will be a figure of shame and cause harm.' Jung's comments here were in response to Spielrein's news that Jan's brother-in-law, Karl Liebknecht, had been murdered by a right-wing militia along with his fellow German Jewish revolutionary Rosa Luxemburg in Berlin, earlier that year. In the letter, Jung offered no condolences. He likened Liebknecht to Lenin and Freud, for spreading 'rationalistic darkness' that would extinguish the lights of understanding.

This is almost the last letter we have of Jung's. His final one addressed his theory of personality types, but the penultimate one is the famous letter that forms the epigraph to this chapter. It has generally been taken as an acknowledgement that his relationship with Spielrein gave rise to the idea of the 'anima' – the ideal female image that each man has within himself, and that plays a central part in guiding his fate. It has also been read as an apology, an expression of remorse, and a confession that he pulled back from their relationship because he felt he was unworthy of her and his sanity might be at risk. These readings are questionable. Jung wrote of 'the love of S for J' but not 'the love of J for S'. In other words, the lessons he believed he learned were from observing her emotions, not his own. It is hard to see how he could find the anima from her feelings, rather than within himself. His own account of how he conceived of the anima, discussed later in this chapter, was entirely different. The 'force in the unconscious that determines our destiny' is not like a description of the anima at all: it sounds far more like Spielrein's sense of a 'higher calling'. Her idea may well have sown the seeds of his belief that each individual had a personal destiny – in other words, exactly what they were discussing in these letters, and by now the central plank of all his thinking and therapy – but that was quite a different concept.

It is also worth recalling that Jung did not 'sublimate' his affair, or return to his work and domestic life, simply because he felt he was 'unworthy'. He initially pulled away because he wanted other mistresses, and then stopped the friendship altogether because he was found out. Afterwards, he resumed the affair, unworthy or not, until Spielrein left him. Nothing he did in relation to the affair did anything to prevent 'delusion and madness'. Those arrived soon afterwards anyway, and another mistress helped him through it. Setting all of this aside, most of what he had written to her otherwise over the previous two years had been critical, and some of it had been poisonous.

As well as marking the closure of the relationship between Spielrein and Jung, these letters were also the last time she ever discussed evolution or the death instinct directly. After that, she turned her theoretical gaze to other questions, mainly to do with child psychology and language. Nevertheless, the concept of the death instinct endured. Two years later, Freud himself took it up. Responding to the scale of destruction in the First World War, and the refractory nature of many mental problems, he proposed that there must be a purely destructive drive in human beings, acting in opposition to the drive of pleasure.[30] In putting this idea forward, he added the following footnote: 'A considerable proportion of these speculations have been anticipated by Sabina Spielrein (1912) in an interesting and instructive paper which, however, is not entirely clear to me: she there describes the sadistic components of the sexual instinct as "destructive".' Freud's death instinct was different from the one Spielrein described. Indeed, someone took the trouble of amending the record of Spielrein's talk at the Vienna Psychoanalytic Society, many years after she had given it, to point this out, and to make sure she was not assigned precedence.[31] Freud did not see the death instinct as an aspect of the reproductive drive. Instead, he believed it existed it its own right. He likened it to the law of entropy, whereby the energy of any physical system declines over time to zero.[32] At the same time, his acknowledgement of Spielrein shows how her 'Destruction' paper set him off on a new train of thought. Freud's version of the death instinct became an important idea for some psychoanalysts, but was rejected by others. Jung dismissed both versions.[33] In later editions of *Symbols of Transformation*, he added a footnote claiming that 'his pupil Spielrein' got her idea of the death instinct from the mythic image of the

'Terrible Mother', and it was then taken up by Freud. In his view, there was no such instinct. The 'Terrible Mother' symbolised 'spiritual life'. These footnotes were the last time either of them mentioned her by name in print.

This was not Jung's final allusion to Spielrein, however. He described her once more, in the autobiography he dictated late in his life to the psychologist Aniela Jaffe.[34] The account is both recognisable and bizarre. Jung spoke of seeing a 'Jewish woman who had lost her faith' as a patient. The night before meeting her, he had a prophetic dream about seeing a woman with 'an unusual father complex'. The next day, the 'highly intelligent daughter of a wealthy banker' turned up for an appointment with him. She told him she had previously undergone an analysis, but the doctor acquired a strong transference to her, and implored her not to return since this would destroy his marriage. After taking her history, Jung suddenly remembered his dream. As the patient did not appear to have a complex about her father, Jung asked about her grandfather instead. She replied that he had been a Hasidic rabbi. Jung inquired if he was a '*zaddik*' [a Jewish saint]. She said yes, and explained that he was credited with second sight. Jung then pronounced: 'Your father became an apostate to the Jewish faith ... And you have your neurosis because the fear of God has got into you.' This struck her 'like a bolt of lightning'. After having a further dream, Jung saw her again the next day. He went down on his knees in front of her 'as if she was a goddess', and told her about his second dream. In a week, her neurosis 'had vanished'. If one can draw any conclusions at all from the story, it is that Jung's capacity to mythologise his past had become boundless. Every detail of the dream, from the wealthy banker to the instant cure, says a great deal about Jung but nothing about Spielrein.

In the same book, Jung finally talked about how he conceived his idea of 'anima'.[35] He described how he had become aware, during his breakdown fifty years earlier, that his unconscious was forming a separate, female personality. Jung recognised this as 'the voice of a patient, a talented psychopath who had a strong transference to me'. He did not mention Spielrein, nor offer any identifying features that might point to her. Subsequently, in his book *A Most Dangerous Method*, John Kerr declared this was undoubtedly Spielrein.[36] Kerr drew his conclusion based on some 'clues' in the story. These clues are highly tenuous. For example, Jung recalled how the woman's voice kept criticising his beliefs by saying '*It is art*', whereas Jung believed they came from nature. Jung said this criticism echoed a remark the same 'aesthetic lady' had once expressed in a letter. Jung explained that he finally broke with the woman in 1918-1919, which happens to coincide with the end of his correspondence with Spielrein.

Kerr took all of this as proof that Spielrein was the origin of Jung's 'anima'. In fact, there is no extant letter from Spielrein expressing this view, nor did she voice this criticism anywhere else. To address such objections, Kerr proposed that Jung may well have 'deliberately misreported' what the voice actually said. Instead, Kerr suggested, the voice may have used their private word for erotic contact and said '*It is poetry*'. It is hard to know whose narrative is more fanciful – Kerr's or Jung's. If Jung really did have Spielrein in mind, it is a pity that his last characterisation of her was as a 'talented psychopath'. It would certainly deflate any claim that he regarded Spielrein as his muse. In reality, we have absolutely no idea how many 'talented psychopaths' Jung broke off with in those years. It is most unlikely that Jung himself had any accurate memory at a distance of almost half a century. Here too, the description of a talented psychopath may tell us more about Jung than it does about anyone else.

As it happens, Jung also presented a case in his autobiography that he described as 'my first analysis'.[37] Yet again, it was different to any previous accounts, and definitely not Spielrein. It involved a woman who had suffered a paralysis of her left leg for seventeen years. After just one session of hypnotism with Jung, she threw away her crutches. The following year she returned to him once more, with violent back pains. After one analytic interpretation, these also disappeared, never to recur. Unaccountably, Jung had never described this miraculous case before.

We do not know when Spielrein stopped sending letters to Jung, but it was probably just before or after his last surviving one from 1919. After that, there is no evidence she ever made contact with him again. She may have finally taken his threatened curses – for being a renegade, a Freudian, a Jewess, and a woman – as a sign that she was not destined to fulfil her 'higher calling' with him, after all.

18

Geneva 1920-1923

We always have to bear in mind that the ancestor is sleeping within each child, and the child within each ancestor. If it was adults who invented language, they originally drew on the childhood stages of their own minds. Do children create language by themselves, or is it only something handed down by adults? My view is that the question should be formulated quite differently, in the following way: is the child a social being by nature, with a need to communicate? If he has inherited a need to communicate, and moves around among speaking people, then he has inherited a need for language, which he in turn will seek out and also invent. Obviously, if adults then proceed to help the young mind in its struggle, through their own talk and by imitating the child, they will encourage him to develop the speech mechanisms for which heredity has prepared him; in this way, mothers and nurses instinctively adapt to the kinds of language that the child is ready to produce; they feel into the young mind, and find the material prefigured in the depths of their own minds, from their own earlier stages of development, and they allow this to speak to the child in an unconscious way.[1]

THIS PASSAGE comes from the opening part of a paper that Spielrein published in 1922. She delivered it originally at the first psychoanalytic congress she ever attended, in the Hague in 1920. Entitled 'On the Origins of the Words "Papa" and "Mama"', it is second in importance only to her 'Destruction' paper in Vienna a decade earlier. It is also strikingly different. Instead of being rambling, it is cogent and tightly argued throughout. It is still that of a pioneer, someone at the forefront of the study of childhood and the treatment of its disorders. Freud's ideas are prominent, but they are not the only ones present. The voice is also one of modern scholarship and observational science. She incorporates ideas from the emerging fields of linguistics and developmental psychology. Some of her familiar themes are also in evidence. There is an emphasis on the special roles of women, and of mothers in particular. If the theory of evolution is not in the foreground, it is a constant presence in the background: it shapes the way she considered how behaviour passes from ancestors to their descendants, from parents to their offspring, and is remoulded in interactions between one person and another. It is also, in terms of modern thinking about language and childhood, impeccable.

We have reached the second of the periods that can be identified as the most creative in Spielrein's career. The first occurred between her qualification as a doctor in early 1911 and her marriage the following year. That was when she first appeared in print, with her dissertation and the 'Destruction' paper. The second period, covered in this chapter, began with her reconnection with the psychoanalytic world through her visit to Holland in 1920. It marked a move from one radical new field of thought and practice – psychoanalysis – to another: the scientific study of child development. It brought her into contact with some of the leading Swiss psychologists, including Jean Piaget. It was also the most productive of her entire career. As we will see later, there was a final brief period when she worked in Moscow alongside Lev Vygotsky and Alexander Luria before returning to Rostov-on-Don. At each of these times she was associated with some of the pioneers of European psychology. Each provides examples of the scope and originality of Spielrein's thought, but also demonstrates how her wide range of interests created a distance between her and her more single-minded contemporaries.

*

The sixth International Psychoanalytical Congress in the Hague was a tremendous success for everyone involved. Two years had passed since the Great War ended. For the first time it was possible to hold a truly international conference. The British Psychoanalytical Society was admitted, with Ernest Jones as its president. So was the (non-Jungian) Swiss society with Emil Oberholzer at its head. The schisms of the previous decade had come to an end for the time being – although Oberholzer was later to fall out with Freud over the question of accepting psychoanalysts who were not doctors. Freud was unassailably in charge of the movement. The list of presenters at the congress reads like a roll call of the people who were to consolidate and develop psychoanalysis over the next twenty years and more. These included Anna Freud as well as Karl Abraham and Max Eitingon. Two significant delegates from Hungary were also there: Sándor Ferenczi and Melanie Klein. In the official photo of the delegates, Spielrein was among them.

It is unclear what led Spielrein to attend after so many years on the periphery.

One factor may be that she no longer needed to fear meeting Jung. But her interest in the psychoanalytic world had never gone away. She kept up her membership of the Vienna Psychoanalytic Society, and maintained correspondence with Freud. She stayed up to date with the journals, and had made a few more contributions to them herself. Now the austerities of war were beginning to recede, it was time to join the mainstream again. She used the Hague congress to urge her colleagues to restore links with Russia, and to translate the proceedings of the event into Russian so people might have access to them. Her compatriot Max Eitingon supported the proposal. She also made an announcement: she was planning to move to Geneva, and to work at the Rousseau Institute.[2] There were doubtless many reasons for her choice. She could remain in Switzerland, where she had lived for most of her adult life. Geneva was Francophone, so she could work in the third of the languages in which she was now fluent – and was using to converse with her daughter. However, the presence of the Rousseau Institute was certainly the most important reason. It was a place where both psychoanalysis and biology were taken seriously. Above all, it was at the forefront of an entirely new field of learning and practice that would have appealed to Spielrein's passion for innovation and science.

The Jean-Jacques Rousseau Institute of Educational Science was founded in 1912 by the leading Swiss psychologist Édouard Claparède. Claparède started out as a natural scientist, and was deeply influenced by an uncle who was a follower of Darwin. He then moved into the field of psychology and education. In his lifetime he published over 600 books and articles. According to a modern successor they were 'striking in the breadth of their intellectual preoccupations, the combativeness with which these are asserted, their uncompromising moral vision and the wide range of social interests to which they confidently appeal'.[3] Claparède also founded the prestigious journal *Archives de Psychologie* together with his cousin Théodore Flournoy – the first professor of experimental psychology in Geneva, whose studies of spiritual mediums had influenced Jung.[4]

Claparède laid the foundations of an approach to education that came to be known as 'functionalist'. It was in essence evolutionary. In Claparède's own words, he examined aspects of psychology 'from the point of view of their role in life, their place within the overall behaviour pattern at any given moment'. He continued his explanation: 'It amounts to asking what use they are for. After wondering what sleep is for, I tried to see what childhood is for, what intelligence was for, what the will was for.'[5] Elsewhere he wrote: 'Childhood has a biological role to play ... One must therefore study the natural manifestations of the child and make childhood activity fit in with them. Methods and curricula gravitating around the child, and not the child turning as best it can around a programme decreed without reference to him; that is the Copernican revolution psychology urges on the educator.'[6] Spielrein would have found Claparède's eclectic approach much to her taste. Her paper delivered at the Hague, on the origins of language, suggests she was already taking a more panoramic view of the field than many of her purely psychoanalytic colleagues.

The Institute had a broad range of aims. It was intended as a research institute for child development, a teacher training college, and an experimental school.[7] Claparède was sympathetic to Freud. He saw his ideas as an important strand that could contribute to enlightened education. He had written the introduction to the French translation of Freud's *Five Lectures on Psychoanalysis*. He was president of the Psychoanalytic Group of Geneva and convened a regular discussion group on the topic. However, he was also critical of the field. Like Bleuler, he reproached psychoanalysts with sectarianism and dogmatism.[8] He had visited Jung to learn word association tests, and invited him to join the Geneva group, although he did not come. Claparède's interests and those of his successor Bovet ranged far more widely than any of the sects of psychoanalysis. The training curriculum at the Institute included many different areas of psychology, as well as paediatrics and that other fashionable subject of the time, eugenics. The Institute hosted the first international conference on industrial psychology, the field in which Spielrein's brother Isaac was now making his name – known at the time as 'psychotechnics'.

After gaining security clearance from the Geneva police,[9] Spielrein and Renata took up residence in the city. The then director of the Rousseau Institute, Pierre Bovet, acted as her guarantor. In February 1921, she gave a lecture on the infant's mind, followed by a weekly discussion group.[10] On another occasion she spoke on Bovet's course on the growth of the sexual instinct, presenting Freud's ideas on the matter. The following winter, she led a weekly course of her own on 'Psychoanalysis and Education'. She gave presentations on a range of topics including 'What children don't tell us', creative children, dreams and compulsions.[11] There were various notices of her activities in the *Journal de Genève*, including one informing readers that Mme Spielrein, 'a former assistant of Professor Freud', would be available every Tuesday evening for free consultation with anyone wanting information on educational and scientific psychoanalysis.[12] Her use of the word 'assistant' was more elastic than one would expect nowadays. Later, in the same vein, she also described herself as 'Claparède's assistant'.[13] Her exact position in the Institute is uncertain, as reflected in an inquiry from Emil Oberholzer, president of the new Swiss Psychoanalytic Society, asking if he should introduce her as a lecturer at the Rousseau Institute or just as someone running courses there.[14]

Spielrein's status was unclear in other ways. Some of her work was unpaid and some not. By December 1921, her mother was able to write congratulating her on having some earnings, while remaining concerned how far this would go.[15] Spielrein received a stipend from the International Psychoanalytical Association, donated from a private source and without clear duties.[16] This allowed her to represent herself as an emissary for psychoanalysis, something that did not go down well with everyone. Bovet described her as 'shy and tenacious'. He described how she arrived 'like a newly appointed governor in a province, like a newly nominated bishop in his diocese'.[17] Ernest Jones wrote to his Swiss colleague, the protestant pastor Oskar Pfister, asking him to inform Bovet about the unofficial nature of the arrangement and 'the lady's mentality'. It is unclear what he meant by this: possibly Abraham or someone else who knew her previously had spoken to him about her past. Freud intervened to prevent anyone undermining her in this way. Conceding that she was not an official representative, he suggested that they should treat her with gentleness. He let them know that she would shortly be publishing on the important topic of child analysis.[18] However, when Spielrein asked him to offer some 'therapy' to the Geneva group to make her work of promoting psychoanalysis easier, he warned her that this would be counter-productive. He cautioned her that all the people in Geneva were 'dilettantes', even Claparède. If he intervened as Spielrein had requested, it would provoke nothing but 'national-patriotic resentment against the old leader who feels entitled to play the psychoanalytic pope'.[19] In his view, it would be better in for her to educate them herself.

In spite of these difficulties, Spielrein gained acceptance in Geneva circles. The historian Mireille Cifali reports on the presence of appreciative letters in the Geneva archive from leading figures of the time in psychology, including Henri Flournoy (the son of Théodore), and Charles Odier, who later founded the Paris Psychoanalytical Society. One strong opponent of psychoanalysis, François Naville, wrote to apologise for his vehemence, saying: 'Freud is great. Spielrein is his prophet.'[20] Summarising these letters, Cifali writes: 'She is praised for her moral qualities, her serene stoicism and her intellectual qualities.' Spielrein moved from the Vienna Psychoanalytic Society to the new Swiss one. Just as Freud had waived her fees in Vienna, Oberholzer paid for her membership this time.[21] He invited her to give a lecture in Zurich on the thinking of a two-and-a-half-year-old, later published as a paper.[22] She and Claparède also seem to have had a cordial relationship personally.

In one of the most notable episodes of her Geneva years, the two went of them together to see the première of a play, *The Dream Eater*, by the French writer Henri-René Lenormand. Claparède himself introduced the play, while Spielrein wrote the review for the *Journal de Genève*.[23] That might be unremarkable, except for the plot of the play itself. It concerned a lecherous psychoanalyst – a 'Don Juan in the guise of a healer' – who uses the analysis to persuade a female patient, Jeannine, to become his lover. In the course of the play, another ex-patient and mistress of the analyst persuades Jeannine that she has killed her own mother through her unconscious wishes. She then supplies Jeannine with a revolver so she can shoot herself, which she obligingly does. Lenormand was fascinated by psychoanalysis and had attended Claparède's discussion group. He claimed to have based the story on personal knowledge but does not seem to have disclosed the identities of the people concerned.[24]

Once can only speculate on Spielrein's feelings as she watched the play. She did not mention these in her review, entitled 'Who committed the crime?' With typical earnestness, bordering on the deadpan, she simply defended psychoanalysis. She pointed out that the attitude of the analyst was incompatible with the method of Sigmund Freud. A true psychoanalyst, she wrote, would behave more sensitively and not invade his patient in this way. 'An astute doctor would have slowly come close to this frail and long-suffering soul,' she wrote. 'What a keen difference there is between this brutal invasion and the tactful method taught by the Viennese psychologist!' Spielrein's comments also revealed something of how she worked herself, by not imposing interpretations on patients until they were ready to understand and make use of them to forgive themselves, not to make their guilt worse. Spielrein ended her review by explaining that both analyst and patient in *The Dream Eater* represented a failure of education, and the waning of religious belief in society. 'We as doctors and educationalists are completely isolated in our efforts to win over the support, at least in the interests of the parents. We are consulted when it is already late, often too late.'

As Richebächer points out, Spielrein had moved on from seeing everything purely in terms of the relationship between analyst and patient, and looking more widely to education and social psychology for producing sound minds. Spielrein's view of psychoanalysis was by now a measured one. She wrote later to Bovet that the treatment 'does not cure anyone, and leaves everyone with their individuality'[25] – giving Piaget as an example of someone who had remained a mystic and contrasting this with another patient of hers who had remained a realist, in spite of both having been in analysis with her. The claim that psychoanalysis did not affect a person's individuality was by now a familiar claim, but the concession that it brought about insight without constituting a 'cure' was unusually frank for its time.

Spielrein appears to have offered short courses of personal psychoanalysis to a number of colleagues, including possibly both Claparède and Bovet,[26] and certainly Odier, who sent a note to Spielrein arranging to pay her.[27] In his autobiography, Bovet described how the Institute 'took an upswing' once Spielrein arrived and began to analyse her colleagues there.[28] Her most notable analysand was Jean Piaget, who joined the Institute in 1921, and whose relationship with Spielrein is one of the subjects of the next chapter. The greatest testimony to the interactions she had with colleagues is her prolific intellectual output from the years she spent with them. Between 1920 and 1923, she made a prodigious total of nineteen contributions to professional journals, more than she made in the rest of her career put together, and more than most psychoanalysts write in a lifetime. Her papers appeared in all three of the movement's journals. Most of them were in the *Zeitschrift*, the journal that Freud had founded in 1912 with Otto Rank. Spielrein's paper on the origin of the words 'Papa' and 'Mama' and two of her other pieces appeared in *Imago*, a journal Freud had launched in 1912, with the specific purpose of looking at the arts, literature and social sciences. By the time she left Geneva, she had also written two papers in French for the *International Journal of Psychoanalysis*, which Ernest Jones had launched to help spread Freud's ideas worldwide. Another French paper appeared in Claparède's *Archives de Psychologie*.

Some of Spielrein's contributions to these journals consisted of no more than a paragraph – a brief case description, the analysis of a dream, or some reflections. In a short paper titled 'Renatschen's Theory of Human Creation',[29] she described her daughter's ideas about the origins of life at the age of four. Renata had believed that humans reproduced by dividing: 'If Renata fell ... then there would be two Renatas ... and if they fell again, two more would appear from each of them.' Spielrein pointed out how her daughter had intuitively understood how creatures like bacteria or other asexual organisms multiplied, and had surmised this was the basis of all reproduction. When Renata was older and aware that children grew inside their mothers, she formed a different theory, based on cannibalism: 'Mummy, swallow me without chewing me, then you will die and I will come out of you.' Later on, she expressed a wish that her mother would die, but then quickly revised this: 'I wish that my mother was dead – no that she doesn't live and doesn't die. I want her to become a little girl again.' In keeping with her 'Destruction' paper, Spielrein saw in this an instinctive realisation that death and reproduction were intimately bound up with each other.

Spielrein drew on her notes and recollections of Renata's early years in a number of other papers. For example, in 'The Weak Woman'[30] she described how Renata wished she was a boy and could grow up to have a wife and children. She contrasted this with her playmate Claude, who had absolutely no wish to belong to the opposite sex. Other papers made it clear that she carried out psychological work with both children and adults, either at the Institute or privately. The approach she described was clearly psychoanalytic, drawing on the free association of ideas and the analysis of dreams. But she also drew on a variety of other techniques as well, including intelligence tests, physical examination and expressive play. In 'A Brief Analysis of a Childhood Phobia',[31] she described how she had helped a seven-year-old boy named Rudi to make a Mummy, Daddy and seven-year-old Rudi out of paper. By adding an 'angry, bad boy', she then made it possible for Rudi to release his aggressive fantasies safely. Anyone who is familiar with approaches to therapeutic work with children today will be struck by the revolutionary nature of Spielrein's work. Given the dates of these accounts, she was almost certainly the first person to develop play therapy with children, as well as being the first to combine psychoanalytic work with children along with the use of methods based on experimental research and paediatrics. These achievements alone might have earned her an enduring reputation had her later circumstances been different.

Some of her papers suggest a continuing preoccupation with the vicissitudes of love in adulthood. 'A Dream and a Vision of Shooting Stars'[32] described 'plump' Miss N., who dreamed of shooting stars that turn out to be rainwater running down a window. Miss N. found this transformation disappointing but also beautiful. Analysis of the dream helped Miss N. to reach the idea: 'I would like to have a great love, an immense love; I am so fearful that it will never happen.' Further association leads Miss N. to think of a man who is going to be her boss, who is rich but not likeable. Spielrein commented: 'the young girl is looking for a paradise on earth, a heaven of love, something immense and pure. At the same time she doubts if it exists. She has recently felt the torments of love herself.' Spielrein explained how the dream showed both desire and its negative side. The positive desire manages to triumph. 'When she discovered it was nothing but water, she was disappointed, but was comforted by the fact that it was beautiful all the same.'

In another paper entitled 'The Motor Car – A Symbol of Male Power',[33] Spielrein analysed the dream of a single thirty-eight-year-old woman who had never been able to marry 'or give herself to a man'. In her dream, the woman struggled to drive a car in the direction she wanted, guiding it with her hands from the outside and at times having to hold it back physically to prevent it crashing. The second night she had the same dream but was certain of reaching her destination. Spielrein explained that the woman wanted an 'immense love'. She had a suitor who had lost his fortune and tried to get a job as a chauffeur. 'She did not want to give herself to him and had great trouble in keeping the relationship at a level of intellectual and moral intimacy that she did not want to go beyond.' It is tempting to believe there is something of Spielrein herself here, not only in the interpretations but in the dreams themselves. It may be no coincidence that she was herself a thirty-eight-year-old woman when the paper was published. If the paper really is autobiographical, she may still have been struggling with the search for 'immense love' and keeping relationships 'at the level of intellectual and moral intimacy'. Like her earlier paper on 'The Mother-in-law', it also testifies to her determination to take a perspective that was feminist as well as psychoanalytic.

Spielrein also carried out some research. In 1923 she published an experiment she had done the previous year with fourteen of her students, to explore the difference between conscious and subconscious thought. She asked them to imagine they could pose three questions of great interest to them. She found that the ones that occurred to them with open eyes were abstract, existential, philosophical and moral questions, while the ones they wrote down some weeks later when asked to do so with closed eyes were highly concrete 'egocentric' questions, removed from socially adapted thinking.[34] She also wrote a paper about the Geneva Psychoanalytical Society, pointing out how favourably Piaget regarded psychoanalysis.[35] She reviewed a book by her brother Isaac about the use of word association experiments.[36] Three of her papers were particularly substantial. Two were influenced by her work with Piaget, and are covered in the next chapter. The other was her article on the origins of the words 'Papa' and 'Mama'. This paper is the focus of the rest of this chapter.

Her paper on the origin of these words is one of her most significant achievements, second only to the 'Destruction' paper. It goes far beyond addressing the origin of these two words. Indeed, it covers the entire nature of language and its relationship to the growth of the mind. Her starting point was an observation from the German Jewish philosopher Moritz Lazarus, a former professor of psychology in Bern. He described how infants become social beings through language. This was a central theme of the paper. Spielrein pointed out that human language does not start off in the form of words but of music:

The language of melody, music, in its most primitive form of rhythm and tone, comes a long time before verbal language. Well before the first signs of verbal speech appear, crying is a reliable way of communicating between the infant and its carer ... Whether intentionally or not, the infant at first expresses his state and his desire through differing rhythms, pitch, tone and intensity of his cry – essentially in a primitive, melodic language ...[37]

Spielrein went on to describe her observations of Renata as she produced her first musical communications. She noted how these were all attempts 'to make a tune from speech'. Later, when the two of them sang folk songs together, she found that her daughter associated one song with another not through the words but by the similarity of their tunes. From such observations, she formulated the views quoted at the beginning of this chapter: mothers 'encourage children to develop the speech mechanisms for which they are prepared by heredity' and 'adapt instinctively to the kinds of language that the child is ready to produce'. She then moved progressively towards addressing her key questions: Why do children of all races use the same comparable terms for father and mother? Why are these the child's first words? How does it come about that a sound produced by a child contains meaning? Taking ideas from both Freud and Piaget, Spielrein distinguished between three stages in the development of language. The first she called an 'autistic' stage: not in the modern sense of a disorder, but in its original sense of something being used for its own sake. She identified the other stages as being 'magical', because the word appears to conjure up a reality, and 'social' language intended for true interchanges with other human beings. Next, she took the reader through her explanation of how the child's first words develop. At the core of this lay her description of how, over time, the word 'Mama' gradually becomes associated with need and sucking, and the word 'Papa' with satiety and letting the breast go:

It is very important to pay attention to how the infant speaks these words. He does not at first say 'Mama' and 'Papa' but 'mö-mö-mö', 'pö-pö-pö': the vowel sound is therefore approximately an ö and the number of syllables originally unlimited ... The act of sucking is present in the 'mö-mö-mö sounds' ... But it is surely the case that the connection between certain movements and their accompanying sensations is already laid down at the earliest age ...[38]

Spielrein argued that there did not have to be clear images of objects in the baby's mind at first. They could be quite vague sensations of warmth, softness, liquid, fullness and so forth. With time and further development, the idea of the mother would gradually become differentiated from the ill-defined cluster of sensations, but the connection between action, word 'Ma-ma' and the object of the mother would persist. The child would then develop an 'I' in relation to the external world. Equally, the mother would subconsciously recall the experiences coming from their own childhood memories, and repeat the words lovingly while at the same time offering the breast to the infant. Hence, the cycle of language, understanding and development would continue. Having traced the development of language through these stages, Spielrein then returned to some observations of Renata, showing how children experiment with 'magical' language until they gradually discover the limits of what language can do and engage in more social negotiations with others. She ended her paper with the following summary:

The word 'Mama' (in baby pronunciation 'mö-mö-mö') reproduces sucking. The word 'Papa' (= 'pö-pö') stems from the phase when the satisfied child is playing with the breast. Both words owe their origins to sucking. Like no other, the act of sucking is fundamental to the most important of the child's life experiences: here it learns the bliss of knowing its feelings of hunger satisfied, but it also learns that this bliss has an end and has to be won again. The infant has its first experience that there is an external world; its contact with the mother's body plays a part in this by offering resistance to the movements of the tiny mouth. And finally the little creature learns that there is a refuge in this external world, which is attractive not only because its hunger is satisfied there, but because it is warm, soft and safe from all dangers. If we have felt once in our lives 'Let this moment linger, it is so beautiful' it was surely at this time. Here the child learns for the first time to love, in the widest sense of the word, that is to perceive contact with another being, independent of nourishment, as the highest bliss.[39]

One of the most impressive aspects of this paper is that Spielrein came up with most of these ideas while living in Lausanne, before she joined Claparède and his colleagues at the Rousseau Institute. We know this because the summary of her presentation at the Hague congress in 1920 set the ideas out in much the same way.[40] She must have worked on the ideas further during the two years before it was published, with her colleagues at the Institute and also with the linguist Charles Bally.[41] Nevertheless the paper is fundamentally her own and not of the 'Geneva school'. What is most impressive of all is Spielrein's view of the reciprocal relationship between parental attachment, feelings, language, and cognition. From the perspective of modern research, this is entirely correct.[42] Alongside this, there is the framework of evolutionary thinking in which Spielrein embeds this view: the influences that help the child learn to speak are moulded genetically by the 'ancestor sleeping within the child', but also through the emotional reawakening in each generation of the 'child within the ancestor'. It was the first attempt anyone had made to connect a theory of language with psychoanalytic ideas. It is also entirely consistent with a contemporary view of the evolution of childhood.[43]

In the course of her paper, Spielrein mentioned another female analyst who attended the Hague congress, Hermine Hug-Hellmuth. The latter was struck by Spielrein's comments. She exclaimed that Spielrein 'had taken the words right out of her mouth'. Hug-Hellmuth was the only other analyst at the time with a claim to be treating children.[44] However, she was not the only woman attending the Hague congress who paid attention to Spielrein's ideas. Anna Freud and Melanie Klein did so too. The two women were to become the pioneers of psychotherapy with children. Each of them moved to London in due course. Their theoretical and personal animosity led the British Psychoanalytical Society to split into three camps – Freudians, Kleinians and 'independents'. As many have pointed out, Spielrein's presentation spelled out an idea that was to become the core of Klein's thinking about the infant relationship with the maternal breast, and one of the most influential approaches to psychoanalysis in the forthcoming century. What Klein did differently was to focus solely on psychoanalysis, rather than to integrate other disciplines. Both she and Anna Freud were also astute politicians. Spielrein was certainly no politician. Where she excelled was in understanding that no aspect of the child could be separated from the other, without a loss of intellectual coherence, and of the full potential for understanding and healing.

19

From Geneva to Moscow 1922-1923

I had a didactic analysis with one of Freud's students. Every morning at eight o'clock for eight months. In Geneva. She was one of Freud's students from Eastern Europe and had been analysed by him ... Everything I saw in it was interesting. It was marvellous to discover all one's complexes. But my psychoanalyst learned that I was impervious to the theory and that she'd never convince me. She told me it wasn't worthwhile to continue ... She'd been sent to Geneva by the International Psychoanalytical Society to disseminate the doctrine. It was around 1921. I was perfectly willing to be a guinea-pig. As I said, I found it very interesting but the doctrine was something else again. In the interesting facts that psychoanalysis showed, I didn't see the need for the interpretation she tried to impose on them. She's the one who stopped ... You see, it wasn't a therapeutic situation or even a didactic psychoanalysis, since I didn't intend to become a psychoanalyst: it was propaganda in the best sense of the term, an extension of the doctrine. She felt it wasn't worth wasting an hour a day on a man who wouldn't accept the theory.[1]

THE SPEAKER here is Jean Piaget, in an interview with the journalist Jean-Claude Bringuier in 1975. Piaget was possibly the greatest child psychologist of the twentieth century, certainly the most influential. Here, he was describing his analysis with Sabina Spielrein. It is the only account we have from any of her patients, and it is doubly fascinating because the patient himself was such a distinguished one. His view of Spielrein was no doubt slanted by his own perspective and by the passage of time. Spielrein was not strictly speaking 'one of Freud's students from Eastern Europe'. She had never been analysed by Freud. The claim that she was sent to the Rousseau Institute to 'disseminate the doctrine' may be an overstatement – although, as we have seen, Piaget was not the only person to have that impression. Elsewhere, Piaget also gave a different account of how his analysis came to an end: 'I felt it was important to engage in a didactic analysis. My analysis was undertaken with a direct student of Freud's until her complete satisfaction. In the jargon of those days, I became a "grandson" of Freud's.'[2] According to another source, he and Spielrein laughed a lot in their sessions.[3] It is a delightful image, and reminds us that Spielrein, despite her earnestness, could have fun.

*

After Jung and Freud, Jean Piaget was the figure with whom Spielrein formed the strongest alliance of her career. His work led to fundamental changes in educational approaches across the world. The early part of the 1920s was the time when he laid down the foundations of his theory. He developed his research method of questioning children to assess the rationality of their thought at different ages. As well writing a number of crucial papers in those years, he also published his major book. *The Language and Thinking of the Child*,[4] setting out how children progress through instinctive to rational modes of thought. Like Claparède, Piaget's initial interest had been in biology rather than psychology. He completed his doctoral dissertation on the taxonomy of molluscs. He no doubt knew about Darwin's study of his beloved barnacles, which provided evidence to support of his theory of evolution. Piaget then moved to Zurich, where he attended Bleuler's rounds at the Burghölzli. From 1919, he spent two years in Paris working on the psychological testing of children. In 1921, Claparède invited him to join the Rousseau Institute. He was originally opposed to psychoanalysis. As a twenty-year-old, he had written a philosophical novel in which he accused Freud of 'pansexualism', a common judgement at the time.[5] Later, he read Freud and other psychoanalytic writing, and heard some of Jung's lectures.[6] His view changed as a result, and in 1920 joined the Swiss Psychoanalytic Association. In the same year he gave a lecture on 'Psychoanalysis and its relationship to child psychology'. The published version testified to his hope that the two fields could contribute a great deal to each other.[7] The Swiss analyst Oskar Pfister affirmed that the movement could 'expect important contributions from this young scholar'.[8]

Spielrein was ten years older than Piaget, but they had a great deal in common. As the historian of science, Fernando Vidal, has pointed out, they both shared an interest in childhood and the development of thought.[9] They were both determined to carry out disciplined observation and research in these areas. They were pupils and admirers of Bleuler, and drew on ideas he had put forward on 'pre-logical' thought. They each saw how important it was for child psychology and psychoanalysis to learn from one another. They rejected Freud's firm distinction between the conscious and unconscious mind, believing it was more useful to talk of a flexible 'subconscious', from which thoughts could emerge into awareness or sink into genuine amnesia.[10] They also shared an allegiance to a functionalist or evolutionary approach: rather than simply examining the nature of behaviour, thought or development, they asked what it was *for*. Each of them observed their own children closely in order to inform and verify their theories, although Spielrein did so much earlier. She began making observations during Renata's infancy from 1913, while Piaget started after the birth of his first daughter in 1925, after his collaboration with Spielrein.

As colleagues, they were generous in acknowledging each other's influence. Spielrein attended Piaget's course on 'autistic' thought at the Rousseau Institute, and quoted his work several times in her papers. They attended the seventh Psychoanalytic Congress in Berlin together in 1922, and gave papers alongside each other. When Piaget spoke, he mentioned ideas he shared with Spielrein, and announced the forthcoming publication of his colleague's 'very suggestive theory of symbolism' – which sadly never appeared. Later, he commented that the audience had 'only looked at Freud, to find out whether or not he was happy with what was being said'.[11] His Berlin paper was subsequently published in Claparède's *Archives de Psychologie*[12] alongside one by Spielrein making comparisons between children's speech, the unconscious mind, and aphasia – loss of speech following a stroke. Their separate observations of the progression of children's thinking were mutually compatible. As Vidal wrote, 'it is tempting to attribute the intellectual initiative to Piaget on account of his later stature ... it seems more accurate, however, to speak of reciprocity and exchange'.[13] However, while they wrote on similar subjects, Vidal points out, they also had 'serious divergences of aim and attitude'.

These differences of aim and attitude came to the fore in Piaget's analysis with Spielrein. By the standards of the time, undertaking analysis daily for eight months was a serious commitment. Later on, and certainly nowadays, patients seeking analysis might attend for several years. In the 1920s, people were still expecting to be seen for a far shorter time. Spielrein had complained that neither Claparède nor Bovet had been willing to continue for long. Oberholzer wrote to her about this: 'In a few weeks ... one cannot effect great changes: on the contrary, it increases the probability of a later rejection.'[14] By contrast, eight months would have been considered a decent period. Equally, there would have been no qualms about analysing a close colleague. Although this would now be frowned upon, it was not the case in Spielrein's time. Piaget's analysis seems to have focussed on helping him become more aware of his mental processes, rather than building any strong emotional bond or exploring the dependent feelings of childhood. He described later how he used his analysis to 'visualise scenes from the past, partly reconstituted ... but with a whole context including shape and colour – a precision I would have been incapable of at any other time'.[15] As the psychologist Eva Schepeler has pointed out, it was probably more of an intellectual exercise for him than a therapeutic experience. This may have been due to limitations on Piaget's part, as Schepeler argues. It may also have been true for many courses of psychoanalysis at the time, particularly when carried out with colleagues.

In spite of this, Piaget seems to have regarded himself by the end of it as a trained analyst. In the interview quoted at the head of this chapter, it is noticeable that he begins by saying he had a didactic analysis – in other words a training to become an analyst – before later contradicting this both in the same interview and elsewhere. On a further occasion, he told the editor of the Freud/Jung letters that his analysis was definitely didactic.[16] We know he undertook the analysis of a young autistic person and saw at least three other patients.[17] His approach to analysis seems to have been the opposite of the one he reproached Spielrein with having applied. In 1924, he offered to analyse a protestant minister, Robert Jequier, who was studying at the Rousseau Institute. In a later interview, Jequier described how he went to see Piaget daily for two months, lay down on the couch and talked while Piaget took notes without making any interpretations. According to Jequier, 'Piaget was not born a psychoanalyst, he was doing this out of interest.'[18] He also attempted to psychoanalyse his own mother in the late 1920s. Piaget's sister, herself a psychoanalyst, recalled how this ended rather abruptly when her mother refused to accept her son's interpretations, affecting him deeply.[19] Following this, Piaget's interest in psychoanalysis lessened. In his autobiography he wrote:

> Though this interest helped me to gain independence and widen my cultural background, I have never felt any desire since then to involve myself more deeply in that particular direction, always preferring the study of normality and the working of the intellect to the tricks of the unconscious.[20]

In his reminiscences, Piaget was clearly critical of what he saw as Spielrein's attempts to convince him of Freud's theories. This contrasts with Spielrein's own claim in her review of *The Dream Eater* that analysts should try to avoid confronting patients with unwelcome interpretations.[21] Spielrein may have regarded Piaget as a potential recruit to the ranks of active psychoanalysts, who would need grounding in theory, whereas he was simply curious to see what it was like in practice. Or perhaps, like so many practitioners, what she did was not exactly as she described. Whatever the case, his personal feelings towards her remained warm. So far as we know, neither Freud nor Jung made any attempt to contact her when she returned in Russia. Piaget evidently did so, although he was unsuccessful.[22] Piaget's critical comments testify to a view of Spielrein and psychoanalysis that was not just personal. By the time he entered analysis, there was growing concern in Geneva that Freud and his circle had become an unscientific sect. Just as Bleuler and Swiss psychiatry had walked away from psychoanalysis, the leaders of Swiss psychology – Flournoy, Claparède, Bovet and now Piaget – became critical of what they saw as its narrow interests, and its dogmatic adherence to one man's ideas. Freud's frustration with their 'dilettante' tendencies, expressed in his letter to Spielrein in 1922,[23] was reciprocated in their view of his approach as 'propaganda'. With their biological backgrounds, they could no longer accept the disconnection of Freud's ideas from any scientific framework.

Piaget's account of his analysis makes it clear that he regarded Spielrein as an entirely orthodox Freudian. He may not even have known of her previous association with Jung. Spielrein would have had no reason to mention it. Piaget was no fan of Jung. In fact, there is little mention of Jung's ideas in Spielrein's papers by now, and no impression that she held on to any significant remnants of his way of thinking about the collective unconscious, archetypes or personality types. Although it is impossible to be certain, his virtual absence from her writing from 1920 onwards (with the exception of some use of his association tests) may signify that by now he was out of her system. There may be further evidence of this in a short paper of 1922, where she reported a pair of dreams that were clearly her own. They purportedly described a 'colleague' who had terminated her own analysis abruptly, without resolving her transference to her analyst.[24] In the first dream, she had to pay excess postage on a letter containing faded photos of a man who symbolised the analyst, but was also by association a 'syphilitic Don Juan'. In another dream, she had forgotten her analyst's name but woke up with a quotation from Nietzsche on her lips: 'Was I ill? Have I recovered?' It certainly reads like an indication that she had finally laid her obsession with Jung to rest.

Two of Spielrein's other papers from this period give a flavour of her thinking. They also show how her emphasis was different from Piaget's concern with cognitive development. In 'Time in the Unconscious Mind',[25] originally delivered at the Berlin congress in 1922,[26] she described how the concept of time is acquired with difficulty in the course of individual development. She argued that time has a direction only in the conscious mind, whereas it lacks direction in infancy, dreams and the unconscious. Instead, it is represented there by space. She based some of her arguments on how Renata had developed these concepts. She also drew analogies with languages that have no time distinctions, and are similar to the language of dreams. She used her skills in foreign languages to compare Russian, German, French and English ways of expressing time, and to demonstrate how verb tenses in some languages express the linkage between time and space in the unconscious mind. This was one of the papers on which she collaborated with the linguist Charles Bally. It was the second paper in which she had looked at the development of language in psychoanalytic terms, and another example of Spielrein's enthusiasm for crossing disciplinary boundaries.

A longer paper, building on her paper to the Zurich Psychoanalytical Society, was her comparison of the thinking of children, stroke victims with aphasia, and the unconscious mind.[27] She recorded the utterances of a child aged two-and-a-half, also probably Renata, and analysed these carefully, showing how small children will tend to assimilate a new idea with a familiar one, rather than identify it as separate. She compared this with the speech of an aphasic patient whose misuse of words was affected by what he had just said. For example, he was able to say 'chambre', but when he was asked to say 'table' immediately afterwards, he mistakenly said 'timbre'. Spielrein took the same view here as in her paper on the words 'Mama' and 'Papa': over time, the child's language, concepts and intelligence develop alongside each other, through interactions and socialisation. However, with brain damage or mental illness, they can revert to more primitive forms. According to her, it was due to the spoken word that thought gradually became logical and adapted to reality, although in mental illness and strokes it could revert 'in some measure to the primitive thinking of the child'.[28]

For Spielrein, such primitive thinking remained a principal mode of thinking for humans. She believed that, harnessed to conscious thought, it could result in creative work. She wrote about the responsibility of the psychoanalyst to study non-conscious thinking in dreams, symptoms and children, in order to help their patients make use of this. Piaget, by contrast, was simply interested in how one form of thinking evolved into another. He argued that 'pre-logical' or symbolic thinking was destined by nature to be supplanted by better constructions of reality – or in Vidal's words, 'a danger to be neutralised'.[29] One incidental feature of her paper on children's thought and aphasia was that Spielrein described the use of word association tests without mentioning Jung. Comparing the two thinkers, Vidal is more positive about Spielrein than he is about Piaget. He argues that 'Piaget's distrust of subjectivity and the unconscious was in opposition to Spielrein's willingness to allow them to exist side by side.' In his view, Piaget tried to restrict himself to what he saw as objective thought and was possibly scared of non-logical thought, while Spielrein was not afraid to value intuition, 'or follow the meanderings of a thought which drew on subliminal life for its nourishment'.[30]

Piaget had talked in 1923 of hoping that he and Spielrein would develop some hypotheses 'together'.[31] By contrast, Spielrein wrote of working on the same topics 'separately'.[32] The contrast between the words speaks volumes. In the end, Spielrein may have decided Piaget's perspective was too limited for them to engage in a full professional collaboration. It is ironic that Piaget's ideas later came under attack from many critics for their excessive emphasis on cognitive processes. As Schepeler points out, students of Piaget's theories have often been puzzled by 'his treatment of young children as little intellectuals who construct cognitive schemas from their interactions with the physical world alone, without any apparent emotional exchanges with their mothers'.[33] There is a parallel here with the way Freud and Jung became subject to criticism for failings that Spielrein tried to correct by making links between psychoanalysis and biology, evolution, child development and observational research.

Spielrein's three years in Geneva were in many ways the most prolific of her entire life in terms of ideas and publications. This was in marked contrast with her personal life. She kept up a sporadic correspondence with her family in Russia during this time,[34] which paints a depressing picture of conditions there, but also conveys a impression that Spielrein herself was living in poverty and isolation. Sabina's youngest brother Emil wrote asking why the Institute could not give her some income.[35] Pavel suggested she should use her sewing talents to earn money.[36] Sabina sent him a photo of Renata, and his reply suggests how concerned it made him. He commented that she looked more like a young woman of fifteen than an eight-year-old girl: 'With her serious eyes, her fine features, her curly hair, her concentrated and knowing gaze, her pursed lips.' He continued: 'Perhaps it is not just the war that was to blame. Perhaps we were more to blame as people, not just the victims of circumstances and fate.'[37] Even if opportunities in Russia were limited, he argued, they should try to live together again. Renata wrote long letters to her father describing their lives, and this distressed him too. He lamented that she could not grow up alongside both her parents and her grandmother. 'It is terrible,' he wrote to Spielrein, 'that the daughter of two doctors should be living on borrowed money.'[38] He pressed his wife to come back rather than standing in charity queues and begging almost like a Russian refugee.[39] Seeming to accept that she would not come straight back to Rostov, he told her she could stay with either of her brothers in Moscow. Writing at a time when Renata was boarding away from her mother, he pointed out that Sabina could barely scrape together a few pennies to go and visit their daughter. In a poignant phrase that Richebächer used as the title of her German biography, he reproached with being impractical by nature and having 'an almost cruel love for science' (*Eine fast grausame Liebe zur Wissenschaft*).

In spite of her circumstances and Pavel's pleas, the idea of a return to Russia could hardly have been an attractive one for her. The civil war had finally ended, but had been succeeded by food shortages and epidemics, as well as hyperinflation. In Geneva, Édouard Claparède was leading a campaign for disaster relief.[40] The revolution had also had a dramatic effect on the Spielrein family. Their 'palace' of a house had been requisitioned by the communist regime and turned into a collective dwelling. Sabina's old bedroom had now become the family apartment. Nikolai was now in Moscow for much of the time, while Eva shared the room with her youngest son Emil, his wife Fanya Burstein, and their first son Mark, who was born in 1921. Pavel visited Eva there almost daily, and they looked together at photos and letters from Spielrein.[41] Pavel had tried to find work in Moscow, and to organise a trip abroad. Both projects failed.[42] He worked for a while directing a group of spas in the Crimea. He did some private practice so that patients could pay him directly with food. Meanwhile, Eva's medical condition deteriorated. She moved to live with Pavel's sister.[43]

On 25 March 1922 Eva Spielrein died. Nikolai was in Berlin on business. Pavel wrote to him movingly, praising her maternal loyalty and her ability to put up with his own moods, as well as lamenting that she never saw her daughter and Renata again before her death. 'She simply wanted to give happiness to her children, like an Earth Mother.'[44] For his part, Nikolai was philosophical about the loss, remarking that death and life belonged together.[45] His comments recall his letters to Sabina when she was in her twenties, as well as the links between life and death that fascinated her. Out of the five children to whom Eva gave birth, only Emil could attend her burial. Emilia had died as a child. Jan was back in Berlin. Isaac was in Moscow, and was refused permission to attend his mother's funeral on the grounds that it was a 'bourgeois' tradition.[46] Sabina had been in Switzerland for most of the past twenty years. We have no record of her reaction to her mother's death (see plate section no. 6). She had not seen her for at least eight years, since before the First World War.

By early 1923, Spielrein was no longer earning enough from private practice and teaching even to pay her rent, let alone for a consulting room. At one point she wrote to Pierre Bovet lamenting her inability to earn money, saying that she should not be left to die like this.[47] Whatever her success might have been in Geneva in terms of ideas and publications, it was clearly no longer possible to stay there. Freud knew of her predicament and advised her to go to Berlin. He pointed out the advantages of the low cost of living and the presence of Russian publishing houses that she could write for.[48] The psychoanalytic world there was thriving. Under the leadership of Karl Abraham, it was attracting people from all over Europe, including Britain and Russia. Spielrein's brother Jan and his wife Sylvia were still there. They now had two children: their first-born, Irina, and another girl called Marianna who had been born in 1918. Both Nikolai and Emil had visited them there.[49] Jan had written to Sabina, offering to find her and Renata some decent accommodation, and praising the progressive school Irina attended.[50] It is unclear whether his sister seriously considered this offer. Her previous experience of trying to make an impact there was no better than in Geneva, and possibly worse. Meanwhile, other Russian Jewish emigrants were making their way to Paris, London, New York or Tel-Aviv. In spite of knowing French, English and at least some classical Hebrew, there is no evidence that Spielrein considered these destinations.

Only two weeks after she had written to Bovet about her dire circumstances, Pavel wrote to Sabina spelling out her options. It was, in effect, an ultimatum. They had been apart now for nine years. Did she want to live together as a family – she, himself and Renata – or did she want to say a definitive 'no'?[51] He referred to a painting they both knew called 'The Unquiet Sea'. It showed a man at the rudder with a woman alongside him, trying to help him steer through the storm. 'What happens next?', he asked. 'Will the waves sweep them to freedom or swallow them up?' He conceded that he was not like the strong man at the rudder, nor was she the weak assistant. He recognised she would not necessarily settle back straight away in Rostov. But her brothers had already spoken about organising a place for her in Moscow, where she could have access to a library and pursue her scientific studies. Emil also wrote, urging her once again to come back to Russia: 'This is no longer the Russia of the Tsars, and the communists look on psychoanalysis very favourably. You can bring your ideas to reality in an educational environment.' He talked of developing psychoanalytic thought in high schools and psychological laboratories – ideas that were close to his sister's heart.[52] Emil himself had recovered from the military service that had seriously affected his health and was studying to be an agronomist.[53]

Their father Nikolai was himself in Moscow, throwing himself with characteristic energy into socialist causes. He had already written to his daughter the previous year to tell her about a new research institute for child psychoanalysis that was looking for specialists.[54] Now he wrote again about her prospects in Moscow: 'There is a lot of work here in psychotherapy, although you will need to compromise over food and accommodation.'[55] Spielrein had kept abreast of developments in psychoanalysis in Moscow. Two years earlier she had published an account covering eighteen of its leading practitioners.[56] She would have been aware there was a new Russian Psychoanalytic Society, and that an Institute of Psychoanalysis had just been set up in Moscow. In spite of all the difficulties the new Russia was facing, psychoanalysis was undergoing a renaissance there.

In the spring of 1923, Spielrein finally decided to visit Russia. She wrote to Freud, telling him of her decision to go to Moscow. His response was encouraging. He agreed that her plan was better than his advice to try out Berlin. She would be able to accomplish important work, alongside the two leading Russian analysts, Moisei Wulff and Ivan Yermakov. In these difficult times, she would at least be on home ground. He concluded by writing that he hoped to hear from her soon 'but would earnestly request that you write your address on the inside of your letter which so few women are inclined to do'.[57] The only other communication from Freud that year was a brief note referring a patient, presumably sent before he knew of her decision.[58] These are his last recorded letters to Spielrein.

Almost a year before Spielrein left Geneva, her brother Isaac – climbing up the political and professional ladder in Moscow – had used his connections to fix up an official invitation for his sister. It came from Grigori Rossolimo, head of experimental and child psychology at the First University of Moscow.[59] Spielrein now used this document to apply for a short-term visa to leave Switzerland temporarily. In her application, she explained that she wished to pay a visit to Russia with her nine-year-old daughter for a couple of months 'for scientific and personal reasons'. She enclosed a letter from Claparède testifying to her continuing value to the Rousseau Institute. Explaining that she would need to use a Bolshevik travel document in order to enter Russia, Spielrein added that she had no interest in politics, no understanding of it, nor any intention to remain in Russia. She stated twice in the document: 'I do not wish to stay there.' The second time she used the word '*keinesfalls*' – 'under no circumstances'.[60] Her brother Jan arranged for her to visit him and his family in Berlin, before progressing on to Riga and then Moscow.[61]

210

In May 1923, Sabina Spielrein packed all her diaries, letters and correspondence from family and friends into a chest in the basement of the Rousseau Institute. After spending the best part of twenty years of her adult life in the west, she did not see herself as a homecoming exile, but as an ambassador for psychoanalysis, who would spread knowledge of it in her country of origin for a while. She seems to have had no doubt that she would return.

20

Moscow 1923-1925

Sabina Nikolayevna Spielrein-Sheftel. Born in Rostov-on-Don. A non-religious Jewess. My father works in Rostov-on-Don for Narkompros. My husband is a doctor in Rostov-on-Don. My three brothers are scientific workers (one a professor of physics, one a professor of industrial psychology), the third works in agricultural science. My child Renata is 10 years old.[1]

IN LATE 1923, Spielrein was still in Moscow. She had not returned to Geneva after all. Instead, she had propelled herself with astonishing speed into the centre of Russian professional life. The details above come from a form she filled in for her employers: Narkompros, the People's Commissariat for Education, or Education Ministry. The form was a questionnaire for employees, asking for details of current work and feedback on job satisfaction. Spielrein completed the form in a typically conscientious fashion. She wrote that she was working 'in psychotherapy, specialising in psychoanalysis'. She recorded that since September 1923 – only four months after her arrival – she had combined three jobs under the aegis of the Ministry. As well as being a researcher at the new State Psychoanalytic Institute, she held the chair of child psychology at First Moscow University. She was also working as a 'pedologist' at a small town named, in typical revolutionary style, after the Third Communist International Congress. Pedology was a new discipline that began in America but become particularly popular in Russia. It was a science of the child that joined together medical, psychological and educational approaches. Given Spielrein's broad interests and her enthusiasm for working across disciplines, it is understandable why she would want to spend time as a pedologist – in addition to her new jobs as a psychoanalyst and university teacher.

When completing the part of the form asking her previous experience, she gave the following impressive account of her connections and credentials. It is noticeable here that she did not focus on her work as a psychoanalyst. Her emphasis was far more on her range of different skills, including psychiatry, neurology, psychology and art:

I worked in the Zurich Psychiatric Clinic (with Professor Bleuler) and in a domestic clinic (with Professor Eichhorst) but when I don't recall. I began to do research very early on, partly on topics I chose myself, partly on the topics proposed by Profs. Bleuler and Jung. Apart from my own work, I worked in a psychiatric clinic with Professor Bleuler, in a psychoneurological clinic with Professor Bonhöffer (Berlin) and in psychoanalysis with Doctor Jung in Zurich and Professor Freud in Vienna. In Munich I worked on mythology, and the history of art, and as a teaching-doctor in psychology in the Rousseau Institute of Professor Claparède in Geneva. I researched source material for the Niebelungenlied and other folktales.[2]

She noted down that she had published around thirty papers and had taken part in many meetings as a teacher, psychologist, psychiatrist, doctor and psychoanalyst. She also entered some frank personal remarks on her form. In answer to a question about property, she wrote: 'I have nothing from anyone.' She observed that had never taken part in political parties, and her objective was 'scientific work'. She said she was abroad 'from 1905 to 1923',[3] removing the first year of her emigration from the record. This was possibly a slip of the pen, or a way of covering up an awkward gap for the ten months she spent in the Burghölzli. She made a point of including the fact that she had studied harmony and counterpoint, and composed music a little.[4] In response to a request for suggestions to the administration, she boldly commented that her workload should be lighter, and she should be given more independence and allowed to have students. Presumably as a criticism, she added: 'In a psychoanalytical institute it would be considered essential to have the children under personal observation, so that talks with the supervisors do not lead to purely theoretical discussion and "platonic" advice given *in absentia*.' In answer to the question 'Do you have any scientific or artistic activities at home?', she replied that she considered her work as a doctor to be both scientific and artistic. Finally, in response to a question about job satisfaction, she wrote: 'I enjoy my work and think that I was born for this job, it is my calling. My life would have no meaning without it.'[5]

*

For anyone whose adult life has coincided with the existence of the Soviet Union, it is hard to think of Russia in the 1920s as a land of opportunity. Yet this is how it appeared to many people at the time. Immediately after the revolution, it opened up new opportunities for some groups in particular. Included among these were three to which Spielrein belonged: non-religious Jews, scientists and psychoanalysts. In retrospect this may seem a tragic illusion, since all these groups suffered terrible oppression later, along with many other groups and millions of individuals. However, hindsight should not prevent us from understanding how things appeared at the time.

Jews played crucial roles in the Russian revolution. Lenin himself had spoken out against anti-semitism in response to the pogroms that characterised the October Revolution and the civil war. The Bolsheviks removed all the civil restrictions on Jews. When Spielrein moved to Moscow, many of the leaders of the Bolshevik party were Jewish, or partly Jewish. These included Zinoviev, Kamenev and, most notably, Leon Trotsky. It was Trotsky who had effectively taken charge of the 1917 revolution, as well as leading the Red Army to victory in the civil war. He was now the presumptive heir to Lenin. Meanwhile, Kamenev was premier, and had allied himself with Zinoviev and Stalin to oppose Trotsky's succession. Later, Stalin was to kill all three of them.[6] Jewish secular intellectuals like Isaac Spielrein found no difficulty identifying with communist ideals. Even those who were dispossessed of most of their wealth, like Nikolai Spielrein, sometimes persuaded themselves that their losses would contribute to a worthier cause in the long run. They found new and productive roles under communism. Nikolai had thrown himself into school reform, as well as using his talents in agronomy.[7] The large-scale picture for Jews was more complex and sinister. Jewish religious institutions were closed down, violent anti-Semitic attacks were still commonplace despite Lenin's injunctions, and thousands of Jews continued to flee to North America and Palestine. All the same, there seemed little doubt that for educated, ambitious and non-observant Jews, the Bolsheviks promised a new dawn.

The position of scientists also appeared to be assured. Russia was far from being a scientific backwater, even in Tsarist times. The biologist Ilya Mechnikov had won the Nobel Prize in 1908 for his researches into the immune system. His ideas about the acceptance of mortality were among many that influenced Spielrein's 'Destruction' paper. Mechnikov belonged to a strong biological tradition in Russia. This included the pioneering physiologist Ivan Sechenov and the neurologist Vladimir Bekhterev, whose wife had appeared to Spielrein in one of the dreams she reported to Jung.[8] Both made contributions of worldwide significance to neuroscience. Like Freud, Bekhterev went on to acquire an interest in psychology and the treatment of mental disorders. He influenced and became a rival of another Russian Nobel laureate, Ivan Pavlov, whose theory of conditioned reflexes was becoming the dominant non-Freudian model for psychology. There were figures of similar distinction in mathematics, chemistry and physics. The Bolsheviks were determined to cultivate science in the interests of the masses. If the future was to be atheist, rationalist and progressive, science would be one of the chief forces leading this. For the Spielrein family, it was especially fortunate that their three sons had trained as physicist, industrial psychologist and agricultural scientist. Given the range of her medical and psychological skills, they would have had no doubt that their elder sister Sabina would also find a significant place in the new Russia – as indeed she did.

The idea that psychoanalysis seemed to face a rosy future in Russia is, on the face of it, more surprising and needs more explanation. Many Russians had travelled and studied abroad before the revolution. In the early years of the twentieth century, universities, spas and literary circles in the west were full of Russian visitors. Educated people took a lively interest in western writers and philosophers. Familiarity with movements such as psychoanalysis was as common as in Paris or Berlin. Aron Zalkind, one of the first to experiment with psychoanalysis in Russia, declared in 1913 that Freud's ideas were accepted more in Russia than in the west.[9] Freud himself had many Russian connections. His mother had lived in Odessa and his father had tried to establish a business there. When Freud studied in Paris, his closest colleague was Liveriy Darkshevich, who later became Lenin's doctor. Most of Freud's early psychoanalytic patients were Russian, including one of his most discussed patients, Sergei Pankeyev, the so-called 'wolf man'. Max Eitingon, now a member of his 'secret committee', was originally Russian. So was Lou Andreas-Salome – an extraordinary figure who inspired infatuation in Nietzsche and had an affair with Rilke before becoming a psychoanalyst and one of Freud's closest women confidantes.[10]

Before the First World War, psychoanalysis had thrived in Russia. In 1910, Nikolai Osipov, a psychiatrist who had studied at the Burghölzli, helped to found a journal called *Psychotherapy*.[11] Serbsky, the director of Moscow's psychiatric clinic, regularly sent interns to the Burghölzli. They came back using Jung's association tests, Freud's theories and a psychoanalytic approach to their work.[12] In 1912, Freud wrote to Jung: 'In Russia (Odessa) there seems to be a local epidemic of psychoanalysis.'[13] The war, revolution and civil war interrupted the development of psychoanalysis in Russia, but afterwards it was taken up with more enthusiasm than ever. Tatiana Rosenthal, who had trained in Zurich at the same time as Spielrein, and then worked with Abraham in Berlin, was now back in St Petersburg, promoting a socialist version of psychoanalysis. She had once exclaimed: 'What a harmony we might have with the combination of Freud and Marx!'[14] A whole new field of 'Freudo-Marxism' began to emerge. The historian

Alexander Etkind writes as follows of the position of psychoanalysis after the revolution:

> In the Russian mind, it was identical with the newest, most 'progressive' developments of radical social thought. Taken as a whole, this rational knowledge was perceived as being able to change history, society and human nature.[15]

As Etkind also points out, Trotsky was a personal supporter of psychoanalysis. He had attended psychoanalytic meetings in Vienna and was friendly with Adler. In a letter to Pavlov, he wrote that psychoanalysis should contribute to the creation of the new Soviet man and woman.[16]

By the time Spielrein returned to Russia, some of the pioneers were no longer on the scene. Osipov had left for Prague and never returned. Rosenthal had worked in Bekhterev's neurological institute for a while and directed a children's clinic, but then committed suicide.[17] A moving obituary in the *International Journal of Psychoanalysis* described her as '36 years old, the mother of a gifted, much-loved child, competent and successful in her profession, but her end came tragically by her own hand'. Despite these losses, psychoanalysis continued to do well. In 1922, a group of enthusiasts set up a Russian Psychoanalytic Society. They included four doctors, four professors of art, two professors of physics, two writers and a couple of administrators.[18] The man responsible for steering it through the corridors of power was Otto Schmidt. He was a polar explorer, astronomer, publisher, future editor of the *Soviet Encyclopedia*, and current member of the State Planning Committee and several ministries. He also headed a commission to explore the artificial crossbreeding of humans and monkeys. His wife Vera was already director of a psychoanalytic children's home in Moscow. Three of the doctors were practising psychoanalysts. One was Yuri Kannabikh, who had previously directed a psychoanalytic sanatorium. The other two were the men Freud had mentioned to Spielrein in his letter approving her decision to return: Wulff and Yermakov. Moisei Wulff had been trained by Abraham before returning to Russia.[19] Ivan Yermakov was an experienced psychiatrist, who became president of the society.[20]

Almost immediately, the new Society established a State Psychoanalytic Institute, with Yermakov as director. They took over a magnificent 'art nouveau' house on Malaya Nikitskaya Street. The house had formerly been the home of the chairman of Moscow's stock exchange, who had fled to the west. Later it was given to the writer Maxim Gorky. Vera Schmidt's psychoanalytic children's home moved in too. The Institute invited a precocious nineteen-year-old student, Alexander Luria, to come and work with them. He was from Kazan, east of Moscow, where he had already set up a psychoanalytical society with the approval of Ernest Jones and Freud. The Institute's activities quickly expanded to include a psychological laboratory, outpatient department, library, lectures, workshops and publications. In some ways it resembled the Rousseau Institute in Geneva, with its combination of an experimental school with a training and research centre. It also tried to emulate the institute that Abraham set up in Berlin in the same year. It was certainly more substantial than anything Freud had succeeded in setting up in Vienna, or Jung in Zurich.

There is no record of Spielrein's work at First Moscow University or of her pedological work while in Moscow, but her file at the Ministry of Education gives details of her career at the State Psychoanalytic Institute. So does the Institute's curriculum[21] and reports in the international *Zeitschrift*.[22] What Spielrein did in many ways continued her work in Geneva. She taught a course on 'The psychology of unconscious thinking'. She ran a training seminar for student teachers on child psychoanalysis and treated out-patients.[23] She read a paper on 'Aphasic and infantile thought' at the Russian Psychoanalytic Society, which was presumably a translation of her earlier paper or a revised version of it.[24] She also worked as a research assistant in the psychological section of the Institute of Scientific Philosophy, where she attended conferences and presented two papers.[25] There are indications of other things Spielrein hoped to achieve. She wrote that she planned to finish two new articles on symbolic thinking – the same intention she declared while at the Rousseau Institute. Once again, it remained unrealised. The Russian psychoanalyst Viktor Ovcharenko believes she was planning a major study based on her work with children,[26] but this too never happened. As editor of a periodical called *Psychology and Marxism*, Luria drafted a contents list for a future volume featuring an article with Spielrein as one of the authors: 'The problem of the unconscious in contemporary psychology in Marxism'. Neither the volume nor the article ever appeared. Etkind speculates that Spielrein was probably contemptuous of her colleagues' servile attempts to toe the party line with a 'mishmash' of Freudian thought and Marxist-Leninist ideology. She published nothing while in Moscow.

Within the State Psychoanalytic Institute, the department to which Spielrein was mainly attached was Vera Schmidt's Children's House, also known as the 'orphanage-laboratory'. The home had been founded in 1921, intended to be not only an orphanage but also an experimental school and laboratory for research into child development. It was supported from a variety of sources, including a

German trade union, and hence bore the additional title of the 'International Solidarity Laboratory'.[27] Luria submitted an account of it to the *Zeitschrift* that may have influenced Anna Freud when she later set up a children's clinic in London.[28] Vera and Otto Schmidt's own son Vladimir lived there. He described how they lived in groups of seven or eight children, and said that everyone in his group called Vera 'Mama'. They spent most of the day in the playroom, and were allowed to develop freely 'without having to suppress their feelings'.[29] Vladimir may have had a rose-tinted memory of the place, since 'Mama' really was his mother. In reality, almost from its outset, the school seems to have become part of the surreal make-believe that was already becoming routine in Soviet life and was soon to define it. Despite its theoretical purpose of looking after orphans and carrying out research, it mainly functioned as a boarding home for the children of communist grandees. Yermakov, the director of the Institute, wrote tactfully: 'Most of them are the children of party officials who spend most of their time doing important Party work, and are therefore unable to raise children.'[30] Luria confirmed many years later that the home largely took care of the children of the politically powerful, including Stalin's son Vasily.[31] In the two years before Spielrein arrived, the staff had dwindled from fifty-one to eighteen, while the number of children was halved from twenty-four to twelve.[32] As Etkind remarks, the apparatus of psychoanalysis, scientific observation and academic oversight had become 'in part a cover for privilege, in part fashionable practice'.[33]

As director, Yermakov had declared his positive intentions for the home. He advised his staff: 'In order that the child might reveal himself fully, we must create an atmosphere of total trust and respect on the part of the adult towards the child, as well as vice versa.'[34] He also drew up careful rules of conduct and a research plan for studying the children daily, including their games, fears, dreams and art. All staff were meant to undergo analysis themselves 'to nullify the injurious effects of their own complexes on the work'.[35] In practice, little or none of this was implemented. The comments that Spielrein wrote in her employee questionnaire presumably reflected her frustration when she discovered the gap between declared intentions and Soviet reality. The 'purely theoretical discussion and "platonic" advice given *in absentia*' that she described may have been a euphemism for practices she regarded as unacceptable from the moment she arrived. Her requests to have a lighter workload, more independence and some students may well have reflected intolerable working conditions.

As well as being fraught with deception, the Children's House was also at the heart of some major, at times farcical, political battles. The home had already been subject to several critical inspections by the time Spielrein arrived, and it was now on probation. While Spielrein was there, a commission at the Ministry proposed a further inspection, with Spielrein herself and Luria as consultants. It sounds from this that at least one faction within the Ministry was genuinely concerned to raise standards in the home. However, as soon as the plan was agreed, it was immediately aborted. The commission was reconvened the same day under a more senior chairman, and ratified a totally different plan. In resounding communist rhetoric, they affirmed the Children's House had 'great pedagogical value ... unique not only in Russia but in Europe as well'. They noted its vital role in pursuing 'methods of forming a personality that is socially valuable'.[36] They recommended that Marxists 'should have a guiding influence on its work' and the 'proletarian contingent' among the children should be strengthened. There was to be no further inspection, and no opportunity for Spielrein and Luria to say what they thought should be done. Etkind believes that only Trotsky himself could have engineered this resolution with such speed, authority, and openly anti-elitist wording.[37] Etkind's case is compelling. Trotsky's presumed intervention took place September 1923 when he was at the height of his power. He was a strong supporter of psychoanalysis, but principally as a means for producing 'socially valuable' personalities. He would presumably have had little interest in the kinds of training standards that Spielrein might have promoted.

Whether or not more proletarian children were enrolled, conditions for the staff went from bad to worse. The following summer, seven teachers wrote a letter of complaint to Otto Schmidt as overall custodian of the school. They said they received no training for the kind of psychoanalytic work they were meant to do. They spoke of their inability to manage the 'transference' from the children. They described how they were being invited to promote strong emotional bonds with the children in their charge, without having the skills to deal with the consequences. They requested that the orphanage should be 'run by someone with more social and educational experience', possibly meaning it should be Spielrein. They asked for proper courses to retrain the staff, with temporary staff engaged to provide cover. They also wrote of their strong dislike for the director of the Institute, Yermakov. They described his lack of respect for their personalities as teachers. Their letter reported total disorganisation at the home, lack of continuity of research, and a turnover of fifty teachers in three years: in short, their 'massive dissatisfaction' with 'an unbelievably difficult atmosphere'.[38] Otto Schmidt and the Russian Psychoanalytic Society immediately distanced themselves from the home, saying they were still willing to train the teachers if asked, but not to administer the place any more.

Within a few months, at the end of 1924, all the teachers were sacked. Otto Schmidt now wrote to the Ministry washing his hands entirely of any responsibility for the Children's House.[39] He explained that 'as the children grew older ... the lack of teachers with psychoanalytic training began to have a more marked effect'. He also pointed out that the political decision the previous year had put it into the hands of the Ministry which had 'moved to utilise the well-situated orphanage as a laboratory not only for psychoanalytic experiments but for all kinds of scientific and educational institutions'. This left the psychoanalysts at the Institute with 'practically no influence'. Understanding such opaque Soviet communications is never easy. However, from Schmidt's account it is clear that the children were behaving badly, and the school had been turned into a political experiment. The comment about the children's behaviour evidently alluded to sexual matters. Rumours were circulating that the children were being subjected to experiments to stimulate premature sexuality. Another inspection took place, reporting that 'sexual phenomena such as masturbation have been observed in most of the children living at the orphanage, while masturbation has not been observed in children just entering the orphanage from families'.[40] There is a certain tragi-comic aspect to this. The children had almost certainly masturbated unobserved at home, as children do. The degree to which they indulged in this would have been increased by prolonged separation from their parents, under the care of untrained staff. The pathological personalities of some of the Party leaders who left their children at the home may have been a factor too. It might not be far-fetched to imagine that the death sentence for the home was sealed when Stalin unexpectedly came across four-year-old Vasily playing compulsively with his penis.[41] However, behind the commission's report one can also sense the same stereotypes of psychoanalysis that had surfaced in many places, including Switzerland: it was connected with licentiousness and immorality.

As for the political problems, Schmidt's report makes it clear that the school had gone in the direction that Trotsky had decreed. Instead of being a centre of excellence for the all-round psychological care of children, it became an experimental laboratory for the production of the new Soviet toddler. At the same time as this was happening, Trotsky's star was waning. Lenin had died in January 1924, and behind the scenes political attacks on Trotsky were becoming outspoken. However much authority his directives had carried the previous year, they were rapidly becoming worthless. Otto Schmidt presumably knew which way the wind was blowing. He would not have criticised the previous year's decision if it was going to damage his career. His judgement was correct. The Children's House was immediately separated from the Institute as he requested.

Unfortunately, without Trotsky's protection, not only the Children's House but psychoanalysis itself was now vulnerable. The Ministry's next decision was to move the Institute of Psychoanalysis to St Petersburg, now known as Leningrad, and to merge it with the Psychological Institute there – an entirely different organisation taking a Pavlovian approach. The merger never happened. In the summer of 1925, the Greater Council of Ministers resolved: 'The Psychoanalytic Institute and International Solidarity Laboratory are to be liquidated.'[42] Trotsky's vision of psychoanalysis as a potential force for creating the new Soviet man no longer had any influence. As in other areas of Soviet life, it was being supplanted by Stalin's world view.

Whether or not Stalin played a direct part in the liquidation of the Children's House is unknown. Since his son had been among the children who lived there, this could scarcely have happened without his knowledge and consent. If the home was going in a Trotskyist direction, it would be doomed anyway. The decision to abolish the Institute along with it is certainly consistent with the triumph of Stalin's despotic vision of communism as opposed to Trotsky's one of continuing revolution. Henceforth, the healthy Bolshevik personality would result not from individual enlightenment, but from correct ideology and social control. For the time being, the Russian Psychoanalytic Society was left intact, but the writing was on the wall. Otto Schmidt and several others began to distance themselves from psychoanalysis. Spielrein's experience at the Children's House must have been awful. For a woman who had no interest at all in politics, the closeness of the Institute and Children's House to the leaders of the revolution must have been distasteful. The nightmarish conditions of the home, with its desperate and untrained teachers, all trying to cope with the disturbed offspring of communist party bosses, must have seemed like some grotesque antitype of the Burghölzli. We will never know what part she played in their protest, what she may have heard privately from some of the teachers, or heard of the narratives they brought to her before they were sacked. The rivalries she had encountered in the west were trivial compared with those in Moscow. Many were to end in execution or murder as Stalin rapidly took the reins of power.

We know little of Spielrein's private life during her time in Moscow, but it may have been similar to how it was in Geneva. A story from the time suggests it was an unhappy experience for Renata. Isaac's daughter Menikha recalled her coming to stay with them in Moscow – possibly because Sabina was unable to look after her daughter while she worked. Menikha said her mother thought Renata was strange and not a good influence. On one occasion, Sabina even asked Menikha's mother Rakhil what she should do because she was worried about Renata's behaviour and her lying, and thought she lived too much in her own fantasy world.[43] At some point during late 1924 or early 1925, Spielrein left Moscow for Rostov. In Luria's report in the *Zeitschrift* in 1925 there is no mention of the children's home, nor of Spielrein.[44] Her departure may have coincided with its closure. However, she left an intellectual legacy behind her in Moscow. Alexander Luria, already a rising star, went on to become one of the greatest neuropsychologists of the twentieth century. His friend Lev Vygotsky, who came to Moscow in 1924, was to equal if not exceed Piaget in importance as a developmental psychologist. Together, Luria and Vygotsky have been described as the Beethoven and Mozart of psychology.[45] Luria is renowned for combining a 'classical' objective and neurological approach to psychology with a 'romantic' one – namely drawing on subjective data and psychoanalytic ideas.[46] This description of his approach defines what many researchers now regard as the most exciting area of neuroscience – the intersection between mind and brain.[47] It is also close to the approach Spielrein had already been following for the previous few years.

With regard to Lev Vygotsky's ideas, Etkind has examined how these reflected Spielrein's. He points out how Spielrein emphasised medical and psychological work with children, while Lev Vygotsky began to do exactly the same after he came to Moscow. Having not produced a single major psychological work before 1924, Vygotsky suddenly produced six in that year. Vygotsky went on to create a psychology that described the relationship between language and thought. He argued that normal child development depended on the child's ability to internalise personal relationships and wider social influences. This has formed the basis of most contemporary thinking about normal and abnormal child development. It echoes Spielrein's combined interest in mother-infant relationships and the social origins of language. Etkind speculated that both Luria and Vygotsky may have attended her course at the Institute. Many years later, Piaget was to acknowledge Vygotsky's originality in developing his ideas.[48] He did not name Spielrein as the 'missing link' between him and his Russian colleague, but more recent scholars have done so.[49] Both Luria and Vygotsky also failed to pay tribute to Spielrein, but in a far more pointed way. In 1925, they jointly wrote the introduction to the Russian translation of Freud's *Beyond the Pleasure Principle*. In doing so, they nailed their banners to the Soviet mast:

Here in Russia, Freudianism commands exceptional attention not only in scholarly circles, but among the reading public at large ... Before our very eyes, a new, original psychoanalytic trend is unfolding in Russia, in an attempt to achieve a synthesis of Freudianism and Marxism with the help of [Pavlov's] conditioned reflex theory.[50]

As Etkind points out, one thing must have struck them more than any other on reading *Beyond the Pleasure Principle*. This was Freud's acknowledgement of Sabina Spielrein as the person who gave him the idea of the death instinct. They would have been fully aware that the founder of psychoanalysis had named her as the person who had prompted him to produce one of his most important concepts. Inexplicably, they made no mention of this, nor of her. It is hard to resist the conclusion that they wished to distance themselves from her. We do not know why they did so. Perhaps she left Moscow with disdain for the untrained psychoanalytic establishment of which they were part. Maybe there were personal animosities. More likely, both of them knew which names it would profit them politically to include in fulsome tributes, and which it would be irrelevant to mention. Sabina Spielrein had joined the ranks of the politically irrelevant.

21

Back in Rostov 1925-1942

Freud's teachings are more far-reaching than any of his detractors or followers. For around the past ten years, Freud has defined neurosis as a social disability and an unsuccessful attempt to make contact with the environment. He has repeatedly said that many neuroses could be prevented if it were possible to change the social situation that has triggered repression.[1]

THE PASSAGE above comes from an address Spielrein gave in 1929 to a conference of psychiatrists and neurologists. She had worked for the previous four years as a pedologist in her home town of Rostov-on-Don, combining it with other work as a psychiatrist. Here, she was mounting a learned and articulate defence of Freud. She was challenging the view of Freud that was now official in the Soviet Union: namely that he paid attention only to the personal, and took no interest in changing the social circumstances in which children were raised. The lecture reads as a 'tour de force'. It completely puts paid to any notion that Spielrein's years in Rostov were a disappointing anti-climax to the rest of her career. Her voice was clear and authoritative. The lecture does not suggest she made any attempt to conceal her past connections. It shows no evidence that she was intellectually dulled, or politically cowed, or that she had stopped seeing herself as part of the movement in which she had played a central formative role. This was probably the last public presentation Spielrein gave. It may well have been the last time anyone spoke publicly in support of psychoanalysis in the Soviet Union for the next fifty years. In Moscow, the ideological battles that surrounded the Children's House had intensified, and had virtually destroyed psychoanalysis in Russia.

Apart from an earlier lecture that was eventually published in 1931, we have no more records of anything that Spielrein wrote after this date. Subsequently, this silence led many in the west to assume she had died during those years. Since her rediscovery, this silence has presented a particular challenge to biographers. It is only thanks to the persistence of researchers such as Ljunggren, Etkind and Richebächer, who searched the archives and interviewed surviving relatives and friends, that we know anything about her later years. The paucity of the record is in marked contrast to her youth, and emphasises how precious her earlier diaries and letters are. During her time in Rostov there must have been many events, friendships, conversations and celebrations about which we know nothing. If we did, her biography would be at least half as long again.

*

In some ways it is puzzling that Spielrein decided to return to Rostov-on-Don rather than to the west. In the nine years since Pavel had gone back, she had met with many opportunities to follow him. She had never done so. Only two years previously, she had the firm intention of returning to Switzerland. The practicalities and politics of doing so would have been challenging but not insuperable. Emigration was not banned until 1926. Although she had never made a proper living in Switzerland, there were many other places in the west she might have chosen. In the end, the main reason for going to Rostov may actually have been straightforward. On 18 August 1924,[2] Pavel had a daughter by another woman, Olga Vasilyevna Snetkova (see plate section no. 12). Born Olga Aksyuk, she was a doctor of Ukrainian origin and a war widow. Effectively, Pavel had followed through the ultimatum he had sent her the previous year: either return or agree on a divorce. Olga was not Jewish. Nor, according to religious law, was their new baby, Nina. The 'Aryan-Semitic' child Sabina had once hoped to bear was now a reality, but born to her husband rather than herself. Since Spielrein had vacillated for so many years, it is unlikely to have been a coincidence that she now went home.

Pavel left Olga and their baby straight away and returned to Spielrein and Renata. Olga departed shortly afterwards with Nina to live in the town of Krasnodar, just south of Rostov.[3] The situation in the reunited household must have been strange. Pavel was intellectually his wife's inferior and was evidently conscious of the fact.[4] They had been apart for nearly a decade. Renata, about to enter high school, had not seen her father since she was an infant. Pavel had a new baby elsewhere, whom he continued to see.[5] Instead of the palatial home Spielrein remembered from her childhood and vacations, they lived in a three-roomed apartment in converted stables in another part of the town.[6] Mother and daughter shared one room, while Pavel's doubled as a consulting room.[7] The town around them had been racked by civil war. For Spielrein, the most familiar features may have been the landscapes she had loved as a child: the River Don, the Sea of Azov, Taganrog, the steppes. For Renata, almost everything must have seemed different from anything she had ever known. Their life together was not easy. Pavel was prone to depression.[8] He had mood swings and lost his temper. He and his wife may have led separate lives for much of the time.[9] In spite of this, they both managed to continue with their medical work. Pavel was already the chief doctor in a children's clinic.[10] Spielrein took on work as a pedologist.[11]

As the star of psychoanalysis waned in the Soviet Union, pedology thrived. The great neurologist Bekhterev became one of its champions. Through the 1920s, battles continued over which scientific fields were compatible with Marxism and which were not. While psychoanalysis was deemed to be unsound, pedology received official approval.[12] Some former analysts and their allies, including Vygotsky, allied themselves with pedology. Pedologists themselves were based in schools, where they provided both a medical and a psychological service. Although accounts of Spielrein's life back in Rostov as a pedologist sometimes imply it was a dark period for her, this may be based on a set of stereotypes and prejudices. Even under Stalin, many professionals in the Soviet Union managed to do productive and fulfilling work. There are certainly no grounds for assuming that work as a generalist in child health in a southern Russian city was in any way a failure by comparison with private practice in a western capital. Her published papers from the later 1920s give every indication that Spielrein threw herself into her pedological work with zeal. She also worked part-time with children and adults in a psychiatric hospital.[13] In addition, it is possible she taught at Rostov University or was involved in an orphanage.[14]

Spielrein's relatives were certainly doing well in the mid-1920s. Jan had returned from Berlin and now lived in Moscow with his wife Sylvia Ryss and their daughters Irina and Marianna. He held the chair of electrical engineering at the Moscow Institute for Energy. At the peak of his career he became a dean and was a corresponding member of the Academy of Sciences of the USSR. Sabina's youngest brother Emil had stayed in Rostov where he was professor of biology and zoology, also rising to the post of dean.[15] Following the birth of their first son, Mark, in 1921, they had another son, Evald, in 1926. Nikolai Spielrein managed to hold on to some of his wealth for a while, and dedicated himself to promoting literacy among young people, a high proportion of whom were unable to read and write. Forever brimming with new ideas, he promoted the use of the Latin alphabet instead of the Cyrillic one for writing Russian.[16] A photo of him with his grandson Evald is labelled in this way, in Nikolai's own writing: 'the oldest and youngest members of N. Spielrein's family' (see plate section no. 8).

The most successful family member was Isaac. He too lived in Moscow, with his wife Rakhil and their daughter Menikha. He had established himself at the head of an entire scientific field in the Soviet Union: industrial psychology or 'psychotechnics'. Like pedology, industrial psychology had its origins in the west but had taken off mainly in Russia. It too acquired a pronounced Marxist-Leninist identity. If anyone was well placed to become its leader, it was Isaac Spielrein. As earlier chapters have detailed, he was already a socialist as a teenager and had impressive academic credentials. He had studied psychology and philosophy in Germany with some of the major figures of the age. He was a scholar of Yiddish just at the time it was fashionable to be a secular Jew in Russia. He had changed his name from one he used in Germany ('Oskar') to the overtly Jewish 'Isaac Naftulovich'. At home, he revived the language of his grandparents at home with Rakhil and his daughter Menikha.[17] In 1922, he founded a laboratory for industrial psychology at the Ministry of Labour, moving on the following year to the Institute of Philosophy at Moscow University.[18] By the mid-1920s, he had published dozens of papers. He carried out research projects on topics including working hours, selection methods for army personnel, and the language of the Red Army soldier. He joined the presidium of 'Vremya', a league aimed at spreading the idea of scientifically organised labour. Trotsky and Lenin were both honorary chairs. By the end of the decade, he had published a Yiddish textbook and a study of how people had changed from Russian to Jewish names, reflecting pride in ethnic identity as religious identity declined. He was editor in chief of *Industrial Psychology and the Psychophysiology of Labour*, and a member of the presidium of the International Society for Industrial Psychology. Later he became its president.[19] By 1930, he was one of the leaders of a discipline that had 3,000 members in the USSR with a plan to involve three million people in the Ministry's professional consultation network. Isaac now proposed setting up a college of industrial psychology[20] (see plate section no 7).

Isaacs's achievements reflect the same appetite for learning and activity in diverse fields as shown by his father and his sister. They now worked in closely related fields. During her time in Moscow, Sabina had lectured at the Institute of Philosophy where Isaac worked. There was an Institute of Psychology, Pedology and Industrial Psychology where both their fields of interest were taught and studied. Yet Isaac and Sabina barely seem to have met over the whole decade. Isaac's daughter Menikha reported meeting her aunt only three times.[21] Perhaps the traumas of their childhood had led to a similar interest in the workings of the human mind, but made them reluctant to spend time with each other. However, in 1931 Sabina attended a congress in Moscow that Isaac had organised on industrial psychology, with an emphasis on its role in the class struggle. Édouard Claparède attended from Geneva.[22] It is irresistible to speculate what conversations she and Claparède might have had, eight years after they had last seen each other, particularly if any of them concerned the papers she had left at the Rousseau Institute.

Spielrein and her husband must have restored at least some intimacy, because in 1926 they had a second daughter. Spielrein was forty when she was born. The girl was called Eva, after her grandmother. The choice of name is striking, especially as Spielrein had kept away from her mother in the last eight years of her life. Unfortunately, we have no information about Eva until her teens. Spielrein herself carried on working. Two years after giving birth to her second daughter, she published a paper in a psychoanalytic teaching journal in the west.[23] She described how she avoided using words when treating children with emotional disorders, getting them to show her their difficulties through play instead. In the same year she also gave a lecture to the Pedological Society of Rostov-on-Don University on 'Children's drawings with open and closed eyes'. This arose from a research project similar to the one she had carried out in Geneva when she asked her students to think of questions with their eyes open and shut. This time she applied the same method to ask groups of children to draw figures of people. She found that with eyes closed, children remained closer to primary bodily feelings, and expressed their personalities more readily, albeit with more primitive pictures. It confirmed her view that visual imagination, as opposed to abstract, logical thinking, had its origins in bodily experience. When the lecture was published in 1931, in the psychoanalytic journal *Imago*, it was the last of her works to appear in print.[24] The translation into German was by her father, Nikolai. Since her mastery of the German language must have at least equal to his, the collaboration was presumably her choice. It may demonstrate some kind of reconciliation in the troubled and ambiguous relationship between them.

Although this was her last published paper, it was not her last known work. That was the presentation quoted at the beginning of this chapter,[25] which she gave in response to a presentation by a Dr Skal'kovski concerning his views of the correct treatment of the mental health problems of children. She tackled him on what she considered to be an excessive emphasis on suggestion, and argued that the neutral clinical approach of psychoanalysis was more correct and more effective. She protested against the simplistic view that Freud considered all mental trouble to be the result of psychological flaws, as opposed to the communist view that these arose from defects in society. As the passage above shows, she quoted Freud to show his awareness of the social influences on personality development. In a theoretical survey of methods used by different psychoanalysts, she took issue with Melanie Klein and Hermine Hug-Hellmuth, whom she believed used intrusive interpretations with children. She argued that if you simply encouraged children to talk, they would find their own way forward. She criticised Skal'kovski himself for taking a position that for her was too reminiscent of Adler, with an emphasis on power. She made it clear she regarded Piaget as just as one-sided as Adler, for his exclusive focus on the stages of cognitive growth. She spoke approvingly of Ferenczi, who by now was advocating an emotionally engaged role for the therapist. The central message of her lecture was about the importance of taking an approach to children that encompassed biological, physiological and social perspectives all together. In the final pages of her paper, she described her active practice with adults and children, paying attention to the practicalities of running a psychoanalytic clinic with limited resources of time, money and staff. In many ways, it sounds like a modern attempt to sustain humane ways of working psychologically, while needing to compromise with economic and political realities. Among other things, she recommended that a trained analyst should spend forty per cent of her professional time supervising others. Among other observations, her lecture also contained her last known mention of Jung.[26]

Her continuing papers and lectures were conscious acts of bravery, all the more so because she published them in the west. The position of psychoanalysis since the Institute and Children's House were liquidated in 1925 was perilous. Two years after its closure, Moisei Wulff had gone to a congress at Innsbruck and defected.[27] Luria resigned from the Russian society. The society itself continued to meet, debated the merits of pedology, and maintained contact with Freud – who observed events in Russia with mounting alarm. The Russian Psychoanalytic Society held its last meeting in 1930 to discuss 'planning' but there is no record of any of the plans coming to fruition.[28]

There are stories from the years in Rostov that convey images of Spielrein at that time. Spielrein's niece Menikha told of how her aunt had once claimed she could have 'cured' Lenin.[29] Her step-daughter Nina remembered how her aunt had once cured a little girl's headache by holding a hand above her head. Spielrein was also known to be in correspondence with a poet or writer from Leningrad whose nickname was Crocodile: she interpreted his dreams and gave him advice.[30] Nina reported seeing in the late 1930s a room in the converted stables where Spielrein lived 'that was totally empty except for a huge, lonely sofa'. It may have been a consulting room. The room had no windows. The psychoanalyst Coline Covington has suggested: 'She wanted to provide her patients with an environment that would resemble the womb but I think this also indicated something about her own state of mind.'[31] This seems unimaginative.

Ovcharenko's description of the risks to people practising psychoanalysis by that time is more pertinent: 'Work of this type was practically speaking already a form of particularly dangerous crime against the State, with all the consequences which could follow from that.'[32] Nina also described home-made shelves in the apartment holding rows of German and French books, including several series that may well have been bound volumes of psychoanalytic journals. It is curious to imagine how Spielrein might have collected these, given the lack of any surviving correspondence from her with the west.

Renata seems to have fared better back in Rostov, and went on to study the cello in Moscow. According to friends, the famous violinist David Oistrakh declared that she would one day be a great player.[33] Although there are no photos of Renata, there is one surviving picture of Eva as a teenager. She looks out directly at the viewer with a gentleness, intelligence and beauty that are heart-breaking, since we know the fate that she was soon to share (see plate section no. 11). Many years later, four of her school friends gave interviews to the film-maker Elisabeth Márton. This is how they described her mother in the 1930s: 'Sabina dressed in dark, old-fashioned clothes, she didn't care very much about what she looked like, and was filled with a passion for science and for her work. She was not at all practical when it came to household matters, for example she hardly ever cooked.'[34] There is no hint of her as a tragic figure, and much to confirm that she was the same woman she had been in Lausanne, Geneva and Moscow (see plate section no. 10).

As time passed, Spielrein's professional field of pedology became inextricably connected with the idea of the Soviet 'new man of the masses', and the idea of reconstructing society from the human personality upwards. Even Pavlov objected, from the perspective of scientific psychology.[35] In spite of this, pedology marched on. Its leader was no longer Vladimir Bekhterev. In 1927 he had written a medical report declaring that that Stalin was paranoid. He was poisoned.[36] His role as ideological lead was taken over by Aron Zalkind, the former psychoanalyst who had once declared Freud to be more popular in Russia than in the west. Now exulting over the victory of pedology, he proclaimed: 'The reinforcement of the dictatorship of the proletariat hammers – once and for all – a pine stake through the heart of Soviet Freudism.'[37] He was now preaching that 'sex should be subordinated to class, in no way interfering with class interests, and serving them in any way possible'.[38] By the early 1930s, he was head of a system of 'regional pedological laboratories' and 'local pedological offices'. In Etkind's words, the state was attempting to construct 'an infrastructure of Utopia'.[39] Zalkind's success was not to endure. One ideology after another fell under suspicion, then prohibition, then a death sentence – sometimes literally. Otto Schmidt, the protean scientist who had once established the State Psychoanalytic Institute, wrote a report for the Central Committee of the Communist Party about correct approaches to Soviet science. 'It is of momentous import that we unmask all breeds of pseudo-Marxism.'[40] Among these unfortunate 'breeds' was pedology. So too was Isaac Spielrein's field of industrial psychology. In 1931, the journal *Under the Banner of Marxism* published an editorial declaring: 'Within the psychoneurological sciences, there has not been enough criticism of ... Comrade [Isaac] Spielrein's system of idealist errors, Comrade Zalkind's Menshevik, idealist eclecticism, and so forth.'[41]

The turgid prose was a code, and a lethal one. Zalkind was sacked as head of his institute and editor of his journal. Pedology sputtered on for a few more years, with contradictory directives either encouraging or condemning it. However, in 1936 the Central Committee finally passed a resolution that brooked no misunderstanding. It was entitled 'On the pedological perversions of the Ministry of Education system'. After reading the resolution, Zalkind had a heart attack and died.[42] If he had lived, he would have seen the entire system of pedological institutions and activities dismantled. The author of the vicious editorial leading to these events later emigrated to the United States, where he wrote his repentant memoirs.[43] Meanwhile, the fate of the other 'pseudo-Marxist breed', industrial psychology, was even more catastrophic. At first Isaac Spielrein offered little response to criticism and carried on at the helm of his journal. Then, in 1934, the network of industrial psychology institutions across the country was summarily shut down. At the same time the journal was liquidated. On 25 January 1935, Isaac and his father were both arrested.[44] Nikolai was tortured and deprived of his remaining property, but then released.[45] Isaac was charged with participating in the Trotskyist opposition. A loyal communist to the last, he wrote to people in high places under the misapprehension that it was a mistake.[46] He protested that the revolution had been his entire life and that he had always followed the party line. Unfortunately, such 'mistakes' were commonplace. Isaac was sentenced to five years' hard labour.[47] He worked in factories and on the roads. In letters, he exhorted his wife Rakhil to keep her faith in the party and expect him to be released, although it might take some time.[48]

Sabina Spielrein could no longer work as a pedologist. She was also sacked from her hospital post in psychiatry.[49] She took on another job as a part-time school doctor,[50] and Renata worked in a nursery to supplement their income. Both daughters occasionally earned some money from playing music,[51] but the family had barely enough money for food. Then, in 1937, Pavel died suddenly from a heart attack at the age of fifty-seven. His daughter Nina, who had maintained regular contact with her father and step-sisters,[52] went to visit Spielrein. Nina later described her: 'She looked like an old woman, although she wasn't that old. She was bent, wearing some old, black skirt that reached the ground. She wore boots with clasps that people now call "farewell youth" boots. I think she had brought them from Berlin. That's how my own grandmother used to dress. It was obvious, she was a broken woman.'[53] Friends later gave similar accounts: 'She led a very lonely life, old before her time and exhausted yet persevering, with her work as a refuge and her daughters, both very talented in music, as points of light in the darkness.'[54] Yet on another occasion Nina painted a different picture, likening her step-mother to Lydia Ginzburg, a writer who was hunched and grey, but was clear-thinking with a great intellect.[55] Her niece Menikha too gave a more positive description, quoted in the next chapter. Although Spielrein's marriage had not been fulfilling, she showed a sentimental attachment to Pavel's belongings. When Nina decided to clear her late father's desk, which had been kept in the same disarray since his death, Spielrein was too upset to let her do it.

After Pavel's death, Spielrein approached Nina's mother, Olga Snetkova, to request a meeting. When Olga declined, Spielrein travelled to Krasnodar to see her. According to Nina, she explained at once that Pavel had only ever really loved Olga.[56] She suggested that if anything happened to either of them, they should take responsibility for all three girls – Nina, Renata and Eva. Olga agreed. On New Year's Eve, the two mothers and three daughters met around the Christmas tree in the bare converted stable room with the couch.[57] Renata was visiting from the conservatoire in Moscow, where she was now studying. Nina described Renata as looking like an actress in her evening gown.

Spielrein was not arrested, but there were more catastrophes to come. Stalin's paranoia led to a purge of real and imagined dissidents on a grotesque scale. Whole sectors of the Russian population were targeted: 'kulaks' or wealthier peasants, anyone within the communist party or army suspected of the slightest disloyalty, along with engineers and scientists. In December, Isaac faced more charges: espionage and membership of a counter-revolutionary organisation. By this time, he may or may not have realised these charges were scarcely 'mistakes'. His wife and daughter were thrown out of their apartment.[58] On 26 December 1937, Isaac was sentenced to death by firing squad. The sentence was carried out at once, and his body was thrown into a mass grave.[59] As his brothers, and as scientists, Jan and Emil were predictable targets. In January 1938, Jan was shot by firing squad. Emil was shot in Rostov in June. On 17 August 1938, Nikolai died. At seventy-seven he was no longer a young man, but there is no record that he suffered from any previous physical illness. All three of the sons he had raised to 'fly to the heavens' had been murdered by the state that they, and he himself, had served so loyally. Whatever the medical cause, it seems he died from a broken heart. At the time of his death, Nikolai Arkadyevich Spielrein left behind his daughter Sabina and seven grandchildren. He had also lived to see his first great-grandchild, a boy named Oleg born to Jan's daughter Irina and her husband Pavel Mikhailov in 1932.

Spielrein may not have learned straight away about her brothers' fate. Some people only discovered years later whether a relative had been imprisoned, deported to Siberia or summarily shot. Isaac's daughter Menikha Spielrein remembered his arrest, which took place on her nineteenth birthday, but was only told in 1939 that he had been 'sentenced to ten years in prison without the right to correspond'.[60] Even if Spielrein entertained hopes in the late 1930s that her brothers might still be alive, the scale and visibility of the purges were too great for her to have many illusions. From 1936 to 1938, between 950,000 and 1.5 million Russians were shot by the secret police or NKVD, a rate of approximately 1,000 people a day.[61] One of the leading historians of the Terror, Robert Conquest, described how 'fear by night, and a feverish effort by day to pretend enthusiasm for a system of lies, was the permanent condition'.[62] People were arrested, tortured, sentenced to years of hard labour or shot on pretexts that would seem surreal if they were not so chilling: being the first to stop clapping after a speech, or letting an object drop on a picture of Stalin in a newspaper. For millions of Russians, each day from 1936 onwards felt like an unexpected reprieve from incarceration and death.

Spielrein no doubt considered it likely she would be next. Fewer women than men were caught up in the Terror, but they were not exempt. Jan's wife Sylvia was arrested and imprisoned, while Emil's wife Fanya fled with her two sons to Kazakhstan to evade arrest.[63] Spielrein herself would certainly have come under suspicion. She had spent more time in the west than any of her brothers, kept German books in her home, was possibly the last person to defend Freud publicly or to write for his journals. In her mind, a future where Olga Snetkova would end up looking after all three of their daughters may have seemed a near certainty.

22

Deaths 1942

In November 1937, my father was in a concentration camp and my mother was exiled to Middle Asia. I could not remain in Moscow. After the arrest of Sabina's eldest brother, I decided to travel to Rostov, to my grandfather ... It turned out I arrived on the morning of the night when Emil was arrested. Upon being ushered into the room by Sabina, she asked me whether I believed what was being written in our newspapers about the cruelties perpetrated by Germans. She added, she had lived for many years in Germany and could not believe what is being printed in our newspapers, since she knows the high level of the German culture, of the people who gave the world Goethe, Heine, Schiller and many well-known and outstanding people. I told her that I believed what was written about the Germans ... Obviously, I was unable to convince her. Otherwise Sabina Nikolayevna was by her upbringing a very well mannered, friendly, and gentle person. At the same time she was tough as far as her convictions were concerned – she could not be convinced of the contrary.[1]

AFTER PAVEL'S DEATH, Spielrein's niece Menikha came to visit her from Moscow. In the passage above, Menikha is describing that visit. At the time she was training as a translator in the German department of the Foreign Languages Training Centre. Many of the teachers there were communist émigrés from Germany who gave their students accounts of Nazi crimes and showed them underground literature on the subject. Menikha had no difficulty in believing them. She was a committed communist, like her father Isaac, and a member of the youth movement. Like Nina Snetkova, she regarded her aunt as 'impractical and out of step with the times, almost helpless in everyday Soviet life'.[2] When her father disappeared and her mother was made homeless, Menikha could make no sense of it and continued her commitment to communism.[3] Like him, she may have assumed it was a mistake that would be rectified in due course, not comparable to the Nazi crimes she was hearing about from the émigrés. Menikha described her aunt as a woman of 'tough convictions'. This is recognisable from everything we know about Spielrein. It is also worth noting her depiction of Spielrein as 'well mannered, friendly and gentle'. This is in contrast to the 'broken woman' that Nina Snetkova described from around the same time. Menikha's memory of her from this time may be more accurate. Menikha was clearly an idealist, but Nina may have been recalling an image of Spielrein mainly from her final days. The way Menikha attributes Spielrein's manner to 'her upbringing' is also striking. That bygone age of wealth and gentility had given her a demeanour that was a rare attribute in Stalinist Russia. In Menikha's eyes she had held on to it despite everything.

Spielrein clearly believed that no crimes the Russians ascribed to the cultured German nation could be as bad as their own. At that point in history, she was entirely correct. In 1937, Hitler and the Nazis were carrying out a systematic campaign to dispossess German Jews of their livelihoods and property, but there were few deaths. The cruelties referred to by Menikha were economic and social ones, not murders. If we look at the late 1930s in the light of the genocide ahead, we risk misinterpreting the way Spielrein would have seen the world. Europe had also known nothing before on the scale of the slaughter of civilians under Stalin. It was unimaginable that these atrocities might pale into significance by comparison with an even greater holocaust. Rather, they established the model for it. The story of Spielrein's final years is inextricably linked with the progression of mass murder in Europe.

*

The Bolsheviks had spent years inculcating the masses with hatred of Hitler and fascism. In August 1939, all that suddenly changed when Russia and Germany made a ten-year peace agreement, known as the Molotov-Ribbentrop pact after the two foreign ministers who signed it. Inside Russia, the masses had to adjust their political views completely. From being a despicable threat to class struggle and the triumph of the proletariat, Hitler and the Nazis were now comrades in the resistance against encirclement by international capitalism. Overtly, the pact was an agreement that neither Russia nor Germany would join a military alliance against the other. The Germans would keep out of the long-running dispute between the Russians and the Japanese. Equally, Russia would not join the alliance that Stalin had formerly sought with France and the United Kingdom against the Nazis. The real plan lay in a secret protocol. Molotov and Ribbentrop agreed to divide continental Europe into two 'spheres of influence'. Effectively this would create two immense totalitarian empires, a fascist one and a communist one.

Within a week of signing the pact, Germany had invaded the western half of Poland, leading to a declaration of war by Britain and France. Two weeks afterwards, Russia invaded the eastern half of Poland. In 1940, Russia occupied the Baltic states and part of Finland. Before the end of the year, Germany had occupied France, the Low Countries, Denmark and Norway. Subsequent events and the outcome of the Second World War were later to alter memories, but it is impossible to underestimate the impact of the agreement and ensuing events on people at the time. Across western Europe, the notion that Britain could prevail alone, or that the United States would even join the war, let alone orchestrate a victory from the other side, seemed improbably remote.[4] By birth, Spielrein was half Polish. She would have been distressed by the terrible fate of that country and fearful for her extended family. She knew Warsaw and had fallen in love there with her Uncle Adolf. Yet she may have been relieved that Warsaw was now in the control of the Germans rather than the Russians, whom she trusted far less. What she cannot have known was that the non-aggression pact, and the swift bisection of Europe that followed, created exactly the conditions Hitler needed to pursue the 'final solution of the Jewish problem'.

In *The Destruction of the European Jews*, the historian Raul Hilberg summarised the history of anti-semitism in a series of three injunctions. The first was: 'You cannot live among us as Jews.' Next was: 'You cannot live among us.' And finally: 'You cannot live.'[5] If Spielrein had believed any of the reports from Germany during the 1930s, she would have recognised how the first and second of these injunctions had been put into practice. Among hundreds of other restrictions, there was now a prohibition on Jews being doctors or lawyers. Shops and businesses were being closed down or sacked; almost every synagogue had been destroyed; and there were arbitrary arrests and relentless pressure to leave. One of those who had little choice about leaving was Sigmund Freud. The Nazis began to burn Freud's books publicly from 1933. At the time, he famously said: 'In the Middle Ages they would have burned me; nowadays they are content with burning my books.' The remark would soon carry terrible ironies.[6] Following the unification of Germany with Austria in the 'Anschluss' in 1938, Freud finally left Vienna. He settled in London, which became the European centre for psychoanalysis. He died from longstanding mouth cancer on 23 September 1939, the day Russia invaded Poland.

If Spielrein had credited reports from Western Europe, she would also have known that many people apart from Nazis were in sympathy with anti-Jewish measures. Others simply turned a blind eye, or failed to criticise them even when they were in a safe position to do so. Somewhere along this spectrum was

Carl Jung. As earlier chapters have shown, Jung was not immune from negative stereotypes of Jews. In 1934, after the Nazis had come to power, he wrote that it had been a very serious mistake for Freudians to apply Jewish categories indiscriminately to Germanic and Slavic Christendom. He asked whether the extraordinary phenomenon of National Socialism had taught them any better understanding.[7] He cherished hopes that his psychology would triumph over Freud's, and that German National Socialism might create the conditions for it to do so. His sentiments were unfortunate, but his actions went further. Jung was vice president and, after 1933, president of the International General Medical Society for Psychotherapy – an organisation to promote the practice of psychotherapy among doctors. He co-edited its journal with Matthias Göring, who led the German branch of the society. Göring was a member of the Nazi party. He was also a cousin of the Gestapo leader, Hermann Göring. He spoke out in far more virulent terms than Jung against 'Jewish' psychoanalysis. He supervised the expulsion of the Jews from membership of the society, and from the institute he had founded. Jung remained as his co-editor, even after the journal announced the adoption of Hitler's *Mein Kampf* as a basic text. Jung allowed others to use their connection with him to promote anti-Semitic causes. Notoriously, he described the Jewish problem in terms of a purulent wound that should not be hushed up in discussions among doctors.[8] He remained president until 1940.[9]

Defences that have been mounted for Jung include naivety, or a hope that he might be able to prevent worse consequences for Jewish psychotherapists in the Third Reich – although it is hard to imagine what these might have been. According to Deirdre Bair, his anti-Semitic sentiments continued after the war, when he allegedly wrote in a private letter: 'Jews are not so damned innocent after all – the role played by the intellectual Jews in pre-war Germany would be an interesting object of investigation.'[10] There seems a terrible inevitability to this final contrast between Freud and Jung: one a dying refugee and the other a misguided bystander at best, or an opportunist and collaborator at worst.

Neither Jung, Freud or Spielrein could have had any foreknowledge of where the Nazis' plans might lead. Even when the German army had occupied the countries around them, there was no systematic plan to kill Jews. During the invasion of western Poland, Hitler gave orders for the murder of the Polish intelligentsia, including Jews. Around 65,000 people were shot in the first three months. The killings were carried out by task forces – 'Einsatzgruppen' – set up for especially that purpose. They included members of the SS, the armed forces, allied soldiers and the police, as well as local ethnic Germans and sympathisers.

Their method of execution by shooting was to be the model for massacres throughout eastern Europe for the next two years. The later system of industrial killing by gas, designed for the mass murder of Jews from the entire continent, was only set up from 1941. Meanwhile, the Einsatzgruppen continued to operate in every area where the Nazis penetrated. They functioned in the same way as Stalin's killing squads had done, except that they shot large numbers of people at a time rather than individuals, often next to mass graves that they had sometimes forced the victims to dig.[11]

In summer 1940, less than a year after the non-aggression pact, Hitler started to plan a surprise invasion of Russia. He had subdued most of western Europe, and the German army now had capacity to conquer the east. On 22 June 1941, he launched his campaign, 'Operation Barbarossa', with more than three million soldiers. The nations allied to Germany, including Italy as well as most eastern European countries, also declared war on Russia. Wherever the German army advanced, the Einsatzgruppen followed, carrying out mass shootings. Initially their targets were adult Jewish males, Roma and communist party officials. From late July 1941, they began to kill entire Jewish communities including women and children. The invasion of Russia marked the beginning of what Hilberg denoted as the final stage of anti-Semitism: 'You shall not live.' The extermination of European Jews had by now moved from being simply an opportunity opened up by total war, to become one of the primary objectives of war.[12] The main purpose of the task forces was now explicit. The head of Einsatzgruppe A wrote to Heinrich Himmler, the head of the SS: 'In view of the extension of the area of operations and the great number of duties which had to be performed by the security police, it was intended from the very beginning to obtain the co-operation of the reliable population for the fight against vermin – that is, mainly the Jews and communists.'[13] By the end of 1941, around half a million Jews had been murdered in the Soviet areas occupied by the German army. This included around 34,000 Jews murdered at 'Babi Yar', a ravine outside the Ukrainian city of Kiev.[14] Rostov-on-Don was around 800 kilometres further east. It had a population of around half a million people. It was an important railway junction, and a major port for the export of oil and minerals. It was clear that Stalin and the Russian army were poorly prepared to resist invasion. There was no reason to halt the invasion short of the Caucasus.

German panzer tank divisions occupied Rostov for the first time on 21 November 1941. Within seven days they were overcome by the Red Army and retreated. There were killings of civilians during that week, but the Einsatzgruppen had no opportunity to organise a systematic massacre. Spielrein and Eva survived. So did Renata, who had joined them from Moscow. Olga Snetkova had moved to Rostov from Krasnodar with her daughter. Nina described how fearful the inhabitants of Rostov were with the German army encamped on the outskirts of the town, waiting to invade again. Nina also described her step-mother's attitude, in the same terms as Menikha. Having lived in Germany and Switzerland, Spielrein could not believe what people described the fascists as doing, although now she did not speak of it.[15] Eva had been staying earlier that year with a family who had chosen to flee Rostov, but she decided to return to her mother and sister instead.[16] Such decisions were common.

Conditions in Rostov over the winter were grim. There were constant air raids by the Luftwaffe. The inhabitants hid in cellars. The house where Spielrein lived was bombed. She and her daughters moved into a communal cellar along with many others.[17] Water and electricity failed in much of the town, and food was in very short supply. In the interval between the first invasion and the next, Stalin's secret police or NKVD massacred thousands of people suspected of collaboration, as well as deporting thousands more from among Rostov's minorities. There is one account that Armenian friends of Renata and Eva, about to leave the city, offered to take the girls with them on false Armenian identity documents. The girls evidently refused to leave their mother by herself.[18] This account may be apocryphal, but Jews certainly were leaving Rostov, and the Soviet authorities were assisting some to do so.[19] It is likely that accounts of massacres in nearby towns had reached Rostov. When the next offensive began, Olga Snetkova was in charge of evacuating doctors from the hospital.[20] She too suggested to Renata that she should leave together with her and Nina. Renata refused. Nina saw her one more time before fleeing with her mother through Chechnya, across the Caucasus, and into Dagestan.[21]

At the beginning of the war there were around 27,000 Jews in Rostov. Refugees from the surrounding areas had now increased the total to nearly 40,000.[22] Around half this number succeeded in leaving before the Germans' final offensive, but Spielrein stayed on. Family members questioned afterwards why she did not leave when so many others did.[23] It has been suggested that this may have been due to fatalism, in addition to her high regard for German culture. It probably makes most sense to see the decision in the context of thousands of other Jews who stayed on in Rostov, and did so elsewhere. They were starving, exhausted, psychologically numbed, and often lacked the physical resources to flee. Some, like Spielrein herself, had suffered multiple bereavements in atrocious circumstances. Many found the stories they heard quite literally unbelievable. Massacres of Jews had been common in Russia as recently as the civil war, but had almost never been carried out by Germans since the Middle Ages. Any accounts they heard of mass cold-blooded killings of men, women and children – entire communities that had endured for hundreds of years, the secular herded along with the religious, the rich standing alongside the poor, judges and professors of medicine shot alongside farm workers and stallholders – simply did not correspond to anything that they had ever heard. Even in Stalin's Russia, massacres of this kind were impossible to imagine.

In July 1942, the German army bombarded the city for eleven days. By 27 July, the Germans had conquered Rostov once more. This time they were to stay for seven months. Atrocities started again. At first these were on an individual scale, including arbitrary killings and the murder of hostages in revenge for a soldier who was found dead.[24] A detail of Einsatzgruppe D was now able to move into the city under the command of an SS storm trooper named Heinrich Seetzen, also known as Heinz Seetzen. He was a lawyer by training, and had joined the Nazi party in 1933, rising rapidly through the ranks of the SS.[25] In Rostov, he was in charge of twenty of his own men from 'Sonderkommando [Special Detachment] 10A' and thirty allied Italian soldiers.[26] They had come there to kill communists, psychiatric patients and Jews. Most of what we know about the remaining days of Spielrein's life is drawn from detailed archival research carried out by Sabine Richebächer. This includes witness testimonies from a secret report that was submitted to the regional communist party secretary the following year, after the retreat of the German army. A copy of the report is in the archives of Yad Vashem, Jerusalem.[27]

Rostov's Jews had never been confined to a ghetto, and the Nazis saw no need to put them into one now. The Jewish population was of a size that could be exterminated in a day or two, and the city was close enough to the countryside for everyone to be conveyed there for the purpose. The only requirement was to make sure Jews identified themselves. Using a common ploy, they engaged the assistance of the leaders of the local Jewish community, reassuring them that the Jews of Rostov would be unharmed, but would need to be concentrated in one part of town for their own safety. Posters went up around the town instructing Jews to register for this purpose. The posters were signed by the chair of the community council, Dr Luriye.[28] Such tactics had been honed in campaigns across eastern Europe since Operation Barbarossa began a year previously. The SS at this stage were usually polite, able to persuade people that rumours they may had heard were exaggerated, that their own community was to be subject to protection, and that the orders were necessary to make sure this happened.

While registration proceeded, Sonderkommando 10A occupied itself with the arrest of 700 Rostov citizens, killing 400 who were partisans or party members.[29] On 2 August, three officers arrived at the hospital. One spoke good Russian and introduced himself as a neuropsychologist. They asked the doctors to make a list of all patients with psychiatric illnesses. When the officers returned the following day, they ordered the doctors to produce the list and to load the named patients onto two trucks, which then drove away. They then commandeered the hospital as a residence for their commandants. The doctors realised afterwards that the trucks were gassing vans. The patients were asphyxiated by carbon monoxide in exhaust fumes from the engines, piped into the rear in the course of the journey from the hospital to their place of burial.[30] Deaths took place as later in the gas chambers: from asphyxiation, or from being crushed as people tried to force open the doors. Some of the psychiatric patients may have been young people not so different from Spielrein on her admission to the Bürgholzli.

When Seetzen was satisfied that registration of Jews was reasonably complete, he distributed a further poster asking them to present themselves two days later with their valuables and keys. They were assigned various assembly points according to the parts of town where they lived. One of these was in Pushkinskaya Street, close to Sabina's childhood home. At 8 am on 11 August, Jews began to assemble. Some of those who understood the murderous nature of the exercise committed suicide; others barricaded themselves in their homes, but were forced to join the crowds now converging on the prescribed locations. Sabina Spielrein, together with Renata and Eva, were in the crowd assembled at Sozialisticheskaya [Socialist] Street. They were crammed into vehicles and driven off. These were ordinary trucks, not gassing vans, and were bound for a ravine five kilometres outside the town, known as the Zmeyevsky or 'Snake' Ravine.[31] The last people ever to see Sabina Spielrein were Russian friends who watched the gatherings of Jews on the street corners of Rostov, waiting for the vehicles that would take them away:[32]

> The last time she was seen was in the summer of 1942, in a column of Jews, destined for annihilation, whom the Nazis were driving in the direction of the Zmeyevsky gully ... Poorly dressed, mortally tired and occupied with thoughts known only to herself, Sabina Spielrein shuffled along in the column together with her daughters.[33]

There were witnesses to what happened to the columns of Jews from then onwards. One was Leo Maar, an ethnic German who worked as a translator for the SS and later gave testimony at a posthumous investigation into Heinz Seetzen.[34] Maar explained how Jews were brought to a house near the ravine and stripped of all their possessions. He worked in the room where the women and children were brought. He described how they were compelled to give up their rings, watches, jewellery and money. They were then told to take off all their clothes in order to go to a bathhouse where they would be allocated new clothes for a work camp.[35] A few hundred metres away, captured Russian soldiers and communist prisoners had been made to dig three huge trenches, each seven by five metres. Local villagers were ordered to leave the village for the entire day and told that a shooting exercise would take place. They were threatened with death if they failed to leave. Some later gave statements to a communist party investigation into the massacres. One described seeing a column of 150 to 200 women and children on the road, and trucks full of men. He also heard the sound of shooting from the woods.[36] In the Nuremberg trials, the commander of Einsatzgruppe D, Otto Ohlendorf, described how platoons shot the victims:

> Men, women and children were led to the execution site which in most cases consisted of an anti-tank ditch in the vicinity. They were then shot, kneeling or standing up, and their corpses were thrown into the ditch ... The commander of the company or persons especially in charge of these things were assigned the task of finishing off those who were still alive.[37]

Three days after Sabina, Renata and Eva died, the villager who had heard the shooting went back to the woods. He found pits full of corpses, barely covered with earth, and with 'rivulets of blood'. Another villager described how the shootings went on well into the night. The total number of people killed there on 11 August was 13,000. A further 3,000 to 5,000 Jews were rounded up and shot in the Jewish cemetery in the ensuing days.[38] At Zmeyevsky gully, shootings continued throughout the summer, together with the repeated arrival of gassing vans each containing fifty to eighty people. On arrival at the grave site, the engines would run for twenty minutes before the doors were opened, and the corpses unloaded into the graves.[39] One villager estimated that 4000 people had already been killed in the week before the Jews.[40] The victims included communists, Red Army soldiers and stray teenagers. The massacres at Zmeyevsky gully ended in September, after three months. Altogether, around 27,000 people were murdered there.

When they were murdered, Sabina Spielrein was fifty-six, Renata Sheftel was twenty-eight, and Eva Sheftel was sixteen. In the words that Sabina's grandfather would have said over the three women: *Zikhronan l'vracha.* May their memories be for a blessing.

23

Legacy

Nothing in biology makes sense except in the light of evolution.[1]

I begin with the fundamental principle of evolutionary biology, that all living organisms have evolved to seek and use resources to enhance their reproductive success. They strive for matings, invest in children or help other genetic relatives, and build genetically profitable relationships. In biology, this is not a controversial proposition, and it follows that organisms will act as though they are able to calculate costs and benefits.[2]

A BIOGRAPHY SHOULD not end with the dead, but with the living. In this final chapter, I want to celebrate the legacy of Sabina Spielrein and her family. First, and most important to mention, are the living descendants of Nikolai and Eva Spielrein. Then there is Spielrein's own direct legacy, in its many different forms. These include her diaries and letters, her professional papers, and the original ideas these contained. Some of these ideas, as we have seen, made an impact on Freud and Jung. A far larger number affected her other contemporaries, either through direct influence or by changing the climate of opinion in psychology, and in the treatment of mental distress.

Finally, there are her beliefs that were ahead of their time. Among these was her passionate belief that people who practise talking therapies should never stop talking to each other, nor to colleagues in related fields of study. Another of Spielrein's beliefs was that we should understand the mind and its disorders in terms of the fundamental biological facts of our existence: we die, and hence we need to reproduce. Everything we do has been moulded by that process, and is directed in some way or another towards that purpose. This includes both the conscious mind and the unconscious. The principle is expressed succinctly in the quotations above, from the Russian biologist Theodosius Dobzhansky, and the contemporary biologist Bobbi Low. In this chapter I summarise the different aspects of Spielrein's legacy, consider its significance, and look at the ways that some of the ideas she first explored are now being developed in the twenty-first century.

*

In the year before he died, Sabina Spielrein's father Nikolai Spielrein had four living children, seven grandchildren and one great-grandson. Four years after his death, all his children had been murdered: Sabina, Jan, Isaac and Emil. Two of his grandchildren, Renata and Eva, had died alongside their mother. However, many members of the family survived.[3] Jan's widow, Sylvia Ryss, had been prosecuted along with her husband and spent six years in prison, but she came out of the ordeal alive. Her two daughters also survived. The elder daughter Irina spent part of the war in Uzbekistan with her husband Pavel Mikhailov and their son Oleg. Although trained as an architect, she volunteered for the Soviet Army and was present at the liberation of Berlin. Her younger sister Marianna was a dancer and choreographer. She too survived. She spent some of the war in Georgia, but then served at the front like Irina. Isaac's widow Rakhil spent the war in central Asia with her daughter Menikha, afterwards returning to Moscow. Emil's widow, Fanya Burstein, remained alive and free in Kazakhstan. Although her older son Mark was killed on military service in 1942, her younger son Evald came through the war unharmed.

For forty years after the war, there was no interest in the west in what had happened to Spielrein, or in whether any of her relatives were still living. After her diaries and letters were finally discovered and published, Magnus Ljunggren, a professor of Slavic studies from Sweden, began to try to find her family. In 1983, he succeeded in tracking down her niece Menikha. He found her in a 'dismal, concrete' apartment block in a Moscow suburb.[4] When he told her about the newly emerging fame of her 'impractical' Aunt Sabina, she found this impossible to believe. Her immediate response was: 'I think I'm going mad.' Menikha was working at the time as a physiologist and biochemist. After she learned about her aunt, she devoted much of her time and linguistic skill to promoting her reputation. Menikha died from a stroke in 2000. Sadly, Isaac Spielrein's line died out with Menikha. Although she had one child of her own, a son named Mark, he had taken his own life in 1992.

Both of Sabina's other brothers have left descendants. Jan's daughters Irina and Marianna each had a child. Irina's son Oleg Mikhailov emigrated with his wife and two daughters to Israel in the 1990s. They stayed there for fifteen years before moving to Canada, where they now live. His side of the family has continued the scientific tradition of previous generations. Before leaving Russia, Oleg was a professor of electrical engineering in the same Institute for Energy where his grandfather had been dean. Now, his elder daughter Katy Zaidman is a professor of mechanical engineering, while her sister Vera Grodek has masters' degrees in both electrical and biomedical engineering. Oleg has two grandsons and three granddaughters. Jan's younger child Marianna Spielrein had a daughter named Marina, who also became a choreographer. Marina Suvorova still lives in Moscow, where her own two daughters, Anastasia Vasilyeva and Ksenya Teplova, also work in ballet and theatre. Marina has a grand-daughter, born to Anastasia in 2007. Emil has left descendants too. His surviving son Evald became a professor of thermo-physics, also at the Moscow Institute for Energy. Like his uncle Jan, he became a corresponding member of the Russian Academy of Sciences. Evald died in 2009 at the age of eighty-three. His son Vladimir Shpilrain emigrated to the United States and is now a professor of mathematics in New York, where he lives with his wife and their daughter Marie. Thus Sabina Spielrein's parents have fourteen descendants in Russia, Canada and the United States.

An appreciation of Spielrein's written legacy must start with her personal papers, her letter and diaries. It is hard to think of any other figure from the last century, especially one so closely connected with its influential thinkers, who left such an intimate account of themselves. It deserves to be much better known, and far more widely read. Over thirty years since its rediscovery, it is astonishing that such a unique collection of writing is only available in an unsatisfactory form – separated across a number of books that are mostly out of print, and in editions and translations that are sometimes of poor quality. We will only be able to do any justice to this legacy when proper editions of these writings are available, supplemented by the hundreds of other documents that have never been released. Apart from anything else, a volume including all the three-way correspondence between Jung, Freud and Spielrein from 1905 to 1923 would allow any interested reader to make their own informed judgement of that crucial period in the history of psychoanalysis.

Regarding Spielrein's intellectual legacy, it is an irony that her reputation currently rests on two ideas to which she made little if any contribution. Freud acknowledged her as the original source of his 'death instinct', and she has been credited with originating this idea ever since. As I showed in Chapter 17, Freud's version of the death instinct did not resemble the one she had put forward in Vienna nine years previously. He may have taken the name from her paper, but he altered its meaning totally. His death instinct was an abstract principle to account for the tendency of individuals, or civilisations, to be drawn to their own destruction. Spielrein's concept was not really a death instinct at all. She described it more accurately elsewhere with the term 'sexual instinct-death instinct'.[5] It was a biological concept, and she used it to refer to the creative and destructive aspects that she believed were intrinsic to the reproductive drive. Freud was speaking truthfully when he acknowledged her paper but described it as 'not entirely clear to me'.[6]

The other source of Spielrein's reputation is as the alleged inspiration for Jung's 'anima'. This too rests on flimsy evidence, namely a single reference by Jung fifty years afterwards to a 'talented psychopath'. If Jung really did recall Spielrein mainly as someone who pestered him with her criticism and turned into a nagging inner voice, it would provide no grounds whatsoever for describing her as his 'inspiration'. More likely, this figure was the creation of a distorted memory. Yet if we are to judge by his contemporaneous comment to Spielrein regarding 'the love of S for J',[7] he does seem to have credited her with an even bigger idea, namely his notion that everyone has to pursue their destined place in the world – what he described as 'individuation'. If we are to believe this claim, it means that her conviction of a 'higher calling' gave him the idea he placed at the heart of his system of psychology and his method of treatment.

In order to do proper justice to Spielrein, we need to look beyond Freud and Jung, and to identify the substantial list of ideas that she put forward in her own scholarly writings. A brief review of her career and published work, in its historical context, shows the true scale of her achievements. For her medical school dissertation, Spielrein wrote the first extended study of schizophrenic speech and its internal logic.[8] It was to be another fifty years before psychiatrists such as R.D. Laing showed how such speech is a vital form of communication about how psychotic people understand the world.[9] This approach is now central to some enlightened, community-based approaches to schizophrenia.[10] Her dissertation was both the first to be accepted for a doctorate using a psychoanalytic approach, and the first to be published in a psychoanalytic journal. The following year, she wrote two more significant papers. One was her 'Destruction' paper, with its evolution-based approach to the 'talking cure', discussed further below. The second was her article on childhood fantasies about pregnancy and childbirth.[11] This was probably the first systematic attempt to describe the imagination of children and the intuitions that underlie it. Such attempts were to become routine from Piaget onwards. She wrote all three of these papers shortly after becoming the first person who had ever progressed from being a hospitalised psychiatric patient to practising psychoanalysis herself.

Of the ten papers she published around the time of the First World War, at least two also explored entirely original territory. Her paper on 'The Mother-in-Law' was the first to take an explicitly feminist perspective on family interactions and the wider social influences that affect them.[12] A paper she published the following year on the brief treatment of a boy's phobia about monkeys was almost certainly the first case report of a child being treated for an emotional problem through talking and the use of memories and associations.[13] Here too, she was at least a decade ahead of Anna Freud and Melanie Klein, who now appear in history books as the pioneers of such treatment. During her three years in Geneva in the early 1920s, Spielrein produced around nineteen further papers. They included a series of articles making links across the fields of psychoanalysis, child development and linguistics for the first time, such as her papers on the origin of the words 'Mama' and 'Papa',[14] and on the similarities between the unconscious mind and the speech of children and stroke victims.[15] As we saw in Chapter 19, her manner of addressing these topics not only influenced her colleague and analysand Jean Piaget, but in some respects went beyond his own work. In writing these papers, Spielrein was also one of the pioneers of observational research into the way children speak and talk. She started this with observations of her daughter Renata many years earlier, although it was Piaget who was later to become famous for this approach. A short paper written during the same period demonstrates that she is likely to have been the first person to use play therapy with children.[16]

When she returned to Russia, Spielrein joined the staff of the world's first psychoanalytic kindergarten and campaigned for proper training of its teachers. Her influence included her effect on the working methods and ideas of her colleagues Alexander Luria and Lev Vygotsky, who both achieved fame for the ways they combined objective and subjective data in their approach to psychology, in the manner that she had introduced. She continued with observational research of children into the late 1920s.[17] Working in the new field of pedology, she developed her own personal adaptation of psychoanalytic methods to address the economic and political circumstances of the Soviet Union, and spoke about these publicly as late as 1929.[18] Her studies from her years back in Russia, along with all her publications from her dissertation onwards, deserve far more attention they have ever received. So indeed do all her papers. Just as there is a need for a scholarly edition of her correspondence and diaries, we also need an edition of her collected professional works, in order to gain a better understanding of the scope of her ideas and their place in twentieth-century thought.

Given this list of her achievements, how can one account for the lack of any recognition of them for forty years after her death – not to mention the continuing inattention to them nowadays? Two of the likely explanations are straightforward, while another two are not. The straightforward explanations are that she returned to the Soviet Union in the early 1920s, and that she died there in the Holocaust. As a Russian, she had always represented a culture that was poorly understood and often denigrated in the west. After her return, it was one that was literally inaccessible. Her murder in 1942 meant that she never lived to see the early stirrings of liberalisation in the USSR, and hence some possible opportunities to contact any former colleagues in the west. She was therefore entirely unknown to the next generation of psychotherapists, psychologists and historians who wrote about the early years of psychoanalysis and child development studies. If she had moved to London or New York and survived, it is unlikely her role would have been written out of history.

The less straightforward reasons for forgetting or undervaluing her work are connected with her own beliefs, and how much they went against the spirit of her times. These were her refusal to join factions or identify herself with any one discipline, and her passion for science. For those outside the world of the talking therapies it is hard to convey the degree to which they have been factionalised and fractious. Even now, people often train exclusively within one of body of ideas and remain within that school of thought throughout their professional careers. If the same practices existed within a professional field like cardiology, people would rightly regard this as preposterous. Therapists, by contrast, still generally follow the traditions that Bleuler described a hundred years ago as having more similarity to religious sects or political parties than to sciences. On the whole, people who are 'purists' or charismatic leaders in the image of Freud or Jung have won prestigious reputations. Those like Sabina Spielrein, who have been more interested in building bridges, have often been undervalued, forgotten, or pathologised. For example, when Carotenuto first published Spielrein's letters, he dismissed her attempt to harmonise the ideas of Freud, Adler and Jung with this comment: 'Any attempt at synthesis can be taken as a difficulty in accepting conflict.'[19] Fortunately, such perverse views are being increasingly seen for what they are. Mutual respect between different schools of thought, and an exchange of ideas between them, are now becoming far more common. In particular, there is more emphasis on what works in psychotherapy, regardless of its label.[20] Acknowledgement of Spielrein's position in the early history of psychoanalysis, and of what she tried to achieve by way of reconciliation between its warring factions, would be an important part of accelerating that process.

If therapists have dug trenches around their rival camps, they have also done so in relation to neighbouring fields of thought. From the 1920s onwards, psychoanalysis went its way largely disconnected from studies in child development. Those who practised talking therapies, even on children, did so in isolation from their colleagues in child research, while the latter often looked on with suspicion at approaches that seemed unscientific. Those who led single professions became eminent, while those who regarded disciplinary boundaries as arbitrary were undervalued. It was only decades later that researchers like John Bowlby[21] and Daniel Stern[22] started to try to build bridges between psychoanalysis and the systematic study of how the attachment between carers and their children develop, and how the minds of infants and children actually work. Once again, such crossing of disciplinary boundaries is commoner than it used to be. Here too, Spielrein set a precedent that needs to be honoured.

Among all the harmful kinds of division that Spielrein tried to resist, probably none was as important as the one between the world of psychoanalysis and that of biology. When she was first admitted to the Burghölzli, there was no such division. It was Forel, both a great evolutionary scholar and an inspirational asylum director, who proposed a unified vision of brain and mind. Bleuler was both a committed biological scientist and sympathetic to the cause of psychoanalysis. At the Rousseau Institute, both Claparède and Piaget had backgrounds in evolutionary studies and tried to nurture psychoanalysis. Mutual hostility and misunderstanding arose for all kinds of reasons, but a central one was the objection held by Freud and Jung to anchoring psychoanalysis in the principles of biology. They never expressed this more forcefully than they did in response to Spielrein's own attempt to do this in her 'Destruction' paper. The day she presented it – the day following Bleuler's resignation from the psychoanalytic movement – was indeed the parting of the ways.

As this book has shown, Spielrein's attempt to set out an underlying evolutionary theory of the mind contained serious flaws. The first time she considered it, in her first 'Transformation' letter to Jung, it was muddled and infused with the idea of sex as 'demonic'.[23] When she presented it three or four years later in her 'Destruction' paper, it was clearer, but still imbued with fantasies of self-immolation. The version she finally articulated in her letter to Jung in 1917 was far more coherent.[24] She had refined it by observing the behaviour of Renata as an infant and considering how this was related to future survival and the imperative for reproduction. She was explicit in offering it as a theory to bring together the thought of Freud, Jung and Adler. Even there, however, she had still not let go of the mystical notion of the 'need to die and be reborn' in a romantic relationship. Despite these limitations, Spielrein succeeded in locating some essential truths about reproduction, sexuality and the human mind that now lie at the centre of evolutionary studies of human behaviour. She recognised the inseparable connection between death and sex: the one necessitates the other.[25] She realised that reproduction involves as much conflict between the sexes as love and collaboration.[26] She knew that women and men have different reproductive interests, and these are reflected in their feelings and behaviour.[27] She understood the tension in human lives between the pursuit of procreation and that of survival.[28] Above all, she understood that the talking therapies would make no sense, either to others or in their own right, unless they could be harmonised with a theory that had earned – and still earns – almost universal credibility among intelligent people.

Since that parting of the ways between psychoanalysis and biology, the two worlds have largely gone in separate directions. On the whole, most biological scientists have regarded Freud and Jung's theories as self-referential and unrelated to any recognisable scientific principles. They have shown little interest in trying to apply their ideas to the talking therapies. Meanwhile, therapists and counsellors have often regarded biology as hopelessly deterministic. Rather than seeing it as an important source of insight into their own feelings, they fear it will lead people to see genes as fate, and prevent them from taking charge of their own lives. Practitioners of talking therapies almost all go through their entire training without reading Darwin, or receiving any grounding in basic evolutionary principles. Many of them reject the whole idea of 'human nature' as outdated and incorrect: they prefer to regard the human mind as a blank slate, affected only by individual experience.

Fortunately the debate has not been entirely polarised, and dialogue is now increasing. In the last decade, a significant group of psychoanalysts, led by people such as Peter Fonagy[29] and Mark Solms,[30] has once again tried to harmonise the talking therapies with the physiology and neurochemistry of the brain, which was where Freud originally started in the late nineteenth century. A number of pioneers in the past twenty years have taken an even more fundamental approach. They have argued that we need to construct an entirely new framework for the talking therapies: one that takes the central concepts of evolutionary theory as a starting point. They have asked the same question that Édouard Claparède posed, and that Spielrein was always implicitly asking: 'What is this *for*?' If the unconscious mind exists, if people suffer from hysteria or other mental disorders, or if they experience the wish for pain, how did such things arise and persist? What is the purpose not only of infant attachment, child development and language, but also of anxiety, envy, rage, joy, love and healing? The answers may be open to huge debate, but without such a debate, we will never find sensible explanations for such things. In the words of the evolutionary scholar Brian Boyd:

Some of the answers proposed in an evolutionary explanation of human nature may be premature, but they will be tested, sifted, and refined in due course. But incorporating deep time into our knowledge of the species adds a dimension whose absence had distorted all our thinking.[31]

Nowadays, many psychologists and psychiatrists are asking exactly these questions. So are biologists, anthropologists and philosophers.[32] What is especially welcome is that some psychoanalysts are finally joining in the dialogue too. In a book entitled *The Adaptive Psyche*, US psychoanalysts Daniel Kriegman and Malcolm Slavin have proposed nothing less than a total reinterpretation of psychoanalysis, to bring it into alignment with Darwin.[33] They talk of the long, dismal history of attempts to distance human psychology from the rest of nature. They share with other thinkers a conviction that evolutionary knowledge leads not to fatalism but to forgiveness. Just as an understanding of past traumas and family conflict can lessen self-blame, they argue, so can an understanding of our shared evolutionary inheritance. In a discussion that is reminiscent of Spielrein, they propose that our motivational system is divided between the two aims of sex and survival, and a central task of our lives is to negotiate this tension.[34]

Since writing *The Adaptive Psyche*, Daniel Kriegman has also contributed to a book called *Genes on the Couch*.[35] This contains essays written by therapists from a number of different professions and viewpoints, including both Freudians and Jungians. They share a belief in the need to understand evolution as a starting point for any treatment of mental distress. In his own essay, Kriegman writes about the need to rediscover the evolutionary baby in the bathwater of psychoanalysis: 'Not only would I suggest that we will find a living baby, I would also suggest that the baby has nearly drowned and is in desperate need of evolutionary biological resuscitation.'[36] Among other points, Kriegman argues that therapists need to be aware of their own evolutionary interests when seeing patients, so that they can make sense of the feelings that arise during therapy. He criticises generations of male therapists who have blamed women patients for their own biological responses.[37] His point uncannily recalls Jung and his response to Spielrein.

This brings us to the most important question of all about Spielrein's legacy. Were her ideas ignored, suppressed and forgotten because she was a woman? There can be absolutely no doubt that she suffered in many ways during her own lifetime on account of her sex. This occurred not only through her abuse as a child, and her seduction and betrayal as a medical student, but also in the way Freud, Jung and others responded to her ideas. Could she have been written out of history for the same reason? In some ways, the answer is not straightforward. Other women, such as Anna Freud and Melanie Klein, achieved unrivalled reputations in psychoanalysis. Indeed, they benefited from the amnesia concerning Spielrein. What seems clearer is that Spielrein was marginalised not simply because she was a woman, but because she wrote and behaved *as a woman*. From her first paper on her schizophrenic patient, and through most of her other writings, she wrote from a woman's perspective. Spielrein approached biology and sexuality from the viewpoint of a young woman who was both tempted by desire and afraid of it. She wrote about the family dynamics surrounding mothers-in-law in terms of gender roles. She described the development of child language and thought from her own experience of motherhood. Unlike the writings of other major women psychoanalysts, it is almost impossible to read any of Spielrein's professional papers without being aware that she is a woman, and expressing a woman's view. The tentative style of much of her writing also goes against the common scientific habit of only displaying certainty. To write in these ways, rather than to ignore gender differences, was unconventional in a male professional world. It is not surprising that her voice was drowned out by more assertive ones.

Her behaviour reflected her position as a woman in the same way. Whatever had happened between her and her father, she stayed close to him to the end of his life. In spite of Freud's insistence that she should uncover her hatred for Jung, she was never disloyal to him. She carried on trying to persuade those two stubborn titans of psychoanalysis to resume dialogue, years after there was any prospect of it. She insisted on combining the roles of lone parent, researcher, writer and clinician, when her husband and others were insisting it was cruel for a woman to do so. She refused to define herself as a Jungian or a Freudian, a doctor or a psychotherapist, a scientist or an artist, when it might have advanced her career to accept a label that other people recognised. She demanded no acknowledgement from others when they took up her ideas and developed them. She never knew how to play politics, or had the slightest wish to do so. She refused to take sides with anyone, or gather a band of zealous followers to promote her own cause. She did not play by the men's rules.

In a conventional sense, Sabina never achieved her 'higher calling'. There was no school of therapy named after her. There was no Spielrein Institute. In every other way, her achievements were formidable. She worked alongside the key intellectual figures of the age, and contributed to some of their most important ideas. More important, she understood the importance of questioning them, challenging their certainties, teaching them, and encouraging them to learn from one another. Above all, she was willing to explore ways of thinking that no one in her time was able to listen to, or comprehend. Her 'higher calling' was to be exactly as she was: independent, open-minded, perpetually curious, and her own woman.

The descendants of Nikolai and Eva Spielrein

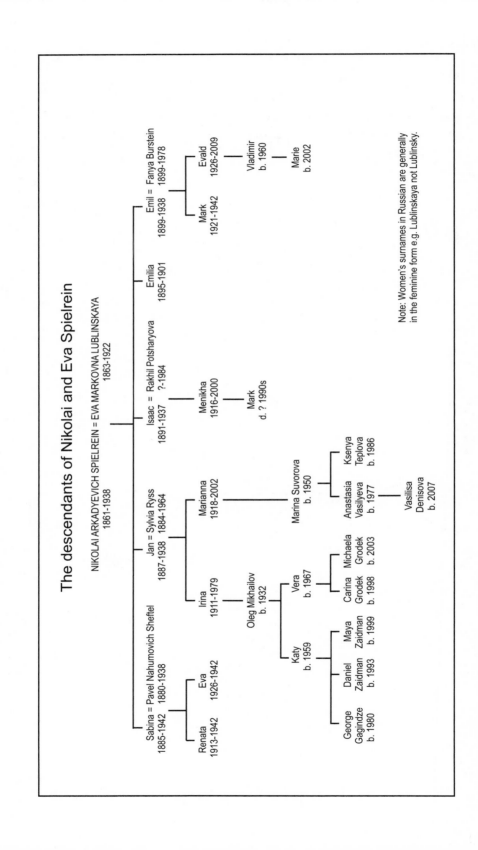

NIKOLAI ARKADYEVICH SPIELREIN = EVA MARKOVNA LUBLINSKAYA
1861-1938   1863-1922

Sabina = Pavel Nahumovich Sheftel
1885-1942   1880-1938

Renata
1913-1942

Eva
1926-1942

Jan = Sylvia Ryss
1887-1938   1884-1964

Irina
1911-1979

Oleg Mikhailov
b. 1932

Katy
b. 1959

George
Gagindze
b. 1980

Daniel
Zaidman
b. 1993

Maya
Zaidman
b. 1999

Vera
b. 1967

Carina
Grodek
b. 1998

Michaela
Grodek
b. 2003

Marianna
1918-2002

Marina Suvorova
b. 1950

Anastasia
Vasilyeva
b. 1977

Vasilisa
Denisova
b. 2007

Ksenya
Teplova
b. 1986

Isaac = Rakhil Potsharyova
1891-1937   ?-1984

Menikha
1916-2000

Mark
d. ? 1990s

Emilia
1895-1901

Emil = Fanya Burstein
1899-1938   1899-1978

Mark
1921-1942

Evald
1926-2009

Vladimir
b. 1960

Marie
b. 2002

Note: Women's surnames in Russian are generally
in the feminine form e.g. Lublinskaya not Lublinsky.

Abbreviations

Sources

AC = A. Carotenuto (ed.), *Tagebuch einer heimlichen Symmetrie: Sabina Spielrein zwischen Jung und Freud* (Freiburg, Kore, 1986)

BB = Brinkmann, E. & Bose, G. (1986), *Sabina Spielrein: Ausgabe in 2 Bänden, Bd. 2 Ausgewählte Schriften* (Frankfurt am Main, Brinkmann & Bose)

CCBW = C. Covington & B. Wharton (eds), *Sabina Spielrein, Forgotten Pioneer of Psychoanalysis* (Hove, Brunner-Routledge, 2003)

COTIPUB = Collection of the International Psychoanalytic University of Berlin https://archive.org/details/CollectionOfTheInternationalPsychoanalytic UniversityBerlin

CSAR = Central State Archives of Russia

CW = C.G. Jung, *The Collected Works of C.G. Jung*, ed. H. Read, M. Fordham, G. Adler & W. McGuire, tr. R.F.C. Hull (Princeton NJ, Princeton University Press, 1953-80)

DS = D. Steffens (tr.), 'Burghölzli Hospital Records of Sabina Spielrein', revised by Barbara Wharton, *JAP* 2001, vol. 46, pp. 15-42

FJL = W. McGuire (ed.), *The Freud/Jung Letters: The Correspondence between Sigmund Freud and C.G. Jung*, tr. R. Manheim & R.F.C. Hull (Princeton NJ, Princeton University Press, 1974)

Geneva = Archives of the descendants of Georges de Morsier, Geneva

HR = Burghölzli Hospital Records

IJP = *International Journal of Psychoanalysis*

IZP = *Internationale Zeitschrift für Ärtzliche Psychoanalyse* (to 1920); *Internationale Zeitschrift für Psychoanalyse* (from 1920)

JAP = *Journal of Analytical Psychology*

Jahrbuch = *Jahrbuch für psychoanalytische und psychopathologische Forschungen*

Minutes = H. Nunberg & E. Federn (eds), *Minutes of the Vienna Psychoanalytic Society* (New York NY, International Universities Press, 1962-75)

SE = S. Freud, *The Standard Edition of the Complete Psychological Works of Sigmund Freud*, tr. under the general editorship of James Strachey (London, Hogarth Press, 1953-74)

SR = S. Richebächer, *Eine fast grausame Liebe zur Wissenschaft* (Munich, BTB, 2008)

TH = T. Hensch (ed.), *Sabina Spielrein: Nimm meine Seele: Tagebücher und Schriften* (Freiburg, Freitag, 2006)

WW = I. Wackenhut & A. Willke, *Sabina Spielrein. Missbrauchüberlebende und Psychoanalytikerin* (unpublished dissertation, Medizinische Hochschule Hannover, 1994)

Yad Vashem = Yad Vashem World Centre for Holocaust Research, Documentation,

Education and Commemoration. Jerusalem, *The Holocaust.* http://www.yadvashem.
   org/yv/en/holocaust/
YIVO = Institute for Jewish Research, New York, *Encyclopedia of Jews in Eastern Europe.*
   http://www.yivoencyclopedia.org/
Zentralblatt = *Zentralblatt für Psychoanalyse und Psychotherapie*

Correspondents

CJ = Carl Jung
ES = Eva Spielrein
IS = Isaac Spielrein
JS = Jan Spielrein
NS = Nikolai Spielrein
PS = Pavel Sheftel
S = Sabina Spielrein
SF = Sigmund Freud

Notes

Preface

1. In the published literature her name is usually given incorrectly as Snitkova.

Introduction

1. The movie was also based on Christopher Hampton's stage play, *The Talking Cure*, which drew on Kerr's book (Hampton, 2002).

2. See for example Bair 2004 on her 'sad life'. For more positive views of her life back in Russia see Cifali 2001, the interview with Elisabeth Márton in Covington 2004, and Appignanesi & Forrester 1992, pp. 204-39.

3. Menikha Spielrein to Henry (Zvi) Lothane, 20 Dec. 1994, Lothane 2007, p. 84.

4. There are three notebooks covering 1 September 1896 to 9 August 1902, of fifty, fifty-three and forty pages respectively (SR, p. 311, WW). In addition, there is an undated diary of forty-two pages, probably from 1906-7 (Moll 2001, p. 155) and a notebook covering the years 1909 to 1912 (AC, p. 31). There are evidently more pages of her diaries in the Geneva archive, although we do not know how many (see SR, pp. 208, 216).

1. Childhood 1885-1904

1. S Diary, 18 Oct. 1910, AC, p. 60.

2. Gilbert 1985, p. 73.

3. There were three grades of guild merchant. Only Guild 1 was allowed to trade abroad.

4. A. Parry, *Rostov Remembered.* http://www.jewishfamilyhistory.org//Rostov.htm

5. Weizmann 1949, p. 95.

6. ibid., p. 102.

7. 'Pogroms', YIVO.

8. 'Rostov-on-Don', YIVO.

9. E.I. Malakhovsky & E.V. Movshovich, *Synagogues and Jewish Prayer Houses of Rostov-on-Don.* http://www.jewishfamilyhistory.org//Rostov.htm

10. S Diary, 18 Oct. 1910, AC, p. 60.

11. ibid., p. 61.

12. ibid., pp. 61-2.

13. HR, 18 Aug. 1904, TH, p. 234. For Mosya as Dr Lublinsky's first name, see SR, p. 30, but no source given.

14. S Diary, 23 Sept. 1909, AC, p. 43.

15. ibid., 18 Oct. 1910, AC, p. 62.

16. ibid., 23 Sept. 1909, AC, pp. 43-4.

17. Ljunggren 2001, p. 79.

18. HR, 18 Aug. 1904, TH, p. 236.

19. Katy Zaidman, personal communication.

20. HR, 18/19 Aug. 1904, TH, pp. 236-7.

21. Ljunggren 2001, pp. 79-80, personal communication from Menikha Spielrein.

22. SF to S, 20 Apr. 1915, AC, p. 127.

23. See Feiga Berg's account of her treatment in Chapter 3.

24. HR, 17 Aug. 1904, TH, p. 233.

25. HR, Dec. 1904, TH, p. 247.

26. She traced the origin of this imaginary word to the French words 'partir' (set out) and 'porter' (carry). It may also have a connection with the word 'parturition', or 'childbirth'.

27. Spielrein 1912c, pp. 57-8.

28. ibid., pp. 60-1. She identifies this uncle as 'Mosya', aged thirteen or fourteen. This is probably not Eva's brother Mosya, whom Jung described as 'an old Russian Jew' sixteen years later. He was presumably a younger brother of Nikolai, with the same name – a diminutive of Moishe or Moses.

29. ibid., p. 60.

30. ibid.

31. In her hospital notes, Jung recorded that the school was in Warsaw, and historians have commented how separation from her family may have affected her. Jung's entry was probably a mistake. In her diary she refers to a visit at home in Rostov from her former Fröbel teacher, and says she remembers being told when the school was opening and they would take the ten brightest children. The implication is that it was local (S Diary, 10 Jun. 1897, TH, p. 21).

32. S Diary, 25 Mar. 1897, TH, p. 19.

33. ibid., 19 Oct. 1910, AC, p. 64.

34. ibid., 2. Feb. 1897, SR, p. 38, WW.

35. ibid., 30 Mar. 1897, SR, pp. 19-20, WW.

36. ibid., 18 Jul. 1898, SR, p. 27, WW.

37. ibid., 3 Feb. 1897, TH, p. 18.

38. ibid., 2 Feb. 1899, TH, p. 30.

39. ibid., 30 Mar. 1897, TH, p. 19.

40. ibid., 25 Mar. 1897, TH, p. 19.

41. ibid., 26 Feb. 1897, TH, p. 18. Ellipses in original.

42. ibid., 8 Nov. 1897, TH, p. 25.

43. ibid., 16 Jul. 1898, SR, p. 36, WW.

44. HR, 8 Jan. 1905, TH, p. 247.

45. S Diary, 18 Oct. 1910, AC, pp. 62-3.

46. ibid.

47. ibid., 28 Mar. 1901, SR, p. 323, WW.

48. ibid., 22 Jul. 1898, TH, pp. 27-8.

49. ibid., 26 Feb. 1900, TH, p. 33.

50. ibid., 19 Oct. 1910, AC, p. 64.

51. Jung 1906c, pp. 20-1.
52. S. Diary, 19 Oct. 1910, AC, p. 66.
53. ibid., 16 Jul. 1901, SR, p. 56, WW.
54. ibid., 11 Jun. 1901, TH, p. 34.
55. ibid., 25 Jun. 1901, TH, p. 35.
56. ibid., 18 Oct. 1910, AC, p. 63.
57. HR, 18 Aug. 1904, TH, p. 235.
58. For example, Carotenuto wrote without comment: 'Sabina was the eldest child; a younger sister died, leaving three younger brothers' (1982, p. 137). Minder, in a sympathetic essay, also reported the fact with no comment (2001a, p. 50).

2. Asylum 1904-1905

1. HR, 18 Aug. 1904, TH, p. 235.
2. Eva was forty-one at the time. We do not know their birth order. It is possible that even her 'youngest' brother was some years older, but he must have been between thirty and fifty. If he is the bearded man in the family photo (see plate section no. 5), he was clearly not old.
3. My reading of Sabina's notes and Jung's case reports has been particularly influenced by the Norwegian historian Petter Aaslestad, who has examined how psychiatrists construct case narratives to support their theoretical frameworks (2009).
4. See Rice 1982.
5. Jung's omission is inexplicable and unprecedented (see Minder 2001a, p. 47). Hysterical symptoms need to be distinguished from ones due to physical illness, so a full medical examination would have been routine.
6. There is no record of a transfer document from the Heller Sanatorium or from Professor Monakov (see Minder 2001a, p. 65 n. 6). Feiga Berg reported that Monakov thought Sabina was schizophrenic (see next chapter).
7. HR, 17 Aug. 1904, TH, p. 235.
8. Graf-Nold 2001, p. 77, A. Forel, *Der Hypnotismus und die Suggestive Psychotherapie* (Stuttgart, Enke, 1902).
9. ibid., p. 75.
10. ibid., p. 79, M. Bleuler, 'Geschichte des Burghölzlis und der Psychiatrischen Universitätsklinik', *Zürcher Spitalgeschichte,* 1951, vol. 2, pp. 377-425.
11. Bair 2003, p. 60.
12. Graf-Nold 2001, p. 79, O. Binswanger, *Die Hysterie* (Vienna, Hölder, 1904).
13. See Witzig 1982.
14. CJ to Andreas Vischer, 22 Aug. 1904, Graf-Nold 2001, p. 83.
15. Although a few writers, including Carotenuto, have gone along with the local Zurich doctor in believing she was psychotic, there is no evidence she had true delusions.
16. Graf-Nold 2001, p. 90, E. Bleuler, *Textbook of Psychiatry,* ed. A. Brill (London, Allen and Unwin, 1936), p. 389.
17. Minder 2001a, p. 57.
18. ibid.
19. ibid., p. 46.

20. HR, 28 Aug. 1904, SR, p. 84.

21. Etkind 1997, p. 137.

22. Kerr records that there were five Russian patients in the hospital in 1904 but does not state his source (1993, p. 34).

23. HR, 17 Aug. 1904, TH, p. 235.

24. Sabina was described as short so this may have been a reasonable weight. If she was over 160 cm in height, she was underweight by modern standards.

25. HR, 18 Aug. 1904, TH, p. 234.

26. HR, 24 Aug. 1904, TH, pp. 239-40.

27. HR, 8 Sept. 1904, TH, p. 241.

28. HR, 26 Sept. 1904, TH, p. 250.

29. HR, 29 Sept. 1904, TH. p. 241.

30. She had probably read Théodore Flournoy's book *From India to the Planet Mars*, describing a medium who claimed to have visited Mars. The book gave Jung the idea for his dissertation. She may have been teasing Jung by imitating the medium in that book or the one in his own dissertation.

31. HR, 18 Oct. 1904, TH, p. 243.

32. HR, undated, TH, p. 256.

33. HR, 25 Oct. 1904, TH, p. 42.

34. HR, 12 Oct. 1904, DS, p. 31.

35. HR, 11 Nov. 1904. TH, p. 246.

36. In spite of the depiction of the scene in the movie *A Dangerous Method*, there is no evidence that Sabina was present on the occasion when Jung carried out the tests on his wife and elucidated her fear of abandonment (see Bair 2003, pp. 92-3).

37. HR, 13 Feb. 1905, DS, p. 34.

38. HR, 28 Apr. 1905, TH, p. 249.

39. BB, p. 230.

40. See the next chapter.

41. Jung 1989, p. 17.

3. Treatment 1904-1905

1. HR, 18 Aug. 1904, TH, p. 236.

2. CJ to SF, 29 Sept. 1905, Minder 2001b, p. 69.

3. 'Fräulein Anna O', *SE*, vol. 2, pp. 21-47.

4. The two others are mentioned in an essay on association, dreams and hysteria. One account mentions an erotic relationship with the doctor. The other patient wanted a sexual relationship with him (Jung 1906b, pp. 392, 394).

5. Jung 1901, pp. 361-8.

6. See Shamdasani 2011, 'Introduction', p. x.

7. HR, 19 Aug. 1904, TH, p. 237.

8. HR, 20 Aug, 1904, TH, p. 238.

9. HR, 22 Aug. 1904, TH, p. 238.

10. The word 'someone' is deleted here.

11. HR, 23 Aug. 1904, TH, p. 239.

12. HR, 24 Aug. 1904, TH, p. 240.

13. Minder 2001a, p. 63.

14. ibid., p. 53.

15. This is virtually the only entry expressing criticism of Sabina's behaviour. It also includes the note 'When I said she had upset her mother, she felt it acutely.' This doctor may not have been fully inducted into the rules of tolerance at the hospital.

16. HR, 8 Sept. 1904, TH, p. 241.

17. HR, 29 Sept. 1904, p. 241.

18. The German is ambiguous: 'Die Patientin hat sozusagen gar keine Ausdauer, wenn sie für sich allein etwas lesen soll, bloss die persöhnliche Gegenwart des Artzes kann sie fixieren, aber dann sehr oft auf Stunden.'

19. HR, 10 Oct. 1904, TH, p. 243.

20. HR, 18 Oct. 1904, TH, pp. 243-4.

21. HR, 4 Nov. 1904, TH, p. 245.

22. HR, 20 Nov. 1904, TH, p. 246.

23. HR, Dec. 1904, TH, pp. 246-7.

24. SR, p. 94.

25. HR, 8 Jan. 1905, TH, pp. 247-8.

26. The other was the first 'analysis' of her foot pains on 18 October.

27. SR, p. 87 n. 31. There is also a report of a final-year Russian medical student undertaking the word association test in 1909, in a compilation published under Jung's supervision. Kerr believed this was Spielrein (1993, p. 126). However, the associations given (e.g. 'Ask/Answer', 'Stubborn/Minded') are too vague to know, and there were fifty-two Russian women medical students in her year (see next chapter).

28. F. Berg, 'Impressions of Psychiatry in Zurich', *Sovremennaya Psykhiatriya*, 1909, vol. 1, p. 13.

29. Berg added: 'These complexes were mainly about her family. The patient was a severe neurasthenic, her mother a hysteric. The father hit the girl very often, and all of this built up inside her mind as enormous and overwhelming suffering. She had no peace. After the patient was able to work through these complexes, she could act in a cooler manner. Her concentration was not disturbed by this suffering any more. Influenced by Jung's psychotherapy, she developed a new interest in her soul, namely an interest in science. Nowadays this young girl studies in Zurich and is absolutely healthy.'

30. HR, 13 Jan. 1905, TH, p. 248.

31. ibid., 29 Jan. 1905, TH, p. 249.

32. Jung 1906a, p. 304.

33. ibid., p. 316.

34. Minder 2001a, p. 55.

35. Graf-Nold 2001, p. 96.

36. CJ to SF, 28 Oct. 1907, *FJL*, p. 95.

37. Her real name was Bertha Pappenheim and she later became a notable social worker. For a brief summary of her case, see Launer 2005.

38. Freud & Breuer 1895, pp. 32-3.

39. Graf-Nold 2001, p. 80. Bleuler reviewed the book and spoke of Freud's ideas at the Burghölzli meetings that Sabina attended.

40. See Vickers 2011.
41. HR, 27 Aug. 1904, DS, p. 30.
42. HR, 10 Sept. 1904, DS, p. 30.
43. HR, 14 Sept. 1904, DS, p. 30.
44. HR, 12 Oct. 1904, DS, p. 31.
45. HR, 25 Oct. 1904, TH, p. 251.
46. HR, 28 Nov. 1904, DS, p. 32.
47. HR, 6 Jan. 1905, TH, p. 252.
48. Jung implied the fright may have happened on New Year's Day but did not specify the date of his three-hour session. This may have occurred before Bleuler's letter of 6 January, or after it.
49. HR, 23 May 1905, DS, p. 36.
50. HR, 31 May 1905, TH, p. 254.
51. HR, 7 Jun. 1905, DS, p. 37.
52. HR, 18 Apr. 1905, DS, p. 35.
53. HR, 27 Apr. 1905, TH, p. 253.
54. Graf-Nold 2001, p. 101.

4. Medical Student 1905

1. 'Junga' is a Russian diminutive of Jung, also meaning 'ship's boy'.
2. S Diary, 24 Apr. 1905, pp. 45-6.
3. 'Nadezhda Prokov'yevna Suslova: The First Russian Woman Doctor', *Zhurnal Zdorov'e*, 1988/9. http://lechebnik.info/511/20.htm
4. BB, p. 223.
5. Weizmann 1949, p. 92.
6. ibid., p. 92.
7. Richebächer 2003, p. 237, *Berner Volkzeitung*.
8. SR, p. 115.
9. SR, p. 152, immigration police records.
10. S Diary, 8 Jun. 1905, TH, p. 47.
11. HR, 17 Jul. 1905, SR, p. 124.
12. S Diary, 29 Aug. 1906, TH, p. 53.
13. S to ES, 26 Aug. 1905, TH, p. 69. TH dates this as 26 Aug. 1908. Lothane has corrected it (1999, p. 1192).
14. SR, p. 99, Louise Rähmi's hospital record.
15. HR, 30 Jul. 1905, SR, p. 121.
16. S to ES, 26 Aug. 1905, TH, p. 69 (see n. 13).
17. Minder 2001b, p. 70.
18. CJ to SF, 25 Sept. 1905, Minder 2001b, p. 69. Barbara Wharton's translation.
19. Minder 2001a, p. 64.
20. I am grateful to Judith Prais for suggesting this construction of the letter.
21. S letter draft to SF, 13 Jun. 1909, AC, p. 100.
22. Jung 1905, p. 98.
23. Jung 1906c, p. 16.

24. CJ to SF, 7 Mar. 1909, *FJL*, p. 207.

25. S letter draft to SF, 11 Jun. 1909, AC, p. 91.

26. ibid., p. 92.

27. Lothane 1999, p. 1193.

28. Bair 2003, p. 108.

29. ibid., p. 155.

30. Kerr 1993, pp. 169, 177.

31. Jung 1905, p. 98.

32. Bair 2003, pp. 93-7.

33. 'Rostov-on-Don', YIVO.

34. Ljunggren 2001, p. 80.

35. ibid., p. 93, based on letters and notes in possession of the Spielrein family.

36. ibid., p. 94, interview with Menikha Spielrein. Photos of Isaac show no facial deformity, so the account may have been exaggerated.

37. SR, p. 152, Elisabeth Márton interview with Menikha Spielrein.

5. Man's Talk 1906-1907

1. S letter draft to CJ, 29 Aug. 1906, TH, pp. 54-5.

2. ibid.

3. ibid., TH, pp. 57-8.

4. S letter draft to CJ, 8 Jun. 1906, TH, p. 51.

5. S letter draft to CJ, 1906, TH, pp. 65-7.

6. S letter draft to CJ, 29 Aug. 1906, TH, p. 55.

7. ibid., pp. 59-61.

8. Copyright costs preclude long quotations from Jung and Freud. For anyone with a copy of the correspondence, referring to it alongside this biography will be enlightening.

9. See Gay 1988, pp. 178-9.

10. S. Shamdasani 2011, p. ix, A. Meyer, *Psychological Bulletin*, 1905, p. 242.

11. CJ to SF, 5 Oct. 1906, *FJL*, p. 4.

12. CJ to SF, 23 Oct. 1906, *FJL*, p. 7.

13. Rice 1982, p. 22.

14. SF to CJ, 27 Oct. 1906, *FJL*, p. 8.

15. SF to CJ, 6 Dec. 1906. *FJL*, pp. 12-13.

16. CJ to SF, 6 Jul. 1907, *FJL*, pp. 71-2.

17. See comments by Vladimir Nabokov, *FJL*, p. 72 n. 2.

18. SF to CJ, 10 Jul. 1907, *FJL*, p. 75.

19. CJ to SF, 25 Jul. 1907, *FJL*, p. 90.

20. CJ to SF, 10 Oct. 1907, *FJL*, p. 93.

21. CJ to SF, 28 Oct. 1907, *FJL*, p. 94.

22. Jung 1906c, p. 16.

23. ibid., pp. 20-1.

24. Jones 1953-57, vol. 2, p. 112.

25. CJ to SF, 4 Sept. 1907, *FJL*, p. 83.

26. FS to CJ, 19 Sept. 1907, *FJL*, p. 87.

6. Woman's Talk 1907-1908

1. S letter draft to CJ, undated, TH, p. 139.
2. See Chapter 9.
3. Lothane 1999, p. 1193.
4. See previous chapter.
5. Spielrein 1912a.
6. S to CJ, 27/28 Jan. 1916, AC, p. 179.
7. S letter draft to SF, 13 Jun. 1909, AC, p. 100.
8. The first woman to be recognised as a psychoanalyst was Margarethe Hilferding-Hönigsberg, who joined the Vienna Psychoanalytic Society in 1910, but left with Adler's group the following year (see Chapter 13). She died in the Holocaust while being deported from Theresienstadt in June 1942, two months before Spielrein and her children were murdered.
9. S letter draft to SF, 13 Jun. 1909, AC, p. 100.
10. S letter draft to CJ, undated, Moll 2001, p. 156.
11. I have summarised these questions following Cifali 2001, p. 133.
12. S letter draft to CJ, undated, TH, p. 131.
13. In TH this appears as the last letter draft. I have followed the order in Moll 2001, which reverses the second and third. This seems to offer a more logical progression from an intellectual essay to an outpouring of emotion.
14. S letter draft to CJ, undated, TH, p. 140.
15. ibid., p. 145.
16. Moll 2001, p. 156.
17. S letter draft to CJ, undated, TH, p. 136.
18. ibid., p. 137.
19. ibid., p. 139.
20. Kerr 1993, p. 154.
21. A second daughter, Gret, had been born in February 1906.
22. Bair 2003, p. 138, hospital records of Otto Gross.
23. CJ to SF, 25 May 1908, *FJL*, p. 153.
24. SF to CJ, 29 May 1908, *FJL*, p. 154.
25. CJ to SF, 19 Jun. 1908, *FJL*, p. 155.
26. Kerr gives a list of analysts who had become romantically involved with patients by this date. They include Gross, Stekel, Jones, Pfister and Ferenczi (Kerr 1993, p. 379).

7. Poetry 1908

1. CJ to S, 30 Jun. 1908, AC, pp. 189-90. Because of copyright fees, the quotations I use from Jung's letters are far shorter than those from Spielrein. The full text of the letters is available online in *JAP*, 2001, vol. 46, pp. 173-99.
2. Bair assumes this to be the case (see Bair 2003, p. 145). The timing fits, although

it seems out of character for Spielrein to mock Jung.

3. CJ to S, 20 Jun. 1908, AC, p. 189.
4. CJ to S, 4 Jul. 1908, AC, p. 190.
5. CJ to S, 12 Aug. 1908, AC, pp. 191-3.
6. CJ to S, 19 Aug. 1908, Lothane 1999, p. 1194 (his translation), Geneva.
7. CJ to S, 2 Sept. 1908, AC, p. 194.
8. ES to S, 1 Sept. 1908, Lothane 1999, p. 1196 (his translation), original in possession of Elisabeth Márton.
9. CJ to S, 28 Sept. 1908, AC, pp. 194-5.
10. S to ES, undated, Lothane 1999, p. 1198 (his translation), Geneva.
11. Ellipsis in original.
12. S to ES, undated, Lothane 1999, p. 1196 (his translation), Geneva.
13. ibid.
14. CJ to S, 4 Dec. 1908, AC, pp. 195-6.
15. The published version indicates the letter is incomplete, but not whether the remainder has been lost or withheld.

8. Crisis 1909

1. CJ to SF, 7 Mar. 1909, *FJL*, p. 207.
2. Richebächer 2003, p. 242.
3. S letter draft to SF, 11 Jun. 1909, AC, p. 92.
4. SF to CJ, 9 Mar. 1909, *FJL*, p. 210.
5. CJ to SF, 11 Mar. 1909, *FJL*, p. 211.
6. Minder 2001a, p. 65 n. 11.
7. CJ to SF, 19 Jan. 1909, *FJL*, p. 198.
8. CJ to SF, 9 Sept. 1908, *FJL*, p. 171.
9. See Chapter 9.
10. S to SF, 30 May 1909, AC, p. 89.
11. SF to CJ, 3 Jun. 1909, *FJL*, p. 226. In the same letter, Freud also responded to a remark by Jung about a visiting Russian doctor, Mikhail Asiatani. Jung described Russians as being 'as ill-differentiated as fish in a shoal'. Freud responded that they were 'especially deficient in the art of painstaking work'.
12. The telegram has not survived.
13. SF to S, 4 Jun. 1909, AC, p. 115.
14. CJ to SF, 4 Jun. 1909, *FJL*, p. 228.
15. This is a puzzling claim regarding Gross, whom he saw in the Burghölzli as paid senior physician.
16. SF to CJ, 7 Jun. 1909, *FJL*, p. 230.
17. 'The Future Prospects of Psychoanalytic Therapy', *SE*, vol. 12, p. 144.
18. SF to CJ, 31 Dec. 1911, *FJL*, p. 476.
19. SF to S, 8 Jun. 1909, AC, pp. 115-16.
20. For Freud's use of this word, see Lothane 1999, p. 1199.
21. SF to CJ, 18 Jun. 1909, *FJL*, p. 235. Rice comments: 'Freud evidently enjoyed these developments and responded to them with merriment' (Rice 1982, p. 24).

22. CJ to SF, 12 Jun. 1909, *FJL*, p. 232.

9. Free Associations 1909

1. S letter draft to SF, 11 Jun. 1909, AC, p. 95.
2. S letter draft to SF, Jun. 1909, Lothane 1999, p. 1199, WW.
3. S letter draft to SF, 10 Jun. 1909, AC, p. 90.
4. S letter draft to SF, 13 Jun. 1909, AC, p. 100.
5. S letter draft to SF, 10 Jun. 1909, AC, p. 91.
6. ibid.
7. S letter draft to SF, 13 Jun. 1909, AC, p. 100.
8. S letter draft to SF, 20 Jun. 1909, AC, p. 104.
9. S letter draft to SF, 13 Jun. 1909, AC, p. 99.
10. S letter draft to SF, 20 Jun. 1909, AC, p. 106.
11. S letter draft to SF, 1909, AC, p. 108.
12. She may have gone to a performance of Siegfried in Zurich in August 1907, possibly giving birth to the idea (Márton, 2002).
13. S letter draft to SF, 1909, AC, p. 108.
14. ibid., 11 Jun. 1909, AC, p. 94.
15. ibid, pp. 91-2.
16. ibid., p. 106.
17. See Chapter 6.
18. S letter draft to SF, 10 Jun. 1909, AC, p. 94.
19. S letter draft to SF, 13 Jun. 1909, AC, p. 98.
20. S letter draft to SF, 10 Jun. 1909, AC, p. 91.
21. SR, p. 179.
22. Lothane 1999, p. 1189.
23. See Chapter 13.
24. I am grateful to Judith Prais for this close reading of the text.
25. Cremerius 2003, p. 73.
26. S letter draft to SF, 20 Jun. 1909, AC, p. 106. Jung's associations are described in detail in Bair 2003, pp. 109-13, 688 n. 22. Binswanger noted in another experiment that Jung had difficulty with the sound 'sh', and drew the conclusion that this related to 'a former female patient whose name begins with this sound who had slandered him'. The tests took place in January 1907, two years before there was any fear of slander, so the inference that this was Spielrein is doubtful.
27. S letter draft to SF, 13 Jun. 1909, AC, p. 98.
28. ibid., p. 106.
29. ibid., p. 101.
30. Lothane 2013, p. 7.
31. S letter draft to SF, 11 Jun. 1909, AC, p. 92.
32. This may be the woman patient she also mentioned in a letter to her mother (see

Chapter 7).

33. S letter draft to SF, 11 Jun. 1909, AC, p. 94.
34. ibid., pp. 95-6.
35. S letter draft to SF, 12 Jun. 1909, AC, pp. 96-7.
36. ibid.
37. S letter draft to SF, 11 Jun. 1909, p. 92.
38. ibid., p. 93.
39. ibid.
40. S letter draft to SF, 12 Jun. 1909, AC, p. 97.
41. S letter draft to SF, 13 Jun. 1909, AC, p. 98.
42. ibid., p. 102.
43. ibid.
44. S letter draft to SF, 10 Jun. 1909, AC, p. 90.
45. ibid., p. 91.

10. Reconciliation 1909-1910

1. S letter draft to SF, 20 Jun. 1909, AC, p. 103.
2. S Diary, 11 Sept. 1910, AC, p. 48.
3. S letter draft to SF, 20 Jun. 1909, AC, p. 103.
4. CJ to SF, 21 Jun. 1909, *FJL*, p. 236.
5. SF to S, 24 Jun. 1909, AC, p. 117.
6. SF to CJ, 30 Jun. 1909, *FJL*, p. 238.
7. CJ to SF, 13 Jul. 1909, *FJL*, p. 240.
8. Cremerius 2003, pp. 63-4.
9. S letter draft to SF, 20 Jun. 1909, AC, pp. 103-4.
10. With the exception of one short fragment, probably from an earlier period, this is when the diary published by Carotenuto begins.
11. S letter draft to SF, 21 Jun. 1909, AC, pp. 42-3.
12. S Diary, 27 Aug. 1909, AC, pp. 39-40. First ellipsis in original.
13. ibid., 28 Aug. 1909, AC, pp. 40-1.
14. ibid., p. 41.
15. ibid, 21 Sept. 1909, AC, p. 42.
16. SR, pp. 152f.
17. S Diary, 23 Sept. 1909, AC, p. 45.
18. CJ to SF, 14 Oct. 1909, *FJL*, p. 252.
19. S letter draft to CJ, undated, TH, pp. 137-8.
20. SR, p. 165.
21. S. Grebelskaja, 'Psychologisches Analyse eines Paranoiden', *IZP*, 1912, vol. 4, pp. 116-40.
22. SR, p. 152.
23. SR, pp. 217-18.
24. S Diary, 8 Sept. 1910, AC, p. 46.
25. ibid., 19 Oct. 1910, p. 66.

26. SR, p. 155 (see also S Diary, 11 Jul. 1912, AC, p. 86).

27. S Diary, 19 Oct. 1910, AC, pp. 64-5.

28. ibid., p. 67.

29. ibid., p. 69.

30. Ellipsis in the original.

31. S Diary, 19 Oct. 1910, AC, p. 71.

32. E. Bleuler to S, 16 Oct. 1909, Lothane 1999, p. 1201, Geneva.

11. Separation 1910-1911

1. S Diary, 11 Sept. 1910, AC, p. 50.

2. ibid., p. 48.

3. ibid., p. 51.

4. The German title was *Wandlungen und Symbole der Libido*.

5. He used the fantasies of an American medium called Mrs Miller. These had been published in 1906 by Théodore Flournoy, who also wrote an introduction commenting on them, although Jung never acknowledged this (see Witzig 1982, p. 146).

6. Hayman 1999, p. 121, although no source is given.

7. S Diary, 8 Sept. 1910, AC, pp. 46-7.

8. ibid.

9. ibid., 14 Sept. 1910, AC, p. 52.

10. ibid.

11. ibid., Sept. 1910, AC, pp. 53-4.

12. ibid., p. 54.

13. ibid., p. 56.

14. ibid., pp. 58-9.

15. Ellipsis in the original.

16. S Diary, 9 Oct. 1910, AC, p. 59.

17. See Chapter 1.

18. See Chapter 10.

19. The reason for this comment is unclear. She may mean that Freud replaced her as Jung's potential soul mate.

20. S Diary, 19 Oct. 1910, AC, p. 70.

21. ibid., 24 Nov. 1910, AC, p. 73.

22. ibid.

23. See Bair 2003, p. 229.

24. Kerr 1993, p. 366.

25. These are the letters from 1908 dated 30 Jun., 4 Jul., 12 Aug. and 4 Dec. (see Chapter 9). This is out of a total of around forty extant communications from Jung to Spielrein between 1909 and 1919, a further twenty-seven to Freud that allude to her, and five to her mother (excluding ones sent from the Burghölzli).

26. NS to S, 10 Jun. 1910, SR, p. 158, WW (dated 10 Jun. 1901 in SR; presumably a misprint).

27. S Diary, 19 Oct. 10, AC, p. 72.

28. ibid., 8 Dec. 1910, p. 78.

29. NS to S, 9 Jan. 1910, SR, p. 162, Geneva.
30. ibid., 26 Nov. 1910, SR, pp. 75-6, Geneva.
31. ibid., 8 Dec. 1910, SR, p. 77, Geneva.
32. ibid., 21 Dec. 1910, SR, p. 79, Geneva.
33. SR, pp. 159-60, Zurich State Archive.
34. ibid., p. 159.
35. SR, p. 160, Zurich State Archive.
36. ES to S, undated, SR, p. 160, Geneva.
37. Ellipsis in the original.
38. S Diary, 8 Dec. 1910, AC, p. 78.
39. ibid., 21 Dec. 1910, AC, p. 79.
40. ibid., 19 Jan. 1911, AC, p. 80.
41. The psychoanalyst Bruno Bettelheim pointed out in 1983 that Jung had fulfilled his primary obligation to Spielrein since 'he cured her' (1983, p. 43). However, his argument was based on the mistaken premise that she was his psychoanalytic patient.

12. Munich 1911

1. S to CJ, 1911, AC, p. 136.
2. S Diary, 7 Jan. 1912, TH, p. 82.
3. S Diary, February 1911, AC, pp. 80-1.
4. JS to S, 7 May 1910, SR, p. 162, Geneva.
5. SR, p. 183, Leipzig University Archive. Wundt had taught Théodore Flournoy, who in turn influenced both Jung and Claparède, who was to be Spielrein's director in Geneva.
6. S Diary, 28 Feb. 1911, AC, p. 82. I have taken 'Du' in the original to mean Spielrein herself.
7. SR, pp. 161-4.
8. SF to S, 20 Apr. 1915, AC, pp. 127-8.
9. S to CJ, 1911, AC, p. 136.
10. Freud 1911.
11. Spielrein 1911.
12. Van Waning 1992, p. 402.
13. Jung 1952.
14. Freud 1911, p. 80.
15. CJ to SF, 12 Jun. 1911, *FJL,* p. 426.
16. CJ to S, 8 Aug. 1911, AC, pp. 199-200.
17. CJ to S, 17/18 Aug. 1911, AC, p. 200.
18. CJ to SF, 29 Aug. 1911, *FJL,* p. 439.
19. Bair 2003, p. 248.
20. CJ to S, 21/22 Sept. 1911, AC, pp. 201-2.
21. However, he had suggested to her in a letter the previous month that she should consult a neurologist colleague in Munich, Leonhard Seif, presumably for this symptom or a similar one (see CJ letter to S, 8 Aug. 1911, AC, p. 199).

13. Sex Versus Survival 1911

1. Spielrein 1912a, p. 466.
2. SF to CJ, 12 Oct. 1911, *FJL*, p. 273.
3. ibid.
4. SF to S, AC, 27 Oct. 1911, pp. 117-18.
5. SF to CJ, 27 Oct. 1911, *FJL*, p. 458.
6. See Chapter 16.
7. *Minutes*, 8 Nov. 1911, vol. 3, pp. 302-3.
8. ibid., 15 Nov. 11. pp. 316-17.
9. CJ to S, Nov. 1911, AC, p. 202.
10. Emma Jung to SF, 6 Nov. 1911, *FJL*, pp. 455-7.
11. ibid., 24 Nov. 1911, *FJL*, pp. 465-6.
12. CJ to S, 24 Nov. 1911, AC, pp. 203-4.
13. P. Federn, 'Sabina Spielrein: Die Destruktion als Ursache des Werdens', *IZP*, 1913, vol. 2, pp. 89-93. Without subscribing to her overall theory, Federn praised her 'sensitivity to emotional relationships' and her 'contribution to the analysis of the mystical modality of thought'.
14. *Minutes*, 29 Nov. 11, vol. 3, pp. 329-31.
15. Kerr 1993, p. 320. I think Kerr understood the stature of Spielrein's theory but not its biological basis.
16. Spielrein 1912a, p. 465.
17. ibid., p. 467.
18. Mechnikov 1903.
19. Etkind 1997, p. 1.
20. Solovyov 1985.
21. Etkind 1997, pp. 152-3.
22. Darwin 1859.
23. Darwin 1871.
24. Darwin 1872.
25. Darwin 1859, p. 576.
26. Romanes 1883.
27. The theory had been put forward by Darwin's leading German disciple, Ernst Häckel.
28. See Sulloway 1979.
29. See Ritvo 1974.
30. See Triarhou & del Cerro 1985.
31. Freud 1914, pp. 78-9.
32. Kriegman & Slavin 1992, p. 35.
33. Modern discoveries in epigenetics have complicated the picture slightly but have not vindicated Lamarck (see Haig 2007).
34. See Stevens 1982.
35. See Clark 1996.
36. See Haig 1993.
37. See Baker and Oram 1998.

38. See Chisholm 1999, pp. 149-202. Chisholm nicely characterises this core dilemma of where to invest human energy as 'sex now or sex later' (personal communication).

39. This area is a minefield in evolutionary psychology. However, there have been legitimate attempts to understand variations like homosexuality as adaptations that allow alternative contributions to group survival, or to act as social signals that create paradoxical opportunities for reproduction (see, for example, Buss 2003 and Zuk 2003).

40. S to CJ, 27 Nov. 1917, AC, pp. 143-4 (see also discussion in Chapter 17).

14. Aftermath 1912

1. S to CJ, early 1912, AC, pp. 138-9.

2. Bleuler to SF, 11 Mar. 1911, Alexander & Selesnik 1965, p. 5.

3. The split between Bleuler and Freud, and its implications for the division between psychiatry and psychoanalysis, are covered in Falzeder 2007.

4. SF to CJ, 30 Nov. 1911, *FJL*, p. 468.

5. In German the difference between 'Ihr' (meaning 'yours') and 'ihr' (meaning 'hers') is simply the capital letter.

6. In the original: 'ΨA *fara da se.*'

7. CJ to SF, 11 Dec. 1911, *FJL*, p. 470.

8. CJ to S, 11 Dec. 1911, AC, p. 205.

9. CJ to S, 23 Dec. 1911, AC, p. 206.

10. SF to CJ, 17 Dec. 1911, *FJL*, p. 471.

11. *Totem and Taboo*, *SE*, vol. 13, pp. 1-161.

12. *Moses and Monotheism*, *SE*, vol. 23, pp. 7-140.

13. S Diary, 7 Jan. 1912, AC, pp. 82-3.

14. All ellipses in original.

15. S Diary, 17 Feb. 1912, AC, p. 84.

16. Richebächer 2003, p. 243.

17. CJ letter to S, 18 Mar. 1912, AC, pp. 206-7.

18. Kerr 1993, p. 403.

19. CJ to S, 25 Mar. 1912. AC, pp. 207-8.

20. Appignanesi & Forrester 1992, p. 219.

21. CJ to SF, 1 Apr. 1912, *FJL*, p. 498. The quotation is from *Ars Poetica*, 'Unity and Harmony', lines 1-6: 'Supposing a painter had chosen to set a human head on a horse's neck, and covered a mixture of limbs with multi-coloured plumage, so what was a lovely woman, at the top ended repulsively in the tail of a fish: if asked to view this, could you stifle laughter, my friends?'

22. SF to CJ, 21 Mar. 1912, *FJL*, p. 494.

23. CJ to SF, 1 Apr. 1912, *FJL*, p. 498.

24. See for example Covington 2003 and Britton 2003.

25. SF to CJ, 21 Apr. 1912, *FJL*, p. 499.

26. See Chapter 17.

27. Freud 1915, p. 165.

28. Spielrein 1912c.

29. SF to S, 14 Jun. 1912, AC, p. 119.
30. S Diary, 11 Jul. 1912, AC, p. 85.

15. Berlin 1912-1914

1. S Diary, 11 Jul, 1912, AC, pp. 85-6.
2. She used the German version of his name, Paul, only in her diary entry of 11 Jul. 1912, see previous chapter.
3. SR, p. 178.
4. Covington suggests Spielrein was now having sexual fantasies about Freud instead of Jung (2003, p. 5).
5. SR, p. 177, CSAR. In her diary, Spielrein accidentally wrote '14.1.' instead of '14.J.' (see TH, p. 85).
6. ibid., Munich city records, Vienna police register.
7. ibid., p. 177.
8. S Diary, 17 Feb. 1912, AC, p. 84.
9. PS to S, 5-11 Jan. 1922, SR, p. 179, Geneva.
10. SF to S, 20 Aug. 1912, AC, p. 120.
11. SR, p. 183.
12. ibid.
13. ibid., pp. 182-5.
14. SF to S, 13 Dec. 1912, AC, p. 121.
15. SR, pp. 184-5.
16. SF to S, 20 Jan. 1913, AC, p. 121.
17. SF to CJ, 3 Jan. 1913, *FJL*, p. 539.
18. CJ to SF, 6 Jan. 1913, *FJL*, p. 540.
19. SF to S, 20 Jan. 1913, AC, p. 122.
20. CJ to S, 11 Apr. 1913, AC, p. 209.
21. SF to Karl Abraham, 27 Mar. 1913, Falzeder 2002, p. 181.
22. Grosskurth 1991.
23. SR, p. 190.
24. Karl Abraham to SF, 15 Jan. 1914, Falzeder 2002, p. 216.
25. SR, p. 199.
26. ES letter to S, undated, SR, p. 184, Geneva.
27. Esther Aptekmann to S, 1 Oct. 1913. SR, pp. 193-4, Geneva.
28. Rebecca Ter-Oganessian to S, 1913, SR, p. 195, Geneva.
29. NS to S, 13 Jun. 1913, TH, p. 154.
30. Spielrein 1913a.
31. Spielrein 1914a.
32. Spielrein 1912c.
33. Van Waning 1992, p. 406.
34. Spielrein 1913c.

35. ibid., p. 591.
36. ibid., p. 592.
37. ibid., p. 590.
38. Van Waning 1992, p. 408.
39. Spielrein 1913b.
40. Spielrein 1914b.
41. CJ to S, 24 Aug. 1913, AC, p. 210.
42. Spielrein's letters to Freud are not available after 1914, and we do not have her letters to Jung from this period either, so have to infer their contents from the replies.
43. SF to S, 8 May 1913, AC, p. 124.
44. ibid., 28 Aug. 1913, AC, p. 124.
45. Rebecca Ter-Oganessian to S, 1913, SR, p. 195, Geneva.
46. S to CJ, 27/28 Jan. 1918, AC, pp. 182-3.
47. SR, pp. 196-7.
48. CJ to S, Dec. 1913, AC, p. 211.
49. Freud wrote 'Sie' with a capital 'S', referring to Rider Haggard's famous novel depicting 'She who must be obeyed'. He was also making a pun on 'Sie' [she] as opposed to 'Siegfried'.
50. SF to S, 29 Dec. 1913, AC, p. 125.
51. S to SF, Dec. 1913, SR, p. 196, Geneva.
52. SR, p. 198.
53. ibid., pp. 197, 200.
54. SF letter to S, 15 May 1914, AC, p. 125.
55. SF to S, 12 Jun. 1914, AC, pp. 126-7.
56. Karl Abraham to SF, 14 Jun. 1914, Falzeder 2002, p. 247.
57. CJ to S, 15 Apr. 1914, AC, p. 211.
58. Storr 1997, p. 89.

16. Switzerland Again 1914-1919

1. S letter to SF, probably 1914, Carotenuto 1982, p. 112, translation taken from there. This is not in the German edition. An endnote records: 'This paragraph appears on the back of a letter sent from Jung to Sabina Spielrein of 15 April 1914 and was probably sent to Freud by Spielrein in the same period.'
2. SF to S, 13 Oct. 1912, AC, p. 121.
3. SR, p. 199.
4. PS to S, 6 Aug. 1914, SR, p. 201, Geneva.
5. PS to S, 1914, SR, p. 200, Geneva.
6. ES to S, 27 Oct. 1914, SR, p. 201, Geneva.
7. Shaina Grebelskaya to S, 16 Jan. 1914, 7 May 1914, SR, p. 202, Geneva.
8. S to CJ, 27 Nov. 1917, AC, p. 141.
9. PS to S, 11 Oct. 1917, SR, p. 201, Geneva.
10. JS to S, 15 Nov. 1915, SR, p. 202, Geneva.
11. SR, p. 215.
12. Bleuler letter to S, 28 Dec. 1914, TH, p. 254. This reminds us how much was lost

from the historical record once people could pick up the telephone.

13. SF to S, 20 Apr. 1915, AC, pp. 127-8.

14. ES to S, 2 Mar. 1915; NS to S, 20 Jun. 1915, SR, p. 205, Geneva.

15. S to CJ, 27/28 Jan. 1918, AC, p. 183.

16. ES to S, 21 Aug. 1915, SR, p. 205, Geneva.

17. ES to S, 9 Dec. 1915, SR, p. 205, Geneva.

18. S to CJ, 27 Nov. 1917, AC, p. 141.

19. SR, p. 215.

20. ES to S, 12 Aug. 1917, SR, p. 211.

21. ES to S, 2 Mar. 1915, SR, p. 204, Geneva.

22. SR, pp. 204-5.

23. SR, p. 215.

24. ES to S, 18 Apr. 1917, SR, p. 210, Geneva.

25. NS to S, 23 Nov. 1917, SR, p. 240, Geneva.

26. S to CJ, 19 Jan. 1918, AC, pp. 175-6.

27. BB, p. 259.

28. S to CJ, 6 Jan. 1918, AC, p. 167.

29. ES to S, SR, 28 Nov. 1917, p. 211.

30. ibid.

31. SR, p. 215.

32. S Diary, 7 Dec. 1919, SR, p. 216, Geneva.

33. SR, p. 218.

34. It also reflects the fact that hundreds of family letters have never been released or published.

35. Spielrein 1915.

36. Spielrein 1918.

37. S to CJ, 19 Jan. 1918, AC, p. 176 .

38. Bleuler to S, 7 Jul. 1919, TH, p. 255.

39. Carotenuto described Spielrein's offers to both Freud and Jung to translate their works as 'strange' (1982, pp. 186-7). I find this odd.

40. SF to S, 2 Aug. 1919, AC, pp. 128-9.

41. Roazen 1990.

42. NS to S, 7 Dec. 1919, SR, p. 216, Geneva.

43. 'Pogroms', YIVO.

44. JS to S, 1 Jul. 1918, SR, p. 214, Geneva.

45. ES to S, 1 Jul. 1919, SR, p. 216, Geneva.

46. Etkind 1997, p. 169.

47. S to CJ, 6 Jan. 1918, AC, p. 167.

48. ES to S, 1920, SR, p. 218, Geneva.

49. SR, p. 218, medical report of Dr S. Zeitlin, 29 Aug. 1918.

17. Your Best Pupil 1917-1919

1. CJ to S, 1 Sept. 1919, AC, p. 223.

2. CJ to S, 13 Sept. 1917, AC, p. 215.

3. CJ to S, 10 Oct. 1917, AC, pp. 213-14.

4. S to CJ, 27 Nov. 1917, AC, p. 141.

5. ibid., pp. 143-4.

6. I have avoided the term 'the selfish gene' because of its unhelpful connotations of 'selfishness'. Every evolutionist, including Richard Dawkins (who coined the term), recognises that this evolutionary fitness requires collaboration just as much as competition, at many levels including the gene itself. For a fuller treatment of this subject, see Launer 2015.

7. CJ to S, 30 Nov. 1917, AC, p. 215.

8. S to CJ, 3 Dec. 1917, AC, p. 145.

9. ibid., p. 147.

10. See Chisholm 1999, pp. 227-38.

11. See Trivers 2011.

12. S to CJ, 15 Dec. 1917, AC, p. 149.

13. ibid., p. 152.

14. S to CJ, 20 Dec. 1917, AC, p. 155.

15. S to CJ, 6 Jan. 1918, AC, p. 161.

16. ibid., p. 164.

17. ibid., p. 165.

18. ibid., p. 168.

19. ibid., p. 173.

20. S to CJ, 19 Jan. 1918, AC, p. 175.

21. Kerr 1993, p. 487.

22. CJ to S, 21 Jan. 1918, AC, p. 219.

23. CJ to S, Jan. 1918, AC, p. 219.

24. S to CJ, 27-28 Jan. 1918, AC, p. 177.

25. ibid., p. 182.

26. ibid., p. 185.

27. ibid., p. 186.

28. CJ to S, 19 Mar. 1919, AC, p. 221.

29. CJ to S, 3 Apr. 1919, AC, p. 222.

30. Freud 1920, p. 55.

31. *Minutes*, 29 Nov. 11, vol. 3, p. 331: 'At first glance it might seem that, under Jung's influence, Dr Spielrein had formulated, many years before Freud, the hypothesis that instinct life ... consists of two opposing drives – the life instinct and the death instinct. Closer scrutiny, however, discloses that she does not express this theory at all, but rather believes that the sexual instinct, the creative instinct itself, contains a destructive component.'

32. For a fuller discussion from a psychoanalytic point of view, see Britton 2003.

33. Jung 1952, p. 328 n. 38.

34. Jung 1963, pp. 137-8.

35. Jung 1963, p. 178. His first published account of the anima was in 1920 (Jung 1920, pp. 467-72).

36. Kerr 1993, pp. 502-7.

37. Jung 1963, pp. 119-20.

18. Geneva 1920-1923

1. Spielrein 1922a, p. 348.

2. *IZP*, 1920, vol. 6, p. 391.

3. Hameline 1993, p. 161.

4. See Chapter 3. As well as drawing on Flournoy's writing for his dissertation, he also used material from séances described by Flournoy as the basis for his *Psychology of the Unconscious* (see Witzig 1982).

5. Hameline 1993, p. 162, from Claparède's autobiography, originally published as a supplement to his posthumous 'Développement mental', reprinted in *Archives de psychologie*, 1940, vol. 38, pp. 1-39.

6. ibid., p. 163, from E. Claparède, 'Les nouvelles conceptions éducatives et leur verification par l'experience', *Scientia*, 1919, vol. 35, pp. 3-5.

7. Vidal 2001, p. 141.

8. ibid., from E. Claparède, 'Freud et la psychanalyse', *Revue di Genève*, Dec. 1920, pp. 846-64.

9. SR, pp. 221-2, Geneva police immigration dossier on S.

10. ibid., p. 226, Institut Rousseau records.

11. ibid., pp. 235-6, Institut Rousseau programme and timetable.

12. *Journal de Genève*, 28 February 1922, p. 5.

13. Vidal 2001, p. 141, after M. Cifali, 'Entre Genève et Paris: Vienne', *Les bloc-notes de la psychoanalyse*, 1982, vol. 2, p. 125.

14. Emil Oberholzer to S, 18 Feb. 1922, BB, p. 257, Geneva.

15. ES to S, 24 Dec. 1921, SR, p. 226, Geneva.

16. Freud would not have had enough money. The most likely person is Max Eitingon: Russian by origin, trained in Zurich, and wealthy.

17. Schepeler 1993, p. 260, P. Bovet, *Vingt ans de vie: L'Institut J.-J. Rousseau de 1912-32* (Neuchatel, Delachaux et Nistel, 1932), p. 101.

18. SR, p. 224, Circular letters of the 'Secret Committee', Oct.-Dec. 1920.

19. SF to S, 12 Jun. 1922, AC, p. 131.

20. Cifali 2001, 19 Nov. 1920, p. 135, François Naville to S, Geneva.

21. SR, p. 231.

22. Spielrein 1923g.

23. Spielrein 1922b.

24. Vidal 2001, p. 140, H.-R.Lenormand, *Les confessions d'un auteur dramatique* (Paris, Albin Michel, 1949), p. 279.

25. S to Pierre Bovet, 11 Sept. 1922, SR, p. 233, Institut Rousseau Archives.

26. BB, p. 257, based on a letter from Emil Oberholzer to Spielrein in the Geneva archive, referring to 'C and B'. 'C' is clearly Claparède. 'B' is probably Bovet, but could also be the linguist Charles Bally, who assisted Spielrein with her paper on the words Mama and Papa.

27. Charles Odier to S, probably 1921, Cifali 2001, p. 134, Geneva.

28. Schepeler 1993, p. 256, Bovet 1932, p. 102 (see n. 17).

29. Spielrein 1920b.

30. Spielrein 1920d.

31. Spielrein 1921b.
32. Spielrein 1923d.
33. Spielrein 1923e.
34. Spielrein 1923c.
35. Spielrein 1922c.
36. Spielrein 1920e.
37. Spielrein 1922a, p. 346.
38. ibid., p. 355.
39. ibid., p. 367.
40. Spielrein 1920a.
41. Vidal 2001, p. 144.
42. See for example Music 2010.
43. See for example Konner 2011.
44. Tragically, she was murdered four years later by her nephew Rolf, whom she had brought up. He alleged she had tried to psychoanalyse him, and had also written about him without his permission in her articles.

19. From Geneva to Moscow 1922-1923

1. Schepeler 1993, p. 259, J.-C. Bringuier, *Conversations libres avec Jean Piaget* (Paris, Editions Robert Laffont, 1977), pp. 122-3.
2. Schepeler 1993, p. 261, J. Piaget, 'Réponse de Jean Piaget au Dr Olivier Flournoy', *Journal de Genève*, 5 Feb. 1977.
3. SR, p. 230, personal communication from Kaspar Weber.
4. Piaget 1923a.
5. Schepeler 1993, p. 256, J. Piaget, *Recherche* (Lausanne, Imprimerie la Concorde, 1918).
6. Schepeler 1993, p. 256, J. Piaget, 'Autobiography', in E.G. Boring (ed.), *A History of Psychology in Autobiography*, vol. 4 (Worcester MA, Clark University Press, 1952), pp. 237-56.
7. Schepeler 1993, p. 256, J. Piaget, 'La psychanalyse dans ces rapports avec la psychologie de l'enfant', *Bulletin de la Société Alfred Binet*, 1920, vol. 20, pp. 41-58.
8. Schepeler 1993, p. 256, O. Pfister, Review of Piaget's 'La psychanalyse dans ces rapports avec la psychologie de l'enfant', *Imago*, 1920, vol. 6, pp. 294-5.
9. Vidal 2001, p. 143.
10. At times Freud also made such a distinction, but in the practice of psychoanalysis the term 'unconscious' came to be applied to repressed memories and desires. The distinction from the 'implicit' unconscious as expressed by Spielrein and Piaget, and used in modern cognitive psychology, became blurred (see Sletvold 2013, p. 1022).
11. Schepeler 1993, p. 261, R. Evans, *Dialogue with Jean Piaget* (New York NY, Praeger, 1981), p. 3.
12. Piaget 1923b.
13. Vidal 2001, p. 144.
14. BB, p. 257.
15. Schepeler 1993, p. 263, Bringuier 1980, p. 124 (see n. 1).

16. ibid., p. 255, personal communication from William McGuire.

17. ibid., p. 264, after Piaget 1920 (see n. 7) and Piaget 1923b; also Vidal 2001, p. 142, after Piaget 1977 (see n. 2).

18. ibid., p. 264, after F. Vidal, 'Piaget et la psychoanalyse: premières rencontres', *Les Bloc-notes de la psychoanalyse*, 1986, vol. 6, pp. 171-9.

19. ibid., p. 269, after Vidal 1986 (see previous note).

20. ibid., 270, Piaget 1952 (see n. 6).

21. See Chapter 18.

22. Rice 1982, p. 31, personal communication from Jean Piaget.

23. SF to S, 12 Jun. 1922, AC, p. 130.

24. Spielrein 1922d.

25. Spielrein 1923b.

26. Spielrein 1922e.

27. Spielrein 1923a.

28. ibid., p. 320.

29. Vidal 2001, p. 150.

30. ibid., p. 151.

31. Piaget 1923b, p. 286.

32. Spielrein 1923b, p. 300.

33. Schepeler 1993, p. 16, J. Bruner, *In Search of Mind: Essays in Autobiography* (New York NY, Harper and Row, 1983).

34. Richebächer cites a total of sixteen letters between 1921 and 1923.

35. Emil Spielrein to S, 26 Oct. 1922, SR, p. 231, Geneva.

36. PS letter to S, undated, SR, p. 231, Geneva.

37. PS letter to S, undated, SR, p. 242, Geneva.

38. PS letter to S, 12 Jun. 1922, SR, p. 236, Geneva.

39. PS letter to S, undated, SR, p. 237.

40. SR, p. 241. Claparède's wife Hélène Spir was the daughter of a Russian Jewish philosopher.

41. ES to S, 24 Dec. 1921, SR, p. 228, Geneva.

42. ibid., undated, SR, p. 228; PS to S, 19 Jun. 1921, SR, p. 242, Geneva.

43. PS to S, 3 May 1922, SR, p. 245, Geneva.

44. PS to S, 4 May 1922, SR, p. 246, Geneva.

45. SR, p. 247.

46. Etkind 1997, p. 169.

47. S to Pierre Bovet, 8 Jan. 1923, SR, p. 239, Institut Rousseau.

48. SF to S, 30 Jan. 1923, SR, p. 238, Geneva.

49. JS to S, 27 Jan. 1922, SR, p. 244, Geneva.

50. JS to S., 14 Apr. 1922, SR, p. 244, Geneva.

51. PS letter to S, 17 Jan. 1923, SR, p. 248, Geneva.

52. Emil Spielrein to S, 30 Jan. 1923, SR, p. 247, Geneva.

53. Emil Spielrein to S, undated, SR, p. 243, Geneva.

54. NS to S, 16 Jun. 1922, SR, p. 237, Geneva.

55. NS to S, 21 Mar. 1923, SR, p. 248, Geneva.

56. Spielrein 1921a.

57. SF to S, 9 Feb. 1923, AC, p. 132.

58. SF to S, undated, Carotenuto 1982, p. 127. This does not appear in the German edition.

59. IS to S, 14 Apr. 1922, SR, p. 249, Geneva.

60. SR, p. 250, Geneva police immigration dossier on S.

61. JS to S, 8 May 1923, SR, p. 250, Geneva.

20. Moscow 1923-1925

1. Ovcharenko 1999, pp. 364-5, CSAR.

2. ibid., p. 365, CSAR.

3. ibid.

4. SR, p. 265, CSAR.

5. Etkind 1997, p. 172, CSAR.

6. Grigory Zinoviev was executed in 1936. Lev Kamenev, whose father was Jewish and mother Russian orthodox, was executed in the same year. Trotsky was assassinated in exile in Mexico in 1940 by Ramón Mercader, who delivered a blow to the head with an ice axe. The mission was organised by Nahum Eitingon who was the lover of Mercader's mother. Eitingon was one of the leaders of Stalin's Terror and a relative of Freud's colleague Max Eitingon, who was implicated in at least one of Nahum's illegal schemes (see Etkind 1997, pp. 248-51).

7. NS to S, 24 May 1921, SR, p. 254, Geneva.

8. S to CJ, 6 Jan. 1918, Carotenuto 1982, p. 168.

9. Etkind 1997, p. 130, A. Zalkind, 'Individual Psychological Analysis of Three Cases of Somnambulism', *Psikhoterapia*, 1914, p. 130.

10. Good accounts of the life of Lou Andreas-Salome appear in Appignanesi & Forrester 1992, pp. 240-71 and in Etkind 1997, pp. 8-38.

11. Etkind 1997, p. 112.

12. ibid., p. 113.

13. SF to CJ, 21 Mar. 1912, *FJL*, p. 495.

14. 'Psychoanalysis in Russia', *IJP*, 1922, vol. 3, pp. 516-17.

15. Etkind 1994, p. 200.

16. ibid., p. 238, Trotsky letter to Pavlov, in L. Trotsky, *Works*, vol. 21, p. 260 [in Russian].

17. *IJP*, 1922, vol. 3, pp. 516-17.

18. Etkind 1997, p. 192, CSAR.

19. Freud regarded him as the only trained psychoanalyst in Russia (see 'On the History of the Psychoanalytic Movement', *SE*, vol. 14, p. 33).

20. Etkind, 1997, p. 194.

21. ibid., p. 200, Archives of Ivan Yermakov.

22. A.R. Luria, 'Russische Psychoanalytische Vereinigung' (Sitzungsbericht), *IZP*, 1924, vol. 10, pp. 113-15.

23. Etkind 1994, p. 196.

24. Etkind 1997, p. 171.

25. Ovcharenko 1999, p. 366, CSAR.

26. Ljunggren 2001, p. 90, personal communication from Viktor Ovcharenko.

27. Etkind 1997, pp. 202-3.

28. A.R. Luria, 'Russische Psychoanalytische Vereinigung' (Sitzungsbericht), *IZP*, 1925, vol. 11, pp. 136-7.

29. SR, p. 262, Regine Kühn interview with Vladimir Schmidt, 2000.

30. Etkind 1997, p. 203, Archives of Ivan Yermakov.

31. ibid., p. 204, interview with A.R. Luria in M.G. Yaroshevsky, 'The Return of Freud', *Psikhologicheskii Zhurnal*, 1988, vol. 9, no. 6, pp. 129-38 [in Russian].

32. ibid., p. 205, J. Mari, *La Psychoanalyse en Russie et en Union Soviétique* (undated).

33. ibid., p. 204.

34. ibid., p. 204, Archives of Ivan Yermakov.

35. 'Psychoanalysis in Russia', *IJP*, 1922, vol. 3, p. 520.

36. Etkind 1997, p. 208, CSAR.

37. ibid., p. 209.

38. ibid., pp. 210-11, CSAR.

39. ibid., p. 213, CSAR.

40. ibid., p. 214, CSAR.

41. After Gorky's death, Vasily Stalin (Dzhugashvili) took over the former Children's House as his residence. He became a military pilot and carried out successful sorties against the Luftwaffe. By 1948 he was commander of the Air Force in Moscow but was dismissed after giving an order that led to a bomber crashing at a military parade. He later managed the national ice hockey team. The team members all died in another air crash and he covered this up by immediately appointing a new team. Following his father's death in 1952, he was arrested and imprisoned for seven years. He died of alcoholism in 1962.

42. Etkind 1997, p. 214, CSAR.

43. Covington 2004, p. 437.

44. Luria 1925 (see n. 28)

45. Toumlin 1978, pp. 51-7.

46. Cole, Bruner & Sacks 2013, pp. 41-9.

47. See for example Solms & Turnbull 2002; Panksepp 2004.

48. Etkind 1997, p. 174, J. Piaget, 'Commentary on the Critical Comments of LS Vygotsky', *Readings in General Psychology* (Moscow, Izd. MGU, 1981), pp. 188-93 [in Russian].

49. Santiago-Delafosse & Delafosse 2002.

50. Etkind 1997, p. 180, L.S. Vygotsky & A.R Luria, Introduction to 'Beyond the Pleasure Principle' in S. Freud, *Psychology of the Unconscious* (Moscow, Proveshchniye, 1989), p. 29 [in Russian].

21. Back in Rostov 1925-1942

1. Spielrein 1929, TH, p. 224.

2. A. Zhuravlyov, personal communication.

3. ibid.

4. Ljunggren 2001, p. 91, personal communication from Valeriya Yel'vova to Magnus Ljunggren.

5. A. Zhuravlyov, personal communication.

6. Etkind 1997, p. 175, Nina Snetkova.

7. SR, p. 268.

8. PS to S, 4 May 1921, 17 ? 1923, SR, p. 269, Geneva.

9. Ljunggren 2001, p. 91, personal communication by Valeriya Yel'vova.

10. PS to S, 5/11 Jan. 1922, SR, p. 268, Geneva.

11. Etkind 1997, p. 176, Nina Snetkova.

12. ibid., p. 263ff.

13. ibid., p. 166.

14. ibid., p. 176.

15. SR, p. 255.

16. Magnus Ljunggren, personal communication.

17. Ljunggren 2001, p. 89.

18. ibid.

19. ibid., p. 91.

20. Etkind 1997, p. 170.

21. Covington 2004, p. 437.

22. SR, p. 277.

23. Spielrein, 1927/8.

24. Spielrein 1931.

25. Spielrein 1929, BB, pp. 207-12.

26. ibid., p. 207. Citing an early work of his in support of Freud, she explained in parenthesis that he was at that time still a 'pure Freudian'. In German translation, this reads: 'Jung war damals noch reiner Freudianer.' It would be delightful to think that Spielrein, or her father as translator, was playing a game or 'Spiel' at Jung's expense, by describing him as 'rein' or pure, in any respect.

27. When the Nazis came to power, he emigrated to Palestine, where he and Max Eitingon founded the Psychoanalytic Society. Eitingon became the first president of the association until his death in 1943. Wulff succeeded him (with a change of title to the Israel Psychoanalytic Association) until his own death in 1953.

28. Etkind 1997, p. 217.

29. Ovcharenko 1999, p. 367.

30. Etkind 1997, p. 176, Nina Snetkova.

31. Covington 2004, p. 436.

32. Ovcharenko 1999, p. 367.

33. SR, p. 284.

34. Covington 2004, pp. 436-7.

35. Etkind 1997, p. 264, V. Samoilov & Y. Vingradov, 'Ivan Pavlov and Nikolai Bukharin', *Zveszda*, 1989, no. 10 [in Russian].

36. Stalin asked Bekhterev to attend to him in connection with his shortened right arm, the consequence of an accident in his childhood. After the consultation, Bekhterev diagnosed paranoia in the country's leader. He died two days later, allegedly from food poisoning. Bekhterev's family and colleagues were convinced that Stalin had ordered the poisoning. The circumstances are discussed in Etkind 1997, p. 365 n. 25, and in A.M. Shereshevsky, 'The Mystery of the Death of A.M. Bekhterev', *Bekhterev Review of*

Psychiatry and Medical Psychology, 1992, 83-7. Bekhterev's many neurological discoveries included the role of the cerebral hippocampus in memory.

37. Etkind 1997, p. 277, A. Zalkind, 'Differentiation on the Pedological Front', *Pedologiya*, 1931, no. 2 [in Russian].

38. Etkind 1997, p. 274, A.B. Zalkind, *The Sexual Question in the Conditions of Soviet Society* (Moscow, 1924) [in Russian].

39. Etkind 1997, p. 268.

40. ibid., p. 280. Among many other distinctions, Otto Schmidt was to become vice-president of the Soviet Academy of Sciences and to win the Order of Lenin three times. He died in 1956. His wife Vera died during a surgical operation in 1937.

41. ibid., p. 281, E. Kol'man, 'Comrade Stalin's Letter and the Tasks on the Natural Sciences and Medical Front', *Under the Banner of Marxism*, 1931, nos 9-10, p. 169 [in Russian].

42. Etkind 1997, p. 277, based on personal communication from M. Yaroshevsky.

43. ibid., p. 281, E. Kol'man, *We Shouldn't Have Lived Like That* (New York, Chalidze, 1982).

44. Etkind 1997, p. 170.

45. ibid., p. 196.

46. Ljunggren 2001, p. 92, V.A. Kol'tsova, O.G. Noskova & Y.N. Oleinik, 'I.N. Spielrein and Psychotechnics', *Novy Mir*, 1990, vol. 2, pp. 111-33.

47. SR, p. 284, Execution lists and Mass graves database, Moscow memorial.

48. IS to Rakhil Spielrein, 1936 and May 1937, SR, p. 286.

49. Etkind 1997, p. 196.

50. ibid., p. 176.

51. SR, pp. 282, 287.

52. A. Zhuravlyov, personal communication.

53. Etkind 1997, p. 176.

54. Ljunggren 2001, p. 93, personal communications from Svetlana Konyaeva and Valeriya Yel'vova.

55. Etkind 1997, p. 176.

56. SR, p. 285, Nina Snetkova in interview with Regine Kuhn and Eduard Schreiber, 2000.

57. Etkind 1997, p. 177.

58. SR, p. 287.

59. ibid., Execution lists and Mass graves database, Moscow memorial. Jan, together with his brothers Isaac and Emil were posthumously rehabilitated under the Khrushchev government in 1956. The Nobel laureate Igor Tamm delivered a eulogy to her father (Ljunggren 2011, p. 44).

60. Etkind 1997, p. 170, based on personal communication from Menikha Spielrein. This is a discrepancy here with the five-year sentence reported by Richebächer, and with the fact that Menikha's mother received a letter from Isaac (see nn. 46, 47).

61. Ellman 2002.

62. Conquest 2007, p. 434.

63. Katy Zaidman, personal communication.

22. Deaths 1942

1. Menikha Spielrein to Henry (Zvi) Lothane, 20 Dec. 1994, Lothane 2007, p. 84 (his translation).

2. Ljunggren 2011, p. 44.

3. ibid.

4. My parents, who were Jewish refugees in England, told me they cried with relief when they heard that Germany had invaded Russia, as there seemed no prospect of defeating the Nazis without the Red Army.

5. Hilberg 2003.

6. His four sisters all remained in Vienna and were deported to death camps where they were murdered.

7. Jung 1934a, p. 166.

8. Jung 1934b, p. 539.

9. Bair 2003, pp. 431-63, includes a full and relatively sympathetic review of Jung's relationship with Nazism.

10. Bair 2003, p. 444, CJ letter to Mary Conover Mellon, 24 Sept. 1945.

11. 'The Implementation of the Final Solution: The Death Camps', Yad Vashem.

12. 'The Beginning of the Final Solution: Wannsee Conference', Yad Vashem.

13. Headland 1992.

14. 'The Beginning of the Final Solution: The Invasion of the Soviet Union and the Beginning of Mass Murder', Yad Vashem.

15. SR, p. 291, Nina Snetkova in interview with Regine Kuhn and Eduard Schreiber, 2000.

16. ibid., p. 358.

17. SR, p. 293.

18. Mirzabekova 2003.

19. A. Etkind, personal communication.

20. A. Zhuravlyov, personal communication.

21. SR, p. 293, Nina Snetkova in interview with Regine Kuhn and Eduard Schreiber, 2000.

22. 'Rostov-on-Don', YIVO.

23. Katy Zaidman, personal communication.

24. SR, p. 294, Yad Vashem.

25. Stone 2002.

26. SR, p. 294, Federal Archive, Berlin.

27. ibid., pp. 294-302. Secret Report to Rostov Regional Communist Party Secretary Dvinski, 24-25 August, 1943.

28. ibid., pp. 295-7, Secret report to communist party secretary.

29. ibid., p. 295, A. Angrik, *Besatzungspolitik und Massenmord: Die Einsatzgruppe D in der südlichen Sowjetunion 1941-1943* (Hamburg, 2003).

30. SR., pp. 295-6, Secret report to communist party secretary.

31. ibid., pp. 296-8.

32. ibid., p. 302, Nina Snetkova in interview with Regine Kuhn and Eduard Schreiber, 2000.

33. Ovcharenko 1999, p. 368, from an account by Nina Snetkova of conversations with friends in 1944.

34. Seetzen committed suicide in 1945.

35. SR, pp. 298-9, Investigation into Heinz Seetzen, Federal Archive, Ludwigsburg.

36. ibid., pp. 300-1, Secret report to communist party secretary.

37. Arad, pp. 14-15.

38. 'Rostov-on-Don', YIVO.

39. SR, pp. 301-2, Secret report to communist party secretary.

40. ibid.

23. Legacy

1. Dobzhansky 1973, p. 125.
2. Low 2001, p. xiii.
3. I am indebted to Vladimir Shpilrain and Katy Zaidman for the family details.
4. Ljunggren 2011, p. 44.
5. S Diary, Sept. 1910, TH, p. 58 (see Chapter 17).
6. Freud 1920, p. 55.
7. CJ to S, 1 Sept. 1919, AC, p. 223.
8. Spielrein 1911.
9. Laing 1960.
10. See Seikkula and Olson 2003.
11. Spielrein 1912c.
12. Spielrein 1913c.
13. Spielrein 1914b.
14. Spielrein 1922a.
15. Spielrein 1923a.
16. Spielrein 1921a.
17. Spielrein 1931.
18. Spielrein 1929.
19. Carotenuto 1982, p. 187.
20. See for example Fonagy & Roth 2005; Imel & Wampold 2008.
21. Bowlby 1973.
22. Stern 1985.
23. See Chapter 6.
24. See Chapter 17.
25. See Clark 1996.
26. See Haig 1993.
27. See Buss 2003.
28. See Chisholm 1999.
29. Fonagy et al. 2002.
30. Solms & Panksepp 2012.
31. Boyd 2009, p. 41.
32. For a review see Launer 2015.
33. Kriegman & Slavin 1992.

34. ibid., p. 281.
35. Gilbert & Bailey 2000.
36. Kriegman 2000, p. 71.
37. ibid., pp. 77-8.

Bibliography

Works by Sabina Spielrein

All Spielrein's papers from *Imago*, *IJP*, *IZP*, *Jahrbuch*, *Zeitschrift für Psychoanalytische Pädagogik* and *Zentralblatt* are available online at COTIPUB.

1911
'Über den psychologischen Inhalt eines Falles von Schizophrenie (Dementia praecox)' [On the psychological content of a case of schizophrenia], *Jahrbuch*, 1911, vol. 3, pp. 329-400 (reprinted in BB, pp. 11-93).

1912
a. 'Die Destruktion als Ursache des Werdens' [Destruction as the cause of coming into being], *Jahrbuch*, 1912, vol. 4, pp. 465-503 (reprinted in BB, pp. 97-144). In English: *JAP*, 1994, vol. 39, pp. 155-86.
b. 'Über Transformation' [On transformation], *Zentralblatt*, 1912, vol. 2, p. 478 (reprinted in BB, pp. 238-40). In English: *Minutes*, pp. 329-31.
c. 'Beiträge zur Kenntnis der kindlichen Seele' [Contributions to an understanding of the child's mind], *Zentralblatt*, 1912, vol. 3, pp. 57-72 (reprinted in TH, pp. 146-52).

1913
a. 'Mutterliebe' [Mother love], *Imago*, 1913, vol. 2, pp. 523-4.
b. 'Das unbewußte Träumen in Kuprins "Zwiekampf"' [The unconscious phantasies in Kuprin's 'Duel'], *Imago*, 1913, vol. 2, pp. 524-5. In English: *JAP*, 2001, vol. 4, p. 201 (reprinted in CCBW, pp. 263-4).
c. 'Die Schwiegemutter' [The mother-in-law], *Imago*, 1913, vol. 2, pp. 589-92 (reprinted in TH, pp. 158-62). In English: *JAP*, 2001, vol. 4, pp. 201-20 (reprinted in CCBW, pp. 267-70).
d. 'Traum von "Pater Freudenreich"' [The dream from 'Pater Freudenreich'], *IZP*, 1913, vol. 1, pp. 484-6 (reprinted in BB, pp. 147-52).
e. 'Selbstbefriedigung in Fussymbolik' [Self-gratification with foot symbolism], *Zentralblatt*, 1913, vol. 3, pp. 263.

1914

a. 'Zwei Mensesträume' [Two menstrual dreams], *IZP*, 1914, vol. 2, pp. 32-4.

b. 'Tiersymbolik und Phobie einem Knaben' [Animal symbolism and a boy's phobia], *IZP*, 1914, vol. 2, pp. 375-7. In English: *JAP*, 2001, vol. 4, pp. 525-7 (reprinted in CCBW, pp. 264-7).

c. 'Die vergessene Name' [The forgotten name], *IZP*, 1914, vol. 2, pp. 383-4.

1915

'Ein unbewußter Richterspruch' [An unconscious judgement], *IZP*, 1915, vol. 3, p. 350.

1918

'Die Äußeungen des Ödipuskomplexes im Kindesalter' [The utterances of the Oedipus complex in childhood], *IZP*, 1918, vol. 4, pp. 44-8.

1920

a. 'Zur Frage der Entstehung und Entwicklung der Lautsprache' [On the question of the origin and development of speech], *IZP*, 1920, vol. 6, p. 401. In English: *IJP*, 1920, vol. 1, pp. 359-60.

b. 'Renatschens Menschentstehungstheorie' [Renatschen's theory of creation], *IZP*, 1920, vol. 6, pp. 155-7 (reprinted in TH, pp. 178-9).

c. 'Das Schamgefühl bei Kindern' [The sense of shame in children], *IZP* 1920, vol. 6, pp. 157-8.

b. 'Das schwache Weib' [The weak woman], *IZP*, 1920, vol. 6, p. 158.

e. 'Resenzion: Isaak Spielrein, Über schwer zu merkende Zahlen und Rechenaufgaben. Ein Beitrag zur angewandten Gedächtnislehre' [Review: Isaac Spielrein. On numbers that are difficult to retain, and calculation tasks. A comment on the applied science of memory], *IZP*, 1920, vol. 6, pp. 172-4.

f. 'Verdränkte Munderotik' [Displaced oral eroticism], *IZP*, 1920, vol. 6, pp. 361-2.

1921

a. 'Russische Literatur. Bericht über die Fortschritte der Psychoanalyse in den Jahren 1914-1919' [Russian Literature. Report on the progress of psychoanalysis in the years 1914-1919], *Beihefte der IZP*, 1921, vol. 3, pp. 356-65.

b. 'Schnellanalyse einer kindlichen Phobie' [Brief analysis of a child's phobia], *IZP*, 1920, vol. 7, pp. 473-4.

1922

a. 'Die Entstehung der Kindlichen Worte "Papa" und "Mama"' [The origin of the child's words 'Papa' and 'Mama'], *Imago*, 1922, vol. 8, pp. 345-67 (reprinted in BB, pp. 153-80; also in TH, pp. 180-203). In English: CCBW, pp. 289-309, tr. B. Wharton.

b. 'Qui est l'auteur du crime?' [Who committed the crime?], *Journal de Genève*, vol. 93, 15 January 1922.

c. 'Schweiz: Die Genfer psychoanalytische Gesellschaft' [Switzerland: The Geneva Psychoanalytic Society], *IZP*, 1922 vol. 8, pp. 234-5.

d. 'Briefmarkentraum' [A stamp dream], *IZP*, 1922, vol. 8, pp. 342-3.

e. 'Psychologisches zum Zeitproblem', Bericht über den V11. Internationalen Psychoanalytischen Kongreß in Berlin (25-27 Sept. 1922) [Psychology of the problem of time. Report of the 7th International Psychoanalytical Congress in Berlin], *IZP*, 1922, vol. 8, pp. 496-7.

1923

a. 'Quelques analogies entre la pensée de l'enfant, celle de l'aphasique et la pensée subconsciente' [Some analogies between thinking in children, aphasia and the unconscious mind], *Archives de Psychologie*, 1923, vol. 18, pp. 305-22 (reprinted in Delafosse 2010, pp. 161-77).

b. 'Die Zeit im unterschwellingen Seelenleben' [Time in the unconscious mind], *Imago*, 1923, vol. 9, pp. 300-17 (reprinted in BB, pp. 183-210; also in TH, pp. 207-22).

c. 'Die drei Fragen' [The three questions], *Imago*, 1923, vol. 9, pp. 260-3.

d. 'Rêve et vision des étoiles filantes' [A dream and a vision of shooting stars], *IJP* 1923, vol. 4, pp. 129-32. In English: *JAP*, 2001, vol. 46, pp. 211-14.

e. 'L'automobile: symbole de la puissance male' [The motor car as a symbol of male power], *IJP*, 1923, vol. 4, p. 128. In English: *JAP*, 2001, vol. 46, pp. 209-10.

f. 'Ein Zuschauertypus' [A spectator type], *IZP*, 1923, vol. 9, pp. 210-11 (reprinted in TH, pp. 204-6).

g. 'Die Gedankengang bei einem zweieinhalbjährigen Kind. Schweizerische Gesellschaft für Psychoanalyse. Sitzung am 13. Januar 1923' [The train of thought in a two-and-a-half-year-old child. Session of the Swiss Psychoanalytic Society, 13 January 1923], *IZP*, 1923, vol. 9, pp. 251-2.

1927/8

'Einige kleine Mitteilungen aus dem Kinderleben' [Some brief comments on childhood], *Zeitschrift für Psychoanalytische Pädagogik*, 1927/8, vol. 2, pp. 95-9.

1929

'K'dokladu Doktora Skal'kovskovo' [On Dr Skal'kovski's Lecture], *Trudy 1-vo Sovyeshchaniya Psikhiatrov i Nevropatologov Severo-Kavkazskovo Kraya, Rostov na Donu, 1929* [Proceedings of the 1st Congress of Psychiatry and Neuropathology of the North Caucasus Region, Rostov-on-Don, 1929]. In German: BB, pp. 205-12; also in TH, pp. 224-30.

1931

'Kinderzeichnungen bei offenen und geschlossenen Augen' [Children's drawings with open and closed eyes], *Imago*, 1931, vol. 17, pp. 359-91, tr. from Russian by N.A. Spielrein.

Diaries, correspondence and hospital records

In German:
AC: Diary extracts 1909-1912; Letters to Freud 1909-1914; Letters from Freud 1909-

1923; Letters to Jung 1911-1918; Letters from Jung 1908-1919.

TH: Diary extracts 1897-1912; Letter to mother 1905 (misdated 1908); Letters to Freud 1909; Letter drafts to Jung (probably 1907); Letter to Jung 1911; Letters from Freud 1913, 1923; Letter from father 1913; Correspondence with Jung 1918-1919; Hospital records.

In English:

Carotenuto 1982: Diary extracts 1909-1912; Letters to Freud 1909-1914; Letters from Freud 1909-1923; Letters to Jung 1911-1918.

CCBW: Referral letter from Jung 1905; Letter drafts to Jung (probably 1907); Letters from Jung 1908-1919; Hospital records. Also includes extracts from correspondence in essays by Graf-Nold, Lothane and Richebächer.

JAP, 2001, vol. 46: Referral letter from Jung 1905; Letters from Jung 1908-19; Hospital records.

Other sources

Aaslestad, P. (2009), *The Patient as Text: The Role of the Narrator in Psychiatric Notes, 1890-1990* (Abingdon, Radcliffe).

Alexander, F. & Selesnik, S.T. (1965), 'Freud-Bleuler Correspondence', *Archives of General Psychiatry*, vol. 12, pp. 1-9.

Appignanesi, L. & Forrester, J. (1992), *Freud's Women* (London, Weidenfeld).

Arad, Y. (undated), *The Holocaust of Soviet Jewry in the Occupied Territories of the Soviet Union* (Yad Vashem, Jerusalem), pp. 14-15, Nuremburg Trial Documents.

Bair, D. (2003), *Jung: A Biography* (Boston MA, Little Brown).

Bair, D. (2004), 'Comments on the Film "My Name was Sabina Spielrein"', *JAP*, vol. 49, pp. 443-5.

Baker, R. & Oram, E. (1998), *Baby Wars: Parenthood and Family Strife* (London, Fourth Estate).

Bettelheim, B. (1983), 'Scandal in the Family', *New York Review of Books*, 30 June, pp. 39-43.

Bowlby, J. (1973), *Attachment and Loss*, 2 vols (London, Hogarth).

Boyd, B. (2009), *On the Origin of Stories: Evolution, Cognition and Fiction* (Harvard MA, Harvard University Press).

Brinkmann, E. & Bose, G. (1986), *Sabina Spielrein: Ausgabe in 2 Bänden, Bd. 2 Ausgewählte Schriften* (Frankfurt am Main, Brinkmann & Bose).

Britton, R. (2003), *Sex, Death and the Superego: Experiences in Psychoanalysis* (London, Karnac).

Buss, D. (2003), *The Evolution of Desire: Strategies of Human Mating* (New York NY, Basic Books).

Carotenuto, A. (ed.) (1982), *A Secret Symmetry: Sabina Spielrein between Jung and Freud* (New York NY, Random House).

Carotenuto, A. (ed.) (1986), *Tagebuch einer heimlichen Symmetrie: Sabina Spielrein zwischen Jung und Freud* (Freiburg, Kore).

Chisholm, J. (1999), *Death, Hope and Sex* (Cambridge, Cambridge University Press).

Cifali, M. (2001), 'Sabina Spielrein, A Woman Psychoanalyst: Another Picture', *JAP*, vol. 46, pp. 129-38.

Clark, W.R. (1996), *Sex and the Origins of Death* (Oxford, Oxford University Press).

Cole, J., Bruner, J. & Sacks, O. (2013), 'A Dialogue about Alexander Luria', *PsyAnima, Dubna Psychological Journal*, vol. 5, pp. 41-9.

Conquest, R. (2007), *The Great Terror: A Reassessment* (Oxford, Oxford University Press).

Covington, C. (2001), 'Comments on the Burghölzli Records of Sabina Spielrein', *JAP*, vol. 46, pp. 105-16.

Covington, C. (2003), 'Introduction', pp. 1-14 in C. Covington & B. Wharton (eds), *Sabina Spielrein, Forgotten Pioneer of Psychoanalysis* (Hove, Brunner-Routledge).

Covington, C. (2004), 'An Interview with Elisabeth Márton', *JAP*, vol. 49, pp. 435-41.

Covington, C. & Wharton, B. (eds) (2003), *Sabina Spielrein, Forgotten Pioneer of Psychoanalysis* (Hove, Brunner-Routledge).

Cremerius, J. (2003), 'Foreword to Carotenuto's "Tagebuch einer heimlichen Symmetrie"', pp. 63-80 in C. Covington & B. Wharton (eds), *Sabina Spielrein, Forgotten Pioneer of Psychoanalysis* (Hove, Brunner-Routledge).

Darwin, C. (1859), *On the Origin of Species By Means of Natural Selection: Or, the Preservation of Favoured Races in the Struggle for Life* (London, John Murray).

Darwin, C. (1871), *The Descent of Man, and Selection in Relation to Sex* (London, John Murray).

Darwin, C. (1872), *The Expression of Emotions in Man and Animals* (London, John Murray).

Delafosse, O.J.M. (2010), *Sur la langue de l'enfant: Choix de textes de 1876-1962* (Paris, L'Harmattan).

Dobzhansky, T. (1973), 'Nothing in Biology Makes Sense Except in the Light of Evolution', *American Biology Teacher*, vol. 35, pp. 125-9.

Ellman, M. (2002), 'Soviet Repression Statistics: Some Comments', *Europe-Asia Studies*, vol. 54, pp. 1151-72.

Etkind, A. (1994), 'How Psychoanalysis was Received in Russia', 1906-1936', *JAP*, vol. 39, pp. 191-202.

Etkind, A. (1997), *Eros of the Impossible: The History of Psychoanalysis in Russia* (Boulder CO, Westview Press).

Falzeder, E. (ed.) (2002), *The Complete Correspondence of Sigmund Freud and Karl Abraham, 1907-1925* (London, Karnac).

Falzeder, E. (2007), 'The Story of an Ambivalent Relationship: Sigmund Freud and Eugen Bleuler', *JAP*, vol. 52, pp. 343-68.

Fonagy, P., Gergely. G., Jurist, E.L. & Target, M. (2002), *Affect Regulation, Mentalization and the Development of the Self* (New York NY, Other Press).

Fonagy, P. & Roth, A. (2005), *What Works for Whom? A Critical Review of Psychotherapy Research*, 2nd edn (New York NY, Guilford Press).

Freud, E. (ed.) (1960), *Letters of Sigmund Freud*, tr. T. & J. Stern (New York NY, Basic Books).

Freud, S. & Breuer, J. [1895], *Studies in Hysteria*, *SE*, vol. 2.

Freud, S. [1911], 'Psychoanalytic Notes on an Autobiographical Account of a Case of Paranoia', *SE*, vol. 12, pp. 9-84.

Freud, S. [1914], 'On Narcissism', *SE*, vol. 14, pp. 73-102.

Freud, S. [1915], 'Observations on Transference Love', *SE*, vol. 12, pp. 145-56.

Freud, S. [1920], 'Beyond the Pleasure Principle', *SE*, vol. 18, pp. 7-66.

Gay, P. (1988), *Freud: A Life for Our Times* (London, J.M. Dent).

Gilbert, M. (1985), *Jewish History Atlas*, 3rd edn (London, Weidenfeld).

Gilbert, P. & Bailey, K. (eds) (2000), *Genes on the Couch: Explorations in Evolutionary Psychotherapy* (Hove, Brunner-Routledge).

Graf-Nold, A. (2001), 'The Zürich School of Psychiatry in Theory and Practice: Sabina Spielrein's Treatment at the Burghölzli Clinic in Zürich', *JAP*, vol. 46, pp. 73-104.

Grosskurth, P. (1991), *The Secret Ring: Freud's Inner Circle and the Politics of Psychoanalysis* (Reading MA, Addison-Wesley).

Haig, D. (1993), 'Genetic Conflicts in Human Pregnancy', *Quarterly Review of Biology*, vol. 68, pp. 495-532.

Haig, D. (2007), 'Weismann Rules! OK? Epigenetics and the Lamarckian Temptation', *Biology and Philosophy*, vol. 22, pp. 415-28.

Hameline, D. (1993), 'Édouard Claparède (1873-1940)', *Prospects: the Quarterly Review of Comparative Education*, vol. 23, pp. 159-71.

Hampton, C. (2002), *The Talking Cure* (London, Faber).

Hayman, R. (1999), *A Life of Jung* (London, Bloomsbury).

Headland, R. (1992), *Messages of Murder: A Study of the Reports of the Einsatzgruppen of the Security Police and Security Service, 1941-1943* (London, Associated University Presses).

Hensch, T. (ed.) (2006), *Sabina Spielrein: Nimm meine Seele: Tagebücher und Schriften* (Freiburg, Freitag).

Hilberg, R. (2003), *The Destruction of the European Jews*, 3rd edn (New Haven CT, Yale University Press).

Imel, Z. & Wampold, B. (2008), 'The Importance of Treatment and the Science of Common Factors in Psychotherapy', *Handbook of Counseling Psychology*, 4th edn, pp. 249-62. (London, Wiley).

Jones, E. (1953-1957), *Sigmund Freud: Life and Works*, 3 vols (London, Hogarth Press).

Jung, C.G. [1901], 'Freud and Psychoanalysis. Sigmund Freud "On Dreams"', *CW*, vol. 18, pp. 361-8.

Jung, C.G. [1905], 'Essay on Cryptomnesia', *CW*, vol. 1, pp. 95-106.

Jung, C.G. [1906a], 'Psychoanalysis and Association Experiments', *CW*, vol. 2, pp. 288-317.

Jung, C.G. [1906b], 'Association, Dream and Hysterical Symptom', *CW*, vol. 2, pp. 353-407.

Jung, C.G. [1906c], 'The Freudian View of Hysteria', *CW*, vol. 4, pp. 10-24.

Jung, C.G. [1920], *Psychological Types*, *CW*, vol. 6.

Jung, C.G. [1934a], 'The State of Psychotherapy Today', *CW*, vol. 10, pp. 157-73.

Jung, C.G. [1934b], 'A Rejoinder to Dr Bally', *CW*, vol. 10, pp. 535-44.

Jung, C.G. [1952], *Symbols of Transformation*, *CW*, vol. 5.

Jung, C.G. (1963), *Memories, Dreams, Reflections* (London, Routledge & Kegan Paul).

Jung, C.G. (1989), *Analytical Psychology: Notes of the Seminar given in 1925 by C.G. Jung*, ed. W. McGuire (Princeton NJ, Princeton University Press).

Kerr, J. (1993), *A Most Dangerous Method: The Story of Jung, Freud and Sabina Spielrein* (New York NY, Alfred. A. Knopf).

Konner, M. (2011), *The Evolution of Childhood: Relationships, Emotion, Mind* (Harvard MA, First Bellknap Press).

Kriegman, D. (2000), 'Evolutionary Psychoanalysis: Toward an Adaptive, Biological Perspective on the Clinical Process in Psychoanalytic Psychotherapy', pp. 71-92 in *Genes on the Couch: Explorations in Evolutionary Psychotherapy*, ed. P. Gilbert & K. Bailey (Hove, Brunner-Routledge).

Kriegman, D. & Slavin, M. (1992), *The Adaptive Design of the Human Psyche: Psychoanalysis, Evolutionary Biology and the Therapeutic Process* (New York NY, Guilford Press).

Laing, R.D. (1960), *The Divided Self: An Existential Study in Sanity and Madness* (Harmondsworth, Penguin).

Launer, J. (2005), 'Anna O and the "Talking Cure"', *QJM*, vol. 98, pp. 465-6.

Launer, J. (2007), 'The Problem with Sex', *QJM*, vol. 100, pp. 669-70.

Launer, J. (2015, in press), 'Sex and Sexuality: An Evolutionary View', *Psychoanalytic Inquiry.*

Ljunggren M. (2001), 'Sabina and Isaak Spielrein', pp. 79-95 in F. Björling (ed.), *On the Verge: Russian Thought between the Nineteenth and Twentieth Centuries* (Lund, Lund University).

Ljunggren, M. (2011), 'Memories of a Land in Stagnation', *Baltic Worlds*, vol. 4, pp. 42-6.

Lothane, Z. (1999), 'Tender Love and Transference: Unpublished Letters of C.G. Jung and Sabina Spielrein', *IJP*, vol. 80, pp. 1189-204.

Lothane, Z. (2007), 'The Snares of Seduction in Life and Therapy, Or What Do Young Girls (Spielrein) Seek in Their Aryan Heroes (Jung) and Vice Versa?', *International Forum of Psychoanalysis*, vol. 16, pp. 12-27, 81-94.

Lothane, Z. (2013), 'The Real Story of Sabina Spielrein: Or Fantasies vs. Facts of a Life', Presentation at the annual meeting of the American Psychoanalytic Association, 19 January.

Low, B. (2001), *Why Sex Matters: A Darwinian Look at Human Behavior* (Princeton NJ, Princeton University Press).

Márton, E. (2002), *My Name was Sabina Spielrein* [Documentary film] (Denmark, Idéfilm).

Mechnikov, I. (1903), *The Nature of Man: Studies in Optimistic Philosophy*, tr. P. Chalmers Mitchell (New York NY, Putnam).

Mirzabekova, N. (2003), 'Freud's Forgotten Pupil: Woman who Could Have Surpassed the Teacher', *Pravda*, 7 March.

Minder, B. (2001a), 'Sabina Spielrein. Jung's Patient at the Burghölzli', *JAP*, vol. 46, pp. 43-66.

Minder, B. (2001b), 'A Document. Jung to Freud 1905: a Report on Sabina Spielrein', *JAP*, vol. 46, pp. 67-72.

Moll, J. (tr.) (2001), 'Unedited Extracts from a Diary (1906/7?)', *JAP*, vol. 46, pp. 155-71.

Music, G. (2010), *Nurturing Natures: Attachment and Children's Emotional, Sociocultural and Brain Development* (Hove UK, Psychology Press).

Ovcharenko, V. (1999), 'Love, Psychoanalysis and Destruction', *JAP*, vol. 44, pp. 355-73.

Panksepp, J. (2004), *Affective Neuroscience: The Foundations of Animal and Human Emotions* (Oxford, Oxford University Press).

Piaget, J. (1923a), *Le langage et la pensée chez l'enfant* (Neuchâtel, Delachaux et Niestlé).

Piaget, J. (1923b), 'La pensée symbolique et la pensée de l'enfant', *Archives de psychologie*, vol. 18, pp. 275-304.

Rice, J. (1982), 'Russian Stereotypes in the Freud-Jung Correspondence', *Slavic Review*, vol. 41, pp. 19-34.

Richebächer, S. (2003), '"In league with the devil, and yet you fear fire?" Sabina Spielrein and C.G. Jung: A Suppressed Scandal from the Early Days of Psychoanalysis', pp. 227-50 in C. Covington & B. Wharton (eds), *Sabina Spielrein, Forgotten Pioneer of Psychoanalysis* (Hove, Brunner-Routledge).

Richebächer, S. (2008), *Eine fast grausame Liebe zur Wissenschaft* (Munich, BTB).

Ritvo, L. (1974), *Darwin's Influence on Freud: A Tale of Two Sciences* (New Haven, Yale University Press).

Roazen, P. (1990), *Brother Animal: The Story of Freud and Tausk* (Piscataway NJ, Transaction Publishers, 1990).

Romanes, G. (1883), *Mental Evolution in Animals* (London, Kegan Paul).

Santiago-Delafosse, M.J. & Delafosse, O.J.M. (2002), 'Spielrein, Piaget and Vygotsky: Three Positions on Child Thought and Language', *Theory and Psychology*, vol. 12, pp. 723-47.

Schepeler, E.M. (1993), 'Jean Piaget's Experiences on the Couch: Some Clues to a Mystery', *IJP*, vol. 74, pp. 255-73.

Seikkula, J. & Olson, M. (2003), 'The Open Dialogue Approach to Acute Psychosis', *Family Process*, vol. 42, pp. 403-18.

Shamdasani, S. (2011), 'Introduction', in *Jung Contra Freud: The 1912 Lectures on the Theory of Psychoanalysis*, tr. R.F.C. Hull (Princeton NJ, Princeton University Press).

Sletvold, J. (2013), 'The Ego and the Id Revisited: Freud and Damasio on the Body Ego/Self', *IJP*, vol. 95, pp. 1019-32.

Solms, M. & Panksepp, J. (2012), 'The "Id" Knows More than the "Ego" Admits: Neuropsychoanalytic and Primal Consciousness: Perspectives on the Interface between Affective and Cognitive Neuroscience', *Brain Science*, 2, 147-75.

Solms, M. & Turnbull, O. (2002), *The Brain and the Inner World: An Introduction to the Neuroscience of Subjective Experience* (Other Press, New York).

Solyovov, V. (1985), *The Meaning of Love*, tr. T. Beyer (New York NY, Lindisfarne Press).

Stern, D.N. (1985), *The Interpersonal World of the Infant* (London, Karnac).

Stevens, A. (1982), *Archetypes: A Natural History of the Self* (London, Routledge & Kegan Paul).

Stone, L. (2002), 'From Law Student to Einsatzgruppe Commander: The Career of a Gestapo Officer', *Canadian Journal of History*, vol. 37, pp. 42-73.

Storr, A. (1997), *Feet of Clay: A Study of Gurus* (London, Harper Collins).

Sulloway, F. (1979), *Freud: Biologist of the Mind* (London, Burnett).

Toumlin, S. (1978), 'The Mozart of Psychology', *New York Review of Books*, vol. 4, 28

September, pp. 51-7.

Triarhou, L.C. & del Cerro, M. (1985), 'Freud's Contribution to Neuroanatomy', *Archives of Neurology*, vol. 3, pp. 282-7.

Trivers, R. (2011), *Deceit and Self-Deception: Fooling Yourself, the Better to Fool Others* (New York, NY, Allen Lane).

Van Waning, A. (1992), 'The Works of Pioneering Psychoanalyst Sabina Spielrein', *International Review of Psychoanalysis*, vol. 19, pp. 399-413.

Vickers, N. (2011), 'Canonicity and the Psychoanalytic Case History', pp. 103-12 in A. Calanchi, G. Castellani, G. Morisco & G. Turchetti (eds), *The Case and the Canon: Anomalies, Discontinuities, Metaphors between Science and Literature* (Göttingen, V & R Unipress).

Vidal, F. (2001), 'Sabina Spielrein, Jean Piaget – Going their Own Ways', *JAP*, vol. 46, pp. 139-53.

Weizmann, C. (1949), *Trial and Error* (London, Hamish Hamilton).

Witzig, J.S. (1982), 'Théodore Flournoy – A Friend Indeed', *JAP*, vol. 27, pp. 131-48.

Zuk, M. (2003), *Sexual Selection: What We Can and Can't Learn from Animals* (California, University of California Press).

Index

Aaslestad, Petter, 261n.3
Abraham, Karl, 2, 35, 158-60, 165, 168, 190,
    193, 209, 216, 217, 218
abreaction, 44, 50, 69
Academy of Sciences, USSR, 227, 247,
    284n.40
Adaptive Psyche, The, book, 253
Adler, Alfred, 136, 165, 175-9, 217, 266n.8
Aisenstadt, Rabbi Moisei, 14
America, United States of, 112, 118, 213, 215
amoeba, 74
Amsterdam, 1st International Congress of
    Psychiatry, Neurology and Psychology
    (1906), 69-70, 73, 91, 107
anal eroticism, 66-8, 107
anamnesis, 25, 30, 32, 42, 46
Andreas-Salome, Lou, 266, 281n.10
anima, 6, 184-5, 186-7, 248, 277n.35
'Anna O', 8, 48, 50, 69
'Anschluss', 237
anti-Russian prejudice, 25, 55, 227, 250,
    267n.11
anti-Semitism, 6, 14, 97, 157, 176, 215,
    237-9
aphasia, 203, 206
Appignanesi, Lisa, 151
Aptekmann, Esther, 35, 73, 111, 121-2, 160
archetypes, 144, 205
Archives de Psychologie, journal, 191, 195, 203
art history, 129
Asiatani, Mikhail, 267n.11
astrology, 133
attachment, 178, 200, 251, 252
autistic thought, 198, 203
Azov, Sea of, 13, 21, 226

Babitskaya, Rebecca, *see* Ter-Oganessian,
    Rebecca
Babi Yar, 239
Bair, Deirdre, 60, 238
Bally, Charles, 199, 206, 278n.26
Basel, 28, 29, 132
Bekhterev, Madame, 173

Bekhterev, Vladimir, 215, 217, 227, 231,
    283n.36
Berg, Feiga, 4, 35, 46, 47, 63, 64, 111,
    261n.6, 263n.29
Berlin
    psychological community in, 35, 112, 203,
        205, 214, 216, 218
    Spielrein and, 2, 23, 108, 109, 155-66, 168,
        209, 210
    Spielrein family and, 12, 16, 62, 172, 184,
        227, 246
Berlin Psychoanalytic Institute, 35
Berlin Psychoanalytic Society, 158, 160
Bern, 197
Bettelheim, Bruno, 271n.41
Binswanger, Ludwig, 28, 100, 131, 268n.26
biogenetic theory, 143, 144, 272n.27
biology
    Freud's and Jung's view of, 3, 142-4, 147,
        149, 179
    Piaget's view of, 202
    Rousseau Institute and, 191
    Spielrein's view of, 2, 72-4, 135, 139, 144,
        178-9, 207, 245, 254
Bion, Rudolf, 26
Bleuler, Eugen
    and Freud, 66, 77, 143, 263n.49
    and Gross, 68
    and Jung, 28, 39, 49-51, 77, 89, 102, 108,
        110-11, 114-15, 119, 124, 148, 192
    and Piaget, 202
    and psychoanalysis, 131, 133, 147-8, 159,
        161, 205, 250, 251
    approach to psychiatric care, 27-8, 29, 30
    as Spielrein's teacher, 56-7, 169, 171, 214
    ideas, 135, 139
    letters to Nikolai Spielrein, 32, 33, 48-51
    supervision of Spielrein's dissertation, 110-
        11, 114, 115, 119
    treatment of Spielrein, 5, 31, 32, 34, 35, 43-
        5, 48-51, 125, 264n.48
Bleuler-Waser, Hedwig, 27
Bohemia, 129

Index

Wackenhut, Irene, 8
Wagner, Richard, 72, 97-8, 99, 117, 140, 164
Warsaw, 12, 16, 21, 23, 24, 237, 260n.31
Weismann, August, 65, 73, 142, 144
Weizmann, Chaim, 13, 55
White Army, 172
'will to power', 177
Willke, Anke, 8
'Wolf Man', *see* Pankeyev, Sergei
Wolff, Antonia (Toni), 117, 124, 133
women psychoanalysts 73, 136, 200, 254
word association tests, 27, 28, 29, 34, 46-7,
      48, 60, 65, 66, 97, 192, 197, 206, 263
Wulff, Moisei, 210, 217, 230, 283n.26
Wundt, Wilhelm, 130, 271n.5

Yearbook, see Jahrbuch
Yekaterinoslav, 12, 13, 35
Yekaterinskaya Gymnasium, 14, 20, 25,
      271n.5

Yermakov, Ivan, 210, 217, 219-20
Yiddish, 10, 16, 158, 228

Zaidman, Katy, 247
Zalkind, Aron, 216, 231-2
Zeitschrift, journal, 165, 195, 218, 219, 223
Zentralblatt, journal, 153, 169
Zinoviev, Grigory, 215, 281n.6
Zionism, 14, 55, 164
Zmeyevsky Ravine, 242-3
Zurich
   as city, 54
   Lake, 54, 77, 80, 99
   Russians in, 30, 31, 35, 53, 54, 55, 64, 65,
      111ff., 118
   University, 26, 31, 50, 51, 53-4, 56, 61, 63,
      66, 67, 73, 102, 111
Zurich Psychoanalytic Group, 133